Princeton Radicals
of the 1960s,
Then and Now

Princeton Radicals of the 1960s, Then and Now

William H. Tucker

McFarland & Company, Inc., Publishers

Jefferson, North Carolina

LIBRARY OF CONGRESS CATALOGUING-IN-PUBLICATION DATA

Tucker, William H., 1940–
    Princeton radicals of the 1960s, then and now / William H. Tucker.
        p.   cm.
    Includes bibliographical references and index.

    ISBN 978-1-4766-6301-2 (softcover : acid free paper) ∞
    ISBN 978-1-4766-2291-0 (ebook)

    1. Student movements—New Jersey—Princeton—History—20th
century.   2. Radicals—New Jersey—Princeton—History—20th
century.   3. Political activists—New Jersey—Princeton—History—
20th century.   4. Princeton University—Students—History—20th
century.   5. College students—Political activity—New Jersey—
Princeton—History—20th century.   6. Radicals—New Jersey—
Princeton—Biography.   7. Princeton University—Biography.
8. Radicalism—New Jersey—Princeton—History—20th century.
9. Students for a Democratic Society (U.S.)—History.   10 Princeton
(N.J.)—Politics and government—20th century.   I. Title.

LD4616.T83 2015
378.749'65—dc23   2015030961

BRITISH LIBRARY CATALOGUING DATA ARE AVAILABLE

Front cover: Blair and Buyers Hall on the campus of Princeton
University (Photograph by David Goehring)

Printed in the United States of America

McFarland & Company, Inc., Publishers
  Box 611, Jefferson, North Carolina 28640
    www.mcfarlandpub.com

For all those who opposed the Vietnam War,
both in and out of uniform

Acknowledgments

I am deeply indebted to the nine people who shared with me their reflections and their life stories; obviously this book would not have been possible without their assistance. For helpful discussions about SDS at Princeton, I am also grateful to Ron Butler, David Lenson, and Paula Bassoff.

My profound thanks to the following people who read earlier drafts of portions of this manuscript and made suggestions that improved the final version immeasurably: Ellen Chances, Seth Friedlander, Steve Freidus, Rosemarie LoPresti, Priscilla Read, David Schankler, and the person who used to be Robby Nerenberg. While the book has benefited from their comments, naturally they bear no responsibility for the opinion and analysis, which are mine alone.

As always, my greatest debt is to Monica for keen reading, astute judgment, constant encouragement, and love.

Table of Contents

Introduction:
Latter Day Images

Upon being told of his son's leftist activities, French prime minister Georges Clemenceau remarked that if a man were not a socialist at age 20, then he had no heart, but if he were still a socialist at age 30, then he had no brain. Almost five decades ago masses of college students in the United States demonstrated that, according to Clemenceau's standard, they had heart in abundance, taking to the streets by the hundreds of thousands in a movement for social justice and an end to an "imperialist" war, and thereby provoking the most dramatic conflict between large portions of the population and its own government since the Blue and the Gray shed each other's blood.

Although the students who once occupied buildings to express their displeasure with the established order are now grandparents heading into retirement, the tumultuous era of their youth has continued to play a divisive role in public discourse. In the 2008 presidential election, Barack Obama was accused of "palling around with terrorists" for his marginal association with Bill Ayers, the former radical now recognized as a national authority on early childhood education. Indeed, it is not only in the United States that the battles of the 1960s are being refought decades later; in the French election of 2008 the eventual winner, Nicholas Sarkozy, devoted what the *New York Times* called one of his "fiercest campaign speeches" to an attack on the 1968 movement and its contemporary heirs for having caused "a continuing crisis of 'morality, authority, work and national identity.'" At the end of his account of the 1968 Democratic national convention—during which members of the Chicago constabulary waded into a crowd of anti-war demonstrators, swinging their nightsticks indiscriminately in what an investigative commission characterized as a "police riot"—Norman Mailer predicted that "we will be fighting for 40 years," a comment that now appears to have been an underestimate.[1] As a Faulkner character remarked, "The past is never dead. It's not even past."

1

However, this continuing focus on the battles of the 1960s has diverted attention from the more interesting question, the one at the root of the second half of Clemenceau's observation: whether rational people would naturally become more conservative with age. This book is composed of two parts. Part I describes the context that produced radical activists and the campaigns that evolved from that context at one Ivy League institution. Part II traces the subsequent lives of nine of the students who led those campaigns to see what effect their involvement has actually had on their subsequent political opinions and careers.

Participants in the radical movement at the time were certain that they had experienced a life-changing transformation, one that would forever inform their values and the way they saw the world. Reflecting on the movement in 1973, Elinor Langer, who went on to become a well-known journalist, predicted that "whatever we become individually we will be radicals to our graves if for no other reason than that we will never want 'in.' We started out 'in' and didn't like it." And Charles A. Reich—the Yale law professor, whose trendy 1970 book, *The Greening of America*, coined the term "Consciousness III" for a new sense of values that rejected commercialism, materialism, and competition in favor of an emphasis on relationships, the environment, personal liberation, and community—confidently explained that this new consciousness was a deliberate choice, one that, once made, was "not ... reversible. Once a person reaches Consciousness III, there is no returning to a lower consciousness."[2]

The latter day images of 1960s radicals have not exactly confirmed this certainty that the commitment to their youthful idealism would endure; indeed, the most common portrayals of aging activists have suggested quite the opposite: the abandonment of their principles. One frequent stereotype suggests that, in Todd Gitlin's memorable phrase, former radicals have gone "from '*J'accuse*' to Jacuzzi,"[3] becoming liberal materialists whose former devotion to collectivist principles has not precluded personal financial success, enabling them to enjoy an effete and elitist lifestyle, foreign to mainstream Americans; apparently Consciousness III has been no match for the bourgeois comforts of life, after all. This meme was best encapsulated in the political attack ad sponsored by the conservative "Club for Growth" in opposition to Howard Dean during his campaign for the 2004 Democratic presidential nomination. Asked their opinion of his tax policy, an elderly rural couple responds—the man providing the first half of the denunciation, his wife chiming in with the remainder without missing a beat—that Dean should take his "tax-hiking, government-expanding, latte-drinking, sushi-eating, Volvo-driving, *New-York-Times*-reading, body-piercing, Hollywood-loving, left wing freak show back to Vermont, where it belongs." Though the ad made no mention of former activists, it was unmistakably an updated version of the campaign against George McGovern, the 1972 Democratic presidential nominee, labeled by Republicans as "the candidate of the three A's: acid, amnesty, and abortion." In either case the strategy was to define the candidate as the choice of an alien group far outside the cultural mainstream, but in addition the characterization of the Dean supporters as a "freak show" was code for 1960s hippies, for whom "freak" was used as a synonym. The fact that Dean was the governor of Vermont, a state once known as a hippie haven and now home to Bernie Sanders, the only declared socialist in the Congress, provided even more reason for viewers to link the Dean campaign to the earlier radical movement. It was not for naught that Vermont's largest city was often referred to as "the People's Republic of Burlington."

In another popular image, aging radicals have been depicted as hypocrites, whose personal lives make a travesty of the values they claim to espouse. In *The Believers*, for example, Zoë Heller's novel about a hilariously dysfunctional family headed by two 1960s radicals who claim to have kept the faith, the father is a William Kunstler figure, who defends an Arab American accused of participating in an Al-Qaeda training camp but has also bribed a superintendent so that his girlfriend and love-child can get into a rent-controlled apartment; the mother had once been a cute girl with a short fuse, a brash style, and a foul mouth—a more intelligent and politically astute version of the Monkey from *Portnoy's Complaint*—but has become an embittered and resentful middle-aged woman, who feigns a chummy equality with her cleaning lady while expecting deference, and whose stream of obscenities, now emanating from a harridan rather than a comely young woman, has lost whatever charm it once enjoyed. Despite having been raised by dedicated leftists, the two daughters, named "Karla" and "Rosa" in homage to members of the leftist pantheon, have difficulty finding happiness or meaning in their lives. The former, overweight and emotionally abused by both her parents and her husband, seeks comfort in an adulterous relationship with an Arab immigrant, while the latter, having spent four years in Cuba, turns to orthodox Judaism, forsaking her parents' atheism but trading in one set of dogmas for another. An adopted son, the biological child of ex-radicals—one parent died while constructing a bomb; the other is serving a life sentence for having killed a police officer during a bank robbery—is mired in drug use and petty crimes. Having begun with the intention "of subverting traditional models of family life," these radical parents had only created their own maladjusted version of it.[4]

In perhaps the most common portrayal, many 1960s activists went on to constitute a large proportion of the next generation of academics, giving rise to scholarly fields receptive to a leftist ideology that had been rejected by the polity. In one episode of the popular television show *Law & Order*, for example, a former radical has become a professor of comparative literature. "Here's his latest contribution to the revolution," sneers a detective, noting the title of the professor's book: "*The Whale Is Red: A Neo-Marxist Interpretation of Moby Dick*." Interestingly, another former activist in the same episode has adopted a new identity and, married to an accountant, lives in an affluent suburb, where she is "den mother of the year."

Indeed, conservative critics have accused former activists of instigating the present day culture wars, polluting the intellectual atmosphere and stifling free debate on university campuses through their imposition of authoritarian speech codes, insistence on (leftist) ideological conformity and the introduction of an identity-based approach to scholarship, especially in the humanities and social sciences. This characterization began in 1990 when the art critic and conservative social commentator Roger Kimball published *Tenured Radicals: How Politics Has Corrupted Our Higher Education*, which maintained that the student protesters of the 1960s had ensconced themselves in the academy and were using their secure positions as professors and deans to achieve "indirectly in the classroom, faculty meeting, and by administrative decree what [the movement] was unable to accomplish on the barricades."[5] And the purpose of their campaign, according to Kimball, was "nothing less than the destruction of the values, methods, and goals of traditional humanistic study." Whether the academics cited by Kimball were in fact pursuing such a nihilistic agenda, he presented little evidence linking any of them to the 1960s student movement, and in most cases their involvement was highly improbable if only on chronological grounds: many of the culprits in his analysis had entered the professoriate either before or well after the onset of student protests. Milton scholar Stanley Fish, for example, whose "antifoundationalist" views about literary interpretation elicited a 23-page denunciation, obtained his doctorate in 1962, and Cornel West, another of Kimball's targets, was only 15 years old in 1968.

Particularly odd was Kimball's claim that former activists were to blame for the putative triumph of relativism in the academy. "We know something is gravely amiss," he wrote, "when teachers of the humanities confess—or as is more often the case, when they boast—that they are no longer able to distinguish between truth and falsity."[6] However, even a cursory glance at the pamphlets or newsletters published by radicals during the 1960s indicated their firm belief in an absolute truth, one that they were certain they possessed and were eager to convey to everyone around them; while the activists may have been arrogant, they were hardly relativist.

Although Kimball did not use the term "political correctness," which was just coming into vogue, he cited the efforts to "ban politically unacceptable speech" through "directives ... from the dean's office or Faculty Senate" as another tactic by which the same people who had attempted "to destroy our educational institutions physically" in the 1960s were now "subverting them from within." Kimball was not alone in making this connection; among others, the writer Kurt Andersen too has characterized "the earnest and awful Marxist-Leninist notion of 'political incorrectness'" as part of the legacy of the sixties.[7] Although it's true that the phrase "politically correct" emanated from the radical movement, at the time it had nothing to do with unacceptable speech, a perversion that came long afterwards, but was applied rather to behavior only superficially consistent with one's professed political commitments. Avoiding the purchase of table grapes in the 1960s, for example, was considered to be "politically correct" because the United Farm Workers led by Cesar Chavez were on strike to win collective bargaining rights, safer working conditions, and an increase in their miserable wages. Along with a serious political intention, behind this usage was always an element of self-mockery, a verbal elbow in the ribs, reminding fellow activists that they were substituting a consumerist gesture—well intended to be sure and probably helpful to the cause, but of little personal risk—for the act of putting their bodies on the line in support of their beliefs; it was easier to avoid grapes in the supermarket as a sign of political purity than to march with Chavez.

The most recent incarnation of Kimball's argument is contained in David Horowitz's 2006 publication *The Professors: The 101 Most Dangerous Academics in America*, a collection of brief profiles of each of the villains alluded to in the subtitle. According to Horowitz's introduction, many of the "anti-war radicals in the Vietnam era ... stayed in school to avoid the military draft" and then, after earning their PhDs, set out to "do away with the concept of the ivory tower," converting the university from "a temple of the intellect" into a vehicle for promoting "their political interests." While the list of 100 academics did include a dozen or so 1960s activists—Bill Ayers and his partner, Bernadine Dohrn, among them—Horowitz provided little information about what actually transpired in their classes, focusing instead on rehashing what they did decades ago and on their subsequent opposition to the war in Iraq. For that matter, scant information appeared about the classes of any of these "dangerous" professors, their major sin in most cases—leaving aside the

profiles' egregious inaccuracies[8]—being to have expressed a political position
with which Horowitz disagreed, especially concerning events in the Mideast.
Some of the examples in *The Professors* bordered on the grotesque: Suzanne
Toton, for example, a professor of theology at Villanova, was castigated for
requiring her students to read the work of Dorothy Day, described by Horowitz as "a Marxist ...who in the 1930s helped found the Catholic Workers
Movement, which was both socialist and pacifist." He made no mention of
the fact that in 2000 the Vatican gave approval to open Day's Cause for Beat-
ification and Canonization, thus beginning the formal process leading to sainthood for this woman who spent much of her life in voluntary poverty caring
for the needy; her candidacy received unanimous support from the United
Conference of Catholic Bishops. To Horowitz, however, assigning students
at a Catholic university the writing of a woman on the path to sainthood
marked the professor as "dangerous."[9]

The books by Horowitz and Kimball suggest two conclusions. First, it
is hard to escape the impression that many of the complaints that 1960s radicals are intent on destroying the academy are merely a way of attacking views
that the authors oppose. And second, the fact that so few of their targets had
anything to do with the protests of the 1960s suggests that whatever the zeit-
geist of that era may have contributed to the political correctness that arose
a generation later, the dynamic by which this occurred was more complex
than the simpleminded notion that the former activists now occupy the offices
into which they once barricaded themselves.

Aside from these questionable stereotypes of materialist, hypocrite, or
intolerant academic ideologue, the other source of information about activists' lives comes from their own writing. There has been no shortage of memoirs about the radical movement, though much less has been written about
life after it. And even in the former category the literature that does exist is
hardly representative of the typical experience, written, as it has been, almost
exclusively either by the movement's early stars—such well-known names as
Tom Hayden or Todd Gitlin, two of the first three presidents of Students for
a Democratic Society—or, more sensationally, by its later extremists. Bill
Ayers, Mark Rudd, and Cathy Wilkerson, all former members of the Weatherman collective, which believed that street riots and clandestine bombs were
the best route to social change, have all published reflections on their experiences, though only Wilkerson's book suggests any truly critical thought
about her involvement and its subsequent effect on her life (a second, more
recent memoir by Ayers focusing on his post-underground years is also an
exception). While Ayers and Rudd are passionate about their opposition to

the Vietnam War, their accounts read like caper books, emphasizing the excitement, romanticism, and Hefneresque sexual activities of life in the movement—a confusion of hedonism with heroism. Deciding that he had been anointed as the "iconic student leader and New Left media star," Rudd, for example, did not hesitate to take full advantage of the position. As he put it in describing the many women who "would present themselves" after one of his talks at a college campus, "I saw these one-night stands as perks of my minor stardom."[10]

However, there have been few personal chronicles centering on the experiences, during or especially after the movement, of the dedicated but less publically prominent grass-roots activists. How do they view their participation now and how did it affect their lives and choice of careers? In addition to describing their collective activities five decades ago, this book is an attempt to answer these questions for nine activists in the leadership of SDS at Princeton University. Thus, while it cannot claim to be a representative sample of the larger movement, it does have the advantage of tracing the lives of a group of persons who shared a common experience as student radicals.

Although the media preferred the designation "New Left," those involved in 1960s radicalism more typically identified themselves as part of "the Movement," a term with overtones of restlessness, activity, and dynamism. This catchall rubric subsumed a hugely diverse set of organizations, approaches, and agendas, all directed toward remaking the society in a more egalitarian and democratic direction: the movement for black liberation, Native American rights, Chicano rights, and Puerto Rican independence; the movement for women's liberation; the anti-war movement, the connecting link for all the different movement components, with its myriad of more specific organizations opposed to the presence of American military in Vietnam, such as draft resistance networks, underground military newspapers, and the "Coffeehouse Movement," which sprung up near military bases as a source of support for GI resistance to the war. In addition to these efforts to change existing institutions, the movement also included numerous attempts to create alternatives: alternative media, such as Liberation News Service, Newsreel, and the Underground Press Syndicate; research groups that issued reports and pamphlets, such as the North American Congress on Latin America and the Radical Education Project; alternative schools, clinics, and the free-university movement, offering an educational experience both more radical and more relevant; radical theater groups, such as the San Francisco Mime Troupe or Bread and Puppet Theater; environmental groups and so-called "back-to-the-landers," interested in alternative sources of energy, organic agriculture, and a simpler, more self-sufficient lifestyle.

Intertwined with the movement was the sixties counterculture, which fused the Beat Generation's sexual libertinism and drug experimentation with the joy and excitement of what was still a relatively new musical genre at the time, producing that infamous troika of sex, drugs, and rock and roll. The fact that society's authorities disapproved of these activities only added to their appeal for a movement that viewed proximity to power as a sign of immorality. Agreement on the larger issues of opposition to the war and support for racial equality did not prevent conflict between the more political and the purely countercultural elements of the movement; those who thought that "personal liberation" was the necessary prerequisite to social change tended to eschew interest in the details of political theory or the hard work of organizing in favor of "doing their own thing," which usually meant a focus on lifestyle (often communal), sartorial "self-expression" (beads and bell-bottoms), and all things psychedelic—not only the use of marijuana and hallucinogenics, but also a style of music called "acid rock," and an Eastern- influenced pacifist philosophy that manifested itself as "flower power." In his explanation of Consciousness III, a construct solidly on the cultural side of this dialectic, Charles Reich maintained that, "despite their bravery," sacrifices, and "endless unrewarding work," the "political radicals" had it all wrong, believing, as they did, "in structural change *before* a change in consciousness."[11] The politically committed in the movement insisted that only the former could produce the latter.

The most well-known radical organization at the time was Students for a Democratic Society, founded in 1960 as the student branch of the League for Industrial Democracy, an inconsequential social-democratic organization characterized by one writer as "a decrepit ... holdover from another age." In 1962, however, an SDS conference held at an AFL-CIO retreat an hour northeast of Detroit culminated in the adoption of the Port Huron Statement, a generation's call to conscience. Crafted by Tom Hayden, the 25,000-word document marked the end of the silent generation's apathy and its replacement by the idealism of a new college cohort dedicated to institutional reform based on a true "participatory democracy," in which "the individual [could] share in those social decisions determining the quality and direction of his life." For its first few years SDS focused on two initiatives. Working closely with the Student Nonviolent Coordinating Committee, the major force behind the Southern sit-ins, it organized support for the civil rights movement. It also launched a summer community organizing project, in which hundreds of students moved into some of the nation's poorest urban areas and lived collectively at subsistence levels while attempting to organize neighborhood residents to work for improvements in housing, education, and employment. Realizing the condescension implicit in the notion of students engaging in this project as a summer activity, some participants dropped out of school to continue their involvement on a permanent basis.[12]

Yet despite these idealistic undertakings—or perhaps because of them, considering the Spartan demands of the community project—SDS remained a small organization for some time. Three years after its founding and six months after adopting the Port Huron Statement, it still had fewer than 1,000 members nationwide and only nine campus chapters; by the end of 1964, with 2,500 members SDS was less than half the size of Young Americans for Freedom, its counterpart on the right, similarly founded in 1960, which had recruited 5,400 members for the "Draft Goldwater" movement that succeeded in nominating the Arizona senator as the Republican candidate for president. The catalytic event for SDS, producing an exponential increase in membership and propelling the organization to national prominence as the most important voice of the Left since the heyday of the Old Left three decades earlier, was its sponsorship of the April 1965 Washington, D.C., demonstration against the Vietnam War. Initially reluctant to focus on foreign policy issues, which it viewed as a distraction from the more fundamental problems of racism and poverty, SDS was forced to add the war to its agenda when, in 1965, Lyndon Johnson initiated the bombing of North Vietnam and announced a massive commitment of ground troops and a concomitant increase in the draft. Almost overnight the war became the dominant political issue on campus, and the spring demonstration, which SDS hoped would bring as many as 5,000 students to the nation's capital, actually drew five times that number. As Kirkpatrick Sale observed in his history of the organization, Lyndon Johnson became "the most successful recruiter SDS was ever to have." By the fall of 1965 membership had grown to 10,000 in almost 90 chapters, but it was only the beginning of the surge. At its peak three years later, SDS estimated membership at somewhere around 100,000 with a chapter on almost every major university campus, and even this figure was probably a gross underestimate of the number of participants in SDS meetings and activities; lots of students who had never officially joined considered themselves members by merely showing up.[13] Also by 1968, with no end to the war in sight, SDS was now composed largely of students who had abandoned the reformist vision animating the Port Huron Statement issued two full undergraduate cycles earlier in favor of a militant Marxist rhetoric. Whatever the exact number of its membership, a radical group, seeking fundamental change in American institutions, had become the largest student organization in the history of the country.

I arrived at Princeton University in the summer of 1967 as an incoming graduate student in psychology and joined SDS not long after, attracted by its opposition to the Vietnam War and support for racial equality, though an analysis of these apparently separate issues was not yet informed—not on my part and not yet on the part of many SDS members—by the organization's more radical critique that would soon comprehend both the war and racial discrimination as manifestations of a deeper, structural problem in American society.

I spent the next three years more involved in political activities than graduate studies. While none of Princeton's SDS members were ever in any academic difficulty—indeed, many of the undergraduates earned excellent grades and almost all the graduate students eventually completed their dissertations—"student" was often not their primary identity; they—we—were political activists taking courses. Life was a series of chapter meetings, caucuses, planning sessions, leafleting, and discussion groups, occasionally interrupted by the necessity to attend class.

By the time I finished graduate work SDS had fragmented into a number of factions, the sum of which was much less politically significant than the whole had been. In addition, as anti-war sentiment increased throughout the population, involving millions of people who could hardly be considered radical, the student movement became successively less important, and by the time that, in 1973, Richard Nixon announced the end of American involvement in Vietnam, the student Left, which had been the core of the American Left, had largely disappeared.

But did the values and beliefs that informed their participation disappear along with the movement? Did these people drift rightward, as Clemenceau expected? Or become Horowitz's and Kimball's academic culture warriors? Did their involvement exert an important influence on their lives and careers? And if so, of what sort? What do they think now of what they did then? The answers to these questions are explored in the second half of this book for nine of the leading activists in the Princeton chapter of SDS between 1967 and 1970—the organization's most radical period. Before turning to the profiles of their lives, however, it is necessary first to have a sense of why the events of the 1960s elicited such passionate activism and what specifically occurred at Princeton. These are the respective topics of the next two chapters.

1. Moral Imperatives:
The Reasons for Radicals

"Vietnam"

This land
A map
her people paper dolls
to burn
villages dots
to juggle with
and trees knocked down
like dominoes
how can she touch us,
this small land,
this toy of ours—
how can we feel
between us
the ocean swirl with tears?
—*Author unknown*

"What are you rebelling against, Johnny?" a girl asks the surly character played by Marlon Brando in the 1954 movie *The Wild One*, to which he answers, "Whaddya got?" This was a common trope about youth in the 1950s: rebellion for rebellion's sake. And the simplistic explanation for such immaturity was offered in another canonical movie of the era, *Rebel Without a Cause*, in which adolescent defiance was attributed to parental incompetence, especially on the father's part: the three main characters, all troubled teenagers, have fathers who are, respectively, spineless, absent, and coldly insensitive, paired with mothers who are carping, distracted, and vain. Rebelliousness on the part of young people was thus primarily an intra-familial psychological problem, the expected result when parents were reluctant to play their prescribed gender roles, the father setting appropriate limits and the mother providing emotional support.

A decade later there was little doubt about the reasons for youthful upheaval, but they had nothing to do with family psychodynamics. A survey of college students at the end of the 1960s documented the reasons for their dissatisfaction. Asked their reaction to a number of criticisms of American society, few students considered them unfounded: only 21 percent disagreed with the statement that "the war in Vietnam is pure imperialism"; only 11 percent disagreed with the statements that "basically, we are a racist nation" and that "economic well-being ... is unjustly and unfairly distributed"; a slightly less pessimistic 26 percent disagreed with the observation that "today's American society is characterized by 'injustice, insensibility, lack of candor, and inhumanity'"; and a mere five percent disagreed with the assertion that "business is too concerned with profits and not public responsibility."[1] These students were rebels *with* a cause.

In addition to knowing *why* they were rebellious, 1960s activists knew precisely whom they were rebelling against. Although the media referred to "the establishment" as the object of student opposition, no self-respecting radical would use such a politically vacuous term. Sometimes people in the movement talked about "the State" in the Marxist sense of that governmental power standing above society, which, while appearing to be neutral, in fact acted to exert the will of the dominant class. The use of this sort of jargon could produce humorous results: when a member of Princeton SDS once told a local print journalist that the organization's goal was to seize "state power," the reporter concluded that SDS was interested in winning control of the New Jersey legislature in Trenton.

However, the more common description of the movement's enemy was the "ruling class," another Marxist concept referring to those large corporate interests who finance, own, and control the means of production and in whose benefit the state typically acts. As the social scientist G. William Domhoff described the system in 1972, political parties in the United States had little to do with actually crafting policy, whether foreign or domestic. Rather, he wrote,

> policy formation is the province of a bipartisan power elite of corporate rich and their career hirelings who work through an interlocking and overlapping maze of foundations, universities, institutes, discussion groups, associations, and commissions. Political parties are only for finding interesting and genial people (usually ambitious middle-class lawyers) to ratify and implement these policies in such a way that the underclasses feel themselves to be, somehow, a part of the governmental process.

This idea of capitalist interests as dominating the state had populist roots as well. In Frank Capra's classic film *It's a Wonderful Life*, the banker,

Mr. Potter, played by Lionel Barrymore, is described as "the richest and meanest man in the county." While meeting with one of his financial advisers, Potter is informed that his congressman "is here to see you," to which he gruffly replies, "Tell the congressman to wait"—a forceful reminder of who is subservient to whom in the relationship between government officials and the owning class. This notion of a small powerful clique with interests adverse to the majority of the population helped the movement to define both its opponent and its goal. As a slogan for a student strike called by SDS put it, "No class today, no ruling class tomorrow!"[2]

Although SDS had regular national conventions, at which position papers were debated, resolutions passed, and programs of action approved, none of these initiatives were binding on individual chapters, which could do what they pleased. As a consequence, different chapters employed different tactics and often focused on parochial issues related to local campus conditions; even caucuses within chapters sometimes acted autonomously, depending on their specific political orientation. What kept this diversity from becoming anarchy was agreement on two issues: black liberation and the conflict in Vietnam. It was the history of these two struggles that attracted students to radical ideologies to begin with.

Seeking Equality

It is difficult to conceive of an issue with greater moral clarity than the centuries-long struggle of black citizens to achieve equality. Before the Civil War most blacks had been brought to the United States in chains after enduring the horrors of the Middle Passage, the trip across the Atlantic during which 15–20 percent of the "cargo" were thrown overboard after perishing from disease or starvation. Although the South's "peculiar institution" was supposedly ended by the Thirteenth Amendment, in fact until the 1940s hundreds of thousands of Southern blacks were kept in a kind of neo-slavery even worse than their antebellum condition. Rounded up by local law enforcement officials on charges such as using obscene language, breaking a work contract, vagrancy, or eavesdropping, they were imprisoned and leased as cheap labor in growing Southern industries, thus helping to build the new South and enrich corporate owners while literally working their lives away in conditions that resembled a Nazi concentration camp. Lacking the financial incentive that had motivated slaveholders to provide some minimal degree of nutrition and health care for their investment and knowing that a dead worker was an easily replaceable resource, the overseers in this prison-industrial complex dispensed contaminated food, leading to deaths from intestinal illness, whipped those who did not meet their work quota, and imposed other forms of punishment, including an early version of what is now called "waterboarding." As David Oshinsky's aptly titled book put it, prison labor was *Worse Than Slavery*.[3]

Those Southern blacks not ensnared by the prison labor system were subject to a combination of legal statutes and local customs that enshrined the remnants of America's original sin, maintaining a system of white supremacy in which blacks were kept separate and very unequal—prevented from exercising the franchise or serving on a jury, relegated to inferior facilities in public transportation, education and health care, and excluded from many public recreational facilities and libraries. Blacks foolish enough to challenge their prescribed station were treated with a savagery ironically mirroring the trait that supposedly made them unfit for participation in white society. "Negro barbecues," the public lynchings of transgressors, became major social events as huge crowds gathered, with "reserved seats" for business leaders and government officials, to enjoy refreshments while watching the victim be horribly tortured before dying, according to the customary explanation, "at the hands of parties unknown."[4]

As is well known, shortly after the end of World War II the Second Reconstruction arose, seeking finally to dismantle the system of American apartheid. However, the civil rights movement's eventual success did not occur without great human cost; in the name of preventing racial equality, between 1954 and 1968 41 persons were murdered, many of them either by police and local sheriffs or with their complicity. After the Supreme Court, in 1960, struck down segregation in interstate public transportation, interracial groups of "Freedom Riders" boarded buses heading to the deep South, only to be met by mobs that stoned or firebombed the vehicles and attacked the passengers as soon as they exited; these travelers were not the fist-waving militants or black power advocates who emerged later in the decade, but neatly dressed, well-groomed, and politely spoken young idealists—the men in ties and jackets, the women in church-going clothes.[5] Trained in non-violent resistance, the riders curled up into fetal positions but were beaten unconscious with metal pipes, chains, and baseball bats, and left lying in pools of blood, while officials—FBI agents as well as state and local authorities—watched the mayhem, finding no reason to intervene; indeed after being brutalized, the victims were often arrested on charges of "breach of peace." Countless other demonstrators seeking equal treatment from local businesses were attacked by police dogs, dispersed with cattle prods, beaten with nightsticks, and subjected to high pressure fire hoses.

Through at least the early 1960s, the FBI, the federal organization officially pledged to enforce the laws of the United States, remained singularly uninterested in offenses committed against black citizens, an indifference informed largely by the segregationist sympathies of bureau director J. Edgar Hoover, who preferred to focus investigatory attention on *supporters* of civil rights, maintaining voluminous files on just about every well known person who had ever issued the mildest statement in favor of racial equality.

Of course, the FBI was responsible first to the attorney general's office and ultimately to the White House, but, quite apart from whatever leverage in opposition to the civil rights movement that Hoover could exert based on his knowledge of the president's energetic sex life, at its onset the Kennedy administration displayed little inclination to expend political capital on the rights of blacks; the president's famous commitment to "pay any price, bear any burden, meet any hardship, support any friend, oppose any foe" to assure liberty was a message to the communist world and not intended to apply to those denied their freedom at home. Having won many of the Southern states in close races, Kennedy was eager to keep their Democratic members of congress in the fold, and any sort of civil rights initiative would endanger the rest of his legislative goals. As a consequence, not only were civil rights a low priority, but he appointed arch-segregationists to lifetime federal judgeships in the South.[6]

Besides, after an election in which the main issues were the defense of Quemoy and Matsu, two islands claimed by what was then Nationalist China (now Taiwan), and a supposed missile gap between the Soviets and the United States, foreign policy took front and center in the new administration, a priority that only became strengthened when, within the first two years of his presidency, Kennedy had to respond to erection of the Berlin Wall and the placement of Soviet missiles 90 miles from Florida. In this context, the civil rights controversy was worse than a distraction, not merely diverting attention from more important matters but creating a public relations disaster for America's image in the international community. To the Kennedys, "the struggle against racism" thus became, as one historian summarized it, "a conundrum to be managed, not a cause to be championed." In a particularly crass example, after unsuccessful efforts at persuasion, the administration attempted to buy off civil rights activists: according to James Farmer, one of the founders of the Congress of Racial Equality, Robert Kennedy promised to get CORE a tax exemption, if only "you'll cut out this Freedom Riding and sitting-in stuff."[7]

Eventually the federal government was forced to take more aggressive action on civil rights, if only out of apprehension over the damage being done to the nation's image. With the United States trumpeting the virtues of democracy in the midst of the Cold War, brutal assaults on black citizens seeking no more than equal participation in the society and the polity was hardly going to help win over the unaligned nations, many of them populated by people of color. In addition, the transition from newspapers to television as a major source of news information exposed the nation to disturbing images of peaceful marchers being bitten by dogs and swept down the street like so much refuse by fire hoses. "Television became a window into America's soul," observed the anthropologist John L. Jackson, Jr., and the view wasn't pretty.[8] The final straw compelling the federal government to act was the martyrdom of white youth from Northern families: the 1964 murder of a college student and a social worker—both whites from New York—together with a local black man, who were arrested by the deputy sheriff, himself a Klan member, and handed over to fellow Klansmen for slaughter. Missing for six weeks, the bodies were found buried in an earthen dam. But there was not much doubt that, had James Chaney met his fate alone, rather than in the company of Andrew Goodman and Michael Schwerner, he would have been just one more Negro who vanished into the Mississippi night, his disappearance hardly of interest to the local authorities much less the subject of a massive search effort involving federal resources. Indeed, the search for the three missing men turned up the bodies of seven other blacks, whose disappearance had attracted little attention beyond the surrounding community.

Beginning under Kennedy and continuing under Johnson, the White House had no choice but to support the end of American apartheid: first the 1964 Civil Rights Act outlawed segregation in employment and public facilities, and then the 1965 National Voting Rights Act prohibited the states from imposing barriers such as the literacy test to prevent blacks from exercising the franchise. But activists were under no illusion that a beneficent state had suddenly seen the error of its ways and decided to extend the constitution to blacks. Nor did the passage of these laws put an end to the sacrifices. In 1968, for example, students from historically black South Carolina State College in Orangeburg were beaten and arrested after protesting their exclusion from a local bowling alley, which still maintained a "whites only" policy four years after such a practice became illegal. When demonstrations continued over the next few days, state troopers fired into the crowd, leaving three students dead and scores wounded; FBI agents on the scene submitted false statements in an attempt to cover up for the perpetrators.[9]

Almost as appalling as the loss of so many lives was the inverted moral calculus that transformed the victims into villains—radical extremists and troublemakers whose insistence on respect for the constitution was the real threat to the society. Civil rights demonstrations in this view were criminal rather than political, an indication of disrespect for law and order. Horribly beaten by thuggish mobs, the Freedom Riders were the ones who were regularly hauled off to jail. When Viola Liuzzo, a white housewife from Detroit who had headed South to join the struggle for civil rights, was murdered by a group of Klansmen, one of whom was a paid FBI informant, the bureau claimed falsely that she was a promiscuous drug user. And after the killings at Orangeburg, the only person convicted of any offense was the Student Nonviolent Coordinating Committee's state coordinator, a proponent of non-violence who was present as an observer and was shot in the arm; originally charged with arson, conspiracy, and assault with intent to kill, he was eventually found guilty only of "riot" and served seven months of a one-year sentence. Although the incident had begun with a clear violation of the law by the owner of the bowling alley, the governor of South Carolina attributed the disturbance to "black power advocates," and the local newspaper called for an investigation of the "black power movement."[10]

Widely regarded as the biggest troublemaker of all, Martin Luther King, Jr., was denounced by one newspaper as "one of the most menacing men in America," and pursued obsessively by the FBI, which tapped his phones with the approval of Attorney General Robert Kennedy, bugged his hotel rooms, tried to turn his wife against him, deliberately withheld information about death threats, hinted that he should commit suicide, and generally attempted to destroy his life. Now that the designation of his birthday as a national holiday has officially confirmed King's status as secular saint, it is easy to forget that, having openly defied legal segregation, he was roundly blamed for his own assassination. "We are witnessing the whirlwind sowed years ago," wrote Senator Strom Thurmond, "when some preachers and teachers began telling people that each man could be his own judge in his own case." And to Ronald Reagan, the "tragedy ... began when we began compromising with law and order, and people started choosing which laws they'd break."[11] It was only after his death that King went from reviled to revered, as the increasing unacceptability of overt racism led many of his former critics to recall after the fact that they had really agreed with him all along.

However, one accusation about the civil rights movement was undeniably accurate: some of its most devoted supporters were communists—with both a large and a small "c"—as well as fellow travelers, socialists, and other leftists.

In her book *Defying Dixie: The Radical Roots of Civil Rights, 1919–1950*, the Yale historian Glenda Gilmore has documented the oxymoron that, during the first half of the 20th century, so many of the persons and groups involved in the struggle to gain the full rights of American citizenship for blacks were considered "un–American." Before the war, only Communists, eventually joined by others on the radical left, sought not just to overturn Jim Crow but to win full equality between the races, social as well as political; as Gilmore notes, "It was Communists who stood up to say that black and white people should organize together, eat together, go to school together, and marry each other if they chose." Indeed, open support for the rights of blacks during the McCarthy era was ipso facto grounds for suspicion of one's loyalties. As one member of a legislative committee designed to root out subversive influence observed, "If someone insists there is discrimination against Negroes in this country ... there is every reason to believe that person is a Communist."[12]

Although many others joined the civil rights movement in the post-war period, leftists continued to be an important presence. King's closest circle of advisers included Stanley Levison, formerly a prominent Communist Party operative and manager of the party's finances. King himself, according to the historian Thomas F. Jackson's award-winning book, *From Civil Rights to Human Rights*, developed a social and political philosophy that recognized the inequalities inherent in "monopolistic capitalism" and believed in an economic democracy along more socialistic lines.[13] The FBI and numerous groups opposed to racial equality harped relentlessly on this connection between radicals and the civil rights movement, oblivious to the possibility that, rather than persuading people to turn against the movement, it might encourage them to admire and respect communists. To the cohort of youth from which the core of SDS would emerge, the struggle to end legal, racial discrimination was an important step in transposing its sense of who were the real sources of moral authority in the society and who were the obstacles to social justice.

By the time that SDS had become a significant, national organization, the civil rights movement had produced dramatic progress in reducing the most blatant forms of discrimination; though still far from egalitarian, it was undeniable that American society had begun the 1960s racially Ptolemaic but ended it Copernican. But this elimination of the most glaring injustices still left unresolved the inequities that systematically relegated blacks to substandard housing, the worst jobs, and inferior education. Indeed, it was the economic plight of the working poor that drew King to his fateful trip to Memphis, where two miserably paid sanitation workers had just died when their garbage truck, known to have a malfunctioning compactor, mashed them to death, leaving their wives and children destitute.[14] These more impersonal, economic problems, more deeply rooted in the institutional structure of the society, pushed SDS toward a more radical critique of capitalism: the systematic marginalization of so many blacks was not personal, just business—and profitable business, at that.

However, even though the black freedom struggle had exerted a major radicalizing influence on many SDS members, this analysis did not lead to a fruitful, practical agenda for an organization composed almost entirely of college students. Many chapters provided support for the demands of black student groups on campus and pressured their universities to divest from companies doing business in South Africa, but these were hardly efforts with the potential to have any tangible effect on the larger society. Some chapters also issued statements of solidarity with the Black Panther Party, which not only shared SDS's Marxist view of racism as a byproduct of capitalism, but was outspoken in its desire to form alliances with like-minded white activists. But with the exception of the urban projects in its early years, SDS could point to few significant efforts of its own to address racial inequality. In contrast, the student movement played a leading role in the opposition to the Vietnam War.

"We were *the wrong side"*

While the long struggle for racial equality is familiar to most Americans, the facts of the Vietnam War are less well known. Yet it was the war that provoked such intense hostility to the government, drawing hundreds of thousands of people into the streets in the largest demonstrations in the history of the country. To understand the movement's fervor, it is necessary to provide a detailed description of what occurred in Vietnam and how the United States reacted to it.

Two weeks before the 2004 presidential election, the journalist Ron Suskind described how a White House advisor had dismissed the "reality-based community"—those who actually believed in policies based on the "judicious study of discernible reality"—for failing to realize that "that's not the way the world really works anymore." Instead, explained the aide, "we're an empire now, and when we act, we create our own reality."[15] Although this observation was intended to apply to 21st century events, in fact the movement against the Vietnam War was largely an attempt by the reality-based community to inject some truth into the fictional narrative constructed by an empire intent on creating its own reality. Indeed, despite the outcome of the war—defeat of the world's greatest military power by a Third World country—the official version of the conflict has continued to privilege the fabrication over the facts. In a 1982 press conference, for example, Ronald Reagan, responded to a question comparing his policy in Latin America to the intervention in Vietnam with the following statement:

> If I recall correctly, when France gave up Indochina as a colony, the leading nations of the world met in Geneva with regard to helping those colonies become independent nations. And since North and South Vietnam had been, previous to colonization, two separate countries, provisions were made that these two countries could, by a vote of all their people together, decide whether they wanted to be one country or not.
>
> And there wasn't anything surreptitious about it, that when Ho Chi Minh refused to participate in such an election—and there was provision that people of both countries could cross the border and live in the other country if they wanted to. And when they began leaving by the thousands and thousands from North Vietnam to live in South Vietnam, Ho Chi Minh closed the border and again violated that part of the agreement.[16]

As Mary McCarthy observed about Lillian Hellman's writing, every word in this statement is a lie, including "and" and "the."

"The most ignoble kind of betrayal": The French War

For most of its existence Vietnam had struggled against foreign domination. Descending in the shape of a fishhook from China's southern border, "Nam Viet"—Chinese for the "land of the Southern Viets"—had been controlled by its larger and more powerful northern neighbor from the expansion of the Han dynasty more than two centuries before the Christian era until China's political fragmentation some 1150 years later; even then, Vietnam was periodically forced to fend off invasion from the Chinese or the Mongols, developing a culture of resistance and a national identity that valued independence highly. When the European powers colonized Southeast Asia in the 19th century, Vietnam, along with its neighbors, Cambodia and Laos, became French protectorates. Secure in the superiority of their culture, the French declared their own language the colony's official tongue, outlawed the word "Vietnam" in favor of "French Indochina," and bulldozed centuries-old Buddhist pagodas to make room for Roman Catholic churches. More economically oppressive, they imposed high taxes on land, causing many peasants to lose their small subsistence plots and forcing them to become either sharecroppers on what had once been their own property or workers in French-owned rubber plantations and coal mines. As one historian observed, to the Vietnamese, "France was a nation of police, soldiers, pimps, tax collectors, and labor recruiters."[17]

In the standard practice of 19th century colonialism, the French relied on an indigenous elite to do their bidding, presiding over the local population in exchange for choice government posts, large estates, and landlord rights to collect rents on lands that had once belonged to peasant farmers. Because colonial rule was justified by the supposed necessity to bring civilization to the uncultivated, these Vietnamese collaborators, the interface between colonizer and colonized, spoke French, were educated in French schools, and practiced Roman Catholicism instead of the Buddhism of their less cultured countrymen.

Accustomed to resisting foreign domination, Vietnam soon developed a movement of opposition to French rule. Near the end of World War I, a Vietnamese patriot, later to take the name Ho Chi Minh—"He Who Enlightens"—submitted a set of demands to the Paris Peace Conference that included full equality before the law for all Vietnamese people and Vietnamese representation in the French parliament, thus propelling himself to heroic status and leadership of his homeland's nationalist movement. In addition to his fierce nationalism—or more accurately, because of it—Ho also became a communist, attracted to the ideology by its analysis of colonialism, which provided an explanatory framework for both European exploitation of less developed countries and for the complicity of local elites, along with a correspondingly twofold solution: a movement to expel the French imperialists and an internal revolution to wrest control of Vietnamese society from their Francophile allies.[18]

However, for Ho communism was not to be confused with subservience to any other country's interests; not only did his dedication to Vietnam's independence prevent him from becoming subject to instructions from either Moscow or Beijing, but he distrusted the former and feared the latter. When the Soviet Union responded to Prague Spring—the former Czechoslovakia's 1968 attempt at "communism with a human face"—with tanks and troops, much to the Kremlin's displeasure Ho condemned the invasion despite the fact that, with the war against the United States at its peak, he was heavily dependent on Soviet military aid.[19] And even while the main threat was coming from Washington, China's historical role as the country's traditional enemy remained deeply rooted in Ho's thinking, as it was in Vietnamese consciousness generally. Indeed, not long after the departure of American troops, Vietnam fought its larger neighbor in the "Third Indochina War," a month-long

bloody conflict that began with the incursion of Chinese troops into Northern Vietnam.

World War II provided the nationalist movement with its most hopeful
opportunity for independence since the beginning of French intervention.
A month before American entry into the conflict, Roosevelt and Churchill
had released the Atlantic Charter, a joint declaration outlining the principles
that were expected to inform international relations in the postwar world,
among them "the right of all peoples to choose the form of government under
which they will live"; Third World peoples viewed the charter as a commitment to their self-determination. But in addition, Vietnam had made important contributions to the allied war effort. When France surrendered to
Germany only six weeks after the onset of hostilities between the two countries, the Third Republic was replaced with the collaborationist Vichy regime,
and only months later Japan, Germany's ally, began its occupation of Vietnam,
taking control of the entire country within a year; just as Vichy did the Reich's
bidding, its colonialist administrators performed the same function for the
Japanese. In response, Ho established the Viet Minh—the League for Vietnamese Independence—a mass organization uniting workers, peasants, professionals and intellectuals, and dedicated to freeing Vietnam from both the
French Scylla and the Japanese Charybdis; by the end of the war the Viet
Minh had 70,000 persons under arms and governed large sections of the
country.[20]

An ardent admirer of the United States, which he viewed as a former
colony that had won its own independence from a European power, Ho also
worked closely with the Office of Strategic Services, the predecessor of the
CIA, gathering intelligence on the movement of Japanese troops, providing
haven for downed American fliers, and offering trained guerrillas for deployment in the American effort against the Japanese. At this point Ho felt
indebted to the United States, having received more support from the Americans than from any other country, and formally expressed his gratitude not
only for material assistance but "most of all for the example the history of
the United States had set for Viet Nam in its struggle for independence."[21]

Nor were these words merely a diplomatic courtesy. On the same day
that Japan surrendered to General Douglas MacArthur, Ho Chi Minh, now
recognized throughout Vietnam as the leader of the forces of national liberation, proclaimed the Declaration of Independence of the Democratic Republic of Vietnam before a crowd numbering in the hundreds of thousands,
jubilant at the nation's emancipation from 80 years of French colonial rule.[22]
Quoting the Jeffersonian creed on "inalienable rights" from the analogous

document in the history of his closest ally, Ho went on to explain that "this immortal statement ... in the Declaration of Independence of the United States of America in 1776 ... means: All the peoples on the earth are equal from birth, all the peoples have a right to live, to be happy and free."[23] Following Ho's proclamation, Vo Nguyen Giap, the Minister of the Interior, singled out the United States as one of the new nation's special allies; there was no mention of the Soviet Union.[24] At celebrations later in the day United States officials were honored guests, a Viet Minh band played "The Star-Spangled Banner," and the new nation's flag was dipped to the Stars and Stripes.[25]

Ho's optimism over independence quickly proved unfounded and his faith in the United States misplaced. The allied victory brought British troops to Vietnam, led by officials concerned about the decline of their own empire and no more sympathetic to the Viet Minh than the French had been. The British commanding general rearmed not only French army units and Legionnaires, but also Japanese soldiers, with the result that, after joining in the effort to win the war, the Viet Minh now found themselves in conflict a second time with the forces they had just defeated; additional French troops, transported in American ships, soon arrived, as France moved to reinstate the status quo ante. Some American officers were outraged. It made MacArthur's "blood boil" to see this "most ignoble kind of betrayal": our allies reconquering "those little people we promised to liberate."[26] When Chinese troops occupied the northern part of the country, Vietnam found itself confronted with all its enemies, old and new, at the same time.

Eventually the British, Japanese and Chinese withdrew, but the French remained, determined to reassert control over what it considered its possession; as French general Jean Leclerc bluntly put it, "I did not come back to Indochina to give it back to the Indochinese."[27] The country that had betrayed the allies, collaborated with the Nazis at home, and capitulated to the Japanese in Southeast Asia demanded the return of its colony, which had fought with the allies and had been promised self-determination at the end of the war. Nevertheless, the United States could find no reason to question French sovereignty over Vietnam.

French attacks soon forced Ho and the Viet Minh out of many cities, especially in the South, and back into the countryside, where they still exercised de facto control. To create the illusion of independence, the French installed Bao Dai as head of their puppet government, a role for which he was uniquely qualified, having performed in the same capacity for the Japanese. A racecar-driving playboy known more as a roué than a ruler, Bao Dai had to be brought back to Vietnam from his real homeland in the Riviera, along with, as one historian dryly noted, his "tennis rackets, cases of Scotch, guitars, and a red-headed flight attendant named Ester."[28]

For the next eight years the Viet Minh waged a bloody war of attrition against the French, while France turned increasingly to the United States to foot the bill for the attempt to preserve its empire. A trickle of funds under Truman progressed to a torrent under Eisenhower, and by 1953 the United States was supplying most of the French war expenses at a cost of more than a billion dollars a year—more than eight billion adjusted for inflation. According to CBS correspondent David Schoenbrun, who covered Vietnam for more than two decades, "It was the first time in American history that we directly and openly aided a colonial power in the reconquest of a colony and the crushing of a subject people's struggle for independence."[29]

Although the French enjoyed superior technology and firepower, the Viet Minh prevailed, forcing the French to surrender after being surrounded at Dienbienphu; the asymmetry in materiel and body count—almost 14 Viet Minh killed for every French death[30]—foreshadowed the circumstances of the next conflict with a Western power, in which the Vietnamese again would outlast a more technologically sophisticated and better armed opponent. According to Georges Bidault, then French Foreign Minister, as the loss of Vietnam became imminent, John Foster Dulles, Eisenhower's secretary of state, twice offered to have the United States drop atomic bombs on Viet Minh forces.[31]

"80 PERCENT OF THE POPULATION": GENEVA AND ITS AFTERMATH

In July 1954, the French forces and the Viet Minh signed a cease-fire agreement, and the next day the participants in the "Geneva Conference"—representatives from not only the adversaries but also Laos and Cambodia, as well as the United States, Great Britain, the Soviet Union, and the People's Republic of China—issued a "Final Declaration"; together these two documents comprised the so-called "Geneva Accords." There were three main points to these statements. First, all French troops and their allies among the Vietnamese would withdraw south of the 17th parallel, and all Viet Minh troops would withdraw north of that line. Both the cease-fire and the final declaration were explicit that "the military demarcation line is provisional and should not in any way be interpreted as constituting a political or territorial boundary"; its sole purpose was to allow regroupment of the parties to the conflict on one side or the other. Agreement on the 17th parallel represented a major concession by the Viet Minh, which had firm control of the north and enjoyed substantial support in the south as well. Thus the 17th parallel, temporary though it was intended to be, divided Vietnam into two approximately equal-sized zones, despite the fact that the Viet Minh controlled far more than half the country and could well have insisted on a line considerably further south, confining what was left of the French forces to a much smaller area. In any event, it was clear that the accords recognized Vietnam as a single nation, whose "sovereignty, ... independence, ... unity, ... and territorial integrity" were to be respected by all parties to the conference.[32]

A second point in the accords—and the reason that the Viet Minh did not feel the need to press for a military demarcation farther south—mandated that "general elections shall be held in July 1956 under the supervision of an international commission." Anticipating that, as the patriotic organization that had fought for the nation's independence, they would win these elections handily, the Viet Minh were willing to settle for a temporary separation line neither favorable to their interests nor accurately reflective of the facts on the ground.

Finally, the accords stipulated that there was to be no foreign intervention of any kind in Vietnam—a prohibition of "the introduction ... of foreign troops and military personnel" and an agreement that "no military base under the control of a foreign State may be established" in either of the two zones.[33] In short, Vietnam was recognized as a single nation, temporarily divided for the period leading up to national elections, and free from all foreign military presence. While the United States was not a formal signatory to the accords, its representative, Undersecretary of State Walter Bedell Smith, pledged to respect them, emphasizing America's "traditional position that peoples are entitled to determine their own future."[34]

In a reversal of the conventional wisdom, which claimed that communists could never be trusted to honor an agreement, the United States quickly violated each of the Geneva provisions. A covert CIA team attempted to create havoc in the North. The group oversaw the mass distribution of counterfeit money and fake leaflets with information about supposed monetary reform, leading to a 50 percent decrease in the value of Viet Minh currency. Paramilitary teams contaminated the oil supply of Hanoi's bus company, attempted to sabotage its railroad, and destroyed weapons supplies, while smuggling military equipment into the North. Less covert was the beginning of American military assistance to South Vietnam, which caused the International Control Commission, charged with monitoring compliance with the Geneva agreement, to cite the United States for breaching its provisions.[35]

In addition, the United States treated the 17th parallel as a boundary between separate nations rather than a temporary partition, recognizing South Vietnam as an independent state. Knowing that Bao Dai could not be taken seriously, the United States orchestrated his replacement by Ngo Dinh Diem, the choice of the "Vietnam Lobby," an influential group of American politicians and Catholic clergy. Unlike his sybaritic predecessor, Diem led an ascetic existence, having once studied for the priesthood and then maintained his vow of celibacy even after leaving the seminary; when tapped in 1954 to be prime minister of "South Vietnam," he had been living for the previous three years at Maryknoll Seminaries in New York and New Jersey. After attending the French Lycée, Diem had graduated first in his class from the French College of Administration in Hanoi; a provincial chief and then Minister of the Interior, he appeared well on the path to becoming prime minister of a colonial state. However, much to his credit, in 1933 Diem resigned his position in protest over French domination, an act that his supporters in the United States thought would make him acceptable to nationalist elements in Vietnam, even though he was a Roman Catholic ruling an overwhelmingly Buddhist country.[36]

With American support Diem announced that his regime refused to participate in the arrangements mandated at Geneva for a general election, the results of which were to unify the nation under a single government. Though the cancelation was ostensibly based on the inability of the North to engage in a free and fair election, more significant was the immense popularity enjoyed by Ho and the Viet Minh, a fact acknowledged even by staunch anti-communists. According to the head of the OSS/CIA mission in Vietnam, the Vietnamese peasantry revered the leader of the Viet Minh. "I have never talked or corresponded with a person knowledgeable in Indochinese affairs," wrote Eisenhower in his memoirs, "who did not agree that ... possibly 80 percent of the population would have voted for the Communist Ho Chi Minh." And in 1955, when the conservative journalist Joseph Alsop visited the countryside in the South, he was chagrined to find that the "Southern Vietminh were not guerrillas at all," but rather the heads of a popular "self-contained Vietminh state with a loyal population" that enjoyed direct participation in the government through village meetings; not only were the people happy and proud of the victory over the French, but "the countryside looked perceptibly more prosperous ... than the French controlled territory." Astonished at this discovery, Alsop concluded that "a whole nation has been deceived and tricked": these contented people were "completely ignorant of the true character of the world Communist conspiracy."[37]

Clearly no chicanery on the Viet Minh's part was necessary to win a nationwide election, but just as clearly, such an outcome was unacceptable to Washington. In addition to the "loss" of Vietnam for the "free world," a victory for Ho would have been a devastating blow to the notion that no nation would choose communist leadership in a fair election; it was always the anticipated result, rather than the legitimacy of the process, that the United States found objectionable. After the election was canceled, an article about Diem in *Life* soberly explained that he had "saved his people from this agonizing prospect" of a Viet Minh victory "simply by refusing to permit the plebiscite."[38] One can only imagine the degree of cynicism that would have greeted a communist country's explanation that it had decided to cancel an election in order to shelter the population from the consequences of its own political preference.

High ranking American officials and influential journalists vied with each other to see who could lavish the most praise on Diem. *Time* claimed that "all Vietnamese recognize" Diem as "the father of his country," *Newsweek* described him as "one of the ablest Asian leaders," and Senator John F. Kennedy called South Vietnam's "political liberties an inspiration." When Diem visited the United States, he was given the key to the capital and lauded by Eisenhower as a "truly very great leader" who had displayed "courage and statesmanship." Such effusiveness was informed in large part by pride of ownership: the United States was pouring huge amounts of money into supporting the South, the bulk of it devoted to military expenditures. Diem himself declared that "the borders of the United States extend to the 17th parallel."[39] South Vietnam had gone from a French colony to an American client state.

Notwithstanding the fawning tributes to Diem, what the United States actually received for its investment was an iron-fisted dictatorship. Although he had refused to participate in a country-wide election allegedly because of Viet Minh untrustworthiness, Diem held his own rigged process, a farce in which he received 98.9 percent of the vote. Once in office, Diem took measures to crush all opposition, preventing newspapers from even publishing the names of opposing candidates for the National Assembly. When one political opponent nevertheless won a seat in the Assembly, Diem had him arrested and sent to a "re-education" facility. In the countryside, local elections for village councils were abolished, eliminating a traditional process that had flourished even under the French; now deprived of their autonomy, villages were run by corrupt officials loyal to the Diem regime rather than the local population. Even while praising him as Vietnam's "miracle man," *Life* noted that "behind the façade of photographs, flags and slogans," there lurked the "grim structure of decrees, political prisons, concentration camps, milder 're-education centers,' secret police."[40]

Distrustful of anyone outside his immediate family, Diem turned to his siblings to assist in administering this police state. One brother was put in charge of the northern region of South Vietnam, ruling as a warlord with his own secret police and private army. Another brother, Ngo Dinh Nhu, controlled the southern region through similar means while accumulating a fortune from a network of criminal enterprises, including drug trafficking, smuggling, currency manipulation and extortion of money from Saigon businesses that paid for "protection." Since Diem remained true to his vows of celibacy, it was Nhu's wife who served as de facto first lady; described by the *New York Times* as "the most feared person in South Vietnam," the imperious Madame Nhu used her own police force to have people arrested for, among other offenses, crimes against good taste. Two other brothers also played important roles while enriching themselves. As Hans J. Morgenthau, the most prominent scholar of international relations at the time, described the polarization: "on one side, Diem's family, surrounded by a Pretorian guard; on the other, the Vietnamese people, backed by the Communists, declaring themselves liberators from foreign domination and internal oppression."[41]

Immediately upon solidifying control of South Vietnam, Diem set about physically eliminating the people who had won the country's freedom from French domination. In the resulting reign of terror, tens of thousands of South Vietnamese were executed, and more than 100,000 sent to concentration camps. In a measure reminiscent of his earlier association with the colonial regime, Diem revived the French Revolution's famous method of capital punishment, dispatching military courts with mobile guillotines to the countryside to behead "Viet Cong" members—the slang term for insurgents in the South—their sympathizers, and other dissidents under a vague law that prescribed the death penalty for, inter alia, "anyone who ... distorts truth concerning the present or future situation in the country or abroad."[42]

While not the object of attempts at extermination, two groups suffered in particular under the Diem regime. When the Viet Minh administered the countryside in South Vietnam, they confiscated the latifundia controlled by the French and their allies among the Vietnamese elite, and gave them back to the peasant farmers, from whose families the land had been expropriated and who had been working these plots as tenants for generations; the Viet Minh did tax the peasants to support the war against the French but at rates far below the rents that had been charged by the absentee owners. Under Diem, however, all the land titles granted to peasants by the Viet Minh were invalidated and the property returned to the absentee landlords, who wanted back payments. Pressured by the United States, which was concerned that such treatment of the peasantry was creating support for the communists, Diem adopted a "land reform" policy allowing the government to purchase holdings in excess of 247 acres and sell them to the peasants, who paid for the land through installments indistinguishable from the amount of the former rents; under the rubric of "reform," peasants could now buy back at exorbitant rates the land that they had owned under the Viet Minh. As one journalist summarized the policy, "in its actual operation, land reform legitimized the return of the landlord to the countryside he had fled, to collect rents he had ceased to collect, and to receive money for land he had long abandoned."[43]

Buddhists, too, were the object of discrimination due to policies that systematically favored the Roman Catholic minority. After a government decree prohibited display of the Buddhist flag at a religious celebration in Hue, the ensuing peaceful protest was met with gunfire from government troops, killing nine people and injuring many more. A month later, as a dramatic protest, an elderly monk sat down on the grounds of one of the largest pagodas in Hue and, after fellow monks poured gasoline on him, lit the match himself and then remained serene in the lotus position while the flames enveloped his body; the photograph of his death appearing in newspapers throughout the world and the additional self-immolations that soon followed elicited widespread sympathy for the Buddhist cause.[44]

The killing of Viet Cong cadre was not only acceptable to the United States but favorable—indeed, the reason for Diem's selection as head of state to begin with. And the oppression of peasants in the countryside was easily overlooked as a small price to pay for keeping South Vietnam out of communist control. But ruthless suppression of the Asian religious majority, especially when accompanied by a widely circulated photograph of a martyr, was not helpful to American interests, focusing international attention on a police state and leading the United Nations to appoint a special commission to investigate religious persecution in South Vietnam.[45] Diem had to go.

In fall 1963 CIA officials in Saigon informed South Vietnamese senior military that Diem and his family had to be removed from power, though the United States could not be publicly associated with the operation. Having dictated Diem's installation, the United States now dictated his de-installation; as the old blues song put it, we "were paying the cost to be the boss." Although Diem and Nhu surrendered without resistance, they were executed anyway. In the next 14 months South Vietnam experienced one seizure of power after another, its government changing hands 13 times, three times during a single week in August 1964.[46] The national emblem for the South could have been a turnstile.

"Deluding Ourselves in Vietnam": The Beginning of the American War

For some time after Diem took power, Viet Minh in the South—now the Viet Cong—did little to fight back while their cadres in the countryside were being executed. The main reason for this restraint was the expectation of victory at the polls; anticipating a unified Vietnam with Ho Chi Minh as its head of state, the Viet Cong did not wish to provide any pretext for the election called for by the Geneva Accords to be canceled. Even a State Department White Paper took note of "the Communists' calculation that nationwide elections ... would turn all Vietnam over to them," acknowledging that, as a consequence, the primary focus of their "activity during the post–Geneva period was on political action." When it finally became obvious that hopes for peaceful reunification were a fantasy, cadre in the South could no longer stand by while their supporters were being wiped out. Selective in their choice of targets, the Viet Cong assassinated corrupt village officials appointed by the Diem government; though indisputably brutal, these acts often enjoyed the support of the peasantry, regarded in much the same way as the assassinations of Vichy collaborationists by French patriots. At the same time, the resistance movement was strengthened by the return of Southerners who had withdrawn to the North as part of the cease-fire agreement with the French; according to the agreement, their presence north of the 17th parallel was only temporary, and when the elections were canceled, they headed home to resume the struggle for unity and independence.[47]

In 1960 the National Liberation Front was founded as the umbrella organization representing Southern resistance. Though much of its leadership had been Viet Minh and were now Viet Cong members, many were also independent professionals, intellectuals, and other non-communists opposed to the Diem regime. According to Gareth Porter, a political scientist serving as Saigon Bureau Chief for a news service during the war, the NLF quickly became "the de facto government of thousands of villages," enjoying "the clear allegiance of the majority of peasants" without having to fire a shot because the government officials "had no legitimacy in the eyes of the people." Once in control, the Front returned land to the peasantry that the Diem administration had given back to landlords. A *New York Times* correspondent described it as a "golden age" for the local population: "Taxes levied by the insurgents were low; there was no landlord to demand 40 percent of the crop, and once again the farmers were given the opportunity to elect their own village council." Soon after its formation, the NLF controlled land that included 3.5 million people and could call on a revolutionary force of close to 200,000, all Southerners; by 1965, an American estimate calculated that the organization controlled about two-thirds of the population and four-fifths of the territory of South Vietnam. Between the Viet Minh and the NLF, an entire generation of peasants was raised knowing no other government.[48]

Even before Diem was assassinated, the Saigon regime was on the brink of collapse as the NLF escalated its attacks, and there was nary a Northerner in sight. This is not to say that the NLF had no connection to Hanoi; it was indisputably the Southern wing of a national movement. Thus, while advised and supplied by the North, the NLF represented an uprising of the South's population against a repressive government propped up by a foreign power. Although the United States had assigned military advisors to this unstable ally, had provided extensive funding for its army, and had been dropping bombs and napalm on NLF strongholds since 1961—killing mostly apolitical peasants—there had not yet been a large scale commitment of American ground troops. Behind the scenes, however, the American military was in the spring-loaded position: President Lyndon Johnson's administration had made plans for involvement in the conflict but lacked the justification for implementing them. He certainly could not announce that American troops were necessary to protect a tyrannical regime from its own people.

Then, with the South's government shakier than ever, in a convenient coincidence an American destroyer was supposedly attacked by North Vietnamese torpedo boats while in international waters in the Gulf of Tonkin. It later turned out that no attack had occurred and the ship's radar and sonar signals had been misread in stormy seas, but even at the time the mission's operational commander informed the Pentagon that "freak weather effects and overeager sonarman" had probably accounted for the episode. Nevertheless, President Johnson now had a pretext for intervention.[49] A compliant congress, voting unanimously in the House and with only two dissents in the Senate, approved a joint resolution authorizing military force.

While the Tonkin "attack" produced air strikes on North Vietnam, the infusion of combat ground troops did not begin until some months later, after the State Department had produced a White Paper justifying the action as a response to North Vietnam's "Campaign of Aggression Against South Vietnam." In a *New York Times* article titled "'We Are Deluding Ourselves in

Vietnam,'" Hans Morgenthau treated this claim with the contempt it merited:

> The United States has decided to change the character of the war by unilateral declaration from a South Vietnamese civil war to a war of "foreign aggression." "Aggression from the North: The Record of North Vietnam's Campaign to Conquer South Vietnam" is the title of a white paper published by the Department of State.... While normally foreign and military policy is based upon intelligence— that is, the objective assessment of facts—the policy is here reversed: a new policy has been decided upon, and intelligence must provide the facts to justify it....
>
> Let it be said right away that the white paper is a dismal failure. The discrepancy between its assertions and the factual evidence adduced to support them borders on the grotesque.... The government fashions an imaginary world that pleases it, and then comes to believe in the reality of that world and acts as though it were real.

In his April 1965 address announcing the escalation of American troops, Johnson reiterated the justification "that North Vietnam has attacked the independent nation of South Vietnam: its object is total conquest."[50] At the time there were no North Vietnamese combat units in the South. But after more than a decade of supporting a reign of terror in the South and sabotage operations against the North, after four years of bombing NLF strongholds in the Southern countryside and almost a year of launching strikes against the North, the Johnson administration had defined the problem as North Vietnamese aggression. As Jon Stewart observed about a later administration, apparently the real goal of American foreign policy was to spread irony throughout the world.

Government officials and public figures extolled the nobility of the American effort. President Johnson declared that the United States "wanted nothing for ourselves, only that the people of South Vietnam be allowed to guide their own country in their own way." "In Viet Nam today," echoed National Security Advisor McGeorge Bundy, "we have to respond, in all that we do, to the real needs and hopes of the people of Viet Nam." Former secretary of state Dean Acheson stated that the purpose of our involvement was "to preserve and foster an environment in which free societies may exist and flourish." And the influential *New York Times* journalist James Reston explained that our action in Vietnam was informed by the "guiding principle of American policy ... that no state shall use military force or the threat of military force to achieve its political objectives." All these assertions were risible. The major attempt to achieve political objectives by force emanated from the United States; left to their own devices the people of South Vietnam would certainly have found the NLF to express their "needs and hopes" more closely than the dictatorship du jour supported by American arms.[51]

The conflict between rhetoric and reality became even more severe when the cycle of coups plaguing South Vietnam ended with the seizure of power by the Ky/Thieu regime in June 1965. Appointed prime minister by an 11-man directory of generals—the latest military junta to take control of South Vietnam—Air Vice Marshall Nguyen Cao Ky was a swaggering aviator with a pair of pearl handled revolvers and a penchant for garish colored flight suits, purple scarves, and yellow gloves; one journalist referred to him as "a kind of Asian Captain Marvel." Originally a Northerner, Ky wound up in the South after the Geneva Accords because he had been trained as a fighter pilot by the French and then fought on their side against the Viet Minh-led independence movement. General Nguyen Van Thieu, who also fought with the French, served as head of state. *New York Times* correspondent Neil Sheehan, initially a supporter of the American military presence in Vietnam, described both men, as well as most other generals in the ruling junta, as quislings, who had been officers in the French colonial forces: "During the First Indochina War these Vietnamese, with a stake in the traditional society which a French presence would preserve, cooperated with France. Now the same Vietnamese, for identical reasons, cooperate with the United States."[52]

Two years later, under pressure from the United States to give the ruling clique a facade of legitimacy, a presidential election was held with the more businesslike Thieu now at the top of the ticket and the flamboyant Ky as his vice presidential running mate. "Pro-communist" and "neutralist" candidates were barred from appearing on the ballot and opposition newspapers shuttered. Shortly after the election a number of opposing candidates were imprisoned, including the second place finisher, a lawyer whose platform had called for recognition of the NLF and immediate peace negotiations; after drawing a sixth of the vote, he was arrested and sentenced to five years of hard labor for the content of his speeches during the campaign.[53]

The Thieu/Ky regime was even more oppressive and corrupt than Diem and his family. More than 100,000 political prisoners were incarcerated in so-called "tiger cages"—six by nine cells containing as many as 12 persons at a time. After meeting some former prisoners, a *Time* correspondent wrote that "it is not really proper to call them men any more. 'Shapes' is a better word—grotesque sculptures of scarred flesh and gnarled limbs," most of them paralyzed below the waist: "Years of being shackled in the tiger cages have forced them into a permanent pretzel-like crouch. They move like crabs, skittering across the floor on buttocks and palms."[54]

Also under Thieu and Ky, smuggling became larger and more well organized, as every high ranking official got in on the action. In addition to the opium trade, which had flourished under Diem's brother, South Vietnam's capital became the hub for distribution of heroin and morphine. The drugs were flown in by the South Vietnamese Air Force or shipped in by its navy, unloaded under the supervision of customs or port authorities, and distributed by the army and national police. Saigon's Tan Son Nhut International Airport was a major center for this activity; according to an official report prepared by a United States customs advisor, "the sole function of customs at the airport seems to be to assist the smugglers to bring in their contraband without hindrance," not only smoothing the path through the examination counters but even accompanying the smugglers to taxis. Beginning in 1970, much of the heroin entering the country was peddled to American GIs, creating an epidemic in which some 10 to 15 percent of enlisted men became regular users. When South Vietnam eventually fell, high ranking officials fled with suitcases full of gold, winding up in the United States where, according to investigative journalists, they were involved in organized crime.[55]

It was to defend this government, detested by the majority of the Vietnamese people, whose elections were a farce, whose leaders enriched themselves through the drug trade and other criminal enterprises, and whose tiger cages were filled with political prisoners that in 1965 the United States began the escalation of combat forces. Between 1965 and 1973 almost 2.6 million Americans served in South Vietnam with a peak troop strength of 540,000 in 1969.

IRRESISTIBLE MILITARY FORCE VS. IMMOVABLE POLITICAL OBJECT

Asked how he would reciprocate if The United States stopped bombing his country, North Vietnam's prime minister Pham Van Dong replied, "If you stop bombing Hanoi, we will stop bombing Washington." In addition to being a sardonic comment on American aggression, Pham's response was a reminder of the absurdly asymmetric nature of the conflict, one of the most logistically inequitable contests in modern warfare. On one side, the best equipped, professionally trained, technologically sophisticated army in the history of the world; on the other, especially at the onset of the conflict, a group of ragged guerrilla fighters lacking any of the standard equipment of modern warfare—planes, helicopters, ships, tanks, trucks, or artillery—and trying to defend themselves against jet planes and bombers with rifles and other small arms. Even after North Vietnam began to deliver more powerful arms and munitions to the South and then sent its own army into battle, the United States and its ally in the South still had total command of the air and sea, as well as a huge numerical advantage in fighting strength. In addition to the half million American ground soldiers, air power, and naval fleet, South Vietnam had its own force of almost a million soldiers, supplied by the American government with state-of-the-art equipment. Indeed, the United States left South Vietnam with the fourth largest army in the world, the fifth largest navy, and the fourth largest air force.[56] At the height of American involvement, there was approximately one person in uniform, serving in either the United States or South Vietnamese military, for every 11 inhabitants of North Vietnam. Based solely on firepower and troop strength, a war between North Vietnam/NLF and South Vietnam/United States was a high school football team up against the Pittsburgh Steelers.

Yet somehow the high school team won. One explanation for this outcome has been the Rambo myth—the paranoid delusion, embodied in the pair of movies starring Sylvester Stallone as a Vietnam veteran—that scheming politicians prevented victory in Vietnam. The American military could have defeated the enemy, but, as Rambo bellows to his former commanding officer, "somebody wouldn't let us win." In a reversal of reality, Rambo is depicted as a guerrilla warrior, relying on a knife and a bow and arrow (though with explosive arrowheads) to fight heavily armed Vietnamese regulars. The Rambo myth has been the preferred interpretation at the highest levels of government. While seeking the Republican presidential nomination, Ronald Reagan told a convention of the Veterans of Foreign Wars that "we will never again ask young men to fight and possibly die in a war our government is afraid to let them win." And in an address only hours after commencement of the air attacks on Iraq during the first Gulf War, President George H. W. Bush declared that "this will not be another Vietnam.... Our troops ... will not be asked to fight with one hand tied behind their back."[57]

The truth, however, was exactly the opposite: the United States employed every tactic short of nuclear weapons, devastating not only large parts of North Vietnam but obliterating much of the South Vietnamese countryside in an indiscriminate bombing campaign that massacred civilians and destroyed the homes and villages of the people supposedly being rescued from communism. According to one study of the air war, the firepower used on Vietnam exceeded the amount used in all previous wars combined; in just the 1968–1969 period, "the United States dropped over 1½ times more tonnage on South Vietnam alone than all the allies dropped on Germany throughout World War II." Another analysis calculated that the United States "dropped 70 tons of bombs for every square mile of Vietnam ... and ... over 500 pounds

of bombs for every man, woman, and child" in the country; American superiority over the NLF/North Vietnamese in ordnance expended "was *in excess
of 450 to 1*" (emphasis in original).[58]

These attacks also surpassed all previous warfare in their technological
sophistication. The "Daisy Cutter," a 7½ ton bomb, creating a blast almost
the power of an atomic weapon, was "dropped by parachute and detonated
above the ground, flattening all trees and structures in an area with a diameter
equal to ten football fields." Describing "the swimming-pool maker"—a bomb
a fifth the size of the Daisy Cutter—a pilot noted that even this smaller explosive "sent out a visible ripple of shock 'like a small atomic bomb.'" Two American scientists estimated that, in 1968 alone, bombing left 2.6 million craters
in the South, "making the country look like the surface of the moon."[59]

The resulting scale of human devastation was staggering. Just between
1965 and 1969, more than a million civilians were killed in South Vietnam,
the majority from the "friendly fire" of American forces, and another 2.25 million wounded—equivalent in the contemporary United States to almost 22
million killed and 46 million wounded. Nearly half the rural population either
lost their homes or were killed or wounded.[60] If this was political restraint
of the military, then an unfettered policy would have left no one for the
Thieu/Ky junta to govern.

The real reason for the inability to prevail in Vietnam was simple: the
United States was not fighting the communists or the North Vietnamese, but
rather the people of Vietnam. Whatever the South Vietnamese may have
thought about communism, they were certainly in favor of being reunited
with the North and led by a government that had spent three decades fighting
foreign oppressors. The NLF may not have been Robin Hood's band of merry
men, but to most of South Vietnam, the Thieu/Ky regime was indisputably
the Sheriff of Nottingham, its base of support centered in Washington rather
than in Vietnam, where most of the population viewed it as merely the most
recent instrument of foreign control and no more legitimate as an expression
of the national will than any of the Soviet puppet states. Despite the substantial South Vietnamese military created by the United States, without
American forces there was never much of a conflict. As Daniel Ellsberg, the
military analyst who released the Pentagon Papers to the *New York Times*,
concisely put it, "we weren't *on* the wrong side; we *were* the wrong side."[61]

The contrast in the field between the South Vietnamese military and
the enemy was particularly instructive. The official Army of the Republic of
Vietnam (ARVN, pronounced "Arvin") suffered desertion rates as high as 50
percent and tended to flee from the battlefield, leaving their weapons to be

picked up by the guerrillas so often that American troops referred to some ARVN units as "Vietcong PXs." Those soldiers who remained typically seemed more interested in fleecing the peasantry than fighting the enemy. As part of their propaganda campaign, NLF cadre told villagers that the government forces would beat, rape, and plunder them, and the ARVN rarely failed to meet expectations. American correspondents in Vietnam regularly reported observing ARVN units steal villagers' food, livestock, and furniture, rob civilians at gunpoint, and back up military trucks to local stores, carrying off large quantities of merchandise. Although the NLF soldiers were no slouch at assassination—typically of government officials who had enriched themselves at the peasantry's expense—they also provided education, medical care, and assistance to the elderly and the widowed in harvesting their crops; particularly important, they did not take anything for personal gain.[62]

Most dramatic was the difference in determination between the two sides. Generally reluctant to engage the enemy despite their superior equipment, ARVN troops were a reflection of the government they represented, essentially mercenaries lacking commitment to a cause. In contrast, NLF forces were notable for their fierce dedication, exhibiting a willingness to fight and die that could only be informed by idealism and the deeply held belief that they were fighting for their country's independence. The American military was chagrined to discover that they were stuck with the "wrong" Vietnamese, deriding their allies' timidity while expressing a grudging respect for the enemy's bravery. One general recounted how a lone guerrilla held up an entire American infantry company by firing all his ammunition, then throwing back the grenades that were tossed at him, and finally hurling rocks in a last gesture of defiance before being shot. "If one of our men had fought like that," the general remarked, "he would have been awarded the Medal of Honor." And a Special Forces major called his adversaries "the finest soldiers I have ever seen in the world except for Americans." There was only one plausible explanation for this difference. "From the contrast in behavior of the two sides," wrote Neil Sheehan, "I can only conclude that Vietnamese will die more willingly for a regime which, though Communist, is at least genuinely Vietnamese and offers them some hope of improving their lives, than for one which is committed to the galling status quo and is the creation of Washington."[63]

Thus, the huge asymmetry in arms, equipment, and troop strength, which conferred such military advantage on the ARVN/American forces, proved no match for the asymmetry in determination and popular support enjoyed by the guerrillas. Even administration officials and staunch anti-communists acknowledged that the majority of the population sided with the NLF. The state department analyst Douglas Pike, author of a book on the organization, called the NLF the only "truly mass-based political party in South Vietnam." After visiting South Vietnam, the conservative journalist Arnaud de Borch-grave reported, "Not only do the Viet Cong remain the only disciplined polit-ical force..., there is no other political party worth mentioning." And the series of "Motivation and Morale" studies conducted by the Rand Corporation—the think tank funded by the military to conduct behavioral research—con-cluded that the guerrillas had won the hearts and minds of the peasant population by offering dignity and respect, in contrast to the "unbridled indul-gence" and "senseless brutality" exhibited by South Vietnamese officials. The United States' own intelligence data on the allegiance of the villages in the countryside confirmed these assertions: in the middle of 1967, only 168 of more than 12,000 villages could be counted as entirely loyal to the government in comparison to almost 4,000 entirely loyal to the guerrillas; the other 8,000 villages were contested to varying degrees.[64]

PACIFICATION, DEFOLIATION AND MASSACRES: CONDUCT OF THE WAR

The popularity of the NLF in the countryside posed a tactical dilemma for the United States: how to fight a war on behalf of an ally, the majority of whose population sympathized with the enemy. If, as the Maoist notion of "people's war" had it, the guerrillas were fish swimming in the sea of the peo-ple, the American military decided not to focus on catching the fish but on removing the water, rearranging the country through the forcible removal of people whose families had resided on the land for generations. This approach represented a massive expansion of a program initiated under Diem, in which farm families were moved into specially constructed developments called "agrovilles."

Eventually involving thousands of villages and millions of people, the relocation program was retitled with various euphemisms—"Operation Sun-rise," "pacification," "strategic hamlets," "New Life hamlets," and, most bizarre, "prosperity zones"—but the concept always remained the same: remove the residents of entire villages at gunpoint, destroy everything left behind—homes, household belongings, trees, gardens, crops—and then herd the people into "fortified" settlements. The process of demolition was notable for its thoroughness. As detailed by an observer, first gasoline was poured on the houses, which were set afire with torches. Then bulldozers flattened what was left. Finally, American jets bombed the deserted ruins, "as though, having once decided to destroy it, we were now bent on annihilating every possible indication that the village ... had ever existed." The former residents became refugees in what was a cross between concentration camp and shanty town, ringed by barbed wire, watch towers and moats, and described by one reporter as "squalid, jerry-built, often without dependable water supplies or even primitive sanitation," resulting in total lack of hygiene, widespread malnutrition and illnesses such as dysentery, malaria, and infectious hepatitis. In one observer's characterization of the pacification program, "We were taking people from an area they liked, where they had plenty of land, and moving them to where they didn't want to go to protect them from someone they didn't necessarily think was an enemy."[65]

American officials offered Orwellian interpretations of the relocation process. While one hamlet was being burned to the ground and protesting peasant families forcibly evacuated, banners proclaimed that "we will root out all the Viet Cong who destroy our villages." Then at the settlement camps the villagers, sobbing or sullen after being wrenched from their homes, were greeted by signs announcing "welcome to the reception center for refugees fleeing communism." In an echo of Teresienstadt—the Nazi concentration camp presented as a model Jewish town—one of the settlement camps, built by forced peasant labor, was set up as a showpiece for visitors despite its encircling walls of bamboo stakes, watch towers, barbed wire, and submachine toting guards. In the most grotesque instance, General Maxwell Taylor explained that the people whose homes and villages had been blasted out from under them had been "liberated from Vietcong control," having "preferred to abandon all that they own ... rather than live under Communist rule."[66]

Villages thought to have assisted the NLF were subjected to less cordial measures—bombed without their residents first being escorted elsewhere. Sometimes the bombing was preceded by warning leaflets dropped from planes, which were often ineffective because many peasants were illiterate. In any event, there were frequent mistakes, in which faulty information or misread maps led to the bombing of "friendly" villages and the deaths of peasants with no connection to the enemy. Asked by a journalist whether civilians weren't killed by the bombings, a non-commissioned officer "answered with a laugh, 'What does it matter? They're all Vietnamese.'"[67]

While the demolition bombs were intended to make a village uninhabitable, anti-personnel bombs, designed to inflict maximum pain and suffering on individuals were also deployed on a massive scale. The most controversial weapon, producing a campaign of demonstrations against its manufacturer, Dow Chemical Company, was napalm, a jellied gasoline that, when ignited, splattered widely, clinging to skin and melting human flesh into barely recognizable forms. Dropped on a peasantry, napalm turned a village into an oven, leaving what one journalist described as a pile of "charred bodies of children and babies." In 1965, a humanitarian medical organization solicited assistance from the State Department to fly out of Vietnam a few hundred of the many thousands of napalmed children for treatment but was rebuffed; photos of burned children were unlikely to engender support for the war.[68]

But whether an area had been razed after evacuation, or bombed after being determined sympathetic to the NLF, or only leafleted with instructions for its residents to leave, it was then declared a "free fire zone," which meant that anyone who remained was considered an appropriate target. Villagers who had trickled back to their homes after having waited out the bombing elsewhere became fair game for "skunk hunting"—essentially target practice. The victims were typically reported as part of the enemy body count under the standard practice of categorizing "anything that's dead and isn't white ... [as] V.C." As one captain succinctly put it, when asked how he knew that the man he had just shot was an enemy: "I know he's a VC by the nine bullet holes in his chest."[69]

Of course, civilian casualties are hardly a rarity in war. Tens of thousands of noncombatants were killed by the allied bombing of the Reich, and many more perished from the use of atomic weapons on Hiroshima and Nagasaki. But this loss of life occurred when one side in a war attacked the other and, for all its cruelties, eroded the enemy's morale and will to resist, increasing the likelihood of surrender. In Vietnam, however, American forces attacked the *South* Vietnamese, alienating the people whose liberation was claimed to be the purpose of the conflict. "They say this village is 80 per cent VC supporters," remarked one American officer after his unit had entered a rural area; "By the time we finish ... it will be 95 per cent."[70]

The evacuation of villagers and the bombing of the countryside also produced dramatic changes in the demography of South Vietnam, driving millions of people into cities and towns. In a short period of time the country's population went from 85 percent rural to 60 percent urban, as Saigon alone grew tenfold, becoming a Dickensian nightmare: women forced into prostitution, black marketeers, beggars, pickpockets, and packs of abandoned children, living and sleeping on the streets. Infant mortality skyrocketed and disease—especially tuberculosis, but also cholera, smallpox, typhoid, intestinal parasites—ran rampant in a city, whose water and sewer systems were unable to accommodate the strain of such rapid population increase. "I have sometimes thought, when a street urchin with sores covering his legs, stopped me and begged for a few cents' worth of Vietnamese piastres," wrote Neil Shee-han, "that he might be better growing up as a political commissar. He would then, at least, have some self-respect."[71]

Nor was this transfer of the rural population an unfortunate but unin-tended byproduct of the conflict. As an American diplomat candidly observed, "to make progress it is necessary to level everything. The inhabitants must go back to zero, lose their traditional culture." Forced "urbanization" was thus the core of the American strategy, as outlined in the influential journal *Foreign Affairs* by Samuel P. Huntington, Harvard Professor and Chair of the Council on Vietnamese Studies. Because the Viet Cong was such a powerful force in the villages, Huntington suggested that the only way to deprive the enemy of its base was "depopulation of the countryside" through "forced-draft urban-ization and modernization." While conventional firepower might be ineffec-tive in defeating a rural movement, it could be applied "on such a massive scale as to produce a massive migration from countryside to city," so that "the Maoist-inspired rural revolution is undercut by the American-sponsored urban revolution." Although Huntington acknowledged that the urban slum might seem "horrible to middle-class Americans," for the Vietnamese peas-antry, their immiseration in the city constituted the "gateway to a new and better life."[72]

However, because leveling villages and relocating inhabitants were insuf-ficient to dislodge the guerrillas from a countryside whose crops yielded nour-ishment and whose vegetation provided physical cover, pacification had to be augmented by defoliation: the American military declared war on the land itself. Although there were initial attempts to burn down forested areas by dropping huge quantities of diesel fuel followed by incendiary bombs as igni-tion, eventually the military decided to poison the biological environment. Beginning in 1961 and continuing for a decade, massive amounts of herbi-cides were sprayed on the most fertile areas of South Vietnam in a program of "vegetation control" that sought to destroy crops that might benefit the enemy, oblivious to the fact that the rural civilian population was more affected by the resulting loss of food than the guerrillas. South Vietnam went from being the "Rice Bowl" of the region, a major exporter, to importing 850,000 tons, and other food crops suffered a similar decline. The purpose of the program was later changed to elimination of the foliage that concealed the enemy, thus depriving them of the ability to ambush American troops. Over its 10 years "Operation Ranch Hand"—the more benign name for the program; the official code name was "Operation Hades"—dropped almost 20 million gallons of herbicides, or about 50,000 tons, on thousands of villages, saturating six million acres.[73] In one of the war's iconic quotations, an American major famously declared that "we had to destroy the village in order to save it." It became increasingly apparent that the major's view was being applied to the entire countryside.

About 60 percent of the chemical defoliants sprayed on South Vietnam was "Agent Orange," a name derived from the color of the stripe encircling the drums in which it was shipped. Though used at concentrations less than a pound per acre by farmers in the United States, in South Vietnam the concentrations reached 50 times that amount, not only killing crops and foliage but contaminating the soil and seeping into the water supply; occasionally a plane with engine trouble was forced to jettison its entire load on a single village, producing a concentration 130 times the level considered safe. While the operation was taking place, research sponsored by the National Institutes of Health found that, even in small dosages, Agent Orange produced birth deformities in mice and rats, and a study by a Japanese agronomist documented dead river fish, poisoned livestock, and the deaths of local residents exposed to air polluted by the herbicide; although the American government attempted to keep the NIH report secret, it came to public attention after a Harvard geneticist obtained a bootlegged copy.[74]

The scientific community was outraged over what it termed "ecocide"— a premeditated attack on a nation's bioenvironment. Even before the information about birth defects emerged, 5,000 scientists, including 17 Nobel Laureates and 129 members of the National Academy of Sciences, signed a petition to President Johnson calling for an end to the employment of anti-crop weapons. An even stronger statement by the Federation of American Scientists condemned the use of chemical agents as "barbarous," representing "an attack on the entire population of the region." And after the study on birth defects, the American Association for the Advancement of Science called for the Department of Defense to "immediately cease all use" of Agent Orange.[75]

In the years following the war, concerns about the effects of Agent Orange were sadly confirmed as American veterans suffered from elevated levels of various cancers and fathered children with birth defects. For decades the Veterans Administration reacted by insisting that Agent Orange was not harmful to humans or by blaming the victims. One VA official suggested that the whole controversy was a scam—"a few Vietnam veterans simply unable or unwilling to adjust to the larger society" and seeking "financial compensation." Finally, in the 1990s the National Academy of Sciences began a series of congressionally authorized reviews to determine the specific medical conditions associated with exposure to Agent Orange—a list that now includes leukemia, bone cancer, cancers of the lymph glands, respiratory tract and prostate, and disorders of the liver and nervous system, as well as birth defects.[76]

As serious as the ailments affecting American veterans, of course the more severely afflicted were the Vietnamese. In the early 1980s, Philip Jones Griffiths, a photojournalist who had covered the war, returned to the areas that had been sprayed and documented the effects in a book filled with images that pain the sensitive and repel the insensitive: children born with severe spina bifida, with missing or malformed limbs, without retinas or with empty eye sockets. According to Griffiths, six percent of school children in a random sample suffered from congenital malformations, and in one village one out of every ten children was born deformed—statistics that did not include the large number of pregnancies resulting in stillbirths or degeneration of the fetus into "a formless blood-soaked sponge-like mass." Many of the photographs were also of fetuses preserved in formaldehyde—"grimacing Siamese twins" or "with half-formed jaws, collapsed skulls, deformed jaws and monstrously twisted pelvises and spines." Long after its departure, the American military had left behind a genetic time bomb.[77]

Although the large number of South Vietnamese civilian deaths was undeniable, until the late 1960s it was possible for the military to claim that they were either an accident or the result of the victims' failure to obey instructions—rural families returning to villages they had been ordered to leave. In fall 1969, however, an event that had occurred 20 months earlier came to light, in which hundreds of unresisting civilians were massacred at close range. In March 1968, an infantry platoon led by Lieutenant William Calley entered My Lai, a village known to be sympathetic to the Viet Cong. Meeting no resistance and finding no guerrillas, or even men of military age, they slaughtered all the people they did find—old men, women, children, and infants. Young women and girls were raped and in some cases mutilated before being killed. Because whole families were exterminated, leaving no one to report the deaths, an exact count of victims was not possible, but based on the bodies later recovered from mass graves, it appeared that 450 to 500 people were slain.[78]

Despite the presence of a military journalist, the operation was described as a great success, a lopsided victory for the American military in the face of enemy fire; the brigade press officer later explained that, had anyone on his staff acknowledged the occurrence of a massacre, "I would have lost my job." Everyone lined up behind the official account: the *New York Times* reported that American soldiers had caught the enemy in a pincer movement, killing 128 guerrillas in a daylong firefight; the brigade commander praised the officers in charge for "expert guidance, leadership and devotion to duty"; and the lieutenant colonel in charge of the mission declared that "the combat assault went like clockwork," adding, incredibly, that civilians "caught in fires of the opposing forces" were helped to leave the area.[79]

The true facts about My Lai surfaced only because one of the soldiers in Calley's platoon described the events to Ron Ridenhour, a friend in another infantry company. After his discharge Ridenhour sent a letter to 30 public officials—senators, house members, the secretary of defense, secretary of the army, and high ranking army officers—insisting that "something rather dark and bloody" had occurred at My Lai and calling for a public investigation. A perfunctory internal investigation resulted in denials that anything noteworthy had taken place, accompanied by accusations that the claim was communist propaganda. But the charge became impossible to deny when an army photographer who had accompanied the troops and was now discharged provided color pictures documenting the slaughter to *Life Magazine*. The military journalist, also a civilian by this time, came forward as well to share his account of what had occurred. Both men stated that they had kept silent while in Vietnam for fear of reprisal.[80]

The responses to disclosure of the My Lai massacre were almost as disturbing as the incident itself. Previous denials suddenly gave way to a flood of acknowledgements that My Lai was merely the tip of a very large iceberg. The commanding officer of the brigade including Calley's platoon maintained that every large combat unit in Vietnam had committed similar atrocities, which were unknown to the public only because "every unit doesn't have a Ridenhour." And a soldier attached to the company that included Calley's platoon observed, "It was just like another day in Vietnam. Something like this is always happening." Indeed, on the day of the My Lai massacre, some 80 to 90 civilians were murdered in a neighboring hamlet by another platoon in the same battalion. Subsequent investigations later found evidence for hundreds of cases of mass slayings. As the title of a recent book concisely put it, the rule for American troops was often "Kill Anything That Moves."[81]

The slaughter at My Lai and similar bloodlettings represented the inevitable culmination of the tactical approach to the war. If the victims had all been hideously burned or blasted to smithereens by bombs and napalm dropped from 50,000 feet, there would have been no reason for concern, because such air attacks were official policy for villages known to be sympathetic to the enemy; indeed, retired General James Gavin, who had led paratroopers in the D–Day invasion, called it "tragic" that Calley was convicted of a crime but not the "officers flying bombers." The face-to-face shooting of unarmed civilians was merely the next logical step, justified in the minds of many soldiers by the same rationale that informed the bombing. Asked to account for their acts, participants at My Lai and similar events explained that even women and children could throw grenades or sit by, knowing the location of a booby trap yet saying nothing while an American soldier took the step that cost his life; "the only good dink is a dead dink," one GI bluntly told a reporter. A government analyst expressed the dilemma more elegantly: "the Vietnamese communists erased entirely the line between military and civilian…. Not even children were excluded…. All people became weapons of war."[82] From the military's point of view, the failure to distinguish between civilians and combatants was thus the result of the former's identification with the latter, acting as their accomplice, safe haven and source of logistic support, a rationale implicitly acknowledging the true sympathies of much of the country. Besides, since the Vietnam War was not a traditional conflict in which the geographical battle lines were clearly defined, the military turned to body count as the metric by which success was determined, and if field grade commanders and their superiors were going to rate units on number of bodies, then, by God, line officers and NCOs would give it to them.

There are two separate and independent senses to the concept of war crimes. "Jus ad bellum" refers to whether the decision to declare war—the determination by one nation to use military force against another—has appropriate justification; "jus in bello" has to do with moral conduct in the prosecution of the war—for example, respecting the distinction between combatants and civilians. The initial impetus for the antiwar movement had been the belief that the United States was in violation of the former sense, having created "South Vietnam" as an invention to justify an intervention. However, even before revelation of the events at My Lai, the lack of justification as reason to oppose the war was becoming subordinated to the more compelling, because less abstract, issue of the means by which the war was being conducted. Earlier attempts to call attention to the evidence of atrocities had been discredited with ad hominem attacks or ignored. When, for example, Bertrand Russell held hearings on war crimes, a columnist for the *New York Times* described the famous philosopher as "an unthinking transmission belt for the most transparent Communist lies"; another article in the *Times* called him "a full-time purveyor of political garbage." Then, when a group of religious leaders—including Martin Luther King, Jr., 10 bishops, the president of the American Jewish Congress, and the heads of mainline protestant denominations—commissioned a study of the conduct of the war, they could not find a recognized publisher and had to have the book printed by an obscure press; despite its documentation of war crimes, committed not as renegade acts but as official policy, *In the Name of America* went largely unnoticed and unreviewed.[83]

After My Lai, however, the floodgates opened. Whatever one thought about the purpose of the war, its means were revealed as undeniably evil. The *New York Times*, which had found Bertrand Russell's efforts so objectionable, now provided a bibliography of 33 books as part of an essay-review suggesting an affirmative answer to its title question: "Should We Have War Crime Trials?" One book was written by Telford Taylor, Professor of Law at Columbia University, who had been brigadier general and chief counsel for the prosecution in the trials of Nazi war criminals. *Nuremberg and Vietnam* argued that senior American officials should be held to the same criteria applied to the enemy after World War II. If the precedent of General Tomayuki Yamashita—a Japanese commander hanged for atrocities committed by his troops— were applied to the United States, Taylor suggested that not only Army chief of staff General William Westmoreland but cabinet level officials, such as Dean Rusk, Robert McNamara, McGeorge Bundy, and Walt Rostow "would come to the same end," even hinting that Lyndon Johnson might be included. Indeed, in contrast to the case against the Japanese officer, whose troops had acted without his knowledge or approval, the use of free-fire zones, forced evacuation, and other tactics that Taylor judged war crimes had been planned and approved at the highest levels of government.[84]

CONFLICT IN THE CONFLICT: MILITARY OPPOSITION TO THE WAR

Recognizing that they were being used to support a government despised by the majority of its own people, many American soldiers turned against the war. As early as 1965, when the escalation of troops was just beginning, Master Sergeant Donald Duncan, a member of the elite "Green Berets," returned from Vietnam and immediately resigned from the army. A staunch anti-communist with family roots in the 1956 Hungarian uprising, Duncan was chagrined to find that "We are the Russian tanks blasting the hopes of an Asian Hungary." This was not some raw recruit disenchanted by the realization that real warfare was less heroic than the Hollywood version. A specialist in operations and intelligence who had briefed Secretary of Defense Robert McNamara, Duncan had a chest full of fruit salad, including two Bronze Stars, the Legion of Merit and a Silver Star, and had been recommended for a battlefield commission.[85]

Many average grunts came to the same conclusion. William Ehrhart, who became critically acclaimed for both his poetry and prose about the war, joined the Marine Corps right out of high school, rejecting offers from colleges, out of the belief that "if we did not fight the Communists in Vietnam, we would one day have to fight them on the sands of Waikiki"; he then badgered his superiors until they gave in to his request to be sent to Vietnam. As a decorated infantry sergeant, however, he came to the "staggering realization" that "I was a Redcoat," just like one of "the nasty British soldiers that tried to stifle our freedom.... I wasn't a hero, I wasn't a good guy ... somehow I had become everything I had learned to believe was evil."[86]

Nor was this notion confined to enlisted men; once retired and thus free to comment, some of the most highly respected military figures pronounced our actions in Vietnam dishonorable. In addition to General Gavin's opposition to the bombing as morally repugnant, General David Shoup, recipient of the Medal of Honor and Marine Corps commandant from 1959 to 1963, described the conflict as a struggle between "crooks in Saigon" and Vietnamese nationalists. General Hugh Hester, another decorated officer offered the harshest comments, describing Vietnam as "a war of aggression," the conduct of which he called "cowardly and morally indefensible, ... monstrous evils ... inflicted by the U.S. Government upon these peasant people who ... could not threaten the U.S. security in any way whatever, even if they wished, which they do not."[87]

Opposition to the war within the military was expressed in various ways. During the peak years of American involvement, the rate of desertion in the army increased to seven soldiers per hundred, while AWOL ("absence without leave") rates rose to 17 per hundred, the highest levels in modern history; unlike desertions in previous conflicts, which typically occurred under fire, most during Vietnam took place away from the battlefield, an indication of dissent rather than a reaction to danger. Also, as the war went on, incidents of "combat refusal" became common, as some units balked at following orders. In August 1969, for example, an infantry company, ordered to proceed into a dangerous area, simply refused; later in the year, while network television captured the event, a rifle company from the illustrious 1st Air Cavalry similarly refused an order to advance in a dangerous area. Sabotage also became a problem, especially in the navy, where a number of ships destined for service in Vietnam were put out of commission by acts of vandalism; in the largest single case of sabotage in naval history, a crew member set a massive fire in the aircraft carrier, U.S.S. *Forrestal*, causing millions of dollars of damage and delaying its deployment for more than two months. In the ultimate act of resistance to authority, some soldiers resorted to "fragging" a superior whose enthusiasm for engaging the enemy exposed his men to unnecessary risk—murdering him with a fragmentation grenade. While accurate statistics about the number of fragging incidents were naturally difficult to compile, it is estimated that there were 550–600 such attempts in Vietnam. In 1971, "The Collapse of the Armed Forces"—an article in the *Armed Forces Journal* written by a marine colonel, the former director of the Corps' History Division—called the "morale, discipline and battleworthiness of the U.S. Armed Forces ... lower and worse than at any time ... possibly in the history of the United States."[88]

In more organized opposition, underground newspapers proliferated—at least 250 by one count—published on or near military bases and distributed on post by soldiers. Unlike the more traditional gripes about service life—the overregulation and petty harassment that soldiers call "chickenshit"—these publications reported approvingly on combat refusals, fraggings, and other acts of resistance, and encouraged outright rebellion against military authority. "In Vietnam," a typical article pointed out, "the Lifers, the Brass, are the true Enemy, not the enemy." Even officers organized: the Concerned Officers Movement, composed of some 3,000 members on active duty, demanded official recognition of their right to oppose the Vietnam War and rented a billboard just outside Norfolk Naval Base with the message "Peace Now."[89]

The anti-war movement within the military culminated with the establishment of Vietnam Veterans Against the War, the first group ever formed of American veterans opposed to a war in which they had fought while it was being waged. VVAW led numerous marches and demonstrations, including the famous event in Washington in which, one by one, hundreds of veterans threw their medals over the wire fence, erected to protect the Capitol Building from men who had fought in Vietnam. The first soldier in this ceremony, a former marine sergeant, announced that "we now strip ourselves of the medals of courage and heroism ... and cast these away as symbols of shame, dishonor, and inhumanity." In the procession that followed, many battle-hardened veterans sobbed, while the pile of discarded honors grew, eventually including 14 Distinguished Service Crosses—the nation's second highest military decoration behind only the Medal of Honor—100 Silver Stars, and more than 1,000 Purple Hearts.[90]

Servicemen also found a safe haven and a sympathetic ear in the antiwar movement, which had always regarded them as victims of an immoral policy and had made systematic attempts to reach out to them. In 1967, the coffeehouse project began operation, an alternative to traditional NCO clubs and USO centers, where soldiers could find anti-war literature and military counseling along with food and entertainment; coffeehouses soon operated near most of the military posts in the United States, each one drawing hundreds of visitors a week. And despite being the despised "Hanoi Jane" to supporters of the war, when Jane Fonda's political vaudeville troupe toured military bases as an alternative to USO shows, it drew throngs of soldiers cheering a performance that encouraged insubordination and condemned American presence in Vietnam and many other places around the world.[91]

Although stories of conflict between anti-war demonstrators and veterans later arose, in fact activists worked hard to befriend veterans. In particular, the notion that opponents of the war spit on returning soldiers and called them "baby killers" is a meme encouraged by the Rambo movies among other sources and spread by repetition to the point of widespread belief despite the fact that it is probably a myth. Neither the print nor the electronic media reported any such incident at the time—at least none perpetrated by *opponents* of the war. Reports do exist in which antiwar activists, Jane Fonda and Abbie Hoffman among them, were spit on and physically assaulted by supporters of the war; some of these attacks took place against anti-war veterans, including one case in which a VVAW member had a drink thrown in his face. There is also no report at the time of any physical altercation between soldiers returning from Vietnam and demonstrators spitting on or insulting them, and it is difficult to believe that veterans fresh from armed conflict would eschew responding to such abuse forcefully.[92] In any event, there is no denying that, in the latter years of the anti-war movement, much of its leadership came from the ranks of the men who had fought in Vietnam.

ACCEPTING THE INEVITABLE

Faced with rising opposition to the war especially after My Lai, President Richard Nixon turned to "Vietnamization" of the conflict, systematically reducing American ground forces while expanding the role of the South Vietnamese army. After a year of escalated attempts to crush the North Vietnamese—bombing campaigns, a naval blockade, and the mining of Haiphong Harbor—in January 1973 the United States signed an "Agreement on Ending the War and Restoring Peace in Vietnam," accepting provisions that had been available at any time during the previous decade. Indeed, the Agreement began by reaffirming the accords of two decades earlier, committing the United States to "respect the independence, sovereignty, and territorial integrity of

Vietnam as recognized by the 1954 Geneva Agreement on Vietnam." Also in the same language as its predecessor, the 1973 Agreement called the 17th parallel separating so-called North and South Vietnam "only provisional and not a political or territorial boundary."[93]

No longer propped up by American troops, the South Vietnamese government soon collapsed, as everyone knew it would. Presidential tapes released decades later revealed that, behind the scenes, even Richard Nixon and his National Security Adviser, Henry Kissinger, acknowledged that Saigon's fate was inevitable and were concerned only to "find some formula that holds the thing together a year or two, after which ... no one will give a damn." Although, as they hoped, the end was prolonged for two years after American withdrawal, it is nevertheless considered the only war the United States ever lost. The very name of the conflict has become a synonym for disaster: "The housing market is the Vietnam War of the American financial system," stated one analyst discussing the Great Recession. But the reflections on American loss have tended to regard the experience of the Vietnamese as merely the ground from which emerges the more noteworthy figure: the service and suffering of American troops, who sustained more than 58,000 deaths, more than 300,000 injuries, and countless cases of PTSD and chemical-related illnesses. Understandable though it may be, this focus treats the war as something that happened to *us*—to America and Americans. The United States invaded a predominantly peasant country, napalmed its rural population, and devastated its countryside, defoliating forests, deliberately uprooting masses of people from their traditional culture and forcing them into urban poverty, rendering one quarter of the population of South Vietnam homeless—equivalent to more than 70 million Americans—and leaving a legacy of birth defects, congenital deformations, and unexploded ordinance; according to *Time*, since the war ended, more than 100,000 Vietnamese have been killed or injured by land mines or other abandoned explosives.[94] More than three million Vietnamese were killed during the war, two-thirds of them noncombatants. The Vietnam War was not primarily a tragedy suffered by the United States; it was an agony and a degradation that the United States inflicted on the Vietnamese.

I have dwelt at length on the war because only by appreciating its obscenity is it possible to understand the degree of anger and passion that fueled the movement. The war was an intolerable evil, and opposing it became an obligation of conscience. As the literary scholar H. Bruce Franklin, himself a former antiwar activist, observed decades later, the tens of millions of people who sympathized with the Vietnamese suffering and identified with their struggle for independence represented "the finest American behavior." Indeed, absent the pressure exerted by the antiwar movement, who knows what additional measures the government would have employed? Tapes of discussions in the Oval Office later revealed that Nixon considered using the nuclear bomb on North Vietnam and bombing the country's dikes; told that the latter action would drown 200,000 civilians, the president responded, "I don't give a damn." However, in his memoir Nixon acknowledged that, especially after the fall 1969 moratorium, in which more than two million people participated in protests, he was mindful of the effects of military escalation on public opinion.[95] As bad as the war was, without the movement the carnage might have been much worse.

The Real Lawbreakers

In response to the movement, law enforcement engaged in behavior criminal as well as unconstitutional. Most of these acts were committed against persons whose sole offense was to express some political opinion deemed unacceptable in official circles; that is, their "crime" consisted of nothing more than thinking the wrong thoughts or uttering the wrong words. At the time many activists believed that the government was keeping tabs on the movement, but their warnings were often dismissed as paranoia or grandiosity; in fact, their suspicions fell far short of reality. Relying on information provided not only by their own agents but also by *informelle Mitarbeiter* on campuses and in communities, the FBI compiled dossiers on hundreds of thousands of persons in a massive surveillance program, in some cases proceeding to tap phones, open mail, and search homes and offices in the middle of the night. For example, the offices of the Socialist Workers Party, a perfectly legal political organization, were burglarized almost 100 times within six years by FBI agents, who stole financial records, correspondence, and other documents, including the defense strategies of members involved in federal court proceedings; as Noam Chomsky pointed out, the Watergate break-in, though trivial by comparison, produced much greater outrage because it was intolerable to "direct ... against the political center a minor variant of the techniques of repression that are commonly applied against radical dissent."[96]

Nor was amassing this information an end in itself, but rather the beginning of efforts to disrupt the lives of individuals and the functioning of groups in which they were active—campaigns approved by an FBI director as obsessed with order as he was disdainful of law. The bureau sent letters to parents of many SDS members, unsigned but claiming to be from one of the student's friends, or another parent of a politically active child, or just a "patriotic American," warning that the student was involved in activities detrimental to both the country and him or herself; some of these letters informed parents, falsely, that their child had contracted a sexually transmitted illness. Another campaign targeted politically active faculty and teaching assistants, sometimes achieving their dismissal, again for no reason other than their support for civil rights or opposition to the war. Some initiatives attempted to sabotage a group's activities by distributing misinformation: sending members notices of meetings that did not exist, canceling meetings that did, or otherwise creating chaos. When a national antiwar organization sought to find housing for people coming to Chicago, the FBI flooded its office with hundreds of fictitious names and addresses, supposedly from local residents volunteering to put up the visitors—a ruse that caused lengthy, frustrating attempts to locate these non-existent possibilities.[97]

More scurrilous, the FBI used its favorite tactic, the anonymous letter, to create personal animosities and sow conflicts both within and between groups. Some members of SDS received letters claiming that other members were FBI agents or were addicted to drugs or were, in what the bureau regarded as a smear, "homosexual." In an effort to manipulate others to do their dirty work, the bureau also sent fake letters to the leaders of organized crime, supposedly written by members of the Communist Party, falsely accusing them of having bombed the party's New York office. When the comedian and civil rights activist Dick Gregory complained about mob activity, the FBI again moved "to alert La Cosa Nostra to Gregory's attack"; the bureau wanted to ensure that a criminal syndicate realized it was being denounced by a social activist.

The campaign against black leaders and groups was particularly vicious. While mainstream organizations such as Martin Luther King's Southern Christian Leadership Conference were targets for FBI disruption, the Black Panther Party received special attention, including attempts to foment violence against its members. One anonymous letter erroneously warned the leader of a Chicago street gang that the Panthers had placed a hit out for him. Another letter, purportedly from the parent of a member of the Panthers, was sent to Rabbi Meir Kahane, leader of the militant Jewish Defense League, describing "a plan to force Jewish store owners to give [the Panthers] money" to be sent to Arabs, "or they would drop a bomb on the Jewish store"; the FBI was gratified to see that members of the JDL subsequently picketed the Harlem branch of the Black Panther Party. In an even more sinister manipulation, knowing that a feud between the Panthers and Organization U.S., a black nationalist group in California, had led to a shoot-out, the Los Angeles FBI office produced a sequence of poison pen letters and cartoons, alerting one side of the other's plans to kill its leaders, in the hope that such measures "will result in an 'U.S.' and BPP vendetta." When four Panthers were murdered within an eight-month period, the FBI viewed it as a "tangible result" of their efforts. In one attempt to "neutralize" Panther leadership the bureau eschewed manipulative letters and took matters into their own hands, combining with the Chicago police in a pre-dawn raid on an apartment where they shot two Black Panther Party members—Fred Hampton and Mark Clark—asleep in their beds. Although no one was charged criminally despite substantial evidence of premeditated murder, a civil rights lawsuit produced a $1.85 million settlement. While it is undeniable that some Panthers eventually turned to criminality—extortion, arson, beatings, even murder—all these FBI actions to decimate the party took place before its descent into thuggery and, in any event, had nothing to do with any unlawful acts by the victims. Hampton, in particular, was regarded as a hero, eulogized by the civil rights leadership for his work with Chicago youth.[98]

The FBI also employed agents provocateurs posing as activists to persuade opponents of the war to engage in activities that would both justify their repression and foster public outrage against the movement. Indeed, in addition to encouraging illegal acts, these operatives often provided the materiel and technical expertise without which demonstrators would never have been able to commit them. Claiming to be an SDS organizer, for example, "Tommy the Traveler," an undercover police agent, frequented a number of upstate New York schools—Cornell, Syracuse University, Alfred University, Hobart College, and others—offering guns and grenades to students, along with instructions on bomb construction; at his urging and with his assistance, students at Hobart firebombed an Air Force ROTC office on campus. One of the most militant members of Weatherman turned out to be an FBI plant. Larry Grantwohl, a demolitions expert who taught his fellow Weathermen how to make bombs and delayed fuses, castigated other radicals for confining their targets to property; "true revolutionaries," he told them, "had to be ready and anxious to kill people." And a paid FBI informant offered explosives to the Black Panther Party, encouraging them to blast their way into armories to seize weapons. Perhaps the saddest case of entrapment resulted in the death of the person lured into the act. An informer working for both the FBI and the Seattle police paid $75 to a decorated Vietnam veteran with a clean record, provided him a bomb, and drove him to the scene of the planned explosion, where the police were waiting; when the veteran tried to flee, though unarmed and surrounded, he was killed by shotgun fire.[99] Although no systematic study of violent acts committed by activists in the Vietnam era has been conducted, agents of law enforcement were indisputably involved in many of them.

Finally, at the beginning of the Nixon administration, the nation's highest law enforcement agency set up a paramilitary group—the Secret Army Organization, created from the remnants of the far right Minutemen—which, on instructions from the bureau, attacked anti-war demonstrators and engaged in various acts of terrorism, including bombings, shootings and an attempt to assassinate a politically active university faculty member; when the attempt failed, wounding a different activist instead of the intended victim, the FBI agent acting as "control" for the group concealed the weapon used in the attack from the local police investigating the shooting. In addition to funding these activities, the FBI provided the SAO between $10,000 and $20,000 worth of weapons and explosives, the equivalent of five to six times that amount adjusted for inflation.[100]

By the late 1960s, much of the movement had arrived at a pessimistic view of the possibility of reform, as the suspicions that had arisen in response to official toleration of the denial of rights to blacks hardened into dogmatic certainties with the events in Vietnam. Those who crafted and administered policy appeared to enforce the rights of minorities only when compelled to do so, were intent on annihilating a small Asian nation seeking independence, and attempted to discredit and disrupt the lives of domestic opponents through a system of spies and provocateurs. Many activists, a number of Princeton students among them, became convinced that the ruling class and the government that served it was their enemy.

2. "Even Princeton"

The fourth oldest institution of higher education in the United States, Princeton University was founded three decades before the Declaration of Independence and played an instrumental role in the nation's early history. The university's president was a signer of the Declaration, and the delegates to the Constitutional Convention included nine alumni; in 1783 the Continental Congress met in Nassau Hall, making it briefly the capitol of the United States. In the nation's first quarter century, this college with a student body rarely numbering more than 100, produced 21 senators, 39 house members, 12 governors, three Supreme Court justices, a vice president and a president.[1]

Originally chartered as the College of New Jersey, the school took the name Princeton University during its sesquicentennial celebration in 1896. The title of the keynote address at the event—delivered by Woodrow Wilson, Professor of Jurisprudence and Political Economy—provided the university its motto: "Princeton in the nation's service"; seven decades later student radicals omitted the fourth word as a sarcastic reminder of the school's involvement in the war effort. Perhaps the smallest of the nation's research universities, Princeton has nevertheless compiled an extraordinary record of academic accomplishment, including, between faculty and graduates, 32 Nobel Laureates and 11 recipients of the Fields Medal, considered to be the mathematicians' equivalent of the Nobel.

As the sociologist Jerome Karabel has documented in *The Chosen*—his exhaustively researched study of admissions at Harvard, Yale, and Princeton—through at least the first half of the 20th century, each of the "Big Three" employed practices designed to ensure an entering class composed mainly of privileged, Anglo-Saxon young men, but Princeton surpassed its two rivals both in the degree of rigidity of these policies and the hostile reception endured by the few ethnic exceptions allowed through the admissions filter. Unlike Harvard and Yale, both of which had a history of accepting a small number of black applicants, for almost its first two centuries Princeton refused to enroll a single black student. The preferred institution for Southern families reluctant to expose their sons to abolitionist sentiments in New Haven and Cambridge, the university contributed its alumni in equal measure to the fallen on both sides of the Civil War. In the first decade of the 20th century, Woodrow Wilson, now elevated from his faculty post, brought to the presidency of the university the Southern sensibilities that he later brought to the presidency of the country: a view of slavery as a patriarchal institution both necessary for an "ignorant and inferior" race, but also benevolent, ensuring that blacks were treated "indulgently and even affectionately" by their noble masters. *Great American Universities*, a study published during Wilson's leadership, called the exclusion of "Negroes" an "injustice in which Princeton is unique among the universities."[2]

Wilson's departure produced no change in this policy. Indeed, in the late 1930s the admissions office accepted an applicant from a selective public school and awarded him a full scholarship, not realizing that they had admitted a black student until he arrived on campus. Yanked from the registration line and escorted to the dean of admissions, he was bluntly informed that he was not welcome at the university. Nor was this exclusionary policy imposed by an illiberal administration on a more egalitarian-minded student body. When, in the midst of the war against Nazi Germany, the editors of the student newspaper, the *Daily Princetonian*, attacked the exclusion of blacks as a policy "more characteristic of our enemies," a subsequent poll revealed that 62 percent of students opposed their admission. As four freshmen put it in a letter to the paper, "we hope the day will never come when Negroes, as they now exist and live, will wave their hats with our sons 'in praise of old Nassau.'" The university finally admitted a few black students in the middle of World War II only when forced to do so as part of the navy's wartime V-12 program. However, their arrival signaled only the most trivial change: for the decade between 1946 and 1955, Princeton enrolled a total of four more blacks, and even in 1960 the entering freshman class included exactly one black student.[3]

Although student opinion had become more liberal by 1960, Princeton was still regarded as the Ivy League school of choice for the sons of Southern gentry. Early in the year a group of demonstrators, including faculty members, who were protesting segregated commercial facilities, was physically attacked by a mob led by Southern undergraduates. As the dean of the college candidly observed in 1963, many blacks thought of Princeton as the best Southern college in the North, an impression that confederate flags on the walls of a number of undergraduate dormitory rooms did little to dispel. Even a year later, a group of Princeton students organized the Committee for Racial Reconciliation to promote the writings of Carleton Putnam, the leader of an attempt to overturn the *Brown v. Board of Education* decision on the basis of science; invited by the Committee to give a speech on campus, Putnam declared that integration was destructive to society due to what he claimed was the scientifically proven genetic inferiority of blacks. In an inspired response a group of opposing students attended the meeting held to choose officers and, noting that in its charter the Committee had claimed to represent "the Southern viewpoint," elected one of the few black undergraduates vice president on the grounds that not everyone in the South supported segregation. For responding to suppression with satire they were denounced both by the student newspaper as having executed an undemocratic coup and by a humorless university president for having violated the rights of the original members of the Committee.[4]

As Karabel has also documented, until after World War II Jews fared only slightly better than blacks at Princeton, regarded much as the five families in *The Godfather* regarded traffic in drugs: they were permitted but controlled. Quotas imposed a maximum on the number of Jews—an easily determined judgment by the admissions office because until 1950 the application form asked for religious affiliation. But in addition, their social isolation once admitted acted as a disincentive for Jews to apply in the first place. *Great American Universities* reported that, "Anti-Semitic feeling seemed ... more dominant at Princeton than at any of the other universities," quoting a university official who observed that, "If the Jews once got in, they would ruin Princeton as they have Columbia and Pennsylvania." The principal deterrent to Jewish interest was the system of private eating clubs—Princeton's version of Harvard's "final" clubs and Yale's secret societies—which for many years refused to accept Jews, effectively ostracizing them from the mainstream of social life; unlike the other two institutions, at which the clubs or societies were highly selective, offering membership only to a small percentage of undergraduates, almost every non–Jewish student at Princeton received an invitation to join a club, the more prestigious the better, during the "bicker" process in the middle of sophomore year. As the university secretary wrote to an alumnus in 1922 concerning Jews, the "strongest barrier is our club system": as long as "the undergraduate bicker committees ... make the admission of a Hebrew to a club the rarest sort of thing," he did not expect "the Hebrew question ... [to] become serious."[5]

As the number of Jews increased in the post-war period, students petitioned for a policy of 100 percent bicker, in which everyone was to be guaranteed an invitation from at least one club. However, there were still occasions when the policy was not successfully implemented, leaving a group of rejects, the great majority of them Jewish. But even when no one was found to be "unclubbable," bicker remained a cruel and humiliating process, in which each sophomore was visited for a few minutes by members of one club after another, and then, on the basis of this superficial encounter, rated on a seven-point scale from "ace" at the top to "lunch" (short for "lunchmeat") at the bottom. The results were predictable, as well turned-out boys who had been "prepared" at the right private schools and whose families belonged to the right country clubs received invitations from the most prestigious clubs; Ivy, which stood at the top of the social hierarchy, did not extend its first invitation to a public school graduate until 1951. As the sociologist C. Wright Mills noted in his classic study *The Power Elite*, for the upper classes a Princeton degree did not mean much unless one had been a member of Cottage, Tiger, Cap and Gown, or Ivy. Jewish students, typically public school graduates, were relegated almost entirely to the four lowest-status clubs, comprising more than half the membership of Prospect, the bottom of the food chain, being more of a cooperative whose members did all the work as opposed to the other clubs, which were staffed by paid employees.[6]

A column in the *Princetonian* in 1960 explained that the clubs' reluctance to admit Jews occurred "not ... because of Jewishness, but because of ... differentness." The clubs sought to find new members who would "fit in"—other students whom the present members would find "congenial"—and it was an unfortunate fact of life, according to the columnist, "that Jews seem to be more 'alien' in personality to the clubs than any other easily recognizable and self-conscious group." Even when a few Jewish members were accepted, it was important to set a quota, wrote another student, in order "to protect the non–Semitic integrity of [the] club in this Christian dominated Princeton community." However, as late as 1964 there were indications of a different motivation when the highest ranking student in his class declared in the *Princetonian* that Jews were characterized by "a deep seated feeling of inferiority in physical conflict and military affairs."[7]

In addition to its more severe social prejudices, Princeton was also distinguished from the other members of the Big Three by its reputation for what *Great American Universities* called "excessive juvenility." Or as the protagonist in an F. Scott Fitzgerald novel put it, the university enjoyed an "alluring reputation as the pleasantest country club in America." Well into the 1960s there was still good reason for this image, partly due to a rivalry between freshmen and sophomore classes that could have sprung directly from a Frank Merriwell novel. In the name of class spirit, roving gangs from one class looked for isolated members of the other in order to hold the victim down and carve their graduating year into his hair with shears or razors; the melee accompanying this amateur barbering often resulted in physical harm and property damage. In one instance, interclass rivalry culminated in a gang fight involving 600 students, until their eagerness to brawl was dampened by a tear gas bomb thrown by one of the combatants.[8]

Even more juvenile were the spontaneous riots that occurred regularly near the end of the spring semester. While white students from other Northern universities were getting ready to put their bodies on the line in summer campaigns for civil rights in the South, at Princeton rampaging undergraduates set fires, destroyed anything in their path, and fought with police. The worst such event occurred in 1963 when 1,500 rioters blocked traffic by hurling debris into the streets, proceeded to the local train station where they tried to overturn train cars, breaking their windows and starting a fire on the tracks, then caused property damage at the university president's house and the official residence of the governor of New Jersey, and finally wrecked campus equipment including a one-ton air compressor. To quell the riot it was necessary to call out the campus police, the entire Princeton police force, and New Jersey state troopers; 14 students were arrested, two sent to jail, many injured, and 47 suspended from the university. At the time such eruptions were usually attributed to the failure to provide a more appropriate outlet for male hormones on a campus that had not yet decided to admit anyone lacking a Y chromosome, an unfulfilled libido presumably leading to an uncontrollable urge to burn and riot. However, there was also a sense on the part of officials that such behavior, though inexcusable and to be punished, was a not entirely unexpected ritual of youth. The university president put it down to "springtime, fire engines, exams and young men," and the governor of New Jersey commented, drolly, that "it's spring and the sap begins to run." But whatever the explanation, spring mayhem produced damage and disruption of both the university and the community that dwarfed anything resulting from the political upheavals only a few years later.[9]

From Lyndon to Lenin

The sixties did not reach Princeton until the decade was half over. Indeed, when a senior organized a small Princeton Socialist Club in 1961, 20 undergraduates, offended at the expression of such ideas, burst into his room in his absence and trashed its contents, including the senior's graduate school applications. The political controversy on campus during the 1961-62 academic year was whether, in the event of nuclear war, the public should be allowed into fallout shelters constructed by the university. As the newspaper later observed, in the early 1960s the university was considered a "bastion of conservatism." An air of snobbishness still characterized the campus, a sense that students were accepted to the university not as recognition for what they had done but as confirmation of who they were. As an administrator observed in 1964, "Education for the Princeton man may be no more than the proper attire for a party to which he has already been invited."[10]

Faculty at the time were more liberal than their students. In early 1965, when almost 100 Princeton professors signed a *New York Times* advertisement opposing policy in Vietnam, hundreds of students, including the presidents of both the Princeton Young Republicans—the dominant political force on campus—and the Princeton Young Democrats, responded by forming a committee in support of the war; in a separate effort six months later, 400 undergraduates signed a telegram to General William Westmoreland, commander of U.S. forces in Vietnam, voicing their approval of the war. Cognizant of the school's reputation, the first contingent of SDS members to participate in an anti-war demonstration in Washington shortly after the chapter's formation in fall 1965, marched under an orange and black banner proclaiming, "Even Princeton." And the headline of an article in the *Princetonian* at the end of that academic year reflected a widely held view: "Princeton Students for a Democratic Society: Radical Activism in an Unlikely Place."[11]

For the first year of its existence, Princeton SDS was unliked as much as it was unlikely, becoming the object rather than the initiator of protests. At one of its earliest meetings, more than 200 students—most of them clean shaven and wearing ties and jackets in deliberate contrast to the less well-groomed SDS members—burst into the meeting to express their displeasure. "We've come to protest these protesters," declared one of the intruders. And an editorial in the *Princetonian* pronounced "campus opinion ... almost unanimous in condemning" SDS, whose "political stance" it called "repugnant to the majority of Princeton students." The major reason for such hostility was the claim that SDS's opposition to the Vietnam War was "assisting the progress of Communism." Nor was this concern assuaged when one of the Princeton chapter's first acts was to follow the lead of the national SDS office, voting to repeal from its constitution the exclusion clause, which had banned from membership any advocate for a totalitarian ideology, whether left or right. As a Princeton SDS member noted at the time, there was no danger that the organization would be "swamped by Marxist-Leninists, since they are non-existent on this campus"; besides, noted another spokesman, "most communists are over 30." At the end of its first year of activity, the *Princetonian* called the "SDS label ... almost invariably pejorative," adding that "the social condemnation one discovers after joining SDS can no doubt be traumatic."[12]

Yet less than two years later, the same *Princetonian* pronounced SDS "one of the most powerful student organizations on campus," and a prominent SDS member had been elected president of the Undergraduate Assembly, the student governing body. In an indication that the newspaper had not exaggerated, at the beginning of May 1968 1,500 people attended a demonstration called by SDS, many of its members having abandoned the liberalism that had informed the organization's creation and now espousing Marxist ideology and the need for socialism. The *Princetonian* called SDS "unrivalled on campus" as a political force, contrasting it with the Undergraduate Assembly, which "has proven itself to be ... impotent." Within less than the span of a single college class, a substantial number of students at a school known for the politically conservative nature of its undergraduates and its regular alcohol-fueled spring riot had gone from beers to barricades. Indeed, one of the chapter's most prominent members during its early years had begun college as an admirer of Lyndon Johnson, the president's picture adorning the wall of his dormitory room; initially an outspoken opponent of eliminating SDS's communist exclusion clause, he later visited Cuba where he met with members of Vietnam's NLF and upon his return joined the violent Weatherman sect, "ready for well-nigh total commitment to the revolution."[13]

What happened at Princeton was not uncommon at the time. Similar transformations were taking place at campuses and in SDS chapters across the nation, as tens of thousands of college students unhappily concluded that the normal political processes were inadequate to produce the kind of dramatic change they believed necessary. In 1964 national SDS's slogan had been "half the way with LBJ"—a play on the Johnson campaign's official motto proclaiming "All the way" and an indication not only that the organization found some merit in his domestic policies, but that SDS members still viewed elections as meaningful events deserving of their participation. Four years later an article from the official SDS newsletter, distributed to antiwar activists during the Democratic convention in Chicago, dismissed elections as an institution designed to perpetuate the existing system of power and thus useless as an instrument for its transformation. When the convention then nominated Lyndon Johnson's vice president, Hubert Humphrey, who had not bothered to participate in the primaries but enjoyed the support of Democratic power brokers, the presidential contest began to seem like a sham even to many people who did not consider themselves radical. As the title of a leaflet distributed by the Princeton chapter succinctly put it, "Elections Are a Hoax—Don't Vote, Organize!"[14]

The primary catalyst of such rapid radicalization was, of course, the Vietnam War. The anti-war movement had begun, perhaps naively, with the notion that the problem was lack of information and that the nation could be persuaded to take the appropriate action if only everyone knew the facts: that Ho Chi Minh was more popular in Vietnam than any satrap supported by the United States; that Vietnam was a single country whose division was an artifice designed to prevent an electoral victory by the Viet Minh; that the NLF was an indigenous movement in the South in opposition to the military dictatorship supported by the United States; and that, rather than extending China's influence in the region, the fear of which was offered to justify the presence of American troops, their departure would again focus Vietnam's attention on its traditional threat from the north. Thus, one of the most common tactics in the early days of opposition to the war was the "teach-in," a day-long event combining lecture, debate, audience participation, and entertainment, as thousands of people gathered to hear from academic experts, political activists, journalists and performers. Foreign policy officials were regularly invited to present the government's case, and their refusal to appear was regarded as implicit acknowledgement that justifications for the war could not withstand serious scrutiny. At a 12-hour "nation-wide teach-in" held in Washington, for example, the featured event was a debate—attended by 5,000 people and broadcast on radio and television by a special connection to more than another 100,000 on 100 campuses—in which the administration's policy was to be defended by McGeorge Bundy, the "special assistant for national security affairs" (now called the "national security advisor"). The announcement that he had been detained by government business and would not be able to appear, received only moments before the scheduled beginning of the debate, was met with snickers from the audience, which intensified into outright laughter when Bundy's message went on to declare, "I looked forward to this meeting, and I hate to miss it." A week later at the 36-hour Berkeley teach-in, attended by 30,000 people, an empty chair labeled "Reserved for the State Department" was placed on the stage during the discussion.[15]

While the teach-ins turned much of academia against the war, they had no effect on administration policy. But to much of the movement the obscenity of the war began to destroy the illusion of a heroic America committed to democracy, freedom, and human rights. Born at the end of the "Good

War," college students in the 1960s had been raised to believe that the United States was a moral exemplar among nations, reluctant to intervene in the affairs of other countries, but also unhesitant to take up arms when necessary to defend basic principles of decency and morality—a role that it claimed to find increasingly unavoidable as the post-war leader of the Free World. The integrity of America's motives was presumed to be above reproach, and opposing nations and their leaders were presumed to be inherently malevolent. The nation's behavior in Vietnam, however, pulled the cover off the heroic image, revealing underneath a bully with a huge military and a ruthless disregard for any real exercise of self-determination if it resulted in a government of which Washington disapproved.

Indeed, it was the realization that the heroic image was a myth that turned much of the movement against liberals, even those opposed to the war. To most SDS activists, "liberal" became an epithet, rarely used without being preceded by some appropriate qualifier like "unprincipled"—opposed to the war only because it was going badly. After all, at its onset it was liberal, elected politicians and the liberal brain trust in both the Kennedy and Johnson administrations, who had planned and supported the war. The two anti-war candidates seeking the 1968 presidential nomination were both for the war before they were against it. More than two years before the Gulf of Tonkin incident, when the American military presence still consisted only of a few thousand "advisors," Attorney General Robert Kennedy visited Vietnam, announced the administration's "full confidence" in Diem, and acknowledged that the United States was involved in "a new kind of war" in the area, vowing that "we will remain here until we ... win." Even after adopting a more dovish position during the Johnson administration, Kennedy still opposed any NLF representation in a South Vietnamese government.[16] And Senator Gene McCarthy, the other standard bearer for anti-war liberals, had voted for the Gulf of Tonkin resolution, authorizing Lyndon Johnson's commitment of American troops.

Most liberals in the media, too, had initially viewed intervention in Vietnam as America's right, voicing no objection while the largest military in the history of the world attempted to pound a small Asian country into submission—until it became clear that the Vietnamese would not submit. Only when the war had become patently unwinnable, did they suddenly find involvement in the conflict problematic—but never because it had been morally questionable to begin with. In his famous commentary acknowledging that "we are mired in stalemate," Walter Cronkite, "the most trusted man in America," maintained that the United States had "lived up to [its] pledge to defend democracy," oblivious to the fact that the real intention had been to subvert it. And even while characterizing American involvement in Vietnam as "a disastrous mistake," the *New York Times* journalist Anthony Lewis referred to the decision to intervene as "blundering efforts to do good." According to the "liberal media," the United States might have made misjudgments, but there was no doubt that American intervention had been informed by benevolent motivation, an instance of honorable purpose translated into poor policy.[17]

To SDS, however, Vietnam was not a mistake, not a morass into which a basically well-intentioned if misguided effort had stumbled, but merely the latest in a long list of actions by the United States, distinguished primarily by the Vietnamese willingness to fight back. Indeed, American intervention in Vietnam acted as an arrow, pointing the movement's attention to the numerous similar—and from the government's perspective more successful—instances of the same model in other developing countries, in which democratically elected administrations were overthrown by coups with American assistance and replaced by two-bit dictatorships more amenable to American business interests, while precisely those leaders most dedicated to what were supposed to be American democratic ideals were rounded up and executed by forces supported by the United States. The standard justification for these actions was the presence of communist influence—allusion to the International Communist Conspiracy sufficing as a reason for the United States to contravene the electoral will of citizens in Third World countries—but in practice they always seemed more effective in thwarting democracy rather than communism. As George Kennan, the intellectual architect of communist containment, explained, it was necessary, if "unpleasant," to impose a repressive dictatorship in preference to an elected government "penetrated by Communists," because the Communists were "essentially traitors" to their own people. However, in contrast to Vietnam, where there really *was* a substantial communist organization, and as a result—in a linkage that did not go unnoticed by SDS—an organized resistance that had already driven out one Western power, in these other instances there was typically no communist movement of any significance. But where the United States claimed to see subversives and conspiracies, SDS saw only hunger and poverty—and governments pursuing policies designed to improve the quality of life of their immiserated populations by redirecting the country's resources and productive facilities toward domestic needs rather than the interests of foreign investors. As Kennan candidly noted in connection with United States policy in Latin America, repressive regimes were required to protect "*our* raw materials" (emphasis added).[18]

In the 1950s and 60s, the United States sponsored or aided coups in many Third World countries: Iran, where the CIA orchestrated the overthrow of a constitutionally elected government, installing the hated Shah and his brutal secret police, the Savak; the Dominican Republic, where, after a military coup deposed a democratically elected president, the United States sent in the marines and the 82nd Airborne to suppress an attempt to restore the popularly elected leader; Indonesia, where a coup aided by the United States overthrew the government, culminating in the murder of hundreds of thousands of people, many of them identified from a list provided by the CIA.[19] However, the example considered particularly instructive within SDS circles was the 1954 overthrow of the Arbenz government in Guatemala, ending that country's decade of democracy and beginning a period of military dictatorships and death squads that lasted through the rest of the century. When Jacobo Arbenz Guzman became president in the first peaceful change of government in Guatemala's history, his administration initiated what an official in the State Department acknowledged was "a broad social program of aiding the workers and peasants," the centerpiece of which was the Agrarian Reform Law, confiscating land that had been owned but never cultivated by the United Fruit Company; this popular policy offered United Fruit compensation for the land and then redistributed it to half a million landless, hungry peasants. A public relations campaign in the United States portraying the Guatemalan government as a Soviet beachhead resulted in a military coup subsidized by the CIA and assisted by American fighter planes; the CIA also provided a list of Guatemalans slated for assassination. Two months later the army colonel at the head of the junta assumed power alone, legitimizing his rule through a nationwide plebiscite, in which, in order to save "unnecessary paper work," voters were required to present themselves before an election board and announce orally whether they wished the new leader to continue in office; 99.99 percent of the electorate found it prudent to answer in the affirmative, a result that *Time* soberly called "reassuring" for stability.[20]

The Guatemalan coup provided SDS a textbook example of the interconnections between business and government that, in the movement's Marxist jargon, exposed the state's role as an instrument of the "ruling class." Secretary of State John Foster Dulles had been one of United Fruit's principal legal advisors; Assistant Secretary of State for Inter-American Affairs John Moors Cabot, had been United Fruit's president; Dulles's brother Allen, director of the CIA, was a member of United Fruit's board of trustees; and undersecretary of state, General Walter Bedell Smith, who had helped plan the coup, was appointed one of United Fruit's vice presidents within three months after overthrow of the Arbenz government. The small number of communists in Guatemala never managed to attract any popular base, enjoyed no support in the military, and exerted little influence. The communist threat was a "good" reason for subverting democracy in Guatemala, offered in place of the real, and less compelling, reason: to ensure that the interests of United Fruit took precedence over the hunger of impoverished peasants. As Carl Oglesby, national SDS president during 1965–66, put it in *Containment and Change*, one of the movement's canonical texts, "Imperialism is thus christened as anticommunism, and our foe is instantly transformed from a human being into a pawn, a dupe or an outright hard-core agent of that International Communist Conspiracy whose ultimate objective (so we are guaranteed) is the conquest of America."[21]

Finally, this change in SDS's perspective, from liberal and anti-war to radical and anti-imperialist produced a corresponding change in its understanding of both the opposition and the solution. The liberal peace movement saw political opponents who had mistakenly involved the country in an unwinnable war and had to be removed from office. The anti-imperialist movement saw not merely misconceived policies but a thuggish and evil system in which the twin traveling companions of the dollar and the bayonet constituted a criminal conspiracy intent on exploiting the labor and resources of less developed countries. This imperialist understanding of the war led, or perhaps pushed, SDS into full-frontal Marxism, a progression that Carl Oglesby viewed as inevitable. "There was no way to resist the truth of the war," he wrote in 1969, at the height of the revolutionary rhetoric, "no way, that is, to avoid imperialism," and "once the policy critique of the war had been supplanted by the structural critique of empire, all political therapies short of socialist revolution appeared to become senseless." The "necessity of a revolutionary strategy," he concluded, "was, in effect, the same thing as the necessity of Marxism-Leninism," the only "*coherent, integrative, and explicit philosophy of revolution*" (emphasis in original).[22] Seeking an explanatory framework for the conflicts of the 20th century, SDS landed smack in the middle of the 19th.

As early as the spring 1965 march on Washington, Paul Potter, the SDS national president immediately before Oglesby, signaled the beginning of this transition to a more radical perspective, one that viewed the war, the oppression of blacks, and the problem of poverty all as sharing common institutional roots. "What kind of system is it," Potter asked, that

> justifies the United States ... seizing the destinies of the Vietnamese people and using them callously for its own purpose? What kind of system is it that disenfranchises people in the South, leaves millions upon millions of people throughout

the country impoverished and excluded from the mainstream and promise of American society, ... that consistently puts material values before human values and still persists in calling itself free and still persists in finding itself fit to police the world.

"We must name that system," Potter declared, while the crowd implored him to do so. Yet without uttering the word itself—he later explained that he thought of "capitalism" as "an inadequate description of the evils of America, a hollow dead word tied to the thirties"—Potter went on to proclaim the movement's moral responsibility:

> We must name it, describe it, analyze it, understand it and change it. For it is only when that system is changed and brought under control that there can be any hope for stopping the forces that create a war in Vietnam today or a murder in the South tomorrow or all the incalculable, innumerable more subtle atrocities that are worked on people all over—all the time.[23]

Within the next four years SDS went from banning communists to waving the Red Book, from calling for negotiations in Vietnam to siding with the NLF, from qualified support for LBJ to opposing "bourgeois" elections—from reform to revolution.

The Movement at Princeton

I entered Princeton's psychology department as a graduate student in the summer of 1967, having arrived through a somewhat circuitous route. I had earlier flunked out of undergraduate school after spending more time with a cue in my hands than a book and spent a number of years hanging out in pool rooms and blues clubs before spending two years of involuntary employment as a military policeman. Returning to college within weeks after being discharged, in my second incarnation as an undergraduate I did well enough to be accepted at Princeton as a Psychometric Fellow—a graduate fellowship for students interested in psychological measurement, funded by Educational Testing Service, the manufacturer of SATs and similar tests for applicants to graduate and law schools. Though a veteran, I was strongly opposed to the war.

The Princeton chapter of SDS was beginning its third year of existence. The first two years had been largely uneventful, and the organization's campaigns against military recruiters and Dow Chemical, the manufacturer of napalm, were generally ignored by the rest of the campus. However, something changed over the summer of 1967, and not just for Princeton students.

In October more than 150,000 people demonstrated at the Lincoln Memorial, after which 30,000 of them surrounded the Pentagon and engaged in civil disobedience—the events chronicled in Norman Mailer's "nonfiction novel," *Armies of the Night*. Refusing to disperse, they were beaten or gassed, and almost 700 were arrested, Mailer among them; a demonstrator placing a flower in the rifle barrel of one of the military policemen bearing down on him became an iconic photo of the time. The same week hundreds of students at the University of Wisconsin occupied a building to prevent Dow Chemical from recruiting on campus; they were removed after a police assault, marked by the first use of tear gas on a university campus.[24]

While nothing so dramatic occurred at Princeton, SDS began the academic year by serving notice of its adherence to the ethos that for many people epitomized the movement: defiance of authority. In the midst of the university president's address to the freshmen class, counseling them not to "divert a major part of their limited time and energy from study to action," two SDS leaders distributed leaflets throughout the audience, urging students to engage in the very activities that the president was cautioning them to avoid. The leaflet called the university a "service station" for an oppressive system, a charge that was elaborated a couple of days later in a letter from the same two activists to the student newspaper: Princeton was "a recruiting center" for corporate executives and government bureaucrats, complicit through its research and investments "in the maintenance of South African racism, poor white poverty, a repressive military machine, and American domination of third world."[25] According to SDS, the university was part of the problem.

My own political involvement began with the Princeton Graduate Draft Union, an organization formed to assist members in finding an alternative to being drafted, after new Selective Service regulations made all first year and prospective graduate students no longer eligible for a student deferment. In addition to distributing literature on topics such as conscientious objection, immigration to Canada, and various sorts of deferments, the union lobbied the administration for a guarantee that graduate students would be readmitted to the university no matter how they decided to respond to the draft—even if they chose prison for refusing induction or departure to Canada. The union's Resistance Committee also sponsored a full-page statement titled "We Won't Go" in the *Daily Princetonian*—a pledge signed by 60 of its members to demonstrate "the depth and sincerity of our opposition to the war."[26] But despite this defiant gesture, it was hard to escape the impression that the union was less concerned with ending the war than with safeguarding its members' careers and protecting them from any personal involvement in the conflict.

The Graduate Draft Union, however, led me to SDS, which viewed resistance to the draft more as a vehicle for opposing the war. Indeed, the one SDS issue in which undergraduates, regardless of their politics, had taken a symbiotic interest was the draft. Even among those students who supported the war, few of them believed their own participation essential to a successful outcome. Shocked to realize that a student deferment was not an exemption from the draft but only a postponement of eligibility, an editorial in the *Princetonian* declared that "as the nation's most important natural resource, ... we, the finest flower, must be preserved at all costs." (And even if they had the misfortune to get drafted after graduation, a pseudonymous series of articles by a former student in uniform observed that the majority of enlisted men were "of very low marble count," assuring Princeton students that they could count on being "reserved for jobs requiring a brain rather than a steady trigger-finger.")[27] Thus, although there was a difference in motives, those desiring to avoid the war and to oppose it both looked forward to the assistance that could be provided by the draft counseling program demanded by SDS from the university.

Of course, SDS also encouraged students to *defy* the draft if they could not avoid it and the organization's Draft Resistance Union had submitted its own "We Won't Go" declaration and list of signatories to the *Princetonian*, announcing that "under no circumstances will we fight in Vietnam." When the two anti-draft groups—graduate union and SDS—began to coordinate their efforts, my own energies shifted from the former to the latter, which seemed less tainted by self-interest.[28] For the next two years, my life centered on political activity.

Being part of the movement was a consuming experience, intensely serious because of what we felt was the significance of our objectives, yet also exhilarating, borne of the belief that we could make a difference—that the actions of ordinary people far from the traditional centers of power could change the course of history. This was an opportunity to lead a life of meaning, a life that reflected your deepest values—or, in Paul Potter's inverse formulation, to choose a life that doesn't make a mockery of them. There was also the excitement that came from idealism combining with optimism: we not only believed in a more just and egalitarian society, but we thought—no doubt naively—that it was within our reach. "The moral arc of the universe is long," Martin Luther King, Jr., had said, "but it bends towards justice"; we didn't doubt the latter but were determined to shorten the former. Though we were not so delusional as to think that this better world would be possible only through our efforts, we certainly believed that it would not happen without them. And then there were the bonds of comradeship, not unlike those I had experienced in the army, which arose among people who worked together in common cause and took physical risks together in demonstrations and on picket lines—what the historian and activist Staughton Lynd had in mind when he described the movement as a "band of brothers in a circle of love."[29]

In addition, an air of intellectual excitement was everywhere, creating the kind of atmosphere outside the classroom that was supposed to be found within it. History, sociology, politics, economics were not just academic disciplines—rubrics under which to organize courses—but topics of immediate relevance to our lives in late night discussions on the institutional roots of poverty and war, the nature of society, the role of education, alternatives to existing social structures, and the possibilities of social change. Many SDS members participated in self-organized reading groups to discuss works such as Baran and Sweezy's *Monopoly Capital* or Harry Magdoff's *The Age of Imperialism*. The movement also generated much of its own literature—hundreds of brochures and pamphlets, some of them reprints of articles from left journals, others based on original research by activists. While much of this literature was circulated nationally by SDS, many leaflets were written by local chapters and distributed only on their own campus; despite the organization's militant rhetoric, SDS's major weapon was always the mimeograph machine.[30]

Even more compelling was the constant sense of urgency. With the American death toll increasing by hundreds each week and the Vietnamese by unknown thousands, the war was a moral miasma hanging over the country. Knowledge of what was taking place in Vietnam brought with it moral obligation. To attend classes complacently, to lead a normal life in such circumstances, was unthinkable, amounting to a complicity in our government's acts no different from the behavior of those Germans who went about business as usual in the 1930s while people were being herded into camps. We began each day wondering and planning what we could do to hasten the war's end, to stop its machinery, to interfere with its prosecution. Life became an endless series of meetings, caucuses, planning sessions, leafleting, door-to-door organizing, and demonstrating. The work was sometimes boring, but the mood was always buoyant.

Yet despite what we perceived as the significance of this goal, in practice the movement rarely did anything without internal controversy. SDS prided itself on being an open, ultra-democratic organization in which no one's right to participate was questioned; whether or not a member in some official sense, whoever showed up at meetings was entitled to take part in the discussion and, no matter how contentious the issue, cast a vote when it was time to make a decision. As a result meetings—not just at Princeton but in every chapter—were famously chaotic; the writer Paul Berman called them "sheer madness," where "the ordinary rules about who has power and who does not were suspended ... and the superdemocratic utopia flickered into reality before your eyes."[31] But an even more significant reason for the conflicts was the presence of people—often some of SDS's most active members—who owed their primary political allegiance to some other group to which they also belonged. While there was a smattering of persons from various Left organizations—Trotskyist groups like the Spartacist League, the International Socialists, or the Socialist Workers Party and its youth wing, the Young Socialist Alliance; the Communist Party and its youth organization, the DuBois Clubs; the Young People's Socialist League, the youth affiliate of the Socialist Party USA—it was the Progressive Labor Party whose student members joined SDS in large numbers, exerting a substantial influence on the organization's direction, and in the process leading to disagreements over both ideology and action.

PL began in 1962 as the Progressive Labor Movement, founded by former members of the Communist Party who had concluded that the party was hopelessly "revisionist"—a "prop of capitalism," encouraging support for "the bosses' lesser-evil candidate," such as John Kennedy; three years later the movement evolved into the Progressive Labor Party. The group's most successful early activity was organization of the May 2nd Movement (M2M), named for the date of the first nationwide mobilization against the war. During the next two years the PL-led M2M mounted one of the first draft resistance campaigns, considered a quite radical step at the time. PL gained additional credibility when M2M's leaders were subpoenaed by the House Un-American Activities Committee as part of hearings on "Assistance to Enemies of U.S." Refusing to be intimidated, they turned the tables on HUAC, denouncing American aggression in Vietnam and attacking members of the committee as a bunch of "yellow-bellied racists, cowards, war criminals, and traitors." In 1966 PL dissolved M2M and instructed its members to join SDS, then emerging as the most important student organization opposed to the war.[32]

Within SDS, PL members created the Worker Student Alliance caucus, which, like M2M, was led by PL but composed mainly of non-party members. Opponents of PL within SDS eventually came to be known as the Revolutionary Youth Movement (RYM), named after a proposal adopted at the December 1968 national convention crafted to counterpose an emphasis on youth as a revolutionary force to PL's more traditional Marxist focus on the working class.[33] Although many SDS members were not affiliated with either group, until the organization's fragmentation in June 1969, most internal disagreements reflected the struggle for SDS's direction between PL/WSA and RYM (pronounced "rim"). The conflicts were more severe at some campuses than at others and particularly bitter at the national level during the quarterly conventions. However, despite their political differences, at Princeton people who identified with RYM and those closer to PL/WSA generally worked together cooperatively; even though I was in the latter group, I thought of many of the former as good friends.

I certainly understood the frustration of SDS members opposed to PL. The normal presumption in a political organization's internal discussions is that it will be possible to persuade people to change their minds if one can offer a sufficiently compelling argument. But no matter how cogent an appeal might be, PL members of SDS were not susceptible to persuasion; as members of a democratic centralist party, they were bound to the positions taken by the party. They were free to voice disagreement within PL's deliberations, but once the party had come to a decision, members were expected to adhere to it in their "mass work." Thus, the vectors of persuasion could point only in one direction within SDS.

But the complaints about PL became as much about personal style as political positions. Accounts of what occurred in SDS, almost all of them written by former activists opposed to PL/WSA, have portrayed PL members as essentially the pod people from "Invasion of the Body Snatchers"—automatons, devoid of emotion, mechanically following orders. Paul Berman wrote that they "struck genuine SDSers as robots." Apparently concerned that this noun was insufficient to make the point unadorned by a redundant adjective, Stephen Kelman, a Harvard student at the time, called them "mechanistic robots." Many of these descriptions emphasized the appearance of PL members, which tended to be more traditional in comparison to many of the other hirsute and unconventionally attired radicals. According to the former activist and author Kirkpatrick Sale, PL people were noticeable for their "starched workshirts and coats-and-ties, fifties-short hair, and smooth-shaven faces." Most damning of all in some quarters, PL discouraged the use of drugs. In her memoir *Flying Too Close to the Sun: My Life and Times as a Weatherman*, Cathy Wilkerson summarized all of PL's suspicious characteristics: they "rarely had a sense of humor and seemed to dress the same—short hair, shirts tucked in, and definitely no bell-bottoms or beads. They opposed all drugs and communal living." As an interpretation for such straitlaced behavior, the sociologist Todd Gitlin, an early president of SDS, explained that PL members had "lashed themselves to the mast of Puritanism" in order to dispense with "bourgeois tendencies," declaring that the party had even voiced "suspicion of rock and roll."[34] It was as if the National Legion of Decency had suddenly opened up a Marxist-Leninist wing.

Of course, these characterizations were largely nonsense, the ironic result of people who had been unfairly stereotyped for their beards and beads now doing the same thing to those who lacked them; the long hairs saw short hair and filled in much of the rest from their imagination, a task facilitated by the convenient consistency of finding that their political opponents were also personally unappealing. My own experience was that PL/WSA members were the opposite of robotic—decent, generous, fun-loving people that you could count on whether you needed someone to help you move, or you were standing next to them at a tense demonstration and the tear gas canisters were headed in your direction. At Princeton, where most people in the PL/WSA caucus were graduate students, they tended to be older than other SDS members and in my opinion more mature; they understood the difference between self-expression and self-absorption. Despite Sale's claim, I never saw anyone in the party wearing a coat and tie. And though it's a small point, perhaps daffiest of all was Gitlin's observation about music. The members of PL/WSA that I knew all loved rock and roll and its forerunner, rhythm and blues, and some of them had huge record collections, which were quickly brought out whenever we got together; one person in the group was an accomplished saxophonist, who has subsequently played behind some of the biggest blues stars in the history of the genre.

It was, however, undeniable that PL/WSA people did tend to have shorter hair, wear more conventional clothes, and, though almost no one in the caucus eschewed enjoyment of the "vegetable of inspiration," they could at least explain why the party wished to discourage drug use; in fact, it was the political rationale for such positions that made the caucus appealing to me. There had always been a tension between the two poles of the movement—between the desire, in the catchphrase of the time, "to do your own thing," and the belief that a certain degree of discipline was necessary for political progress; at its extreme the former tendency could lapse into an apolitical solipsism that made personal liberation a higher priority than social change. No matter how large the number of participants, it was unlikely that a movement composed entirely of college students would be able to end the war by itself; the goal was to convince others to join us, not to alienate them with our appearance. Nor was this concern focused solely on appealing to middle class whites. In "New York, New York," a cut from their groundbreaking 1970 album, the

Last Poets—one of the earliest and most influential, politically conscious rap groups—offered a not uncommon view of the cultural left in the African-American community, referring to "freak looking filthy white rodents ... running around, spreading new kinds of venereal disease, talking about we *love* everybody, we *love* everybody."[35] The image might have been grossly unfair, but it did suggest a barrier to the kind of coalition between the black liberation movement and the anti-war movement that everyone in SDS claimed to seek. In any event, it seemed to me that the reluctance to make a few superficial changes in appearance was an indication of personal indulgence taking precedence over building support for an end to the war; for some people in the movement fire-bombing a government building was a justified expression of opposition to the war, but sacrificing a few locks turned one into a pod person.

The argument against drug use was even more politically compelling. At the time violation of drug laws was being used as a pretext to arrest activists and subject them to sentences out of all proportion to the offense as a way of curtailing their political activity. In 1968 Lee Otis Johnson, SNCC's field secretary in Houston, Texas—where the average prison time for homicide was less than six years—was sentenced to 30 years for passing a marijuana joint to an undercover policeman, who had been hanging around Johnson for two months posing as a fellow activist while waiting for his prey to make a misstep (four years later, Johnson was released pending a retrial, which never occurred). Similarly, in 1969 John Sinclair, poet and chairman of the White Panther Party—a Michigan group modeled after their more well-known black counterparts—was arrested for possession of two joints by undercover officers and sentenced to 9½ to 10 years in prison (two years later he was released after the Michigan Supreme Court ruled the sentence "cruel and unusual punishment"). It was later revealed that FBI Director J. Edgar Hoover had sent a notice to field offices, observing that "the use of marijuana ... is widespread among members of the New Left" and ordering agents to "be alert to opportunities to have them arrested by local authorities."[36] Thus, PL's discouragement of drugs had nothing to do with "puritanism" or the rejection of "bourgeois tendencies"; getting high was just not worth the risk. It was again a question of priorities: working to end the war was more important than hair or dope.

While the rationales for PL's "robotic" style made sense to me, what really clinched the decision to join the WSA caucus was their stance on the draft. I certainly understood the desire to avoid conscription, even if it meant fleeing to Canada or going to prison. After all, who wanted to risk injury or death fighting on behalf of a cause he considered repugnant? At the same time avoiding personal complicity in an immoral war might be comforting to one's superego but would do little to deprive the military of bodies with which to continue the conflict; it just meant that someone else would be drafted. Moreover, there was something troubling about the ease with which most college students—especially those at Princeton and other prestigious universities—were able to find ways out of military service unavailable to their less fortunate peers. Their schools often tried to help them: when Selective Service began to consider class rank in deciding whom to induct, some institutions—Columbia, University of Chicago, and Yale, among others— either abolished ranking students or declined to report the results to draft boards; some instructors announced that, to keep students out of uniform, they would not fail anyone. And students apparently believed that universities had an obligation to help them avoid military service. The Princeton Graduate Draft Union "demand[ed] ... legal, financial, and other resources from the University to aid us in our fight" with the draft board. Moreover, students pursuing specific studies or careers were exempt from service, a consequence that sometimes influenced their occupational choices. This was not an unintended result: an internal Selective Service document titled "Channeling" candidly explained that "the delivery of manpower for induction ... is not much of an administrative or financial challenge" and that a more important concern was "the ever increasing problem of how to control effectively the service of individuals who are not in the armed forces." Thus, the document continued, the primary task of the Selective System was to administer the carrot and the stick—"the reward of a deferment" and "the club of induction"— in order to "drive out ... individuals" from areas considered less important to the national interest and into areas such as science, medicine, engineering, and education. Finally, if all else failed, the well-to-do could usually count on their family physician for a helpful medical certificate.[37]

The aggregate result of all these outlets for college students opposed to the war—and for many unopposed but unwilling to serve—was to ensure that the sons of the working class and the poor were sent to Vietnam. As early as 1967 *Newsweek* noted the charge that the American military had become "a 'poor man's army.'" Some college students viewed this development as an appropriate match between role and abilities. As one Princeton undergraduate told a reporter, "I can make a much more useful contribution than running around the bushes of Vietnam looking for snipers"; another stated frankly that a blue collar youth unable to enjoy a student deferment was "not sophisticated enough to understand or question foreign policy." Others, to their

credit, were at least less sanguine about the inequity. The journalist James
Fallows described how, during his senior year at Harvard, he attended special
seminars, in which "sympathetic medical students helped us search for dis-
qualifying conditions." He was eventually labeled "unqualified" for the draft
after showing up for the pre-induction physical with only 120 pounds on his
six-foot, one-inch frame and then telling an army doctor that he had contemplated suicide. But as they prepared to leave, Fallows and his Harvard friends,
all of whom received deferments for one reason or another, watched the buses
arriving from Chelsea, carrying "thick dark-haired young men, the white pro-
les of Boston," to whom "it had clearly never occurred ... that there might be
a way around the draft." Having "willingly [taken] advantage of this most
brutal form of class discrimination," the Harvard contingent headed back to
Cambridge, "liberated and victorious," while "the boys from Chelsea [were]
sent off to die."[38]

Most activists in the movement were well aware of the war's disproportionate burden on blacks and working class whites but nevertheless did not
hesitate to employ every stratagem at their disposal to perpetuate this injustice.
Mark Rudd, for example, the leader of the spring 1968 uprising at Columbia
and later a member of Weatherman, first tried eating several dozen hard boiled
eggs the night before his physical in order to increase the level of albumin in
his urine, then threatened to create "havoc, even anarchy" in the ranks if
inducted, and finally, when neither of those ploys was successful, used a letter
from his psychotherapist to obtain a deferment.[39] In contrast to such machi-
nations, only PL members took the stance that the student deferment was a
class privilege, which they rejected, allowing themselves to be drafted in the
midst of their studies, committed to entering the army to organize fellow GIs
against the war. Whatever one thought about PL's political positions, this
was principled and courageous behavior. Despite my reservations about the
party's analysis, faced with a choice between PL/WSA's superego and RYM/
Weatherman's id, there was no doubt which side I preferred.

The actual political conflicts between PL and RYM, as is typically the
case between left groups, stemmed from what Freud called "the narcissism of
small differences"—in this case from battles over the arcane details of left
wing dogma that would have been incomprehensible to the vast majority of
people unfamiliar with Marxist minutiae and were often inane even to the
few who understood them; nevertheless each side considered the other's position blasphemous. Concerning the black liberation movement, PL insisted,
in its more traditional, leftist jargon, that blacks were a "super-exploited" sector of the working class—last hired, first fired, and systematically relegated

to the dirtiest and lowest paid jobs—and that their discriminatory treatment acted as a weight on the wage scale, holding down pay for all workers. White workers had a knife stuck in their gut four inches deep, went a common metaphor used by party members, but for black workers it was six inches. However, RYM people maintained, in language right out of Frantz Fanon, that blacks were an oppressed colony within the mother country and thus entitled to self-determination, a matter about which whites were to have nothing to say. Neither of these positions seemed in touch with reality. The idea that blacks were no more than a more highly exploited group of workers ignored a history of slavery and segregation dramatically different from any other ethnic group's experience. And the notion that blacks within the United States in some way *could* plan their own separate destiny overlooked the extent to which, even in the late 1960s, racial integration was fast becoming a fact of American life and black culture was becoming the cutting edge of American popular culture. To me, PL's analysis seemed oblivious to the past; RYM's, to the present and future.

The other cause of conflict between the two sides had to do with their positions on the war, concisely summarized in their respective slogans. PL insisted on "No Deals in Vietnam; U.S. Get Out Now." While this might seem straightforward to the uninitiated, its subtext was a criticism of the NLF/North Vietnamese forces, which were engaged in negotiating with the United States—an act that PL regarded as a betrayal of the Vietnamese people's struggle by their "revisionist" leaders. RYM, on the other hand, marched under the banner "Ho, Ho, Ho Chi Minh; NLF is Gonna Win," a reflection of their infatuation with those fighting the United States. At anti-war demonstrations many members of the RYM contingent carried the NLF flag, its gold star on a background half red and half blue easily recognizable in the crowd. Once again I was not enamored of either position. I thought it took a lot of nerve for a group of college students safely ensconced in their dorm rooms to criticize people being bombed for seeking a negotiated settlement. But at the same time it seemed insensitive to flaunt the colors of the people, no matter how just their cause, who had killed tens of thousands of the sons, husbands, and brothers of our fellow citizens—soldiers who in many cases were conscripted and may not have supported the war; such an action could only alienate those who might otherwise sympathize with the movement, but not if it meant sacrificing their sense of patriotism. Besides, I didn't oppose the war because I thought an NLF victory would be better for Vietnam, but because it was obvious that the Vietnamese people did. In the final analysis I was less uncomfortable with PL's slogan, if only because it was a position one could support without even knowing anything about the NLF/NVN, much less whether they had committed the Marxist sin of "revisionism." The United States just had no business being in Vietnam.

However, these sectarian, internal conflicts did not prevent the organization from emerging in the 1967-68 academic year at Princeton as the leader of a campaign that would dramatically change the university.

The Kelley Committees

"1968" is the title of more than a score of books, usually followed by a subtitle such as "The World Transformed," "The Year that Rocked the World," or "Memories and Legacies of a Global Revolt."[40] In that tumultuous year, hardly a week passed without the occurrence of some historically significant event, often involving college students. On April 23 students at Columbia University began a protest over the school's association with a defense department think tank and its plans for encroachment into the surrounding Harlem community that led to the occupation of five campus buildings; the occupation lasted for a week until 1,000 New York City police cleared out the demonstrators with tear gas and nightsticks, sending 150 people to the hospital and arresting more than 700. One week later, in what *Time* called the "Battle of the Sorbonne," the French national student union led a demonstration of more than 20,000 students and teachers—protesting the closing of a branch of the University of Paris—that escalated over the next few days into violent confrontations, pitting the demonstrators' Molotov cocktails against the police's tear-gas grenades and resulting in a nationwide strike by millions of workers that almost brought down the French government.

In between these two momentous events, Princeton SDS held a demonstration, which, though trivial in comparison to the uprisings in Morningside Heights and Paris, nevertheless drew close to 1,500 participants, an impressive number considering the size of the university—only 3,200 undergraduates and 1,500 graduate students—and the fact that the SDS chapter had, by the most generous definition, perhaps 75 members; indeed, just the planning meeting called three days earlier to formulate the demonstration's demands had drawn 500 people.[41] Although the mood of the crowd was more festive than restive as it filled the lawn in front of Nassau Hall on a spring day, the event was nevertheless sufficient to justify the words on the now infamous banner that led the march: "Even Princeton" had become part of the movement.

THE POLITICAL AND THE PARIETAL

The demonstration's major political focus was the demand for "severance of all institutional ties with IDA," the Institute for Defense Analyses; opposition to Columbia's ties to IDA had played a central role in that university's uprising the previous week. A non-profit organization conducting research for the Department of Defense (DOD), IDA had been established in 1956 by a consortium of five universities in response to a request for assistance by the secretary of defense and the chairman of the Joint Chiefs of Staff. Within the next half dozen years, seven additional universities joined the consortium, the resulting 12 member group soliciting the nation's most talented scientists to advise the Joint Chiefs of Staff on subjects such as "the physical phenomenology of weapons systems" and "the optimum choice among competing weapons systems."[42] In 1966, General Maxwell Taylor became IDA's president; as Chairman of the Joint Chiefs he had recommended the commitment of troops in Vietnam and was then appointed U.S. Ambassador to South Vietnam, before serving as a special presidential assistant on the war.

In the mid–1960s IDA announced its increased attention to techniques with obvious utility in Southeast Asia: development of devices to track down guerrillas in jungles and villages, such as infrared detectors to identify the heat from a distant cooking fire, and personnel detectors sensitive to human body odor; also "village protection systems," designed to prevent any interaction between Vietnamese confined in strategic hamlets and their fellow citizens still in the "unpacified" areas. Although the majority of IDA studies were classified, an unclassified summary of a 1966 study provided a bit of detail. "Constraints on the Use of Weapons and Tactics in Counterinsurgency," conducted by IDA's Economic and Political Studies Division, investigated political constraints on the use of a number of techniques against insurgents, including chemical "incapacitants," napalm, and herbicides.[43] While much of the nation had concluded that military support for the junta in Saigon was illegal and immoral, IDA was drawing on academic resources to support what was essentially a research program in the Vietnam War as an applied science.

In addition, according to the *New York Times*, IDA recommended to a presidential commission on law enforcement the use of a wide range of "supplemental weapons" for riot control, including chemical agents, "super water pistols" that could squirt pepper spray long distance, nets dropped from helicopters, itching powder, and adhesives that would cause people to stick to each other. At a time of numerous civil rights and anti-war demonstrations, there were concerns that these techniques could be used to stifle domestic dissent.[44]

Princeton was not one of IDA's five original members, and, when invited to join early in 1960, declined after the university's Research Board, composed of faculty members, recommended against the affiliation. However, two months earlier the trustees had signed a contract to erect a building for IDA's use, funded by the university and situated on its land, and in October 1960 John von Neumann Hall opened as IDA's Communications Research Division—the organization's only physical facility outside its headquarters in Arlington, Virginia; IDA received a 10-year lease from the university and an option to renew for an additional five years. A year later, when Princeton was again invited to join IDA, university president Robert Goheen ignored the Research Board's recommendation and committed the university to membership on the grounds that Princeton personnel were already working on IDA problems. With Princeton now an official participant, Goheen joined IDA's Board of Trustees, a group composed entirely of representatives of the member universities.[45]

Despite a pair of armed guards on duty round the clock behind an eight-foot high brick wall, IDA's presence on the Princeton campus remained uncontroversial until the fall of 1967, when SDS launched an effort to sever the university's affiliation. The mimeograph machine in the "bat cave"—SDS's basement office—churned out a series of leaflets, making the case for the university's withdrawal. Adding to the momentum, a flurry of articles and sympathetic editorials appeared in the *Daily Princetonian*, and a member of the faculty announced that many of his colleagues were prepared to support the students' campaign. When the issue of Princeton's relation to IDA was placed on the agenda for the Board of Trustees' meeting on Friday, October 20, an SDS spokesman requested permission for a representative to be "heard, formally, before the university's course of action is determined." Denied such an opportunity by the president, SDS then submitted a letter to the trustees, calling for a "free, open, and democratic hearing in which the entire university community" could participate in a discussion. Rebuffed yet again, early Monday morning 50 students showed up at Von Neumann Hall, many of them fresh from the weekend demonstration at the Pentagon, and blocked the entrance until 30 of them were hauled off by the police and fined $50 each. By a week later, a petition criticizing the university's affiliation with IDA had been signed by more than 100 faculty members, many of whom, according to the professor who initiated the petition, expressed admiration for the protestors.[46]

Unable to keep the issue confined behind the closed doors of trustees' meetings, Princeton's president had to take some action. The sixteenth president of the university, Robert Francis ("Bob") Goheen—in SDS circles he was referred to as "BoGo"—was the youngest occupant of the position since the colonial era. Born and raised in India where his father was a medical missionary, Goheen had returned to the United States to be "prepared" at the Lawrenceville School just minutes south of Princeton, and was accepted into the class of 1940 along with half of his fellow Lawrenceville graduates. A brilliant student, he received Princeton's Pyne Prize, the university's most prestigious award for undergraduates, and immediately began graduate work in classics, only to enter the army after his first year of study. Commissioned after attending Officer Candidate School, he rose to Lieutenant Colonel before leaving the service in 1945 to return to his studies, earning a doctorate three years later. Goheen remained at Princeton where he was still what the *New York Times* called an "obscure" 37-year-old untenured assistant professor when the previous university president reached mandatory retirement age. Only eight years removed from being a student himself, he walked into a trustees' meeting believing that they were interested in his views on the sort of person they should seek for the presidency, only to learn their real purpose when he was offered the job along with promotion to full professor.[47] Goheen assumed the position in the fall of 1957 with an expectation that he would serve for the next three decades. In fact, he would leave in less than half that time.

A classics scholar with a specialization in Greek drama, during the quiet generation that preceded the activist era Goheen had lectured students on the importance of the moral dimension of education, but when they actually began to take this theme seriously, it was replaced in his addresses by an admonition to avoid precisely the kind of behavior that a moral sensibility would seem to inspire. Disinclined both by training and nature to break with tradition, Goheen was also smart enough to sense when a break was inevitable; he would never be the first person on board for a trip in a new direction, but neither would he be left on the platform when everyone else departed. Initially opposed, for example, to the admission of women—a prospect he evaluated primarily in terms of how their presence would affect the quality of education for men—he nevertheless quickly grasped the more egalitarian direction in which society was heading and presided over the change in policy that eventually brought women and men to campus in equal numbers. Even then, however, it appeared that a major factor in the decision was Princeton's need to compete for outstanding male applicants, the great majority of whom preferred coeducational schools. But Goheen could also be displeased with those who had been prematurely correct, even when he wound up following their lead. He long supported the war, relying on his faith in Lyndon Johnson's secretary of state Dean Rusk, one of Goheen's best friends. Yet when he finally concluded that the Vietnam adventure had been a "tragic, wasteful, devastating involvement ... taken in ignorance of the history, culture, and aspirations of the people of a far-off land"—exactly what SDS had been maintaining for years—Goheen remained as critical as ever of the radicals for their supposed reluctance to engage in civilized debate.[48]

Yet it was only in response to SDS's month-long campaign culminating in the blockage of the building that Goheen allowed the status of IDA to become a topic of formal discussion. In an open meeting of the university community, called, according to the president, to clear up "misunderstanding," Goheen defended Princeton's involvement against charges that it violated the university's political neutrality but then, knowing that many faculty members as well as students were opposed to the affiliation, he conceded to a procedure for the faculty to express its corporate opinion. That is, faced with resistance to his policy, Goheen did what academic administrators do to defuse such situations: he appointed a "special committee"—in this case chaired by Stanley Kelley, a gentlemanly, well-respected professor of politics, popular with colleagues and students alike.[49]

Over the next few months Kelley and six other faculty members worked conscientiously, holding hearings and soliciting the written opinions of colleagues throughout the university. The majority of the faculty wanted Princeton out of IDA; for many, their position on IDA was inseparable from their opinion of the war. Four members of the Religion Department wrote that the "decision of the university with respect to the continuation of its association cannot be separated from our view of the present government's policy in Vietnam," which they called "politically unwise and morally wrong." And a physicist declared that "we, as individuals bear the moral responsibility for our University's *de facto* endorsement of IDA's pursuits," quoting Justice Robert Jackson's summary for the prosecution at Nuremberg as support. However, some opponents of the university's linkage to IDA decoupled their opposition from any concern about the substance of its research, basing their position on the much narrower academic grounds that, because of the work's secrecy, the university was sponsoring activities, the quality or propriety of which it was unable to evaluate. When the special committee's final report recommended termination of Princeton's sponsorship of IDA, it did so on the latter basis, explicitly rejecting any connection between the decision and the nation's foreign policy and thus ensuring broader support from the faculty. Of course, an end to Princeton's sponsorship would have been entirely symbolic since

IDA's lease could not be unilaterally abrogated by the university, nor could the university preclude any of its faculty members from consulting or collaborating with IDA. Nevertheless, termination would have been a symbolic gesture with considerable significance, especially if, as the Kelley Committee also recommended, Princeton initiated joint action with other IDA members to eliminate university sponsorship altogether. This was not an unlikely possibility: the week before release of the report, a faculty committee at the University of Chicago, another IDA member, had recommended withdrawal of *its* institution.[50]

The Kelley Committee's report was handily approved by the Princeton faculty. There was even an attempt, though unsuccessful, to add an amendment recognizing the role that student activism had played in bringing the issue to the faculty's attention.[51] Although only the Board of Trustees had authority to make the final decision, the expectation was that Goheen would inform them of the faculty's action and they would act accordingly.

However, while the faculty were going through the motions of academic governance, Goheen had been secretly crafting his own solution in conjunction with some of the other IDA trustees and its president, General Maxwell Taylor. Recognizing the unpopularity of the status quo but not wanting anyone to think they might be "giving way to the SDS," the group drafted a proposal, in which Goheen would continue serving on the IDA board, not as a representative of the university but "in an individual capacity"—as if an organization specializing in mathematical models of communication for military use had some need for a specialist in Greek drama on its board, apart from the fact that he was president of the institution from which IDA leased its building and drew much of its talent; a writer in *Science* called the substitution of Goheen the individual for Goheen the university president "a distinction without a difference." This supposed change in the relationship was approved by the Princeton trustees and sent to the faculty in the mail as a fait accompli without any of that civilized debate, the absence of which had been Goheen's chief complaint about SDS.[52]

Dismayed at such an obvious sham, the faculty overwhelmingly passed a resolution expressing their dissatisfaction and urging "Princeton's President and Trustees to undertake further action to achieve [the faculty's] objectives." Some faculty members even raised the possibility of a strike if the trustees refused their recommendations.[53]

Only days after the trustees' action, with the faculty still in high dudgeon at being snubbed, SDS held its demonstration. Under the circumstances the demand for Princeton to sever relations with IDA could hardly be considered outrageous; it was no more than calling for the administration to respect the results of the process it had initiated. But conjoined to the IDA issue was a demand of greater personal significance to students.

Not only did Princeton recruit many of its students from private academies, but until the 1960s much to their displeasure imposed on them a rigid system of rules indistinguishable from the controlled atmosphere they had experienced in prep school. Undergraduates were not allowed to store or operate a car near the campus, and, until the class of 1968 entered the university, freshmen were required to attend religious services half the Sundays each semester. But the greatest source of annoyance was the parietal rule, limiting the visitation hours for women in the dormitories to no later than 7 p.m. on weekdays and 9 p.m. on Fridays and Saturdays. Year after year students approached the administration as supplicants pleading for greater latitude only to have the trustees dribble it out to them an hour at a time—from first, 11 p.m. on Saturdays to, a year later, midnight on Saturdays, and then midnight on Fridays but only for six "big weekends" during the academic year. As an editorial in the *Princetonian* observed in 1966, there was a "profound contradiction" in a university policy that treated a student in class "as an adult taking full responsibility for his actions" but "in the dormitory ... as a child." Two years later—only days before announcement of the president's unilateral action on IDA—in the face of rising student militancy, the trustees suddenly realized that the "existing rules regarding women visitors in the dormitories are not entirely satisfactory" and extended parietal hours to 10 p.m. from Sunday through Thursday and 2 a.m. on Friday and Saturday. But the point at which students might have appreciated such a gesture had passed. An editorial in the *Princetonian*, titled "The Trustees' Travesty," called this belated concession "as amusing as it is senseless and disgraceful," failing to recognize "the basic student right of student management of student affairs."[54]

Capitalizing on this dissatisfaction, SDS's demonstration also called for the complete abolition of parietal rules. It was a winning combination. Demanding that the university end its sponsorship of IDA was sure to draw a supportive crowd given the substantial opposition to the linkage. But adding a demand that, in practice, would allow undergraduates to sleep with their girlfriends—*that* was guaranteed to produce a throng.

In a strategy it would come to regret, SDS decided to connect the political and the parietal through a narrative that focused on the process by which both policies had been crafted rather than their substance. The problem, declared SDS's open letter to the president, stemmed from the domination of decision-making processes by the trustees—"a board of faceless men" who had "not lived on a university campus for decades"—rather than by "those who live in the university and are most seriously affected." Thus, SDS called for "the formulation of a student-faculty committee" that would propose a restructuring of decision making "so that students and faculty have final control over their lives and their institutions." Although SDS's earlier opposition to IDA had centered on its contribution to the war effort, this new emphasis had the advantage of being consistent with the faculty's view of the problem. On the same day as the demonstration, a letter from four professors to the trustees complained that the faculty recommendation, adopted "after long research, open hearings and careful reflection," had been summarily overruled, and they too called for "fundamental changes in the procedures by which policies are formulated." In addition, an increasingly influential element of the movement nationally was encouraging "student power" as the way to achieve "university reform." In a widely circulated underground essay titled "The Student as Nigger," Jerry Farber, an activist and English professor at California State, argued that students were at the subordinate end of a "master-slave approach to education" with "no voice in the decisions that affect their academic lives," aside from "a toy government run for the most part by Uncle Toms and concerned principally with trivia." And in an article that could have been written with Princeton in mind, Carl Davidson, a former vice president and national secretary of SDS, argued that there was "one system responsible" for both "dorm hours and the war in Vietnam," and he called for "the direct participation of students in all those decisions daily affecting their lives."[55]

Although a headline in the *Princetonian* the day before the demonstration warned that "Princeton Could Face Columbia Disaster," and the media, both print and television, descended on the campus in anticipation of an eruption, such fears proved to be groundless. However, with the previous week's debacle at Columbia unavoidably on his mind and knowing that the Princeton event was to focus on how decisions were made, Goheen read a prepared statement to the assembled demonstrators, in which he expressed his "approval for a fresh and searching review of the decision-making processes of the University." Given their own demand for restructuring, it was an offer that SDS couldn't refuse. From the president's perspective, yet another committee would forestall further demonstrations while its deliberations were in progress. The faculty soon chose eight of its members to serve on the "Faculty-Student Committee on the Structure of the University," and once again tapped Stanley Kelley to be the chair. The seven students to serve on the committee included the four officers of the Undergraduate Assembly and three graduate students to be elected by their peers. At the same time the Board of Trustees created its own seven-member committee "to work parallel" to the student-faculty group on restructuring the university's decision-making processes.[56]

THE SECOND KELLEY COMMITTEE

Three members of SDS were named to what was, for a second time, referred to on campus as the "Kelley Committee." As president of the Undergraduate Assembly, a position to which he had been elected only a week before the demonstration, Peter Kaminsky, a junior history major, was an ex officio member. Already chair of the assembly's parietals committee and head of the joint student-faculty committee on draft counseling at the time of the election, he won the presidency with 58 percent of the vote on a platform calling for student control of "the issues that directly concern their personal lives." Quick-witted and unflappable, Peter was always ready with a quotable comeback. Warned that an SDS rally might jeopardize the trustees' decision to allow coeducation at Princeton, he cut to the core of the matter: "That's really stupid," he responded, "the trustees aren't giving us coeducation because we're good boys—they're giving it to us because they're afraid of Yale."[57]

Two of the three elected graduate students were also SDS members. Robby Nerenberg had done his undergraduate work at Queens College, one of the schools in the CUNY (City University of New York) system, and received a fellowship from Princeton to pursue a doctorate in English, intending to become an academic while he wrote the Great American Novel. But during the summer before his arrival at Princeton, he worked as a gravedigger in a cemetery and was struck by the contrast between his own promising future and the dismal prospects of the permanent workers—poor, desolate older men still engaged in punishing physical labor, for whom the notion of upward mobility was a cruel fantasy. Already primed by this experience to embrace a radical critique of the society, Robby was pushed even further when one of his high school friends died in Vietnam from "friendly fire."[58]

I was the other elected graduate student. Actually Robby and I ran as a slate, the pair of us jointly endorsed in a statement signed by 17 of our peers— Robby for his work organizing the planning meeting for the demonstration, and me for my contributions to the Graduate Draft Union's efforts to ensure readmission for students who leave due to the draft. Robby became my closest friend at Princeton.

The first two weeks of the Kelley Committee's existence were devoted to a crash course in the complexities of a research university. In lengthy meetings, held often twice a day, we heard from deans and administrators with expertise in every area of the university's operation: the management of its portfolio, the sources of its income, the process of faculty recruitment and evaluation for tenure, the development of curricula, even the process by which property was acquired and new buildings designed and constructed. At one of these sessions two members of the Board of Trustees suggested that we meet with their parallel committee to avoid the possibility that our group might wind up "locked into positions" that they would find unacceptable.[59] It was that combined meeting that particularly influenced the SDS members on the Kelley committee.

Early on a summer morning the two groups gathered in one of the tiered rooms that Princeton calls a "bowl," with coffee and pastries offered to the participants on silver service. The three of us in SDS were acutely conscious that, for perhaps the first time in our lives, we were face to face with bona fide members of the group that played such a prominent role in our rhetoric: the ruling class. Laurence S. Rockefeller occupied the seat on the New York Stock Exchange once held by his grandfather, oil magnate John D. Rockefeller; John N. Irwin was a Manhattan attorney and diplomat who had been a deputy assistant secretary of defense under Eisenhower and was serving as Lyndon Johnson's representative for Panama Canal negotiations; other members of the trustees' committee were heads of corporations and directors of banks. Robby's entrance introduced a comic element into this sober context. Soon to join PL, at the party's urging he had taken a blue collar job for the summer at a candy factory—the idea was for radicals to experience some small sense of what life was like for the working class. Fresh from his midnight to 8 a.m. shift, Robby showed up covered head-to-toe with powdered sugar. "How are you, son?" said Laurence Rockefeller, extending an avuncular hand. Robby looked at the outstretched palm as if it were a handkerchief into which he'd just blown his nose, and walked away. "What was that about?" I asked. "I'm sharpening my sense of class hatred," was his reply. Though I didn't think it necessary to be deliberately offensive, I understood Robby's point: these were the people we regarded as the enemy.

The meeting did little to change that view, as the trustees made clear that certain areas of the university's operation—the ones we thought most important to change—were none of our business. Student input into curricular decisions, departmental affairs, rules of conduct and other purely academic matters might be tolerable, and even the detested parietals were obviously about to be jettisoned; many undergraduates were already engaged in what the *Princetonian* called "blissful violation" of the rule, and proctors—the university's internal security personnel—had come to regard such violations with a wink and a nod. But there was a line that the trustees would not allow us to cross, and the issues of interest to SDS—the issues that had motivated the three of us to run for the committee—all lay on the other side. In addition to severing ties with IDA, there was SDS's call for the university to liquidate its investments in corporations with holdings in South Africa. In the meeting to formulate the demonstration's demands, divestment had been a high priority and was omitted from the final list only at the request of black students, who did not wish to jeopardize their own meeting with the administration on this subject scheduled for the following week.[60] However, at the meeting of the two committees on restructure, the first mention of the university's portfolio was the last, as the trustees brusquely informed the Kelley Committee that it was not a topic up for discussion.

Frustrated that the most important issues were precluded from consideration, SDS voted unanimously for its three members to resign. There was no need for radical activists to serve on a committee whose deliberations were confined to parochial academic concerns; we had bigger fish to fry. I voted in favor of the recommendation with some feelings of guilt about deserting my responsibility to those graduate students whose efforts had helped get me elected. However, the statement on which I had run emphasized that I would not be satisfied with "token measures," and now it seemed that we were faced with limited opportunities to do otherwise. Besides, I had also promised regular open meetings, only to find such a possibility voted down in the committee despite its support from the three SDS members. Thus, resignation did not seem so irresponsible in view of my inability to fulfill either of the commitments on the basis of which I had asked for other students' support. The actual departure took place at the one public meeting the committee did hold. Each of us read a statement, and then we walked out, asking others to join us; perhaps a quarter of the audience did so.[61]

In retrospect, the walk-out was foolish and shortsighted. Despite our reservations, the committee produced a workable proposal to establish "The Council of the Princeton University Community," a deliberative body with representation from every sector of the institution—not just administrators, faculty, and students but also alumni and staff of all types—with the authority to investigate and make recommendations concerning "any general issue" that its members wished to consider. The Kelley Committee even persuaded the trustees to adopt a proposal for students to elect a graduating senior each year to serve on the board. Although the "U-Council" has undergone a number of revisions in the more than four decades since its establishment, it has in fact shifted the locus of decision-making on a number of issues, allowing more student influence, and has continued to play a significant role in the governance of the university.[62]

The 1968-69 Academic Year: Expanded Efforts

Despite its decision to abandon the Kelley Committee, SDS began the 1968-69 year on an optimistic note when more than 150 freshmen—almost a fifth of the entering class—put their names on the organization's mailing list. While opposition to IDA continued to be a priority, SDS also took more muscular action in other areas related to foreign policy and the war. When CIA recruiters scheduled a visit to campus, SDS announced plans to disrupt the interviews on the grounds that there was no "abstract 'right' to join organizations whose function is to oppress and make war on the peoples of the world." Faced with a confrontation, the CIA cancelled its appearance.[63]

SDS also demanded the elimination of ROTC—the Reserve Officer Training Corps program—as a concrete measure to speed the end of the war by depriving the military of manpower; according to the army's own literature, at the time ROTC was providing "approximately twenty times as many officers as West Point," and SDS chapters at many campuses throughout the nation were making a similar demand.[64] Although in mid–December 400 people turned out for a demonstration, the dean of the college and the Princeton faculty were letting the air out of the SDS balloon with their own proposal to change ROTC's status. Just as the faculty resolution had opposed the university's affiliation with IDA for reasons that had nothing to do with its contributions to the war, they now suddenly realized that ROTC courses did not merit academic credit, essentially reducing them to the level of extracurricular activities and depriving the ROTC program of departmental status. In addition, a faculty committee proposed that the military officers heading the three ROTC units—army, navy and air force—be divested of their professorial titles; the change in their academic rank to "visiting lecturer with the rank of professor" would allow them to participate in faculty meetings but not to vote. Since the ROTC contract with the university stipulated that Princeton would "grant appropriate academic credit applicable toward graduation" for their courses, the proposal was tantamount to terminating ROTC without having to acknowledge any intent to do so. It took time for the proposal to work its way through the process of academic governance, but the program's

eventual elimination was a foregone conclusion. A year later, in the wake of
national outrage over Nixon's expansion of the war into Cambodia, the
recently formed University Council voted to "determine ways to sever any
association" with ROTC, conferring a university wide imprimatur on what
had become a fait accompli.[65]

THE STRUGGLE OVER DIVESTMENT

For Princeton SDS, second in importance to the war was the anti-
apartheid movement, which sought to overturn the racist regime in South
Africa, where the white minority kept the rest of the population—blacks and
"coloreds"—in a state of permanent subjugation. At the time South Africa
was ruled by the Afrikaner Nationalist Party. In opposition status during the
war, leading members of the party had openly supported the Reich, engaging
in sabotage against their own government, which had sided with Britain.
Coming to power in 1948, the party extended the nation's segregationist principles, establishing an elaborate system of laws based on belief in inherent
non-white inferiority similar to the notions of *Rassenhygiene* that had
informed policy under National Socialism. The black 80 percent of the population was stripped of South African citizenship and relegated to 10 "homelands," comprising altogether the most barren 13 percent of the country—the
so called "Bantustans." However, because whites needed cheap labor on farms
and in mines and factories, many black men had to leave their families—their
wives and children deemed "superfluous appendages" and banned from accompanying them—in order to work outside the homelands in menial, dangerous,
and physically demanding jobs, which received legally mandated low wages;
their employment in any other capacity was a punishable offense. Now considered foreigners in white controlled South Africa, blacks were required to
carry a pass at all times, without which they were subject to immediate arrest.
Prohibited from living in white towns and cities even if employed there, these
migrant workers were confined in the degrading conditions of the "town-
ships"—slums with crude dwellings, little sanitation, and no medical care.[66]

In March 1960 the Sharpeville massacre took place, in which the South
African police responded to a peaceful protest against the pass laws by firing
indiscriminately at demonstrators, killing 69 people and wounding hundreds.
The international community was outraged. The United Nations Security
Council called upon the South African government to "abandon ... apartheid,"
and the General Assembly asked UN members to end diplomatic relations
with the country and boycott its goods. While the United States supported

the Security Council resolution, and American statesmen paid lip service to the evils of apartheid, the finance and corporate sector in the United States was less than pleased at the prospect of the fall of a system that had been a source of substantial profit. Fearful that instability in the wake of international condemnation might lead to rebellion, an ad hoc consortium of American banks provided the apartheid government both a $150 million loan (1.13 billion adjusted for inflation) and a revolving credit fund of another $50 million (378 million adjusted).[67]

Five years after Sharpeville a campaign arose to apply pressure on apartheid by encouraging institutions to withdraw their funds from banks providing support for the South African government. Initially led by churches, the "divestment" movement expanded to college campuses, where SDS and other student groups demanded that schools relinquish their endowment portfolios' investments in companies doing business in South Africa in order to reduce the amount of foreign capital used to support the country's economic system. The fact that black South African groups working for liberation supported the tactic gave it added impetus.[68]

At Princeton, where the university's investments included $128 million (860 million adjusted) in more than 40 corporations or banks doing business in South Africa, SDS was one of a coalition of groups calling for divestment; also committed to this issue was the Association of Black Collegians (ABC), the group that had asked SDS not to include divestment in its list of demands. Formed in spring 1967, the organization quickly developed a reputation for effective political action. After the assassination of the Rev. Martin Luther King, Jr., Goheen decided that classes should proceed as usual on the day of the funeral but that all official activities would pause for a moment of silence at noon—until a delegation from ABC visited him at home and persuaded him to cancel classes.[69]

In response to the demand for divestment Goheen appointed the Ad Hoc Committee on Princeton's Investments in Companies Operating in Southern Africa. Chaired by Professor Burton Malkiel, a well-known economist specializing in finance, the committee was composed of four faculty members, the university's financial vice president/treasurer, and five students: two members of ABC, two members of the Committee for Black Awareness (CBA), the black graduate student organization, and a member of SDS. The Malkiel Committee was charged with consideration of the three proposals that the coalition had submitted to the trustees: no future investments in banks, companies, or other financial institutions participating in the South African, Rhodesian, Angolan, and Mozambique economies; a process for the reinvestment of funds presently allocated to these banks and companies; and a commitment to reject "all monies, bequests, and endowments" drawn primarily from profits made in these economies.

When the committee's report appeared six months later, it was signed only by the four faculty members and the university official; none of the students wished to be associated with the document's recommendations. The report began by acknowledging "the horrors of apartheid" and conceded that sale of the "designated" investments would be a powerful statement attesting to Princeton's dedication to the "abolition of racial discrimination." But in the final analysis, it questioned the prudence of using the university's investment portfolio as a vehicle to oppose racism given the financial realities: "the securities proposed for sale" were averaging a return of 14 percent compared to 11.3 percent for the remaining investments, in addition to which there would be "significant transaction costs in changing the composition of the portfolio." That is, having begun by positing the condition of blacks in South Africa as a moral evil, the report concluded that the cost of a stance consistent with the university's values was too high to bear. Besides, the report found no reason to believe that sale of the designated shares would have any effect on either the South African economy or that country's commitment to apartheid; not only would divestment cost Princeton money, but it would be merely a symbolic gesture with no practical impact. But the committee did have other recommendations for producing change in the apartheid regime. Princeton could pressure corporations doing business in South Africa to improve black employees' wages and benefits, and petition the government to liberalize restrictions on blacks—a suggestion undeterred by the irony that, at the same time the committee concluded that the university, an institution dedicated to humanist, non-materialistic values, should not be influenced by moral suasion to jeopardize its bottom line, it also recommended the application of moral suasion to convince entities whose sole raison d'être was the pursuit of profit that they should voluntarily relinquish some of their gains in order to share them with employees and should lobby against the very policies that made them such attractive investments for Princeton's portfolio.[70]

The student members of the Malkiel Committee issued their own reports reiterating support for divestment—one from students representing ABC and CBA, and one from the committee's SDS member, whose statement alluded to a conflict of interest: some trustees served on the boards of banks and corporations with interests in South Africa. A subsequent investigation by the *Princetonian* found that 14 trustees were either directors or officers of banks and corporations in which the university had substantial investments; three of the 14 served on the subcommittee that determined how to invest the university's portfolio.[71]

After Goheen accepted the Malkiel Committee's recommendations, Peter Kaminsky announced SDS's intention to "make the university" relinquish its South African investments, and the campus waited expectantly to see how the organization would back up his words. SDS, however, had decided that ABC should take the lead on this issue; the white radicals would play a supporting role for whatever action the black students wished to take. One morning in early March, ABC members took control of the New South administrative building, a glass and concrete structure on the edge of the campus, housing the university's business departments; the choice of buildings, ABC later explained, had been a calculated decision to "interrupt ... the administrative and financial procedures and not the educative functions.... No professors were harassed. No classes were disrupted. No students obstructed." Half an hour later 40 SDS members, together with a handful of students from the Third World Liberation Front—a group formed only days before the seizure—assembled on the open concourse in front of the main entrance in support of the occupiers, but after an hour and a half of exposure to the frigid temperature and high winds, the shivering radicals were invited into the building. While their supporters left around noon, the black students remained until 6 p.m. and then departed in an orderly fashion, leaving the building in immaculate condition.[72] It was the only building occupation to take place at Princeton in the 1960s and provided an object lesson in how to dramatize an issue without allowing controversy over the tactic to supersede focus on the substance.

The Last (United) Campaign

Hoping to recapture the previous year's enthusiasm, in April 1969 SDS announced a "spring offensive" to be launched once again with a demonstration in front of Nassau Hall, and once again the mood of anticipation was heightened by a building occupation and strike taking place at another Ivy League school—this time at Harvard. The demands still included the abolition of IDA but now also of ROTC, as well as divestiture from South Africa, and an end to military recruiting and counterinsurgency consulting.[73] Missing this time, however, were the parochial issues. With parietals out and coeducation on the way in, it was no longer possible to combine university reform with radical politics so that students could be attracted on the basis of the former but then exposed to harangues about the latter.

Also missing was the previous year's lightheartedness. A nucleus of conservative students showed up to oppose the radicals, and a group of proctors on the fringe of the crowd, "enjoying their newly discovered hobby," as the *Princetonian* put it, took photographs of participants. Some of the rhetoric was also considerably more threatening. Invited to speak, a member of the Black Panther Party advocated ".357 Magnum politics," praised Sirhan Sirhan, dropped numerous F-bombs, and called almost everyone he mentioned a "pig." The one moment of eloquence—the *Princetonian* called it "a note of moderation"—came from an ABC leader, who described the administration as "talking in superlatives but acting in diminutives."[74] Feeling uncomfortable as the speaker following the Black Panther, I made some inarticulate remarks about structural racism in the society being a different and more deeply rooted problem than individual prejudice.

There was a strange personal coda to the event. The demonstration over, I headed back to my apartment where, later in the day, I expected my closest friend from childhood, who was working in Denver but had returned to the East coast for a few days. To my surprise I found him waiting at my door. He had arrived earlier than planned and, finding no one at home, had strolled over to the university to get a closer look at the commotion taking place near the main gate. He had watched for a while, he told me, but after listening to a bizarre rant by a Black Panther, decided not to waste any more time and left. "Not a moment too soon," I told him.

In an effort to sustain the campaign's momentum, a few days later 50 SDS members again blocked the entrance to IDA. Rebuffed in their attempts to enter the building, three employees got into a brawl with the demonstrators, and when Dean of Students Neil Rudenstine—later to become the president of Harvard—attempted to break up the fight, he was decked for his trouble by one of the employees.[75] This event was the last action taken by a unitary SDS. By the beginning of the fall semester two organizations were calling themselves the Princeton chapter of SDS.

Fragmentation and Decline

The first half of 1969 was marked by an increased level of campus upheaval throughout the nation. Three hundred colleges and universities experienced protests, one quarter of them involving strikes or building occupations. A five-month-long boycott of classes at San Francisco State led to 700 arrests, and at Cornell black students, armed with rifles, took over a building. In support of the demand to expel ROTC from campus and to end the eviction of residents from property slated for development by the university, Harvard SDS took over an administration building; when the police cleared Harvard Yard, beating everyone in sight, 10,000 students met to declare a strike, publicized in an iconic poster of the time with a red fist.

SDS, however, was experiencing rising inner turmoil, especially at the national level; each quarterly national convention was bitterer than the previous, as PL/WSA and the different groups aligned with RYM clashed, each side attempting to win over the uncommitted delegates. PL was becoming more influential, though it still could not muster the support necessary to elect any of its sympathizers to a position in the national SDS leadership, which meant that the "NO"—the National Office, located in Chicago—and "New Left Notes," the SDS newsletter, remained firmly in the hands of its opponents. By this time both sides had proclaimed themselves socialist revolutionaries, and the conflicts typically centered on who were the real reds, each group claiming the other to be insufficiently communist. Carl Davidson, vice president and international secretary, captured the atmosphere accurately in his description of the last session of the December 1968 convention:

> Traditionally a time of merrymaking and song at SDS gatherings ... this time the two opposing camps delivered volleys of chants back and forth. "Ho Ho Ho Chi Minh" came from the national collective supporters, answered by "Mao Mao Mao Tse-tung" from the other side. When someone started singing "The Worker's Flag is Deepest Red," the student-worker alliance side of the room came up with "Don't use the red flag against the red flag" and "Defeat SDS's Khrushchev." The final blow came when the singing of "Solidarity Forever" was interrupted by the chant "Defeat False Unity."[76]

The revolutionary fervor dominating all the SDS factions also created logistical problems for the national conventions: universities no longer wished to play host. The March 1969 convention had been scheduled to take place at the University of Texas at Austin, but the chairman of the university's Board of Regents abrogated the agreement and banned SDS from campus. SDS then signed a contract to lease a public facility in Albuquerque, New Mexico, only to have city council determine that the organization would not be welcome in that city either. Finally the Austin churches came to the rescue, allowing SDS to use the campus YMCA as a headquarters and to meet in nearby religious centers.[77]

THE CHICAGO DEBACLE

After more than 50 colleges and universities rejected SDS's request to have the June 1969 convention on their campuses, SDS rented the Chicago

Coliseum; actually a couple of schools in New England would have agreed to act as host, but there was no way the NO would allow the convention to take place in a part of the country known as a PL/WSA stronghold. Sensing that the convention would be the ultimate showdown, both the NO/RYM group and PL/WSA made strenuous efforts to get their supporters to Chicago, and instead of the 500 SDS members who had gathered in Austin a few months earlier, close to 2,000 people showed up in June, about a third of them unaffiliated with either side. PL chartered a bus on which I joined 40 other WSA members for a 20-hour ride. Since the convention was not being held at a university, there were no dormitories, and accommodations had been arranged for us at the homes of local sympathizers, where we spent the nights packed next to each other in sleeping bags on the floor of the living room, looking like a row of oversized manicotti.

Shut down two years later for fire violations and then demolished in 1982, the Coliseum was a huge, unattractive complex whose cavernous main room was also used as a venue for rock concerts. A bank of doors on the right side led into an adjoining room, not quite as large. Tables around the perimeter displayed the literature of numerous left wing grouplets—Trotskyists, socialists of various stripes, anarchists, communists—most of their books and pamphlets unimaginative and predictable, but with an occasional exception; whether or not one agreed with the argument, anarchist Murray Bookchin's "Listen, Marxist!"—its cover featuring photos of Marx, Engels, Lenin, and, in their midst, a winking Bugs Bunny—offered a provocative critique of traditional Marxism. By the end of each day the floor was littered with the mimeographed proposals circulated by the political sects; one of them proposed that all SDS resolutions be made in some obscure language, the name of which I can't recall, on the grounds that they would be just as meaningful to American workers as in English. On the sidewalk outside the hall, passing local residents mixed with obvious police agents, either from the FBI or the Chicago Red Squad, in clichéd trench coats serving to conceal the tools of their trade. The first day of the convention a neighborhood black kid playfully reached underneath the back of one of these garments and pulled down a wire, shouting, "Look! This guy's a monkey. He's got a tail." The operative yanked the wire away, in the process opening the trench coat just enough to offer a glimpse of the clumsy electronic apparatus to which the wire was attached—some sort of 1960s state of the art recording device.

Because I had been a military policeman, someone foolishly thought I should represent the WSA caucus in discussions about convention security. In this capacity I tried to convince representatives of the other factions that, for most people entering the hall, someone could vouch for their identity and we could then question the few "unknowns" more intensively, but the others insisted on individual searches, leading to complaints from a number of women that male security were conducting these pat-downs with unnecessary vigor. In any event, our feeble attempts certainly did not prevent lots of under-cover agents from getting through.

The convention issue of "New Left Notes" featured the longest article ever in the newsletter, a rambling 15,000-word document titled "You Don't Need a Weatherman to Know Which Way the Wind Blows." Named for a line from Bob Dylan's "Subterranean Homesick Blues," it argued that the United States was a "monster," which had become "so rich from its world-wide plunder" that it was able to dole out some "crumbs ... to the enslaved masses within its borders" but that everything enjoyed by Americans—"All of the United Airlines Astrojets, all of the Holiday Inns, all of Hertz's automobiles, your television set, car and wardrobe"—had been produced through the oppression of Third World peoples and rightfully belonged to them. While blacks in the United States were similarly oppressed as "an internal colony," white workers, in this analysis, benefitted from the system, the privileges they enjoyed making them implicit in the "material basis for racism." The role of white radicals was thus to support in whatever way necessary the struggles of the Vietnamese, Cubans, and other peoples fighting U.S. imperialism, espe-cially the black revolutionary movement at home. Third World peoples would beat imperialism from the outside, and blacks, along with their white allies, would "drive a stake into the heart of the monster" from the inside. "Any white who does not follow this ... path," declared the Weatherman article, "is objectively racist"—"objectively" being a favorite term in Leftspeak indicating in this case that whites unwilling to "share the cost" of revolution with blacks were acting in a manner racist in impact, even if not in intent.[78]

Although there had been calls to oust PL as early as the June 1968 national convention, they had been spontaneous outbursts, provoked by frus-tration at the inability to win approval for some proposal that PL and their sympathizers were blocking. In Chicago, however, it became evident that there was an organized plan, foreshadowed by the "Weatherman" article, to put PL/WSA in its place once and for all. PL had recently concluded that all nationalism was reactionary—i.e., counter-revolutionary. According to this analysis, nationalism only promoted the erroneous notion that different classes, whether in Vietnam or the minority communities in the United States, could make common cause on the basis of shared ethnicity or nationality.[79] People associated with the NO/RYM position had never agreed with PL's view of blacks as a super-exploited segment of the working class, but now they were infuriated. Nationalist revolutionary groups like the Panthers, they believed, were the vanguard of the movement, not to mention the target of a government plot to decimate their ranks, and any criticism of them, especially from people who enjoyed "white skin privilege," was considered the ultimate in arm chair radicalism: aiming theoretical ammunition at people whose lives were being threatened by the real thing. As the "Weatherman" statement noted, it was "objectively racist."

Accorded a special status in the movement as the target of government persecution, the Panthers would provide the club to pound PL/WSA into submission or, better yet, out of SDS entirely. On Thursday evening—the first full day of convention activities—the NO had arranged the appearance of a sequence of representatives from revolutionary nationalist groups, clearly chosen to discomfit PL: first a member of the Young Lords, a Puerto Rican organization, and then someone from the Chicano Brown Berets. Finally came the clincher: a delegation from the Illinois Black Panther Party, including the Minister of Information, accompanied in quasi-military fashion by two bodyguards. He started out by castigating PL for its criticism from the sidelines while the Panthers were involved in the fray, but suddenly veered to the women's movement, referring to the importance of "pussy power." Earlier that afternoon there had been a workshop on women's liberation, which included complaints about the subservient role women were asked to play in the movement. The behavior of some of the male security conducting overeager searches had also been raised; of course, none of the offenders had been associated with the "puritanical" PL/WSA caucus. With these preceding experiences increasing the sensitivity to women's issues, the SDS audience, which up to now had listened reverently to the Panther spokesman, began a cry of "Fight male chauvinism," a chant that only increased in volume when he added gratuitously that "Superman was a punk because he never even tried to fuck Lois Lane."[80] While the PL/WSA caucus joined in the chorus because it found the comments genuinely offensive, it didn't hurt that the Panthers had just alienated hundreds of unaffiliated convention members that each side was trying to win over.

A different member of the Panther delegation stepped to the microphone and asked for silence so that he could clarify the situation for these white college students, who had clearly missed the point. "There's no reason that a woman should lay up in the bed with a non-revolutionary motherfucker," he explained, "when there are so many good revolutionaries around." Now the chant crescendoed to new levels, forcing the Panther delegation to head for the door, but not before the second speaker delivered a parting shot: "Women have a strategic position in the revolution," he snapped: "prone." The hall, reported the *Guardian*, "was in pandemonium."[81]

The next evening the Panthers suddenly returned and asked to address the convention with a prepared statement. Demanding that "the Progressive Labor Party change its position on the right to self-determination and stand in concert with the oppressed peoples of the world," the statement threatened that, should PL continue its present course, "they will be considered as counter-revolutionary traitors and dealt with as such." It ended by warning SDS that they "will be judged by the company they keep" and how effectively "they deal with bourgeois factions in their organization." The hall erupted, as the two groups of partisans engaged in a competition of which side could chant its slogans at a higher decibel level. The PL/WSA side went from "Smash red-baiting" to the eloquent "Bull-*shit*!," then "Power to the *workers*"—in deliberate contrast to the Panthers' slogan "Power to the people"—and finally demanded "Rebuttal! Rebuttal!"

As this last call echoed through the Coliseum, six or seven members of the WSA caucus, myself included, formed a wedge around Jeff Gordon, PL's National Student Organizer, and forced our way through the crowd and onto the stage. I stood immediately to his right, looking down at the chaos on the convention floor, as the noise diminished but not the tension; behind me stood a WSA member from Texas, a guy with a power forward's build, and I remember thinking to myself to stay close to him if things got ugly. With a preternatural degree of composure and speaking in carefully measured words, Jeff declared that PL would not be "intimidated out of SDS." PL supported the Black Panther Party, he continued, but offered "comradely criticism" when it believed appropriate. Refusing to be baited into an angry response, Gordon stood his ground without appearing hostile or aggrieved even in the face of obvious provocation.

It was a winning performance, and PL's opponents knew it. Seeing the plan to humiliate PL backfire, Bernardine Dohrn—one of the 11 co-authors of the "Weatherman" document—seized the microphone in a fury, imploring others to follow her into the side room to decide whether they could abide being in an organization with people who refused to defend the right of the oppressed to self-determination. As many of the RYM supporters, caught off guard by the maneuver, slowly began to join her, the PL/WSA caucus chanted "Stay and Struggle" and "No Split! No Split!" Despite the disagreements the last thing PL wanted was a dissolution of the organization that had provided such a fertile hunting ground for new recruits.

On Saturday the dual meetings continued—PL/WSA in the main room, the Weather/RYM group next door, and lots of undecideds moving back and forth between the two. Differences were already beginning to emerge among PL's opponents, leading them to divide into those associated with the Weather statement and a coalition of groups referred to as RYM-II, but for the moment they remained together, united by their common enemy. Finally, after a full day of discussion, they voted to exclude PL and its supporters from SDS, along with all others who did not support a specific set of principles. The fact that the slightly larger group of people who had remained in the main hall, not all of whom were allied with PL/WSA, had been given no voice in this decision was judged to be of no consequence, since their inclusion would have allowed "counter-revolutionaries ... the right to 'vote' on their own counter-revolutionary nature." The minority at the convention was about to expel the majority.

Close to midnight on Saturday, the Weather/RYM forces emerged grim-faced from their 24-hour caucus, their arms folded in emulation of the Panthers' style as they stood along the walls, ominously surrounding the seated group of people in the main room. Bernardine Dohrn took the stage and delivered a denunciation of PL lasting close to half an hour. Then came the punch line: members of Progressive Labor and the Worker Student Alliance were objectively racist and reactionary; they and all others who did not agree with the entire list of principles drawn up by the Weather/RYM coalition were hereby banished from SDS. Ending her fulmination with the same slogan that ended the Weatherman statement—"Long Live the Victory of People's War!" the title of a pamphlet by Chinese Minister of Defense Lin Biao—Dohrn stormed out of the hall followed by the rest of the anti–PL/WSA forces, while their opponents chanted "Shame! Shame!" The next day, two groups, each claiming to be the "true" SDS, met in two different locations and elected national officers, although, at this point, it would be more accurate to say that there was *no* SDS—at least none with a fraction of the strength the organization had once enjoyed.

The "principles" offered as the basis for drumming so many people out of SDS included mandatory support for a number of foreign regimes, among them the Democratic People's Republic of Korea—i.e., North Korea. Not only had an organization originally predicated on a non-exclusionary policy now compiled a set of criteria for membership, but with no sense of irony, the same people who had complained that PL was too "robotic" mandated, as one of these criteria, support for the most highly regimented society on earth. Indeed, one account has it that the Weatherman group sang the tune of "Maria" from "West Side Story," changing the lyrics to suit their deification of the Korean dictator: "The most beautiful sound I ever heard / Kim Il Sung, Kim Il Sung."[82] I wondered if they had given any thought to how the "Great Leader" would react to beads and bongs.

Despite having spearheaded the rejection of PL/WSA, Dohrn and others aligned with the Weatherman statement soon abandoned SDS and went their own way, proceeding on the assumption that almost anything was acceptable, no matter how inane, because, with only a few exceptions, the white working class—i.e., the majority of the country—was the enemy. Over the next few months their activities included picking fights with white working class youth on the assumption that "greasers" would be attracted to toughness; barricading themselves in high schools or movie theaters to lecture a captive audience on the necessity of revolution; or committing outright felonies, even armed robbery. After Weatherman launched the October 1969 "Days of Rage"—in which their members ran through Chicago's affluent Gold Coast smashing windows, luxury businesses, and automobiles—their heroes, the Panthers, rejected the actions as "custeristic."[83] At the time I thought that Weatherman had to be filled with government agents, saboteurs intent on discrediting the movement.

When these tactics failed to attract any new adherents, Weatherman headed further down the path of insanity. A few months after the Chicago action, three members of the collective were killed when a bomb exploded in their Greenwich Village townhouse. Constructed of dynamite wrapped with three-inch nails as shrapnel, this antipersonnel weapon had been intended to "vomit death and destruction" at a dance at the Fort Dix non-commissioned officers club. As Cathy Wilkerson, one of the two survivors of the explosion later recalled, they believed that the suffering inflicted by the bomb would cause its victims to "develop more empathy for how the Vietnamese felt."[84] Quite apart from the utter cluelessness about human emotional reactions revealed in this statement, it suggested that Weatherman didn't understand that the NCO club was for all enlisted men, many of whom were draftees, and their dates or wives. These conscripted soldiers were also victims of American imperialism. The Weather collective, all of whose male members had found a way out of the draft, set out to bomb those who had not been so fortunate, thus victimizing them yet again. It was Weatherman's version of Mort Sahl's quip during the McCarthy era that every time the Russians throw an American in jail, the House Un-American Activities Committee throws an American in jail to get even: every time the government sends a draftee to be killed in Vietnam, Weatherman will kill a draftee in the United States to get even.

With Weatherman going its separate way—in the Left's jargon, too "adventurist" for the rest of the RYM coalition—what had once been SDS was left in three pieces: the PL/WSA faction, the RYM-II faction, and Weatherman. Although the most extreme group was also the smallest, its more sensational activities elicited much greater attention from the media, and, unfortunately, much of the public, unaware of the Left's internal conflicts, regarded Weatherman and SDS as synonymous. However, on individual campuses the other two groups continued their attempts to reclaim the organization's former glory.

Thwarted by Success

Three weeks after the convention, a regional conference of SDS was announced, to be held at NYU's Loeb Student Center at Washington Square. Though the event had been planned by RYM-II, that designation had not appeared in the announcement, and a number of Princeton WSA members headed to New York, seeing no reason that we should be excluded. At the door, every person seeking to enter was required to sign a statement affirming support for the list of principles drawn up in the rump session of the convention; naturally none of the WSA members would do so. A brawl between the two sides erupted, ending only with the arrival of New York's finest with their guns drawn. Although I was involved in the melee, I participated out of loyalty to my friends, who were being attacked; now consumed with differences between factions, all claiming the same goals, SDS was making less and less sense.

As the fall semester began at Princeton, however, the two local SDS chapters managed to go their separate ways without conflict, pursuing activities that reflected their respective political emphases. SDS-WSA supported striking workers at the local General Electric plant and organized a campaign on behalf of janitors at the university, a group predominantly black and poorly paid, but these efforts attracted at most some 60 people. SDS-RYM continued to organize demonstrations at IDA, and together with other campus organizations, co-sponsored a teach-in that featured Black Panther Party Chief of Staff David Hilliard, the attorneys defending the "Panther 21"—then on trial in New York City on conspiracy charges, of which they would be found not guilty—and Afeni Shakur, one of the defendants (Tupac Shakur's mother). Although the event was attended by more than 3,000 people, they were clearly attracted by the speakers rather than by RYM's politics; the group's subsequent demand that the university trustees put up $85,000 worth of property to provide bail for three Panthers awaiting trial in Jersey City received little support. SDS-RYM's other main activity was to "heckle Hickel"—disrupting a speech on ecology by Nixon's secretary of the interior Walter J. Hickel, while President Goheen sat seething next to Hickel on the podium. The aftermath of the disruption led to the largest campaign of the year sponsored by either version of SDS, as RYM organized not around the war or black liberation but to oppose disciplinary proceedings for the disrupters.[85]

Yet despite the diminished influence of a fragmented SDS, the larger anti-war movement was growing like kudzu. The rising tide of opposition might not yet have reached what Richard Nixon called the "Silent Majority," but by fall 1969 it had flooded the campuses, and the president could not visit a major college or university in the nation without sparking a protest and possibly even a riot. More than two million people participated in the first nationwide moratorium on October 15, and a month later half a million people showed up in Washington as part of the second, braving cold winds and tear gas used to disperse the more unruly protesters. But the dam really burst when, on the last day of April 1970, Nixon announced the Cambodian "incursion," provoking nationwide protests. Students at more than 500 colleges and universities went on strike shutting down their institutions; some 50 to 60 percent of college students in the United States were involved in the protests. At that spring's commencement exercises, numerous graduates processed, wearing the war resisters' armband over their academic robes.

Within minutes of Nixon's announcement the Princeton campus was in an uproar, as 2,500 people—only a few of them from SDS—streamed out of dormitories and offices and into the chapel, where they called for an immediate strike. Most remarkable, the eating clubs—the traditional core of conservatism on campus—canceled plans for "Houseparties Weekend," the social highlight of the year, donating the money that would have been spent on the festivities to antiwar organizations. A few days later almost the entire university community—5,000 students, faculty, and staff—crowded into the gym and voted that the university "as an institution oppose the Cambodian invasion, American foreign policy and domestic oppression." The soft spoken Professor Kelley, selected for his level-headedness to chair committees dealing with controversial issues, called for nationwide draft resistance. Some 900 people, faculty as well as students—most of the latter unaffiliated with either wing of SDS—showed up at IDA to protest, and many individual departments passed resolutions condemning the war, supporting a strike, and in some cases calling for severance of all ties with ROTC and IDA. Some faculty members even proposed that the university reject any research funding from the Department of Defense. At a meeting of the entire faculty, a resolution calling for immediate withdrawal of all American military forces from Southeast Asia was adopted by a vote of 261–12. Most surprising, Goheen, who had schemed behind the scenes to thwart the opposition to IDA, emphasizing the university's legal obligation to respect its contract, now sought to terminate the lease as soon as possible.[86] The importance of finding an academic justification to oppose ROTC and IDA lest it appear that the university was "giving in" to the radicals, the desire to avoid creating the impression that the university was taking a political stance—these previous considerations of such importance were suddenly forgotten as the university adopted what had been the entire SDS anti-war agenda just a year earlier.

Thus, even without fragmentation SDS would certainly have declined, paradoxically undermined by achievement of one of its most important objectives: the creation of a mass movement against the war. Before widespread protest, students seeking to express their opposition necessarily gravitated toward SDS. But when almost everyone turned against the war, a fire-breathing anti-imperialist organization was no longer their only option; much of the opposition to the war could now be decoupled from SDS's radical analysis. At the same time, in a kind of rubber band model of politics, the fact that SDS had such an extreme position elongated the left end of the spectrum, making space for what *had* been extreme to become mainstream. Calling for the complete withdrawal of American troops from Southeast Asia in 1967 was considered radical; three years later it was commonplace.

Deprived of its most effective issue as an organizing tool, SDS had little else with which to appeal to students' self-interest in making the case for a radical, socialist alternative. The Old Left had offered its adherents an ideology that fit their personal experience as members of the working class: autoworkers, electricians, longshoremen, miners, labor organizers, and the unemployed. Although the earlier movement had its share of professionals, they too were motivated by a strong sense of class consciousness. Little of this characterization applied to members of the New Left, who were, in the famous first sentence of SDS's founding document, "bred in at least modest comfort," and looked forward to careers rather than jobs. Unable to appeal to students based on their own liberation, the RYM/Weather elements of SDS offered them an ideology based on the liberation of other people. The power of this motivation should not be underestimated; "A life that partakes of ... the chance to take part in battles for the liberation of others," observed Christopher Hitchens, "cannot be called 'meaningless.'" But what began so laudably wound up as an almost servile, worshipful attitude of the North

Vietnamese, the NLF, the Panthers, Fidel, Mao, and any other Third World leader or movement in conflict with the United States; Paul Berman summarized it as "I struggle on behalf of others, therefore I am."[87]

The reductio ad absurdum of this position was Weatherman, which offered the choice of "either joining the world revolution led by the blacks, the yellows, and the browns, or being put down as U.S. imperialist pigs by the people of the Third World." And when the latter, aided by their few stalwart white allies, prevailed over the former, as Weatherman was certain they would, one of the group's theoreticians—Ted Gold, who was killed in the Greenwich Village explosion—proposed that the United States be run by "an agency of the people of the world." (Ironically, when members of Weathermen actually had an opportunity to meet NLF members, their heroes displayed little interest in the attempt to defeat U.S. imperialism from the inside, but wanted young radicals to influence their Republican parents.) The closest Weatherman came to any other rationale for their cause was the desire to achieve personal liberation by engaging in orgies to demonstrate their revolutionary love for each other and indulging in drugs—an inability to distinguish between liberation and licentiousness.[88]

In addition to its emphasis on an alliance with campus workers, SDS/WSA attempted to reenergize its organization with a campaign to oppose racism; over the next few years, the PL-led faction of SDS evolved first into the Committee Against Racism and then, after chapters were established in other countries, into the International Committee Against Racism. The organization focused on both ends of the cultural spectrum: counter-demonstrations against rallies by the Klan, neo–Nazis, and other white supremacist groups, as well as an effort to oppose "scientific racism"—the work of IQ theorists, "hereditarians," and sociobiologists, used to provide intellectual support for racist beliefs and policies. Given that my own academic work has focused on the history of attempts to provide scientific justification for racist social policies, I would be the last person to dismiss this issue as insignificant, but it could hardly provide the basis for a mass movement.

CUTTING TIES

In mid–1970 my own association with SDS/WSA ended. Although the ostensible reason was the full-time position I had been offered in the psychology department at Rutgers University's Camden campus, the truth was that I had become increasingly uncomfortable with both the conflicts within SDS and the direction that the WSA caucus was taking. In addition to the brawl at the NYU student center, two other events contributed to my sense of alienation. Most important was PL/WSA's opposition to the demand for increased admission of minorities to elite institutions like Princeton on the grounds that it would lead to the "bourgeoisification" of the most militant members of the working class. This was chutzpah on steroids—white Princeton students opposing the admission of more blacks, Hispanics, and Asians because it would co-opt them—and I found it embarrassing to be associated with a group that would peddle such nonsense. (In an interesting contrast the Weatherman slogan of "Open them up and shut them down!" called for open admissions but only as a means to an end: the presence of "militant blacks and browns" made it more likely to achieve the group's goal of closing down colleges.) Finally, there was a troublesome personal incident, when someone in the leadership of the caucus saw me reading the Trotskyist Isaac Deutscher's biography of Stalin. "That's not a book you should be reading," he told me; "if you want a book on Stalin, *we'll* give you something to read." That was enough: it was time to leave what remained of SDS. Although I continued to attend any anti-war demonstration within 200 miles, my own focus turned toward community work in the depressed city of Camden on grassroots issues such as education and employment.

While the radical movement no doubt hastened the end of the war, it produced few far reaching changes. The United States continued to overturn the results of democratic elections when they were deemed unacceptable, the victims of these coups typically unable to offer the kind of resistance that had sparked the anti-war movement; Chile, for example, did not have a Viet Minh. ROTC eventually returned to Princeton, as it did to many of the other schools that had banished the program during the Vietnam era. Though having little impact at the time, the South African disinvestment campaign resumed in the late 1970s, peaking in the mid–1980s, when not only a number of universities but also many states, counties, and cities took economic action against the apartheid regime, helping to spur its demise.

In the strange system of categorization that characterizes American politics, it was agreed by everyone, ourselves included, that even before its pivot from reform to revolution, SDS was a radical organization. In fact, most of the movement's initial demands could hardly have been more conservative: respect for the independence and freedom of other people; the extension of constitutional protections and civil rights to everyone; the belief that government officials should not be above the rule of law. When these goals seemed unachievable under the existing system of government, many of us turned to a Marxist framework that seemed to provide both a persuasive explanation for present injustices and a path to a more egalitarian future, unaware that an insightful analysis of the problem was no guarantee that the proposed solution was either feasible or preferable; Marx was much more accurate at describing the predations of capitalism than envisioning the possibilities of communism.

In any event, despite all the lip service at the time, I doubt whether most members of SDS truly believed there was going to be a revolution in the United States. Though there were certainly some exceptions—people genuinely dedicated to an armed uprising—the rhetoric struck me as our version of a scream of protest, a way to call attention to the horrors being perpetrated by our government and in our name.

Four decades later I set out to learn how other activists viewed their involvement and what they had done with their lives. Naturally the first person I sought to find was Robby, but an Internet search provided no clue to his whereabouts. For a moment I thought I had found him in Canada, where there was an English teacher with his uncommon name identical right down to the middle initial, but after a comical phone call in which I attempted to persuade the protesting voice on the other end that he was really my old comrade, I accepted defeat. Then a year later I received an email from a name I didn't recognize, offering greetings from "the person you used to know as Robby Nerenberg." It turned out that in the early 1980s, in anticipation of political repression, PL had obtained new identities for some of its members, and Robby was just now "emerging" after the truth was discovered during an application to have his passport renewed. The charge against him was dismissed because the changed identity had never been used either for personal gain or to perpetrate a fraud; indeed, the only practical effect had been to add unexpected (and unearned) social security credits to the actual possessor of the number Robby had been using. Under his changed name my old friend had used his writing ability and his creativity to fashion an entirely new career doing marketing work in the private sector. Robby and his wife—also a PL member with a changed identity—had remained politically active and had led a campaign to improve the education in their son's largely minority school. They had recently left PL in part over a dispute about the same issue that had hastened my own departure from the WSA but that was more personal in their case: their son had been accepted to Yale, but the party opposed his attending a "ruling class" institution. Although I wanted to include Robby's story in the instant project, he was not yet ready to "speak for the record."

Excluding Robby, I made a list of the most prominent Princeton radicals, the people most recognizable as activists to the rest of the campus. While some of them had held a title of some sort within SDS, I hesitate to refer to them as "leadership" in an organization so opposed to hierarchies. But more important than a title or position, they were among the most committed members of the chapter, the people who endured the interminable meetings, formulated the organization's strategy and tactics, and spoke at the rallies. But in addition to these visible roles, they also wrote the brochures and leaflets, got their hands ink-stained cranking out copies on an old-fashioned mimeograph machine, and went door to door in the dormitories and the eating clubs, encouraging other students' involvement. Activism was work, and these were the people who performed it.

This group is thus representative of the most dedicated activists in one SDS chapter. They were not national figures in SDS, not the organization's generals, but certainly its platoon leaders, and from the government's perspective worth keeping track of. Each of them who had submitted a Freedom of Information Act inquiry received his FBI file, in some cases running to hundreds of pages.

In the Internet age it was not only possible to find all these people but to learn a lot about their careers. Because almost all of them had done a considerable amount of writing, I was able to read their work beforehand, much of which, even when dealing with some specialized field, was a reflection of deeply held values, allowing me to develop a sense of what they believed even before interviewing them. The interviews themselves were semi-standardized, conducted so that approximately one quarter of the questions were identical for everyone and three-quarters tailored to the individual, depending on each person's occupational history and accomplishments. The interviews were conducted between the middle of 2007 and the end of 2008.

3. The Lawyer for Employers

Three Princeton undergraduates were recognized by other students as the face of SDS. Peter Kaminsky, of course, had been president of the Undergraduate Assembly as well as a regular speaker at rallies, and Jimmy Tarlau was known as an organizer and strategist behind the scenes. But it was Doug Seaton, the chapter's chair, who most often spoke for the organization, and his statements in the *Princetonian* reflected the group's growing radicalization. The 1968 presidential election was a "fraud," according to Doug, because "any administration has to accept capitalism and put profit over human needs." No agency connected to the military, including the CIA, ROTC, and IDA, had any right to operate or recruit since they were "part of the military attack on the peoples of the world" and had "no place in the university, or this country or any place in the world." And the South African divestment campaign was designed to strike a blow against racism, imperialism and "the capitalism that is the material basis of that racist and imperialist practice." The solution, Doug wrote, was "to overthrow the system that exploits us black and white workers and students."[1]

The Internet disclosed that Doug had abandoned such rhetoric long ago. Indeed, to the extent that there is a class struggle, Douglas P. Seaton, the founder and lead partner of the Minneapolis law firm of Seaton, Beck & Peters, has changed sides. With a doctorate in labor history earned before his law degree, Doug provides counsel to business owners on actions involving employees: union organizing campaigns, collective bargaining, strike management, arbitration, employee termination, and National Labor Relations Board proceedings.[2]

In summer 2007 I flew to Minneapolis to interview Doug and checked into a Holiday Inn catering to a clientele whose main purpose for visiting was to shop at the Mall of America—2.5 million square feet of retail stores surrounding an indoor amusement park—only a few minutes' walk away. Despite the mall's proximity, a shuttle bus ran back and forth so that guests without a car did not have to lug their purchases back on foot. People entered the Inn's lobby loaded down with purchases, which they piled onto dollies for transport to their room. One couple I spoke to had driven nine hours from their home to spend two days consumering.

The last time I had seen Doug he was the dashing activist photographed in the *Princetonian*, demonstrating outside the New South Building in support of ABC's takeover with a patch over one eye—the result of an infection, though it made him look as if he should be brandishing a sword or maybe a flintlock pistol.[3] I had difficulty recognizing the casually dressed, subdued person with the Mark Spitz mustache who met me at the Holiday Inn. Though still youthfully trim, Doug *sounded* different from his radical self. In contrast to the SDS leader, whose forcefulness and intensity had made him the unanimous choice for chair, the attorney spoke softly, choosing his words slowly and carefully, perhaps a lawyerly trait or prompted by the desire to provide a precise explanation of how the transformation in his views had occurred.

⸻

Douglas Seaton grew up in Cleveland, the son of an electronics expert who had once operated a repair shop but then began a second career teaching electronics in secondary trade schools. While his parents rarely discussed politics, he was fairly certain that his father was a conservative Republican for reasons that Doug began to understand only after studying labor history. In the father's younger days he had worked making radios in a Philco-Ford plant, which was organized by the UE—the United Electrical, Radio and Machine Workers, probably the largest industrial union in which communists and socialists played an influential role—and Seaton père had been involved in battles against the left wing in his plant. Doug suspected that his father had seen a number of fellow workers beaten up and, as a result, decided that "he was not going to wear his beliefs on his sleeve anymore." In any event, though it was clear that his parents disapproved of Doug's political activity, the closest they ever came to an overt expression was the sudden termination of spending money in the middle of his senior year—a gesture that he interpreted as an indication of their displeasure.

After attending a public high school, Doug entered Princeton at a time when the university's emphasis on a more "diverse" student body meant expanding the freshman class beyond applicants from tony prep schools. Though a Goldwater supporter before entering Princeton, he began to attend SDS meetings, influenced by the civil rights movement and the rising opposition to the war, and soon became one of the most active members. A scholarship student who worked in the dining halls as a waiter, Doug was also a model campus citizen; he served as a student trustee of the University Store and was chosen secretary-treasurer of his junior class but declined the office both because its responsibilities would interfere with his SDS activities and because he thought that student government had "no real potential" to accomplish anything of significance. After its sudden growth following the spring 1968 demonstration, SDS could no longer rely on a decentralized committee structure for leadership, and Doug was unanimously elected chair—a rare show of unity in an organization marked by increasing internal conflict.[4] He insisted that "no great charisma" on his part prompted the decision; an anti-hierarchical organization necessarily depended on people's willingness to do the work, and he was always willing. Indeed, his respect for discipline and hard work became a repeated theme in our discussion.

In retrospect, Doug characterized his radicalization as "very intellectual and kind of removed" in the sense that he had no personal experience involving civil rights and, having received a physical deferment from the draft for his poor eyesight, was in no risk of being inducted. This more abstract attraction to the movement was enhanced by his scholarly interest in the history of the Left, the knowledge of which made its idealistic goals all the more appealing. Also, as a history major Doug was influenced by some of his professors who were highly critical of U.S. policy in Vietnam and supportive of the student radicals—in particular Arno Mayer, a leading scholar of the Holocaust whose Jewish family had fled Luxembourg in the wake of the Nazi invasion. Mentioned by a number of interviewees as having had an effect on their thinking, Mayer not only provided outspoken support for the activists but put up bail when they were arrested, and the moral implications of such encouragement from someone with his personal background and field of study was not lost on SDS members. Decades later in Princeton's alumni magazine, Doug attributed his radicalism in large part to being "isolated and very much in this cocoon world of the New Left"—an intellectual environment that left him divorced from any connection to his hometown and the larger society.[5]

At the time, however, Doug felt totally committed to the movement. In addition to his leadership of SDS at Princeton during the academic year, in the summer he returned to Cleveland where he was involved in organizing tenants' unions; another activist working on the same project was Kathy Boudin, one of the two survivors of the 1970 explosion at the Greenwich Village townhouse used by members of Weatherman, and later imprisoned for her role as the getaway driver in the robbery of an armored car during which a guard and two police officers were gunned down. On two occasions Doug was arrested—once as part of an IDA sit-in and once for trying to get onto a bus in order to dissuade prospective army inductees about to be taken to a draft center.

Though part of the RYM faction, Doug considered himself "some sort of free-lance Marxist," taking part in a Hegelian process of inevitable social change; he thought of the movement as "advancing the cause of progress and human kind" with the result that "we'd all be in a better world." In Princeton's senior yearbook, he wrote that he "plans to struggle for socialism and eventually hopes to win the struggle."[6] Doug briefly thought that there would be a revolution, but, shortly after graduating, when he encountered people who were actually ready to take up arms, "the whole idea repelled" him. While he continued to pursue the same radical goals, he decided that violence was "just plain wrong," especially in a "functioning liberal democracy, where you could talk about these issues and theoretically convince people."

Completing his undergraduate work at Princeton, Doug pursued a doctorate in history at Rutgers University, where he remained politically active, helping to organize both the graduate student union and, in the aftermath of SDS's disintegration, an independent group called the Radical Student Movement. Specializing in the history of the American labor movement, he wrote his doctoral dissertation on the Association of Catholic Trade Unionists (ACTU) from the late 1930s through the late 1940s. The purpose of the study had been to shed light on the causes of "American exceptionalism"—why, in comparison to many other countries, radicalism in the United States had "failed to achieve strong organizational roots" in industrial unionism. Doug concluded that one important reason for labor's inherent conservatism was the influence of the church, exercised through the highly disciplined ACTU, which began with a focus on social justice but quickly abandoned that goal in favor of an obsession with cleansing workers' organizations of any left-wing influence, even if it meant weakening the union's bargaining position or ignoring corruption and outright gangsterism.[7] The book resulting from the dissertation was clearly unsympathetic to the ACTU—Doug characterized his work as "the self-righteous student radical's view of what happened in the labor movement." But despite his conclusion, by the time he finished the project, during which he interviewed the organization's remaining leaders and read the complete run of its newspapers, Doug had begun to appreciate the ACTU's perspective and to reevaluate some of his own views.

Now a freshly hooded Ph.D. and intending to become a labor lawyer, Doug enrolled in the University of Minnesota law school but soon transferred to William Mitchell College of Law in St. Paul so that, while pursuing his law degree, he could assume a full time position, on the strength of his doctorate in labor history, as an analyst for the Minnesota state legislature's Labor Committee; after earning his degree he continued to work for the committee as an attorney. In both positions Doug's role was non-partisan, requiring him to provide advice and draft legislation for members on both sides of the aisle. It was during his six years of employment by the Labor Committee that the seeds of doubt, planted during the work on his dissertation, began to sprout into complete disenchantment with the Left, as his Marxist notion of oppressed workers gave way to what appeared to him to be the reality in Minnesota—that, in fact, the labor movement controlled the legislature.

During his last two years at Princeton, Jimmy Tarlau, another SDS activist, became Doug's closest friend; when Doug was a senior and Jimmy a junior, along with some other radicals they shared a crumbling farmhouse in a small town near the university. In an ironic twist Jimmy has pursued a career in the labor movement as a union organizer and official; as Doug put it, Jimmy "has actually lived the life we all thought we were going to be leading." Despite the dramatic difference in the political direction their lives have taken, their friendship has endured. When I was trying to locate former SDS members, Jimmy helped me track down some of the interviewees. Each time I told him I would be visiting some old comrade, Jimmy asked me to convey his "regards," but when Doug's name came up, Jimmy said, "Send him my love."

Even while Doug was going through the transition that would take him to the opposite end of the political spectrum, he still respected the ideals that informed Jimmy's choices and felt the need to explain to his old friend the reasons for his changed views.[8] In a letter to Jimmy, Doug described his experience working for the Labor Committee, in which the chairman would "drop his gavel and leave the committee in midsentence to go to the gallery, not even having the decency to use a smoke-filled room, and ask instructions from the state AFL-CIO President." The result, Doug wrote, was "a workers' compensation law that shocks the conscience, a public-sector bargaining law that includes supervisors and gives mental hospital staff the right to strike, a private sector statute which defines supervisors and transferred employees as strikebreakers" and, under consideration at the time, a law giving "employees the right to refuse to work, with pay, if they think there are evil humors in the plant." Feeling driven out of the legislature by the necessity to remain neutral in the face of such outrages, Doug turned to private practice, which he found just as much of a shock for "an old proletarian romantic." Rather than seeming "noble," the class struggle, from the perspective of the employers' legal representative, struck him as "a series of fraudulent claims, overreaching bargaining and grievance claims, uneconomic wages" and—though there had been a time that he thought the word laughable in this context—"irresponsibility" on the part of employees.

By three years later—a decade and a half after leaving Princeton—it was clear to Doug that the roots of his dissatisfaction were deeper than merely labor's undue influence on state legislators. Rather, he perceived a pervasive societal decline, substantially informed by the ideology of the movement in which he had been an enthusiastic participant. Although he had once walked arm in arm with the Black Panthers through the streets of Newark and was clubbed by the police for his trouble, he now believed that, in the name of black liberation, the Left had condoned a lot of truly dreadful behavior, giving "racism a second life." The problem, as Doug wrote to Jimmy, was that "several generations of liberal leadership and policies (carped at, but largely supported by us radicals) have transformed the minority population and an increasing proportion of the white population into an inert, lumpen, malingering, criminal and quasi-criminal population, as dependent, antisocial and parasitic a class as exists anywhere in the world." It was not their fault, he emphasized, victimized as they had been by a politics of "envy, guilt, greed and what Chesterton called 'incompetent compassion'—the notion that if you do something that makes you feel less guilty, it must automatically be the right social policy." But most of all, it was a "politics of paternalism," resulting in the destruction of "the work ethic, the family unit and the basic habits of civilized life of millions of people." This was a "crime," Doug concluded—one committed by "liberals and radicals, with the best of motives, who didn't and still won't think about or admit to the actual social consequences of the policies they/we pursued." It was very much the Pogo perspective: we have met the enemy and he is us. And the solution, according to Doug, was simple: what the "underclass" needed was "good old bourgeois virtues like work, honesty, thrift, self-reliance, self-denial, abstemiousness, even sexual restraint and shame at charity."

Nor was this change in world view confined to domestic policy. Though Doug felt more "ambivalent" about the international situation, he had come "grudgingly" to the conclusion that Jeane Kirkpatrick's distinction between authoritarian dictatorships and totalitarian—i.e., socialist—regimes was essentially correct. Kirkpatrick, Reagan's ambassador to the United Nations, had famously argued for the United States to support the former despite their oppressive policies because their more traditional economies, organized around private ownership of the means of production and not subject to state control, were better for American interests and more likely to evolve into democracies. Especially in the Third World, where he acknowledged that masses of people lived in impoverished circumstances inconceivable to Americans, Doug was certain that the ruling classes, despite "their scheming and greed and bad taste and scorn for the peasantry and even with their political corruption," nevertheless were motivated by "acquisitiveness," which meant that they carried "the seed of development and democracy"—provided that they adopted those same bourgeois values that had worked so well in the United States. In contrast, the leftist guerrillas, to whom so many SDS members had developed a romantic attachment, now represented for him the path of "political, social and economic death." Although he wasn't completely comfortable with the company in which this analysis placed him, Doug was firmly opposed to Third World insurgent movements, even when the governments they sought to overthrow were themselves repressive.

Even given this transformation in his politics, it was surprising to find that Doug now opposed the goals of the anti-war efforts that he had once led; he was the only interviewee whose analysis of the Vietnam War had changed so strikingly. Some former activists no longer believed that ROTC or CIA recruiters should be excluded from campus but still professed no reservations about having made these demands during the Vietnam era when the military and intelligence services were deployed in support of what they viewed as an immoral purpose. As his opinions began to change, at first Doug sympathized with this attempt to justify SDS's campaigns by contextualizing them, but eventually he concluded that these actions had been wrongheaded even then, a product of the "cartoon vision of imperialism," in which the American presence in Vietnam was an expression of Western domination that had to be opposed in order to improve the lot of the Vietnamese. Having changed his mind about the best route to their improvement, he has decided that it was not the war that was mistaken but rather the "political heavy hand" controlling the way it was fought, which extended the conflict unnecessarily and prevented the kind of Korean-style partition of the country that might have been possible, had the military not been constrained.

Interestingly, the only SDS effort that Doug still supported was the South African divestment campaign. Almost all conservatives at the time had opposed the boycott and divestment movement, insisting that economic aid to South Africa could provide the leverage necessary to transform apartheid— the policy referred to under Reagan as "constructive engagement." Doug, however, not only regarded such economic pressure as appropriate in dealing with a "rogue regime," but actually thought that in South Africa, where there appeared to be no possibility for peaceful change, armed struggle to overthrow the apartheid government had been justified.

Much of his ideological view has been forged in the crucible of Doug's professional career as the "Lawyer for Employers," representing the interests of people who, in his description, "are trying to meet payrolls and get work out of reluctant workers sometimes and fight scams and shams and crazy bureaucrats and all that goes on in the world that is actually trying to get products produced and services rendered." They might not be "seizing any barricades," but Doug regarded them as "the thin red line of capitalist civilization"—the people who were really making a difference—and he was dedicated to their concerns. He identified with them so strongly in part because, as one of the founders of a firm that employed 16 or 17 people, he viewed *himself* as a small business person, whose concerns were the same as theirs: to ensure that the people who worked for him "have a livelihood tomorrow." Doug's practice representing employers meant that he spent much of his time providing advice on how to deal with problem workers: "the employee who never shows up, the employee who steals." In the newsletter published by his firm, Doug himself authored a detailed article on how to document an employee's shortcomings thoroughly in order to prepare the groundwork for termination.[9] (As a grievance officer for a faculty union, representing the rights of employees in proceedings against the administration, I thought all the advice was eminently sensible; a union's position is not to defend egregious behavior but to support employees' rights to due process, ensuring that they are not subject to arbitrary discipline absent appropriate evidence of their failings.)

On behalf of employers, Doug also negotiated with unions. Despite the fact that, as a labor historian he "love[d] the whole idea of the labor movement and what it stands for," nevertheless he felt forced to the conclusion that "Sweeney and company"—John Sweeney was president of the AFL-CIO from 1995 to 2009—had become "dinosaurs"; in Doug's view, the market had solved most of the problems that the movement was once needed to address with the result that unions no longer represented either progress or the interests of working people.

Unsurprisingly, Doug was now an active Republican, who worked hard for the party's candidates and, though he did not say so, apparently exercised some influence within political circles; at the time we spoke, he was chair of the state labor employment law section, and the previous morning had met his state representative for breakfast. Like many Republicans, he admired Ronald Reagan, "the right person at the right time," and as a reminder that "we owe it all to him," Doug prized his own small chunk of the Berlin Wall. Although he thought that George W. Bush—who was nearing the end of his second term when we spoke—had "for the most part done the right things," in contrast to Reagan, he had been the "sorriest communicator," which meant that despite having "the best of intentions" he had not been an effective persuader. Nor was the Republican cause aided by a press that Doug considered "so uniformly on one side of the political ideological divide" that at times he wondered whether, despite the First Amendment, there should be an attempt to invoke antitrust laws.

Yet despite the dramatic political transformation, Doug still resorted to the movement's intellectual framework, referring, for example, to the "ruling class"—an indication that the analysis had endured, though now leading to a different conclusion. Moreover he offered what he acknowledged was a Hegelian explanation of how, as a result of the movement, "things had become their opposite": how what had begun as the strengths of the movement—the goals he had found attractive and continued to support—had reached an inflection point, beyond which they were transformed into its weaknesses. Thus, the advances in racial and gender equality had moved toward the creation of "protected classes" and a "racial spoils system"; the recognition of diversity—of multiple cultures and heritages—had threatened to erode meritocracy; the demand for intellectual tolerance on campus had led to a "dictatorship of left wing intellectuals"; and humanitarian concern for the poor and the disadvantaged had encouraged their dependency and loss of dignity.

But despite what he perceived as its destructive effects, Doug expressed no regrets about his own participation in the movement. He didn't consider any of his actions "a bad thing to do," not even those that had led to his arrest. While he viewed blocking IDA or attempting to dissuade prospective recruits from enlisting as indefensible in a society that offered the means to "convince people to change policies," he didn't do "anything violent" or cause any harm: "all I did was sit there and get arrested; all I did was try to get on a bus."

While it might sound paradoxical, Doug still took pride in his former activities—a sentiment obviously not based on the substance of his efforts but rather on the strength of character he brought to his radical persona and the solidarity he experienced with other activists. His involvement was not a "pose," nor was he a "dilettante." He was sincere, he "really believed in" the cause, and was attracted to the movement not for frivolous reasons, not for the excitement it promised, but because he thought it was "important work," to be taken "seriously." He felt that he had always "acted responsibly" and pursued the movement's goals "in a disciplined and organized way." But most significant for Doug was that willingness to take on responsibility, which had made him the unanimous choice to be the SDS chair: "I worked hard," he emphasized; "I had always been a hard worker at whatever I've done."

Indeed, there was an almost wistful tone, as Doug recalled the sense of high purpose and solidarity that infused the movement: "We were so spirited, we did believe in what we were doing, we were committed, we really tried to do the right thing." Although he certainly felt "closer in ideological orientation" to contemporary students, he worried that "they don't have that sense of commitment to something that we had." It was as if he were searching for some way to reconcile the individualism of those bourgeois values that he considered so important for the society with the idealism and the camaraderie that he had found so appealing in the movement. But on balance it was the erosion of his cherished values—the work ethic, discipline, and respect for authority—that Doug saw as the movement's legacy and the society's burden. Perhaps it was an inevitable consequence of opposition to the Vietnam War, he mused, but "we did undermine the things that I now wish we had more of. I wish we didn't have to argue with everyone all the time to do what they're supposed to do."

More than any of the other former SDS members, Doug's views have substantially reversed. It was not so much that his opinion on specific issues had changed but rather that, in retrospect, he has crafted a narrative about the 60s significantly different from his original perceptions, in which the movement has gone from heroic force for liberation to the source of most of the nation's contemporary problems. But underlying the transition in his politics, Doug emphasized, was a stability in his belief in the importance of individual freedom. While he had once thought that liberty could be ensured by collectivist approaches, he now looked to free enterprise, limited government, and "all that traditional Federalist Papers kind of things" as its guarantor. It was this sense of continuity between the values that motivated him then as a radical and now as a conservative, which allowed Doug to view his own participation with, if not approval, then at least acceptance.

Unlike those whose journey from Left to Right has left them with the convert's enmity against their former beliefs, Doug seemed ambivalent about his past. He was no David Horowitz, bitterly nursing a grudge against his former self and his old comrades, all of whom he still considered friends. As the *Princeton Alumni Weekly* put it in an article on the 1960s, Doug looked back at his activity "as a campus radical with good-natured amusement." And when he told the *Weekly* that, in Minnesota, "I encounter my old self all the time," the observation suggested sympathy more than disapproval.[10]

4. The Erotic Marxist

At the peak of its influence, Princeton SDS proposed a "long term" agenda, outlining both a program of education involving films, speakers, and conferences, and an ambitious plan of action including, along with the usual academic issues, broader efforts to organize campus food service workers, local high school students, and migrant workers in the state.[1] The proposal was authored by Chip Sills, the chapter's internal education secretary.

A ruggedly handsome, motorcycle riding student of the martial arts, usually attired in the appropriate leather jacket and often accompanied by his attractive girlfriend from the local area, Clarence—"Chip"—Sills was Princeton SDS's most dashing member, but as a philosophy major and a particularly well-read member of the chapter, he was also the natural choice to preside over internal education, a responsibility mainly requiring him to organize the scores of pamphlets and brochures produced by and for the movement. Chip was genuinely excited by ideas and any discussion with him invariably produced surprise on his part that you were unfamiliar with some thinker that he regarded as important, followed by a recommendation of texts that you should read—a tendency that could easily be construed as pretentious but that seemed in his case more a consequence of intellectual enthusiasm.

It was a surprise to find that Doug Seaton had become an ardent Republican, but nothing like the shock I experienced when I plugged Chip's name into Google and up popped a photograph, taken only a few months earlier, of "Father Chip Sills' Ordination" in Blacksburg, Virginia, at an Anglo-Catholic Church, which adhered to a particularly conservative interpretation of Anglicanism emphasizing moral absolutes derived from scripture. Indeed, within weeks of Chip's ordination, he was counseling mourners after the massacre at Virginia Tech, also located in Blacksburg. In retrospect, however, there might have been a foreshadowing of this turn to piety, even during his radical days. After the University of Texas canceled its agreement to host an SDS National Convention early in 1969, Austin church groups let the organization use their campus facilities, prompting Chip to observe that "God came to the rescue."[2] In addition to his pastoral role, the Internet also disclosed that Chip was an ardent supporter of libertarianism and its then most visible spokesperson, Ron Paul.

Actually Chip lived an hour from Blacksburg in Greenville, West Virginia, a rural community in the mountains with fewer than 500 residents. I arranged to take Amtrak to the nearest stop and then rent a car the next morning. The nine-hour train trip was not unpleasant, especially the scenic last third where the gently undulating hills slowly merged into Appalachian waves. Late in the day I arrived in White Sulphur Springs, a once popular resort town that had been part of the same social circuit as Bar Harbor and Newport a century earlier but whose Main Street was now lined with businesses that looked like their owners had gone on permanent vacation. The train station was located directly opposite the curved white pillars flanking the entrance to the once illustrious Greenbrier Resort—its proximity probably the main reason for Amtrak to have a station in the town—which had welcomed 26 American presidents, acted as an internment center for Japanese and Nazi diplomats during World War II, and later been the site of a top-secret underground bunker, intended to house the members of congress in the event of nuclear war.[3]

I checked into a nearby motel, where the proprietor's eagerness to be of assistance was ample compensation for the dreary condition of the room; the next morning he happily drove me to the car rental office at the Greenbrier Airport 13 miles away. The facility was a long narrow structure with a couple of airline counters along one wall separated by a baggage carousel, and the car rental companies lined up along the opposite side. But amazingly, the building was completely deserted, and I found myself roaming around an airport all alone in the post–9/11 era.

Twenty minutes later a rental agent appeared, who informed me that the compact car I had reserved was not available but that I was welcome to have the one remaining vehicle at no additional charge—a Silverado 4×4. The last few miles of the drive through the West Virginia mountains were nerve wracking, as I maneuvered the clumsy truck up narrow and unpaved, twisting roads, praying at the beginning of each sharp turn that I would not encounter someone heading in the opposite direction.

Quite apart from its intended purpose, the trip turned out to be worth the effort if only to see Chip's house, nestled organically into a crest of the mountain rather than protruding obtrusively from its summit—"of the hill," as Frank Lloyd Wright once declared a house should be, rather than on it. I was greeted by Chip and his wife, Kelley, a slight, lovely woman who could easily have been taken for a college sophomore, though I learned that she was in her early 40s. The house itself—built by Chip, his wife, and his two sons from a previous marriage—was a work of impressive craftsmanship with few nails and almost all the joinery mortise and tenon. Before the interview we ate lunch at a porch table, the mountain skyline visible on the horizon.

Of the nine interviews I conducted, this was the most animated, the tone of Chip's comments at times bordering on the theatric as he became totally reabsorbed in the emotional context of past controversies. At one point in our conversation a fly landed on his forehead and, with the speed and agility that some large men possess, or perhaps as a consequence of his martial arts training, Chip squashed the intruder with a flick of his hand, so engrossed in the topic under discussion that he continued to speak with no noticeable pause, oblivious to the remains of the fly now visible in part on his forehead and in part on his hand. His thoughts were also the most smoothly phrased, emerging without hesitation in full paragraphs, though he had a tendency to repeat a phrase, not so much for emphasis but rather, it appeared, as a way to temporize while formulating his next thought—a more pleasing substitute for the usual verbal tics. As excited by ideas as ever, at different points in the discussion Chip referred to Michael Oakeshott, Norman O. Brown, Herbert Marcuse, Philip Rieff, Rosa Luxemburg, Lewis Mumford, Murray Rothbard, Eric Vogelin, and a dozen others—occasionally seeming merely like namechecks but more often accompanied by a substantive description of some specific concept relevant to the point. Leavening the serious mood suggested by this list, however, Chip did not hesitate to poke fun at himself—especially when reminded of some of his own decades-old observations—and the interview was marked by frequent outbursts of raucous laughter on both our parts. Even though I had intense disagreements with some of his statements—which I kept to myself only with difficulty—Chip's interview was probably the most fun. And, in an indication that not everything about him had changed, during our discussion he recommended a number of books he thought I should read.

Clarence Sills was, in his own words, "an army brat." His father had intended to be a doctor but after attending a college requiring all male students to take ROTC, he accepted a commission upon graduating. Promoted rapidly during World War II, he decided to make the army his career and retired as a colonel. Chip's mother, the daughter of a production manager for the Knight Newspaper chain, had earned a Master's degree in English at Columbia. While both his parents were extremely intelligent, Chip characterized his father as diplomatic, his mother as confrontational, a trait he acknowledged sharing with her.

As a result of his father's military career, Chip's youth was spent at various times in five different states, including Alaska, and one foreign country, when he, his mother, and his siblings lived in Japan for a year, allowing them to be close enough for regular visits from his father, stationed in Korea. Yet despite this geographic instability, he attended a single high school when his parents decided that their young "smart aleck who liked to correct his teachers" would benefit from the strict discipline of a Catholic boys' school and enrolled him in Ascension Academy in Virginia, an institution whose motto was "*Timor Domini Principium Sapientiae*"—"Fear of the Lord is the beginning of wisdom." Did he believe the motto was true? "It was indeed," Chip conceded, "although I didn't realize it at the time."

At Ascension Chip was an outstanding student but also frequently in trouble. Intellectually precocious and better read than most of his instructors, he did not endear himself to them by flaunting his superior knowledge and was suspended for his "smart mouth" on more than one occasion. Nevertheless he was recruited by Princeton, considered an attractive prospect from the university's perspective because of his high SAT scores and impressive athletic record as captain of his high school's wrestling team.

Although he felt like "a bit of a misfit" at Princeton, his experience at the university left its mark on Chip. For the first time he encountered people who didn't just disagree with him, but who were, he recalled, "more sophisticated than I, and more knowledgeable than I, and even more cocksure than I," basing their arguments on "people that I hardly knew anything about at that point—Nietzsche, Freud, Marx, Darwin, and so forth." Already outraged by what he saw as widespread "oppression," he became particularly interested in Marx for having "a very detailed outlook on what was wrong with the world and what should be done about it." An additional source of appeal was the intellectual challenge of Marxist thought. "Frankly," he acknowledged, "I've always liked complex intellectual explanations, and Marxists are good at that; they sit around and debate all the time, and it was fun for me to sort it all out and come to my own understanding." (Years later, an academic colleague who had co-edited a collection of essays with Chip commented on his preference for complexity, claiming that he seemed to "equate clear writing with simpleminded writing."[4]) Once having arrived at a conclusion, however, Chip harbored no uncertainties about its correctness. "In the excitement of my latest discovery," he admitted, "I was ready to trounce or denounce anybody who saw things as I had seen it a week earlier."

Chip characterized his politics while an SDS member as a mixture of "Lennonism and Leninism"—the idealistic sentiments of "all you need is love" combined with the willingness "to fight to overthrow the oppressors" and to "stand in solidarity" with others who were doing so. Of course, at Princeton solidarity with the oppressed was more rhetoric than reality, but there were also the strong bonds with fellow activists that Chip found "inspirational." One incident, in particular, exemplified for him that sense of comradeship: when he was sick and confined to the infirmary for several days during his senior year, "the guys" sent him a get-well card—a cartoon drawing of Marx and Lenin and Mao, all with their fists raised, and it said something like, "Comrade Chip, get well." "It touched me," he remembered, and "it just made me feel that that part of what we were doing, that solidarity in what we would now call God's work, was something to rejoice in." His ideal at the time was Che Guevara, or at least the romantic image of him—Marxist theorist, revolutionary hero, physician, author and poet, martyr for the cause. "I wouldn't say that now," he added immediately, "but I definitely believed it then."

In an era that ushered in that famous hedonistic trio, Chip loved rock and roll—he still played guitar almost every day—and indulged in his share of pharmacology, which was abruptly terminated when, for the first time ever, he was beaten in arm wrestling after smoking marijuana. But it was the first of the three for which he was particularly known on campus. There was even a much-talked-about SDS meeting during which Chip and his girlfriend engaged in intimacies while everyone else attempted not to notice; while he laughed at other embarrassing events from the past, he looked genuinely sheepish when I mentioned this incident. By the time of graduation, Chip had become what he called an "erotic Marxist"—someone influenced by Marx's class analysis but also by the liberatory notions of sexuality set out in Marcuse's *Eros and Civilization* and Norman O. Brown's *Life Against Death*—and an enthusiastic exponent of "the sixties cult of free love."[5] For others, the sexual openness that characterized much of the counterculture might have been a rebellion against bourgeois convention or just an opportunistic attempt to get laid, but for Chip it was an expression of high philosophical principle.

A couple of years later he described in print the kind of society that he thought the movement had the potential to create: one that would transform "work into play," put an end to "objectifying relations between people," and abolish what he called "museum culture," instead integrating culture into daily life.[6] Reminded of this observation, he characterized it as "young Marx utopianism," explaining that the goal of the revolution, as he then conceived of it, was the society envisioned in Marx's *The German Ideology*, in which people were not tied by economic necessity to one boring and repetitive job but performed different tasks at different times as they wished. In the passage Chip had in mind, Marx had written that, in contrast with the division of labor that "enslaves" a person by forcing upon him "an exclusive sphere of activity … from which he cannot escape," a communist society made it possible "to hunt in the morning, fish in the afternoon, rear cattle in the evening, criticize after dinner," just as one had a mind, "without ever becoming hunter, fisherman, shepherd or critic."[7]

Immediately after graduating, Chip worked briefly as a substitute teacher but still thought of himself as beginning a "career as a revolutionary," whose real task was "to do working class organizing." Eager to learn "how to resist the imperialists" from the people who had already demonstrated success at the task, he joined one of the Venceremos Brigades, traveling to Cuba to help with the sugar cane harvest in order to defeat the United States' attempt to stifle the Cuban economy. Always proud of his physical prowess, he was named a "*machetero vanguardia*"—a leading cane cutter—which entitled him to spend time with Fidel when the Cuban leader came to visit the American contingent. According to Chip, he asked Fidel how to make a revolution in the United States and was "stunned and disappointed" to be told by el Jefe that "you don't need a revolution in America; basically you just have to keep voting Democrat" because the "liberals are bringing about slowly what took an armed struggle in Cuba." The story bore a whiff of implausibility, especially considering that Richard Nixon, the Republican president at the time of the visit, had terminated his two Democratic predecessors' support for covert operations designed to overthrow the Castro regime, but it fit nicely with the eventual transition in Chip's politics to the libertarian belief that liberal policies were infringing on individual freedom.

While Chip's parents had always been "appalled" at his political activity, the trip to Cuba probably had harmful effects on his father's career. Having retired from the army a few years earlier, Colonel Sills had been working in support industries for the defense establishment but suddenly lost the required security clearance and his consulting positions as a consequence, after his son's name appeared in the Congressional Record as a potential subversive— two events that Chip assumed were not unrelated.

In Cuba, Chip became enamored of one of his American co-workers who was involved with a Weather collective in California, and, despite having always considered Weatherman "irresponsible," allowed the fact that he was "in lust" to override his judgment. Returning from the trip, he said goodbye to his girlfriend in New Jersey, loaded his motorcycle onto a trailer behind his car, and headed for the West coast along with four other recruits to the Weather underground. He lasted in the collective less than two weeks. "The noble and inspiring experiences we had had in Cuba," Chip observed, "contrasted wildly with the opportunistic posturing and creepy, manipulative attitudes in the underground," and he soon "realized that I could not stay in there one more day; it was just too crazy." Although he was reluctant to discuss the details, his published review of a book on racism a couple of years later provided some clues to his disaffection with a group that saw its primary task as putting their bodies on the line in support of the struggles of minority groups at home—especially the Black Panther Party—and revolutionaries abroad. "Our fetishization of Blacks" and Third World peoples, Chip wrote, citing the BPP as a prime example, stemmed from "an unexamined self-hatred, repression of one's own (pre-categorical) experience, and a consequent desperate, premature, and self-destructive totalization, which, alienated into its opposite, becomes a 'left-wing' totalitarianism," as exemplified by "life within the underground Weatherman collectives." The movement had become involved in "fighting other people's battles," the review concluded, but had "repressed awareness of our *own oppression*" (emphasis in original).[8]

While Chip now disavowed many of his past pronouncements, in this case he was quick to praise himself. The veneration of what he called "the designated oppressed group"—blacks and Vietnamese at the time—was not informed by a desire to appreciate the "beauty and uniqueness" of different races and cultures or to oppose bigotry against them; rather he called it "a form of genetic determinism all over again," creating as it did an image of these peoples as "basically superman," which they could not possibly fulfill. Indeed, in retrospect Chip saw this trend as the root of the contemporary multiculturalist movement, which he also detested, because, in his opinion, it "basically says that white European Christians have to hate themselves because they're responsible for all the bad things in the world. And if you're male," he added with a laugh, "you might as well die."

Happy to get out of Weatherman with his "skin intact" but not yet ready to give up on the revolution, Chip kept himself together for the next couple of years doing a series of odd jobs, first in Berkeley, where, among other activities, he taught "karate to hippies," and then back in New York City, where he wound up getting a hack license. Then as his political fervor began to wane, Chip became interested in one last radical possibility: he and a few others—most of them connected to *Telos*, a Marxist philosophy journal—attempted to create a Marxist intellectual commune in rural Oregon. However, "it was immediately obvious that it wasn't going to work"; not only was 90 percent of the work performed by 10 percent of the group, according to Chip, but a couple of people, who were not even among the conscientious 10 percent, "just wanted to dominate everything."

Now 26 years old, "a penniless hippie" with no career direction and increasingly disenchanted with the revolutionary ideology he had been espousing, Chip took stock of himself. "I've just been a troublemaker," he realized, "the kind of person who knew a whole lot but never enough in any of the important areas that I was spouting off about to be so cocksure." However, "because I had opinions about everything, people thought I was smart," in addition to which "I had a magnetic enough personality" and an infectious enthusiasm, all of which meant that he had been able "to get other people excited." But now, realizing that he had "misled" them, Chip "came to deeply mistrust" himself and decided he had "to go live in the country" and "dry out"—in an intellectual rather than a physiological sense; he wanted "to be part of something simpler." Influenced by Stewart Brand, author of the *Whole Earth Catalog*—a canonical text of the back-to-the-land movement—he moved to rural West Virginia.

At this point Chip's identity as an "erotic Marxist" had changed to some extent; the noun had been largely abandoned, but the adjective was still appropriate. He met a young woman who was also "a sexual Utopian," and thought to himself, "this is the kind of person I ought to marry." They had what he called "a kind of a marriage ceremony," even though she was adamant that it wouldn't be "a real marriage" because she didn't believe in the institution. She became the mother of his two sons, but it eventually became evident to him that "sexual utopianism and family were not compatible." Ten years later, just as this "marriage" was ending, Chip met Kelley, a student in his karate class, and even though she was almost two decades younger, she already had a commitment to monogamy that, in contrast to his earlier views, he now found attractive. At the time of my visit, they had been together for 24 years and married for 20.

Chip spent his first couple of years in West Virginia working for a county welfare department, supervising juvenile probation and adoption, after which he borrowed some money, bought a backhoe and became a self-employed excavator. After several years as an "earth sculptor," Chip wound up in debt. With no money, two sons to raise, and living "in a little shack" on a piece of land that he had not yet paid off, he decided to go to graduate school. Still a voracious reader and an excellent test-taker, he was admitted to several doctoral programs in the humanities, accepting a prestigious Woodruff Fellowship at Emory University, which provided full tuition and a generous stipend for three years of graduate study. More than a decade older than most of the other graduate students, Chip described himself as a "hotshot" at Emory— "smart, full of myself, and opinionated." Kelley soon joined him at the university, and the money she earned waitressing and tending the university's botanical gardens allowed them to keep up payments on the land in West Virginia on which they would later build their house. He completed his coursework in two years and wrote his dissertation in the third, earning a doctorate in liberal arts.

Chip spent the next two years as a visiting assistant professor, first at Emory and then at the University of North Carolina–Greensboro—a period of transient employment that ended with the stability of a tenure-track position at the United States Naval Academy in Annapolis, Maryland. "What an odd story life is," he reflected; "me, who doesn't like the military—my dad had been in the military, I saw that life, I didn't like it." On the other hand, even though the appointment was in history—the academy did not have a philosophy department—it was an ideal position for someone with Chip's interests, a reason for him to be genuinely excited all over again thinking about it: "It was philosophy!" he exclaimed; "I got to teach philosophy of science, ethics, philosophy of religion and introduction to philosophy." Even better, just after Chip completed his doctorate, the mother of his children asked him to assume custody of the two boys, something he had been hoping for. "I was praying to God at that point," he recalled, "because I started praying again; I said let me raise my kids." He and Kelley bought an old farmhouse in a charming little town on the scenic Eastern Shore—a fixer-upper—and "did the whole middle-class thing for a few years."

Much to Chip's dismay, however, he found the department under the control of "some aggressive and snide liberals," enforcing dogma: "whatever the *New Republic* says you're supposed to be thinking," he elaborated, "that's basically where they all got their ideas." Still intellectually combative and older than the typical junior faculty member, he was "never a good ass kisser," or, as he more euphemistically rephrased it, "I lacked sense about when to be suitably deferential." Chip enjoyed his share of academic accomplishments. Along with co-editing a two-volume collection of essays on *The Philosophy of Discourse*,[9] he helped to submit a proposal to the National Endowment for the Humanities, which was funded for a quarter million dollars, but in practice it only turned out to exacerbate the internal controversies when he used the money to attract traditional conservatives as visiting scholars. He brought in Philip Rieff, the sociologist and public intellectual known as a supporter of traditional authority and critic of the feminist movement and gay rights. Rieff was "my guy," as Chip put it; "he was there because I got him there, and he pissed off everyone," all the more so because he "was smarter than they were, more learned, and could beat them in their own field." The controversy culminated, according to Chip, in a "Stalinist" style meeting, in which everyone in the room was expected to denounce Rieff, but when his own turn came, he announced "how ashamed I was of my colleagues." His possibility for tenure in the history department now decimated, the administration moved him into a program called "leadership, ethics, and law," where he would have another chance.

Chip found his new academic home to be yet another blatant "ideological retraining program," the goal of which, the department chairwoman told him, was "to get young men to take orders from women." "Bullshit!" was his response; "that's not what I do, I won't do it." In contrast to the reputation of a service academy as a bastion of conservatism, from Chip's perspective this was additional evidence that it was just another politically correct institution, in which there were "no unterrorized opinions." Chip's language became particularly intense as he recounted his struggles at Annapolis. Rieff, for example, "would smash" the liberals, an act that, for Chip, had the effect of "slitting my throat," but nevertheless he did not hesitate to "fight back." For him this was intellectual warfare.

Although Chip claimed that the chair of his new department offered him tenure, by this time he didn't "have the heart for it anymore," and resigned. Very unhappy, he sought comfort by returning to the church. Even during his Marxist period, he had never been an atheist, though, surrounded by people at Princeton who scorned the notion of God, he had been "ridiculed out of the affirmation" of his belief; he knew that the critics of religion were "seriously mistaken" but "didn't know how to make the case." Having been raised Episcopalian, he now joined that church in Maryland, only to find that it too was in the grip of political correctness, "ordaining women as if they were men." Hoping to encourage a change in direction, he went to a diocesan synod to raise questions about the church's political agenda but "ended up feeling that the authority structure had completely thrown in with the modernizers: they wanted to make men and women interchangeable," and he knew that "they weren't going to be happy until they started ordaining practicing homosexuals." Feeling that he had no alternative, Chip left the Episcopal Church—"another bridge burnt," he termed it.

Despite the painstaking effort they had invested in renovating the Maryland farmhouse, the family moved back to West Virginia, where Chip opened his own home construction business, its name—"Earthwind"—derived from

Jungian notions: "wind" or "airiness" as a symbol of ideas and ideals, combined with "earth" as a reminder that products of the intellect need to be "grounded." In *The Philosophy of Discourse* he had referred to the Marxist conception of the "intellectual as an alienated product of the division of labor,"[10] and the creation of Earthwind provided an example of an intellectual who didn't fit that model. Thus, along with his pastoral duties, Chip still did construction and renovation, describing how he sang and whistled joyfully while performing hard physical work; the fact that the society may not have attained the ideal that Chip once envisioned had not prevented him from turning "work into play" in his own life.

At the same time, he and Kelley began to home school his children; in Maryland they had found the public school system to be just as politically compromised as the Naval Academy and the church, forcing them to jump through numerous bureaucratic hoops to have the boys excused from what they perceived as particularly harmful parts of the curriculum. Impressed by what Chip and Kelley were doing, other parents in the area asked to have their own children taught by them, and soon they were offered use of a building, where for several years they ran a "small, neat, high-quality program" named "Lindisfarne Academy"; a mile off the coast of Northeast England and known as "Holy Island," Lindisfarne had been a base for Christian evangelizing in the middle ages and the origin of the one of the earliest Old English copies of the Gospels.

In West Virginia Chip also became aware of the "Continuing Church" movement, in which small denominations were created as splits from a parent church after some members objected to the abandonment of traditional doctrines. Finally finding a religious tendency in accord with his own belief in the "authoritative texts," he joined the local branch of the Continuing Anglican Church, which had begun in opposition to what he called the "illegal ordinations of women" and to revisions in the traditional liturgy that inserted "politically correct language." The distrust of state power fueled by his experiences in the Naval Academy and by what he saw in his children's public schools now combined with the adherence to traditional religious beliefs, creating the "Christian libertarianism" by which Chip ordered his life—a fusion of Ron Paul's emphasis on government limitation with the belief in a religiously based natural law. Indeed, he maintained that libertarianism only made sense if "undergirded" by Christianity, which, he emphasized, was what distinguished it from "libertinism"; although state coercion might not be the appropriate method for preventing people from engaging in certain behaviors, they were nevertheless proscribed by natural law, and the way to respond to them—drug use, for example—was to "train people up in self-restraint and trust them to make choices." Many critics of the society's drug policy would agree with Chip's observation that it has "engendered a permanent criminal industry," but few would share his concern that, just as harmful, "the whole thing has helped to demoralize Christian witness in the contemporary world."

At first pleased by their son's return to the church, Chip's parents soon realized that they were just as "appalled" by his traditional religious beliefs as they had once been by his radical politics. Nor was he at all sanguine to see that his parents had joined the modernizers, "embracing the ordination of women and the politically correct liturgy"; his mother—*horribile dictu*—even approved of "ordaining practicing homosexuals." Once harshly critical of his parents' conservatism, Chip was now equally as opposed to their liberal opinions.

Once ordained as an Anglican priest and embarking on a new career at an age when others were anticipating retirement, Chip felt that he had finally found his natural vocation. "All my adult life," he stated, "I've been asking God, what would you like me to do," and at a certain point the answer became clear: "I'd like you to openly and unashamedly abound my name." But he was also attracted to ordination by the opportunity it provided to engage in the sort of activity to which "Christians are called": "corporal acts of mercy," including "feeding the poor, clothing the naked, visiting the prisoners, and caring for the orphaned and the widowed." It was a struggle for him to overcome the "hardline laissez-faire view" that only the "deserving poor" merited assistance, but eventually he realized that the Christian obligation was to "take care of people even when they don't deserve it." Just as libertarianism was tenable for Chip only when qualified by the tenets of Christianity, Jefferson's inalienable rights were also inextricably linked to Chip's religious beliefs. The point of "life" was "to get to the Holy Spirit," while the "pursuit of happiness" meant that "what you own first of all is your sinful self to give to God and then to everybody else."

Chip's Christian libertarianism differed in striking ways from what is usually referred to as the "Christian Right"—the beliefs espoused by, say, Pat Robertson or James Dobson. He agreed with the conventional fundamentalists on most domestic, social issues—that abortion is murder, homosexuality is a "perversion," and Darwinism should not be presented unchallenged in school. However, he had a considerably different view of Jews, Israel, and the Middle East. As Chip perceived it, in his lifetime "Jewish Americans went from thinking of themselves as having to oppose the basic culture of the country, so that they could put themselves in a better position," to many of them believing that there was no longer reason to protest, because "we're in a great position now to let our wishes be known, to have our views prevail." People like Irving Kristol and Norman Podhoretz, major figures in the creation of the neoconservative movement, had begun as Trotskyists or socialists before winding up on the opposite side of the political spectrum, complaining that the people whose opinions they once shared were now the problem. At the same time, just as he "became interested in being a real Christian," he explained, "I noticed the hostility to Christianity"—an unavoidable conflict, he believed, given what he saw as a fundamental disagreement between Christians and Jews about Jesus: the former "believe he is the son of God," the latter that "he's a blasphemous liar." What finally caused Chip's own change of opinion was "the whole Israeli situation"—the sense that the neocons were exploiting religious belief to support their own agenda, together with the realization that the Left's solidarity with Palestinians had diminished. The result, he complained, was that "you can't do anything politically in this country unless you kiss the ass of AIPAC." This analysis was one of the factors that had attracted him to Ron Paul as "the only truly interesting person in national politics." Indeed, Chip had once admired Ronald Reagan for his rhetorical skills in making the libertarian case but became disenchanted with the Great Communicator in part because he presided over the growth of the very state bureaucracies that his rhetoric had skewered, but even more because he helped bring the neocons to power, making "both parties uncritically pro–Israel"— a "disastrous legacy haunting us to this day," in Chip's view.

Thus, despite his own religious traditionalism, Chip opposed the coalition of Christian fundamentalists and Jewish neoconservatives, and the "appalling" attempt by the former to use what he called "bizarre rapture sauce" as a rationale to "crush everybody in the Middle East that Israel doesn't like and say it's because God wants it that way." He was especially outraged at the attempt to "make us loathe the Islamofascists"—a term that "I just hate," he said angrily. Chip acknowledged that many of the Middle East countries were authoritarian and oppressive—hardly the kind of societies that a libertarian would find appealing—but "fascism," he emphasized, "is a specific way of organizing state and corporate power" that he considered in fact more characteristic of the United States than these admittedly autocratic nations. Yet the application of the fascist label, in Chip's opinion, allowed us "to paint a target on people so that we can then throw bombs at them."

Although he expressed great admiration for Jewish intellectuals like Rieff and the conservative political philosopher Paul Gottfried, unfortunately Chip seemed to have conjoined his opposition to American foreign policy in the

Middle East and to the Israeli oppression of Palestinians—both opinions shared by many individuals and groups even within the Jewish community— to the more ominous interpretation of the role played by Jews in American life offered by the evolutionary psychologist, Kevin MacDonald, the favorite academic for numerous neo–Nazi groups; though he did not mention the name in our interview, his description of the Jewish American experience was unmistakably identical to MacDonald's, and I later saw on Chip's Facebook page that MacDonald was the only person listed under the category, "People who inspire Chip." In a three-volume series of books and in scores of articles, MacDonald has argued that Judaism is essentially an evolutionary strategy characterized by a eugenic emphasis on breeding for both high intelligence and the ability to find an ecological niche within a society allowing Jews to create disruption for their own benefit—as in, for example, the civil rights movement or the New Left.[11] Quite apart from this argument's uncharitable substitution of self-interest for idealism, I found it ironic that Chip, a vehement critic of Darwin, should be "inspired" by a theorist whose work is predicated on the notion of traits putatively formed through evolutionary processes.

Chip considered his opposition to the wars in the Middle East to be informed by many of the same principles that had led him to join the antiwar movement in the 1960s. He still thought of the United States as "an imperialist country ... the big bully of the world." "I am proud," he declared, "to have opposed every war waged by the government of my country in my lifetime." He didn't like the military or the state in the Vietnam era, and if anything, his dislike has intensified since the invasion of Iraq. He found it "shameful and depressing that we are defending doctrines of preemptive war" and wondered "why we put those Germans on trial at Nuremberg." Worst of all, he felt "bitterly ashamed" to see government representatives supporting the use of torture. Not only would he still support the elimination of ROTC and think tanks like IDA from university campuses but thought that all other intrusions of the state should go with them. So yes, ROTC and IDA out, Chip agreed, but also all government funding and Pell grants as well; complete separation of school and state was the libertarian goal.

Despite his abandonment of Marxism, Chip still felt "enriched by having read Marx." Indeed, his description of the present political system sounded like it could have come directly from an SDS pamphlet on the ruling class: "a form of international imperial fascism—government by corporations in league with the actual state institutions." What had changed, of course, was that, instead of looking to a collectivist solution, Chip now believed in true, free-market capitalism, which, in his opinion, had not existed since the "debt-based money system took over about a century ago" and the Federal Reserve began to set "the 'price' of money."

While the intervening decades have not altered Chip's staunch anti-imperialism, his greatest regret has been the effect on the society of many of the social changes that he previously advocated. In thrall to "feminist notions," he once "agitated" to have women undergraduates at Princeton but now regarded it "a mistake to require all institutions to admit women." Even worse, in retrospect, was his enthusiastic support for "the cult of 'free love,'" which "ultimately did more harm than good"; the first generation of young women raised with the pill readily available "were tasked with making themselves temporarily sterile," he observed, "so that all could indulge as freely as wanted." The resulting attempt to "demystify" sex not only led "to a lot of sorrow and anger and despair and confused hopelessness," but also facilitated what Chip called "the movement to valorize homosexual relations and the contemporary obsession to make perversions respectable." In the long run it was the "erotic" part of his earlier identification that he considered more harmful than the Marxist.

5. The Poetry of Illness

Although a few other students would eventually join Progressive Labor, the first Princeton PL members were Macklin Smith, a graduate student in comparative literature, and his wife Sallie. Soft-spoken and sensitive, Macklin might have seemed an incongruous choice to be a member of a revolutionary communist party, but he was also analytical and strong-willed. Exceptionally well informed, he organized the study group of WSA members that read Marxist classics like "Value, Price and Profit" and then discussed concepts such as the theory of surplus value, which argued that all profit was derived from the value created by workers in excess of what they were paid for their labor.

The last time I had seen Macklin before interviewing him was the day he entered the army. In keeping with PL's position on the draft, Macklin had relinquished his student deferment as "a device of the ruling class to prevent workers and students from fighting the war together." Happy to oblige, the selective service board reclassified him as available for service, and he was ordered to report for induction—an irresistible opportunity for the WSA caucus to organize a demonstration. On a Monday morning in February 1969, as officially instructed, Macklin boarded a bus in Trenton, which would take him and some 40 other prospective recruits to what is now the Peter Rodino Federal Office Building in Newark, where similar busloads of young men were arriving from around the state to be examined and, if found fit, to begin serving their country in uniform. On the sensible assumption that no one would join such a group unless slated for induction, bus drivers had no list of the persons expected to show up in Trenton, which meant that no one objected when I went along for the ride.

As soon as we left Trenton, I took the rear half of the bus and Macklin the front, distributing his letter to "my fellow inductees," explaining why a married student had decided to refuse the "privilege" of a deferment and join "with other young men who have to work and can't go on to school." He was not a pacifist who opposed all wars, Macklin's letter continued, "only those waged by the bosses to keep their empire of exploitation and people's misery." But now the fight, inside as well as outside the army, was to stop workers and students from being sent to Vietnam "to make giant U.S. corporations richer" or being ordered to "shoot our Afro-American brothers when they justly rebel."[1] Although many of these soldiers-to-be disagreed with Macklin's analysis, none of them was enraged or offended, and an enthusiastic discussion took place throughout the hour-long trip to Newark.

Upon reaching the federal building, we were led into a large room on an upper floor that quickly filled with a couple of hundred young men seated in folding chairs; Macklin and I separated, so that we were sitting far from each other. When all the scheduled buses had delivered their cargo, a non-commissioned officer arose and was just beginning his mechanical spiel about the details of the examination process, when he was suddenly interrupted by a voice shouting, "Question, sergeant." "Yes, what is it?" the NCO asked Macklin. "Why should we be sent to Vietnam to fight workers and peasants on behalf of corporations?" asked Macklin, rising to his feet. "I'll explain that to you later—individually," replied the NCO, surprisingly unfazed by the exchange. "I'd like an answer too," I chimed in, jumping up, and added, "I'll bet I'm not the only one." Before the sergeant could respond to me, Macklin took out the copies of his letter that he had kept under his shirt and began distributing them to other recruits. My request was left hanging, as other NCOs, seeing what was going on, rushed to stop Macklin, which gave me the opportunity to take out my own stash of the letters and follow his example. For a few minutes there was chaos, which quickly subsided as even more uniformed reinforcements showed up to quell the commotion, and I found myself being escorted into a private room by two burly men, who looked at my draft card indicating 4-a—"completed military service"—and literally threw me into the elevator heading down to the lobby. As I landed against the elevator's inner wall, Robby, smartly dressed and looking very official with an attaché case in his hand, was getting off. He looked at me with feigned disdain and nodded sympathetically toward my two attendants, tasked, as they were, with dealing with such riff-raff. But as soon as their backs were turned, he too proceeded to hand out the anti-war literature contained in his case until also bum-rushed out of the building. Both of us wound up joining other members of WSA on a picket line outside.

Macklin's courage and commitment to principle were impressive; he could have avoided the military altogether and no one would have thought the less of him. But in addition, he had to overcome a natural tendency toward passivity. Although he was physically tough—Macklin had been captain of his high school football team—the kind of dramatically assertive behavior at the induction center was uncharacteristic of his more restrained personality, and his wife told us afterward that he had been unable to sleep the previous night, worried that he would not be able to muster the necessary boldness.

I had no further contact with Macklin until I set out to find him almost four decades later; his unusual first name made him easy to track down. Macklin was a Professor of English at the University of Michigan, where, in addition to his scholarly work in Middle English literature, he was also known as a poet and one of the most prominent birders in the country. When, in 1993, the *New York Times* reported on the sudden appearance of a particular bird in New Jersey never before seen in the United States, it turned to Macklin for expert comment, noting that the sighting had prompted him to drop everything and hop a jet east to personally view this rare occurrence. At the time he was ranked fourth by the American Birdwatching Association (ABA) among the "top spotters of North American birds," having personally seen 801 species over the previous 20 years; by 2005, with 873 species, he had risen to first in the "ABA Checklist Area," encompassing the continental United States, Alaska, and Canada.[2] While some of Macklin's poetry has stemmed from his ornithological interests, his most important work was rooted in personal adversity. After being treated for leukemia in the mid–1990s, he converted illness into inspiration, publishing *Transplant*, a collection of almost 80 poems describing his experience of the ordeal in unflinching detail but with dispassion and grim humor; a reviewer called it "masterful."[3]

I was concerned that Macklin might not feel up to being interviewed, but he assured me that he had made a full recovery. Indeed, we had to postpone my visit until he returned from his latest birding trip—to Bolivia.

Arriving in Ann Arbor in late July, I checked into a motel, and walked the mile to Macklin's house. He seemed slimmer than I recalled from decades ago, and his face appeared not so much aged as drained—both effects of his illness, I assumed. But he was still the same sensitive person. The first thing he wanted to know was whether I had other reasons for my trip aside from interviewing him. Hearing that I did not, he seemed both flattered yet uneasy that I had gone to such trouble to see him, and he immediately arranged for himself and his wife, Lynette—Macklin and Sallie having divorced years earlier—to change their own schedule in order to spend more time with me during my couple of days in Ann Arbor.

Macklin Smith spent his first five years in California before his family moved to Newburyport, Massachusetts, just north of Boston; because Macklin's father was a biologist employed by the Fish and Wildlife Service, the family moved regularly to wherever the government assigned him. After seven years in Massachusetts, his father was given the choice between moving to Maine to conduct research, which he preferred, or accepting a desk job in Washington, D.C., the location favored by Macklin's mother. "We moved to D.C.," Macklin noted dryly, where his father wrote reports on foreign fisheries, funded by the CIA. Macklin attended St. Albans, a private school for boys, where many prominent politicians sent their sons; he was two years ahead of Al Gore. Although his mother generally voted Republican, and his father Democratic, Macklin considered them uninterested in politics; neither of them displayed much emotion or voiced any strong opinion during what he characterized as an "Ozzie and Harriet kind of upbringing."

Macklin did his undergraduate work at Princeton, where he was an outstanding student, graduating summa cum laude. Attracted even as a child to "the imaginative world of books," he developed an interest in medieval literature, especially its relation to cultural and historical issues. Not wanting to be an outsider, Macklin joined one of the less selective eating clubs but soon felt awkward as a member, especially after joining SDS. Not only did his antiwar activity tend to isolate him from other club members, but he found them to be "boring people" engaged mainly in "a fair amount of lame partying and drinking."

It was Macklin's relationship with his ex-wife Sallie and her family that began his journey to a more radical politics and eventual membership in PL. In contrast to his apolitical parents, her mother and stepfather were outspoken liberals, interested in social and cultural issues, and all four children—Sallie and her three brothers—were involved in left-wing politics; for Macklin the contrast with his own family was one of her attractions. Sallie's oldest brother became the role model for his three younger siblings. In 1959 he had made an unsuccessful attempt to join Castro's rebellion and had been involved with the Student Nonviolent Coordinating Committee during its multi-racial period, before joining PL himself. Macklin's parents were quite displeased with his political activity, especially after an FBI agent came to talk to his father, who was still working on CIA sponsored projects. In contrast, Sallie's parents were proud of their children's values though concerned for their safety, especially at a time when the McCarran Internal Security Act, providing for the emergency detention of suspected subversives, had not yet been repealed. Quite affluent, her parents had even acquired a house in Switzerland, should their children's sudden departure from the country in the face of government repression seem prudent.

After Macklin graduated from Princeton, he and Sallie married, and he began graduate work at Harvard, while she commuted back and forth to Vassar during her senior year. Influenced by her brother's example, while at Harvard they too joined PL, which was particularly active in Cambridge. However, after an academically unsatisfying year in Harvard's English department, he and Sallie returned to Princeton, where Macklin began work toward his doctorate in comparative literature.

Macklin was attracted to PL partly by what he perceived as its members' greater commitment but also by the party's Marxist analysis, especially in comparison to the politics of other SDS members, who didn't seem to have any idea of class. He found the notion of a ruling class whose ideology dominated a society to make sense of both the feudal system—the context for the literature that was his scholarly focus—as well as contemporary capitalism, which he thought was "pretty awful" and the cause of "a huge amount of social injustice." The only real hope for change, he thought, was a movement led by what PL called a "vanguard" party representing the interests of the proletariat as a class; he actually believed at the time that there would be a socialist revolution. The goal of PL members within SDS was thus to win others to its analysis and recruit them into the party, a task about which Macklin was ambivalent. It seemed not only arrogant to him, suggesting, as it did, that "we know how things really work," but also manipulative—like he was "kind of using people." He also never felt comfortable distributing PL's literature, which he found too extreme, dismissing anyone, even on the Left, whose position differed from the party's as a fascist, a hack, a racist, or a sell-out. But these qualms became less significant when he considered the unappealing alternatives: "the terrorist thing or the hippie movement." It was an interesting comment on life within SDS: of the various tendencies, the self-described revolutionary communist party seemed to him to be the most sensible one.

PL's analysis of racism as a bosses' tool to divide people along ethnic lines also seemed to make sense of Macklin's personal experience in the workforce. As part of the "summer work-in"—an SDS project initiated by the WSA caucus—he took a job at a local copper mill, where molten copper was extruded into long ½-inch rods by being forced through pipes and grabbed with tongs by the "catcher." It was a physically demanding and sometimes dangerous environment, in which red-hot metal was being tossed around, burns were not uncommon, and workers had to take salt tablets to cope with the heat, which could rise to 120 degrees during the height of the summer.[4] Despite widespread dissatisfaction with working conditions, compulsory overtime, and wages—$3 an hour (almost $20 adjusted for inflation)—there was little collective action to gain improvements, largely due, in Macklin's view, to the ethnic differences among the workers: half the employees were black, most of the other half were Hungarian refugees, and the two groups hardly spoke to each other.

Only a year into his graduate studies, Macklin was drafted. Although he subjected himself to induction because it was the party's position to refuse a student deferment, he remains proud of the decision. "Here we were, sort of studying away and getting this deferment because we were reading books," he remarked, and allowing himself to be drafted just seemed "like a fair thing to do." Macklin was initially inducted into the Marines, which was randomly selecting a small number of conscripts during the Vietnam era, but his service in the corps lasted all of two hours, after which he was formally discharged and immediately re-inducted, this time into the army. However, the army didn't seem to know what to do with him. After basic training Macklin was sent to Military Police school in Fort Gordon, Georgia for an eight-week program of instruction, but after five weeks he was pulled out without explanation—perhaps the army suddenly realized that a communist revolutionary was not the best choice to be an MP—and assigned as a company clerk in Fort Knox, Kentucky.

His politics did not prevent Macklin from being highly valued by superiors for his skills as a wordsmith; one of his tasks was to compose language for awards for which the unit's non-commissioned officers were nominated. It became his private joke that what his superiors thought laudable he considered laughable: "ridiculous prose," in which every ordinary NCO was described as "the most outstanding." Yet absurd as these exercises in hyperbole seemed to him, they produced the desired result, achieving commendations for their subjects. Macklin himself was promoted—first to PFC (Private First Class) and then to "Spec 4" (Specialist 4).

In his off-duty time Macklin and Sallie set about accomplishing the task for which he had allowed himself to be drafted. They found access to a printing press off-post and began to publish an anti-war newspaper called "EM-16"—the title combining the military abbreviation for "enlisted man" with the infantryman's basic service rifle, the M-16. It was not illegal to distribute these newspapers off-post, and they handed some out in local trailer parks and other locations frequented by enlisted personnel and their families. The bulk of the papers, however, they left on soldiers' bunks and passed out in other areas on military property, which entailed serious risk—one of the other GIs who worked with them was caught distributing on-post and wound up in the stockade for a couple of months—but no one aware of Macklin's role turned him in. Indeed, the reaction to "EM-16" was largely sympathetic, as more and more enlisted men were becoming disillusioned with the war. FTA graffiti ("Fuck the Army") was common on the post, and soldiers back from Vietnam talked frankly to Macklin about fragging their officers, hiding out and smoking dope rather than engaging the enemy, or going in the opposite direction from where they were ordered. At one point Macklin himself received orders for Vietnam, but a car accident kept him in the hospital for six weeks, leading the army to keep him at Fort Knox for the remainder of his commitment.

Discharged from the army early in 1971, Macklin returned to full time political work—organizing, selling the party's literature, going to meetings and rallies—but he was beginning to harbor doubts about the value of this activity. Already uneasy, he experienced a "conversionary moment" in a discussion with PL's National Student Organizer. In a contemptuous gesture, the organizer, a graduate student in French literature at Columbia, tossed some of the classics in his field onto the floor, commenting that the books were meaningless. At that instant Macklin, who really valued literature, realized that he had "been doing this shit for a long time, it's not doing much good," and he decided to quit the party and return to school. He resumed graduate work in the fall of 1972. Although she too eventually left the party, for a time Sallie went off to meetings while Macklin tended to child-care, an arrangement that pleased him; one of the things he liked most about the movement was its emphasis on male-female equality.

After a 3½-year hiatus, Macklin re-immersed himself in his studies. His doctoral dissertation investigated the relationship between *Piers Plowman*—an allegorical narrative poem about the quest for spiritual truth, considered one of the greatest works of Middle English—and the more popular writing of the time. Remarkably, at the same time that he was writing his dissertation, Macklin also completed *Prudentius' Psychomachia: A Reexamination*, his study of the famous personification allegory by the fourth century Roman Christian poet Prudentius, describing the conflict between virtues and vices. In contrast to the view that early Christian authors were respectful of pagan literature, Macklin argued that Prudentius used Virgil's techniques to reject Virgil's doctrines.[5] With such an impressive record of accomplishment while still a graduate student, he had a number of offers for academic positions and chose the University of Michigan.

While working on his dissertation, as a means of relaxation Macklin began to take a regular walk in the wooded area adjacent to Princeton's housing for married graduate students, not realizing at first that it was a wildlife refuge attracting birders, especially during the warbler migration in the spring. Curious about the many colorful birds he saw on these walks, Macklin bought a book to help him identify the various species. However, he soon began to find the pictures of the birds he had *not* yet seen more interesting than the ones he had, and it was not long before bird watching changed from meditation to obsession, as he would drive to other places for a new sighting; eventually the trips became longer and longer, as he traveled to exotic locations like Attu Island in the Aleutians. Although Macklin attributed his interest to "a collecting impulse," he was also clearly fascinated by the migration process, describing, with a sense of amazement, how a tiny organism could begin in Nome, Alaska, fly across the arboreal forest to Nova Scotia, then non-stop over the ocean picking up the trade winds, and finally end up in Brazil, only to later reverse the sequence and wind up in the same spruce tree in Nome from which the trip had begun.

In fact, it was while on a birding excursion to Attu that Macklin first noticed symptoms of what turned out to be serious illness. It was a three-week tour, for which Macklin and Lynette—he had now remarried—served as staff, thus providing them a free ride. Because the daily activity was so strenuous—a combination of hiking and bicycling over rough terrain, covering as much as 45 miles—he was not concerned at feeling fatigued. However, when his next routine physical revealed a leukocyte count a dozen times higher than the normal range, in retrospect his exhaustion had been an ominous sign: he was suffering from chronic myelogenous leukemia. Six months later he underwent a bone marrow transplant, in which his own diseased stem cells were replaced by healthy ones from an anonymous donor. The procedure was followed by a lengthy, miserable period of what Macklin called "slow motion recovery," marked by anxiety—would the transplant be successful?—weakness, and nausea, unrelieved or perhaps caused by the panoply of drugs he was taking. Good nutrition was an essential part of regaining his health, but everything tasted like cardboard.

When his condition improved, Macklin turned to poetry as a way of re-experiencing what he had been through, but this time with the security of knowing that the outcome was favorable; it was an opportunity to recapture his fear without being fearful. After his long period of debility, writing the poems was an energizing experience; as Macklin told a reporter for the student newspaper, "It was as if a muse had taken up permanent residence in my right shoulder, making me remember everything again." The resulting volume, *Transplant*, became a narrative of Macklin's experience, beginning with the diagnosis and proceeding through the wait for a donor, his month in the hospital, the draining process of aftercare at home, and finally remission. Predominantly poetic but with some prose poems and letters—including those he wrote to the donor, who eventually divulged his identity—the collection was an emotionally powerful work, all the more so for being devoid of sentimentality and filled with matter-of-fact and sometimes humorous observations. "Walking Around with Tubes and Bottles," for example, described how hospital patients, knowing that the number of hanging bottles were an indication of medical progress, "scope out each other's IV stands" while walking around the ward, which led Macklin, at the beginning of his stay, to insist on drinking as much water as necessary in order to avoid being a "one-bottle guy." The poem concluded wryly, "But for those of us up to it, walking around with all hooks hung, / There is that shared thrill. All of us, the men / At least, have already done this, haven't we, cruising."[6] While the sequence of poems provided a narrative structure, the pieces displayed no formal coherence, varying in style and length in a conscious attempt on Macklin's part to recreate what he called "the edginess of the experience itself." In response to the work, he received a number of emails from people who found it a source of comfort in their own struggle with illness.

Actually, Macklin's first attempt at writing poetry had occurred years before his illness though, similarly, as a therapeutic opportunity for emotional expression—in this case, in the context of his divorce from Sallie. Although he had long been interested in poetry as part of his scholarship, before beginning to write poems himself, his focus had been on interpretation: what did the words mean? But in the process of writing, he became more interested in the craft of poetry, in its form, its sound and rhythm—"in how it's meaning what it's meaning."

While this Mcluhanesque emphasis on the relation of form to content exerted an influence on his own poetry—evident in the different rhythms and styles of the poems in *Transplant*—it also led to a new direction in Macklin's scholarly work. He has returned to *Piers Plowman*, the Middle English poem that had been the subject of his dissertation, but now with more interest in its poetics, analyzing how William Langland—presumed to be the poem's author—used a pattern of alliteration instead of an end rhyme to convey a sense of rhythm within a line. But in addition Macklin was interested in the continuities in rhythm between this 14th century poet and contemporary hip hop. In our two-hour interview no other topic made him as animated as his explanation of the similarities between hip hop and Langland's system of versification; the former, he pointed out, had very much the same rhythm as the latter, and it too lacked end rhyme, tying each line together through a series of alliterating words or syllables. Indeed, in his Introduction to Poetry course, Macklin began by asking students whether they had had much experience with poetry and then, in response to the inevitably negative reply, played some cuts from the Grammy award–winning group OutKast to demonstrate not only that the class was more familiar with poetry than they realized but also that what they listened to was as susceptible to literary analysis as more traditional forms.

Although Macklin was no longer politically active, his opinions were still informed by the analysis that had attracted him to PL. One of the reasons he found Langland interesting was the poet's sensitivity to class. Langland wrote at a time when English society was in the process of dramatic transformation caused by a number of factors: the threat of the plague, the transition from feudal relationships to the introduction of a money-based economy in which wages replaced a share of crops as payment, a movement of many people into cities, and pervasive corruption. According to Macklin, Langland was outraged by the society's inequities and sympathetic to the poor; his poem contained the only passage in late medieval literature of which Macklin was aware, describing "what it's really like to live in a cottage and be cold all the time, and not get enough to eat." And, cited by the leader of the peasants' revolt in 1381, the poem actually "had this role as a kind of revolutionary text."

As in his radical days, Macklin still considered capitalism a terrible system, though he was now "really skeptical that there's anything much that can be done"; his analysis of the problem has remained the same, but he no longer viewed socialist revolution as a solution and was "embarrassed" that he had once held such a belief. His disenchantment with both ends of the political spectrum was reminiscent of the old Soviet joke that capitalism is the exploitation of man by man, while communism is the exact opposite. Macklin was particularly troubled by "the U.S.'s economic bullying all over the world," which he still referred to as "imperialism," and he admired small countries, such as Vietnam and Cuba, that had fought back against the "U.S. ruling class."

Despite his dislike of capitalism, Macklin no longer believed that participation in electoral politics was futile; almost sheepishly, as if self-conscious about no longer believing that "bourgeois" elections were meaningless, he acknowledged that he is "now in the system, thinking that one party is worse than the other"—which meant that he has generally liked Democratic presidents and disliked Republican ones. One reason for this change has been Macklin's interest in birding, which has made him more sensitive to climate change, and as a result he particularly admired Al Gore for his environmental activism.

Throughout his life it has been most important to Macklin to tell the truth—"saying what's happening in so far as you can and witnessing that." This motivation has informed each of his major accomplishments—his radical political activity, his poetry, and his scholarship. *Transplant*, in particular was an attempt at describing the truth of "what it's like to be sick and going through the process," a goal all the more important to Macklin because other "cancer literature" was either sentimental or angry; no one else had described the experience "and certainly not in verse." He thought of his work on the poetics of a fourteenth century writer also as an exercise in truth telling, "even though there might be only 100 people directly interested" in the topic. But I was left with the impression that Macklin was no longer an activist in part because he had despaired of what he perceived as the truth about politics.

6. The Talent

As president of the Undergraduate Assembly during the tumultuous 1968-69 academic year, Peter Kaminsky was probably SDS's most recognizable figure to the rest of the campus. He had been elected by following the same strategy as did SDS of combining the political and the parietal: his platform had called for the administration to provide draft counseling and to allow a student "to decide when and how he will 'entertain' ... members of the opposite sex." As head of student government, whenever possible he attempted to have it support SDS's agenda. According to Peter, when Goheen was once asked to name the worst thing that had ever happened to him as Princeton's president, he gave a one word answer: "Kaminsky."

One of the most capable writers among the activists, Peter was able to make the case in much livelier prose than the wooden rhetoric that characterized much of SDS's literature. Opposing the parietal system, for example, he scored the university for a policy informed by "the mentality of the Victorian examiner of bedroom sheets." And in the statement explaining his resignation from the Kelley Committee, in contrast to the usual obligatory reference to capitalism or racism, Peter denounced their effects without using the words themselves. "As students," he wrote,

> we are here to be integrated into a Machine that brooks no questions, demands conformity, and dispenses rewards in the form of inferior goods, boring jobs, and a decaying environment. It's a Machine that would keep blacks poor but happy (or, failing that, poor but unhappy); a Machine that systematizes the lives of working people into a pattern of stultifying work, enervating leisure, and the consumption of mass-produced excrement; a Machine that asks of the bright and lucky that they hold their peace, in return for which they receive expense accounts and federal grants. It's a Machine that can afford to be benign, but once challenged, it reacts with ferocity: in Vietnam, in Chicago, in Morningside Heights, in Trenton.[1]

Smart, funny, and unhesitant to be outrageous, Peter rarely missed an opportunity to épater les bourgeois. During a reunion weekend—a major event at Princeton, in which many of the old guard troop back to the campus, donning various configurations of black and orange apparel—Peter appeared on a student panel on radicalism, intended to give these prosperous alumni a sense of what all the hullabaloo was about. After remarks from the panelists, the first question from the audience asked Peter whether he had any concern that the movement might be attracting "subversives." "You don't understand," Peter replied, with just a hint of patronizing smile signifying the questioner's naïveté; "*we're* the subversives." Undaunted, the alumnus tried again: "But aren't you afraid that you may be associating with the enemy?" "The only enemy we recognize," Peter shot back, "is the United States government."

Peter's quick wit and writing ability turned out to foreshadow his future activities, most of which have involved entertainment and journalism. A comedy writer, producer of comedies and special events, the "Underground Gourmet" for *New York Magazine* and fishing columnist for the *New York Times*, ghost writer or collaborating author of books by chefs, athletes, and politicians, as well as author of his own books on food and fishing, Peter has had more careers than Jane Fonda, but while hers have been sequential, his have been simultaneous.

In late January 2008, I drove to Peter's house in the Cobble Hill section of Brooklyn, a neighborhood designated a historic district for its charming brick and brownstone homes. Having seen photos of a somewhat heavyset author on the website promoting his latest book, I was surprised by how trim Peter looked, but he explained that he had recently shed 35 pounds—no simple task for a food writer—after being told by his physician that he was prediabetic and having the application for renewal of his life insurance rejected; the change in his diet toward healthier but no less flavorful food became the substance of *Culinary Intelligence*, his book describing how to enjoy the maximum flavor per calorie.[2]

Because Peter was scheduled for jury duty that day, we met for lunch, postponing the interview till the evening. Only weeks earlier Barack Obama's victory in the Iowa caucuses had jump-started his transition from long shot to favorite for the Democratic presidential nomination. Enthusiastic at the prospect of an Obama presidency, over Middle Eastern food Peter mused about the composition of his cabinet, predicting—correctly, if prematurely—that Obama would appoint Republican senator Chuck Hagel as secretary of defense; despite having served as his party's deputy whip, Hagel had been critical of the Bush administration's policy in Iraq, and his recently published book, written "with Peter Kaminsky," called the war "one of the greatest foreign policy fiascos in the history of our republic."[3] Before deciding to collaborate with a prominent conservative, Peter explained matter-of-factly that he had asked for advice from Tom Brokaw and Tom Daschle, both of whom encouraged him to pursue the project.

After a leisurely afternoon at the Brooklyn Museum, I returned to Peter's house, and we sat down for the interview in his bedroom that doubled as an office. Peter is a busy man. As we talked, there were brief interruptions, none of them lasting more than a minute, while he answered email and fielded phone calls. At the end of one conversation Peter told the caller that he would speak with "Stevie" about the matter—a reference, it turned out, to the person the *New York Times* calls "Mr. Wonder," that year's recipient of the Gershwin Prize for Popular Song at a White House event for which Peter was one of the producers.

After the interview, I joined Peter and his wife for dinner at a local restaurant, where I saw the food critic side of him in action. When his first choice of wine was not available, he responded with a loud expletive, turning a few heads of nearby diners. A conversation in winespeak then ensued between Peter and the sommelier, little of which I understood despite being conducted in words familiar to me in other contexts, but which resulted in the best glass of syrah I have ever tasted.

Peter Kaminsky was raised in a middle class Jewish family in a New Jersey suburb half an hour west of New York. His father, a comedy writer, had begun to write for Jackie Gleason by the time that Peter finished high school. Both his parents had liberal politics. His immigrant grandfather on his father's side had been a poet and communist, who once traveled with John Reed, translating for the journalist in meetings with Slavic speaking workers; he left Russia after Bukharin fell victim to the Stalinist purges of old Bolsheviks and then wrote for the *New Masses*, a Marxist publication that was part of the pre-war attempt to create a radical culture in the United States. Peter's mother was a nurse, and though her parents were shopkeepers, she too had leftist opinions. In the more verbally genteel 1950s, when "hell" was a considered a profanity and banned from television, the sight of Joe McCarthy on the screen caused her to exclaim "that son of a bitch."

Peter attended an excellent public high school proud of its regular share of national merit finalists and seniors accepted at Ivy League universities. His own high school experience, he characterized as "one of the most delicious passages of my life"; he thought of himself as part of "the cool guys group, a mix of dressers and dancers and brainiacs." As president of Student Council, prefiguring his similar position at Princeton, Peter engaged in his first political activity when he attempted to involve the school in support for the civil rights movement. The day after "Bloody Sunday," when marchers for voting rights in Selma were viciously beaten by state troopers, Peter persuaded student government to send its entire fund to the Southern Christian Leadership Conference, but the decision was vetoed by the administration.

Peter had not intended to apply to Princeton, but in one of those chance encounters that changes life's direction, he was sneaking a cigarette in the janitors' room when a classmate joining him in this misbehavior asked about his plans for college. Knowing that Peter was interested in political science, his fellow malefactor suggested that he consider Princeton for its Woodrow Wilson School, a center for the study of public and international affairs. "That was all I knew about Princeton," Peter said, "and I sent in my 35 bucks." Not only was he accepted, but of the scholarship offers he received, Princeton's was the most generous, paying for everything with no requirement for him to hold a campus job.

Peter became involved in student government at Princeton not for any "noble" purpose but "because a boy that age wants girls around." As chair of the coeducation committee the year before becoming president, he conducted a straw poll of the student body that demonstrated overwhelming support for the admission of women. He also organized a sleep-in—a university version of civil disobedience—in which students called the proctors to turn themselves in for having a woman in the room after hours; although the trustees had yet to make the policy official, in practice it was the end of parietals.

Peter's radicalization was initially rooted as much in 1960s youth culture—especially its music—as politics, and he soon found himself "cut off from more conventional cultural moorings." Naturally, the anti-war movement and the urban uprisings also played an important role, and he remembered thinking after the 1967 riots that "there were more federal troops deployed on U.S. territory than at any time since the Civil War." Then one day, as Peter was walking through the campus, he passed an SDS sit-in at IDA, and the demonstrators, suspecting that he was "a ripe prospect," invited him to join. He did so and was arrested. "After that," he said, "I threw in my lot with SDS."

Once he "stepped into it," as Peter put it, "it was a really quick acceleration," especially after PL became "the engine that pulled SDS leftward," producing, in his opinion, a doctrinaire old-left ideology that no one wished to challenge for fear of appearing "revanchist." Soon he considered himself a revolutionary. "I bought the whole Leninist and Mao line, lock stock and barrel," Peter recalled, together with all the associated jargon—"revolutionary vanguard, petty bourgeois intellectuals," and so on. Because he thought that

Stanley Kelley was such a "great guy," he felt bad about resigning from the Kelley Committee, but "by that time," he concluded, "we were insane." As one of the most visible radicals at a prestigious university, Peter made a number of public appearances in which the audience probably agreed with his assessment. On the Barry Farber radio show, a program hosted by a well-known conservative, Peter declared that he was a "Maoist." And on Voice of America, the government's official international broadcast platform, he was even more outrageous. According to Peter, "VOA thought they were getting Princeton Charlie"—the stereotype of the traditional student from a country club background—only to find someone who sounded as if he were fresh from a stint at the Comintern, urging "our soldiers and peasants to rise up" in revolt.

In retrospect, Peter viewed his "Maoist" period as "misguided." Though still proud of his opposition to the Vietnam War, he felt that the radical movement lost "touch with Americans and their values." Along with so many other activists, however, at the time he found "something very seductive and attractive and intellectually whole" about the ideology. But with the advantage of distance it became more like one thinks of a long past, failed relationship: what did he ever see in it?

A history major, Peter too was influenced by Arno Mayer, who facilitated his acceptance at Birkbeck College at the University of London to study with Eric Hobsbawm, the brilliant British historian and unapologetic communist, famous for his four volumes spanning the history of Europe from the French Revolution through the rise of industrial capitalism to the fall of the Soviet Union. As Peter related to a recent Princeton alumni audience composed largely of former activists, after a few months Hobsbawm told him, "you can stay here and find some very interesting things to do, or you can fart around and smoke a lot of pot." With perfect comic timing, Peter paused and then added, "I chose B."

Returning to the United States, Peter married his girlfriend and spent the next year feeling "kind of lost"—drifting from Princeton to Berkeley to Mexico and back to Princeton. He became interested in "back to the landy stuff," and wound up on a farm, where he "wanted to do something with my hands," and found a job working for a pipe organ builder. After half a year he tired of both pipe building and marriage. For the previous few years he had been what he called a "psychedelic Maoist," having combined revolutionary ideology with acid trips, but "once we stopped taking LSD," Peter realized that he and his wife "had nothing in common." Moving to New York, he drove a cab for a year, smoked more pot, and began graduate study in anthropology at NYU, still thinking of a career as an academic; he thought cultural anthropologists were doing more interesting work in history than historians. Though the top student in his class, Peter was running out of money, and prospects in the field were not encouraging; he didn't want to spend another three years on a doctorate only to find that there were no jobs.

To make money Peter found a job with *Rolling Stone*, where he worked in marketing, writing ads. A book of sample ads that he had composed crossed the desk of the publisher of *National Lampoon*, the edgy magazine specializing in surrealist humor and parody, the more outrageous the better. Impressed by Peter's work, the publisher hired him to be his "flack writer"—to edit and publish his newsletter and other marketing materials. After a few months, Peter became one of the editors—the group that wrote the magazine.

Peter spent close to four years at *Lampoon*; it was the beginning of one of his many careers—in this case, in comedy. His description of the work sounded like a dormitory party: "We sat around," he reminisced, "smoked pot, drank a lot, made each other laugh, and cut each other to shreds." A number of the people in this group went on to become cast members on *Saturday Night Live*, including John Belushi and Bill Murray. Peter became managing editor at the magazine but then was "excused" from his position when an issue appeared three weeks late, costing the publisher a substantial amount of money. In part, the delay was due to the rowdy atmosphere dominating the editorial group, in which people would show up at noon and go drinking at three. But another important factor was his discovery of fishing while on winter vacation in the Florida Keys. With nothing to do and the weather too cold to lie on the beach, Peter saw a roadside sign for people to spend the day on a fishing boat. "It was not a sign from the heavens," he later wrote, "although it might just as well have been."[4] "I fell in love with it," he said, "and it absolutely changed my life."

To convert this new infatuation into a paid endeavor, Peter decided to write about fishing, sensing a journalistic void that he was uniquely qualified to fill. "There was nobody like me," he reasoned, "no New York commie Jew writing for *Field & Stream* or *Sports & Field*," magazines where he was soon appointed an editor. Now headed in a new career direction, Peter became a freelance writer, at first concentrating on fishing but soon branching out to do more diverse "journalism stuff." For magazines he contributed articles on topics such as baseball and Martin guitars, and for television he wrote the series *GI Diary*, in which Lloyd Bridges narrated first-hand accounts of the combat experiences of military servicemen in World War II. Eventually, Peter's various backgrounds in comedy and journalism blossomed into two broad and occasionally overlapping careers: one as a producer and writer for television shows and special events, the other as a gastro-environmentalist and outdoorsman.

The journalist Nicholas Lemann once outlined three different versions of success in the United States—not different definitions of the term but distinct paths to attaining it. The Lifer joined an organization at the beginning of his or her career and then rose through the ranks over time; civil service, the military, and many corporations are typical Lifer careers. The Mandarin, newest of the three paths and particularly characteristic of a meritocratic society, performed well in school and then used these credentials—the more elite the educational institution, the better—to enter professions such as academia, law, and medicine. Finally, the Talent engaged in what Lemann termed "self-initiated activity"—unstructured and requiring neither formal credential nor "passing through a rigidly defined series of stations of the cross"; Talents, he observed, included "most of the celebrated examples of success in America."[5] Unsurprisingly given their Ivy League background, most of my interviewees were Mandarins; Peter was the only Talent. He didn't have a salaried position and relied for income on a succession of journalistic or entertainment projects.

Becoming a producer was the natural segue from Peter's experience at *National Lampoon*. By his own judgment he was "an okay comedy writer," who had written for many well known comics and had a knack for "zoning in on another person's sense of humor," but, he acknowledged, "I wouldn't hire me first if I needed to do a monologue for the Oscars." Rather, producing was what Peter really liked to do. The media equivalent of a general contractor in the construction of a building, a show's producer was responsible for hiring and paying everyone involved—the acts, the band, the set designer—as well as editing the acts and, in the case of a television program, dealing with the network.

Along with numerous television shows—from David Mamet plays to *Spy Magazine*'s *How to Be Famous*, hosted by Jerry Seinfeld shortly before the beginning of his eponymous program—Peter has also written and produced a long list of major public events, such as the winter Olympics and the MTV Video Music Awards. However, a handful have had particular cultural or civic importance. Together with his brother and two other persons, Peter created and produced the Mark Twain Prize for American humor, awarded for each of the past 15 years at a Kennedy Center event. The recipients have included Richard Pryor, Steve Martin, Billy Crystal, and George Carlin. Similarly, in 2007 the same group of producers created the Library of Congress

Gershwin Prize for Popular Song, awarded annually in a ceremony at the White House. Paul Simon was the first year's recipient, and at the time of my visit Stevie Wonder was about to be named the second.

In addition to these award shows, Peter has also produced two special events of national significance. Near the end of the Clinton administration, the President's Summit for America's Future, intended to encourage volunteerism and community service, was scheduled to take place in Philadelphia, chaired by Colin Powell and attended by all the living presidents except an ailing Ronald Reagan, who was represented by his wife Nancy, as well as 30 governors, more than 100 mayors, and numerous celebrities. As Peter told it, Michael Deaver, who had been deputy chief of staff in the Reagan White House, was in charge of the event and had hired someone to write and produce it, but, when "nothing was happening" with only five weeks to go, Deaver called Peter and his brother to take over. "It was insane," Peter recalled, but he also found it very satisfying because "nobody had time to say no, and I really got to pick whatever I wanted to do," including writing speeches for many of the participants.

Of greater emotional magnitude, he was asked to write the two-hour NBC show commemorating the first anniversary of 9/11 and hosted by his friend Tom Brokaw. It was scheduled for 9 p.m. after a day in which viewers had been exposed to death and destruction and funerals since early that morning. Peter decided to "change the mood" with a "cold opening: big American flag in the background on stage and Reba McIntyre singing Woody Guthrie's 'This Land Is Your Land.'" "We killed them," he exulted; "it was great."

Peter's other career—in journalism—has focused mainly on the related topics of fishing and food. Indeed, a number of chapters in his book *American Waters*—a "highlight reel" of his journeys to the best fly-fishing locations in the country—ended with recipes from "some of the greatest chefs in the world." Fishing—especially fly-fishing, in which the angler casts a lure or "fly" using a technique demanding skill and physical coordination—has played a kind of mystical role in Peter's life, both embodying his connection to the natural world while simultaneously transcending it. "When I have a fly rod in my hand and water all around me," he wrote, in the aptly named *Fly Fisherman's Guide to the Meaning of Life*, "time stops. Let me try that again. Time doesn't so much stop as it passes in a different way. I enter a different reality, one in which I am fully alive, fully focused, where each second is a ripe fruit bursting with juice." In part, this reaction seemed to stem from his appreciation of the artistry inherent in the act of casting: "When you execute it properly, it is as if your arms and fingers reach out a hundred feet with the grace of a ballerina gesturing with her arms." But a part of it was also rooted in Peter's Jungian sense of fly-fishing as a contemporary re-creation of "a drama that has been playing out for hundreds of thousands of years"—a direct link "back and back ... to all of the creatures on our family tree until we reach that dusty gorge in Kenya where a little woman that archeologists named Lucy first stood on her hind legs." "I think about fishing," he concluded, riffing on Descartes, "therefore I am human."[6]

Peter's books and magazine articles as well as approximately a hundred "Outdoors" columns for the *New York Times* describe his trips to places that constitute the equivalent of Valhalla for serious anglers: for albacore in the Outer Banks, bonefish in Biscayne Bay, bass in the Everglades, trout in Yellowstone and in Tierra del Fuego, salmon in Alaska's Katmai Wilderness Park and on Russia's Kola peninsula, reached by a two-hour helicopter ride. Unlike most fishing writers, who turned to the pen—or later the word processor—in order to chronicle their experiences with the rod, Peter enjoyed the advantage of being a writer first who then learned to love fishing. Thus he brought to the task a writer's eye for detail together with the cultural literacy that produced allusions not typically found in an account of a fishing trip. Looking for striped bass off Montauk Point at the East end of Long Island, for example, Peter saw "there, on the beach at Turtle Cove, where one year ago the bass beat the water to a froth, three women in long black chadors, their faces covered by veils, ... their robes blowing in the wind. In the background, the lighthouse stood against the sky like a minaret. A scene from a Bergman movie? A Middle Eastern production of 'Macbeth'?" And he had a writer's knack for the inventive phrase. Describing that narrow arc of land curving from Florida's southern coast toward the Gulf of Mexico, he referred to "the indeterminate edge of the Keys where the land doesn't so much end as it stops trying and becomes ocean."[7]

Although he was neither preachy nor strident about it, Peter's fishing columns contained glimpses of his environmentalist sympathies. He has championed the practice of "catch and release," in which reeling in even a prize specimen is followed by its revival and replacement back in the water—an act sometimes recounted lovingly. "I cradled the fish in my arms," Peter wrote about a 25-pound striper he caught off the coast of East Hampton, Long Island, "just the way I carry my new daughter, Lily," before wading into the sea foam to revive the fish and let it swim away. While he has noted that this decision "not to take a life when there is no reason to kill is moral and right," the primary justification for the policy was practical rather than moral, especially in rivers and streams, where trout were the top predator; almost nothing in a stream feeds on a trout. Top predators in any eco-system, whether lions in the savanna or wolves in the forest, are relatively infrequent in comparison to their prey. Thus, Peter explained, "it takes very little pressure to hunt down the lions and very little pressure to degrade a trout stream." The conclusion was unavoidable: "if you want to have good trout fishing, you cannot have your trout and eat him too." But Peter was no fanatic. "I release 99 percent of the fish I catch," he wrote in one *New York Times* column, but "every now and then I get a great kick out of marching down to the harbor ... and catching my dinner, the way the Indians did." Then, too, he appreciated artistry in the kitchen as much as in the stream. "As long as someone is not a "profligate trout murderer," he did not favor sending the person "to trout jail" for a "[once] yearly plate of pan-fried fish, dredged in cornmeal and salt and crisped in bubbling brown butter in a black iron pan."[8]

Peter's first experience as a food writer occurred after he had already become an established television producer and fishing journalist. He had been working with the writer Kurt Andersen on a short lived television program offering a comedic look at current events intended for smart, hip people— the forerunner of shows like Jon Stewart's *Daily Show* or Bill Maher's *Real Time*. Located in offices upstairs from Union Square Café—owned by Danny Meyer, the most successful restaurateur in New York—they would eat at the Café three times a week. When Peter learned that Meyer was planning to open Gramercy Tavern—which quickly replaced the Café as Zagat's No. 1 rated restaurant in New York—he went to Tina Brown, then editor of the *New Yorker*, and pitched the idea of a feature story on the opening of a major restaurant; getting the green light, he followed Meyer around for a year and a half through planning meetings, weekly tastings, various negotiations, and even a trip with Meyer and the architect to Italy. Peter put his "heart and soul" into the resulting article, only to find that, in Brown's opinion, "it just didn't sing"; though handsomely paid for his time, he felt "devastated." But remembering that his friend Kurt, who by that time was the editor of *New York Magazine*, had once said he would "kill for that story," Peter called him to say that killing was not necessary; all he had to do was buy it.

"Why Ask for the Moon When He Already Has Three Stars" was published as *New York Magazine*'s cover story, tracing the complex series of steps necessary to start a top notch restaurant—everything from finding the right piece of real estate to designing the interior, selecting the plates, hiring the staff, and even deciding what artwork should go on the walls. According to Peter, "there had never been a piece like that in the restaurant business," and "it made a lot of noise." It also marked the beginning of a whole new set of journalistic projects. Any time some god of the kitchen opened a restaurant in New York—Sirio Maccioni's le Cirque, Daniel Boulud's Daniel, or Gray Kunz's Café Gray—Peter wrote a cover story for *New York*. He also became the magazine's "Underground Gourmet," writing a column on ethnic food in New York City, and a contributor to *Food & Wine*, which led to the books by some of the foremost chefs, written with Peter as their collaborator. He was ideally suited for these projects. Among his SDS comrades Peter had always been the cook, and even during his time as a cabbie he was "into drive-by dining—if something looked right I would try it." "I love to eat," he enthused, "I love to cook, I really understand food, and I enjoy people who create it." Just as he did with fishing, Peter was able to write about food "as a passionate amateur."

When Peter decided to co-author a book with a well-known chef or other public figure, his goal was to become their voice, not merely to convert their ideas into words but "to come off the page in the reader's mind as if that person was speaking." To achieve this result he needed to see, literally, "where people come from." Thus, in preparation for writing both about and with Daniel Boulud, Peter insisted on accompanying the French chef and restaurateur on a visit to his parents' home in Lyon, France, knowing that his approach to food was heavily influenced by the farm atmosphere in which he had been raised. Peter joined Boulud and his sommelier on a drive from Paris through the Burgundy wine country on what he called "the hundred thousand calorie tour," eating at Michelin three-star restaurants and taste-testing hundreds of burgundies at "the greatest wineries on earth" before arriving at the parental farm, where he could experience the Boulud extended family traditions first-hand: the food made from their own produce and livestock according to generations-old recipes, the "homemade booze," even the games of petanque, a local pastime similar to bocce.[9]

Nor was such ambitious research confined only to practitioners of haute cuisine. Before co-authoring *John Madden's Ultimate Tailgating*—a book about the National Football League subculture in which hundreds of thousands of fans gather from hours to days before a game for the "greatest mass dining event in America," firing up portable grills on the backs of their vehicles for serious barbecuing—Peter spent 44 hours driving cross country on the "Madden Cruiser" with the former coach and NFL broadcaster, who was fearful of planes and traveled in his own customized bus. And for his book with the celebrity Argentine chef, Francis Mallman, Peter traveled to Mallman's home in the Uruguayan countryside to observe the traditional methods for grilling food. Indeed, I later learned that the backyard of Peter's Cobble Hill brownstone contained an Argentine infiernillo—a three-tiered outdoor oven of Incan origin, allowing wood fires, built on both the top and bottom, to cook the food in the middle level—which he had specially fabricated by a local wrought iron shop.[10]

In one instance of Peter's collaboration on a book with a prominent chef, he played a much larger role than usual, developing the theory at the heart of the book as well as acting as the wordsmith who made the culinary expert's ideas accessible to the reader. *The Elements of Taste*, which Peter co-authored with Gray Kunz, proposed a vocabulary for flavor similar to the one used by oenophiles in discussing wine.[11] As Peter explained, it was an attempt to describe "what happens in your mouth" during eating by deconstructing the sensation of flavor into 14 categories, each of which exerted one of four possible effects. This theory then led to an understanding of how different ingredients combined to create a particular taste, thus making it possible to identify both what was missing from a dish, as well as a sense of how a particular sequence of dishes created a natural progression of flavors. It was difficult to imagine a more sophisticated approach to food.

Peter's close connections to so many New York chefs was also instrumental in helping to organize food for the emergency responders in the aftermath of 9/11. Two days after the twin towers fell, Gray Kunz invited him to a meeting, where he was flattered to find himself the only person in the room not a chef; as Peter put it, he got "a journalist's pass." Having difficulty with the logistics of the effort, they thought that Peter might be helpful in putting together a system. Because no one was permitted to drive south of 23rd Street at the time, they arranged for a tour boat to take food, volunteers, and the chefs down to the World Financial Center in lower Manhattan, where a cruise ship with a kitchen was docked at a yacht basin nearby. "I don't want to aggrandize my role," Peter said, "but I was there to set it up," organizing volunteers into shifts of between 80 and 120 at a time. "We thought we were going to feed 1,200 or 1,500 people, and we ended up doing 5,000, then 10,000, then 15,000 a day. And it was great," he recalled; "they'd make mac and cheese but with foie gras and stuff. It was cafeteria food with the greatest chefs in America making it." Along with the chefs, Peter put in 10–12-hour shifts for days, doing whatever was necessary—serving, busing, sweeping the floor.

To Peter, being a food writer and an environmentalist were inseparable roles, two facets of the same gem. Although as a fishaholic he wrote eloquently about how the sport connected him to "the energy, beauty, drama, and peace of Nature," it was the transformation of farming from family business to industrial operation that confirmed for him not just the environment's esthetic and spiritual appeal but its importance to the society's health, its welfare, and even its taste buds. *Pig Perfect*, the story of his odyssey in search of "heavenly ham," offered a persuasive argument for this conclusion. Peter's most impressive literary accomplishment, the book combined his identities as food writer, outdoorsman, and the social scientist he had once planned to become. Describing his pork pilgrimage to Spain, where he experienced the "supernal" Jamón Ibérico—derived from the legendary black pigs raised on acorns and bursting with flavor as well as high in healthy omega-3 fatty acids—Peter felt "kind of like Tony when he first sees Maria in the dance scene in *West Side Story*." He also traveled through the Barbecue Belt in the South, marveling at the ability of local pit masters to begin with a "nearly tasteless" product and create "a culinary silk purse from a factory-farmed sow's ear." But in addition he tracked down academic experts on three continents—specialists in genetics, archeology, biology, physiology, and animal science—to provide an account of the biological evolution of pigs, their domestication by humans, the ecological history of the Iberian hogs' habitat in the fields of the "dehesa," the physiological reasons for their superior taste and nutritional value, and even an explanation for the origin of the taboo against pork in certain cultures. Peter also discovered that descendants of the Iberian hogs existed on Ossabaw Island off the coast of Georgia—their ancestors brought there by Spaniards in the 16th century—and helped to transport 23 of them from a National Institute of Health facility in Missouri, where they were being used in biomedical research, to family farms in North and South Carolina.[12]

Near the end of this tour de force, Peter turned from his quest for the quintessential to focus on the root of the problem—the reason that so much pork in the United States is "dry-as-dust meat whose only flavor attribute is no taste at all." Suddenly the charming narrative of the "hamthropologist's" travels gave way to an impassioned denunciation of the culprit: CAFO—Concentrated Animal Feeding Operation—the industry's acronym for factory farming, a system of mass production in which thousands of hogs were crammed together so tightly that "they cannot even turn around" and wound up "developing open sores from rubbing against the metal of their pens." This was not the kind of farm to which kindergarten students would ever make a class trip, Peter wrote, lest they "hear the ceaseless screams of pain and fear," experience the overwhelming stench, and see the "brutality, misery, and filth of these places where the fact that pigs are living creatures is seen as an inconvenience to be borne in the pursuit of lean, insipid meat and the profits it brings." But more serious than the animals' suffering, as disturbing as it might be, was CAFO's threat to the environment, and ultimately to public health.

In North Carolina nutrient pollution caused by factory farming—of poultry as well as hogs—was producing a tiny one-celled organism that caused bleeding sores in the local river's fish, killing over a billion in a six-week period. Moreover, to prevent the transmission of disease among animals in such cramped conditions, they were administered antibiotics, consuming 80 percent of all such medications annually in the United States and risking the development of disease-resistant bacteria. With the number of hogs in North Carolina alone generating more fecal matter than one third of the United States population, Peter warned of the potential for this "poisonous broth" to provide the "conditions for incubating new and devastating plagues." Yet because such operations were legally classified as farms rather than factories, he noted, they were not subject to the same environmental laws requiring cities to construct sewage processing plants for human waste, and the most influential politicians in the state, all of whom profited from industrial pork, were not about to burden business with what they called "overregulation."[13] It was probably the most overtly political passage in Peter's substantial corpus of published work.

Although Peter valued the environment, he was not a "tree hugger"; just as his support for catch and release was more concerned with consequences than morality, there were practical reasons for his concern about the environment. "Often, environmentalists ... appeal to our sense of guilt and shame," Peter observed in *Pig Perfect*, "but the world will not change because of a guilt trip. The real heart of the matter is our survival. Destroy nature and you destroy our home, and so far there are no other planets to provide us with a new one."[14]

Although Peter's politics were still left of center, his attraction to Marxism ended after a trip to Cuba with Jack and Margaux Hemingway to do a film on their famous father. As a student activist, Peter had contemplated joining one of the Venceremos Brigades. But instead of encountering "socialist brothers," for the first time Peter found himself "in a place where there were no *things*; you could get the Collected Works of Lenin, but on a tropical island you could not get a mango." In addition, the Cuban version of the KGB followed the film crew, except for early in the morning; in a communist country, he discovered, "nobody really worked when they didn't have to." By the time he left the island, Peter was "cured."

Peter characterized his politics now as being "a classic Isaiah Berlinist liberal," after the philosopher and political theorist known for emphasizing the importance of value-pluralism—the conception, in Berlin's words, "that there are many different ends that men may seek and still be fully rational."[15]

Or as Peter succinctly put it, "I have a great belief in live and let live." As a practical matter, he thought that "what's important in the world is having enough food and an economy that works" and has concluded that "capitalism is more resilient and productive than I gave it credit for; it seems to do a lot well." However, he added, "it may also be its own undoing."

One attraction from the 1960s has endured, leading to Peter's work on popular music with the Library of Congress, institutional sponsor of the Gershwin Prize. "For a guy who's loved rock 'n' roll his whole life," he said, "I think pop culture is so important." Decades ago what was considered the music of the "counterculture" had played a significant role in Peter's radicalization, and now he was helping to enshrine it as part of the national cultural heritage.

7. Studying the Divide

In early March 1969 a statement in the *Daily Princetonian* announced formation of the Third World Liberation Front (TWLF), the counterpart of an organization at San Francisco State and Berkeley. Noting "America's exploitation and oppression of non-white peoples," the statement invited all Third World people—Asians, Africans, Latin Americans and American non-whites—to join the "militant coalition of non-whites" in the belief that "the recognition of unity is foremost in the understanding of the common enemy before us: namely the racism and imperialism perpetrated by the American (i.e., 'free') system throughout the world." Interviewed by the newspaper, Gordon Chang, a TWLF leader and the statement's primary author, explained that racism in the university could "not be defeated until racism in society is eliminated by the abolition of the capitalist system"; the group was anti-capitalist, he emphasized, not anti-white.[1]

"The first official TWLF act," the announcement of its formation declared, was "to give complete support" to the demand for divestment from companies doing business in South Africa. Indeed, when the Association of Black Collegians occupied the New South Building five days later, the *Princetonian*'s front page article on the takeover featured a photograph of two supporters demonstrating outside the entrance: Doug Seaton, a patch over one eye, and, holding the microphone, Gordon, looking almost cloak and daggerish—the lapels of his overcoat turned up against the March wind, his moustache curling slightly down the sides of his upper lip, and his long dark hair in bangs covering the tops of his wire-rimmed glasses.[2] Gordon himself referred to the picture as "barbarians at the gates"; "I was pretty scary looking," he commented.

Gordon H. Chang—not to be confused with Gordon G. Chang, a conservative pundit specializing in commentary on China and North Korea—is now a member of the History Department and the Olive H. Palmer Professor of Humanities at Stanford, as well as a founding member of the university's

Asian American Studies Program and editor of the Stanford University Press series on Asian America. I arranged to interview Gordon in March 2008, just as the nation was being exposed to the footage of fiery sermons once delivered by a certain Chicago pastor and spiritual advisor to Barack Obama. Arriving in Palo Alto in the middle of the night, I checked into a small hotel in one of the city's two separate downtown areas a mile and a half apart—a consequence of the fact that what had once been the township of Mayfield was annexed decades ago by its newer but faster growing neighbor to the North.

Gordon had offered to pick me up late the next morning, leaving me time to confirm Palo Alto's reputation as a bastion of liberalism, its mixture of personal liberation and anti-war sentiment a contemporary version of the sometimes vexed alliance between hippies and radicals decades earlier. Posters on a bulletin board in the middle of the commercial area announced such events as an "Impeach the Terrorists Peace Concert and Rally" to mark the anniversary of the Iraq "war that never should have happened," a free workshop in "spiritual experience" promising to provide attendees "new and advanced ways for exploring your inner worlds," and a series of lectures on "The Ethics of Food," the latest of which was titled "What to Eat: Personal Responsibility vs. Social Responsibility."

The SUV that slowed down in front of my hotel at the specified time indicated Gordon's arrival, though otherwise I never would have recognized him, now smooth shaven and short-haired with tinges of professorial gray. We drove to his townhouse in a complex for Stanford faculty, removing our shoes before entering, and sat down at the dining room table; the stunning art work on the walls, I learned, had been painted by his father.

Gordon Chang was raised in Piedmont, California, an almost entirely white middle and upper middle class community surrounded by Oakland. His father, Chang Shu-chi, an artist who died when Gordon was nine years old, had been sent to the United States by the Chinese Nationalist government shortly before World War II as an "ambassador of art," after being commissioned by Chiang Kai-shek to create a large painting in honor of Roosevelt's election to a third term. However, after Pearl Harbor prevented his return, he remained for the next five years, becoming, according to a volume on Asian American art edited by Gordon, the most widely known Chinese artist in America, his paintings exhibited in shows at the most prominent museums, his solo demonstrations drawing thousands of spectators, and his work "the subject of films, a radio broadcast narrated by Pearl Buck, and a feature in *Life* magazine." Although he spent a couple of years in his native land at the end of the war, the country's civil conflict led to his return to the United States, this time permanently. Though also of Chinese background and multilingual, Gordon's mother was a third generation Californian who had earned a bachelor's degree at Berkeley; having met her husband during his first period in the United States, she accompanied him during his brief postwar stay in China, and Gordon was actually born in Hong Kong. An astute woman and an amateur painter herself, upon her husband's death she took over the family business—the Chang Art Studio, which reproduced his paintings on greeting cards and stationery.[3]

While Gordon's mother was a Stevensonian liberal, his father's politics were more complicated. As Gordon learned from biographical research long after his father's death, the senior Chang had close friends and relatives on both sides of the struggle between the Nationalists and the Communists. Not only had he been given such an important mission by Chiang Kai-shek, but he was one of the painting teachers for the generalissimo's wife, who gave Gordon's parents a large landscape of her own on the occasion of their wedding; indeed, Gordon still owned artwork done by the two of them in collaboration and signed by both his father and Madame Chiang. And because intellectuals and political figures in China had always been close, his father "knew all the Nationalist Party bigwigs." Yet at the same time his father also had ties to the Communists. In the 1930s he had used his political connections to help secure the release of a relative, a prominent member of the Chinese Communist Party arrested by the government—a favor that was not forgotten. In addition, during the short-lived period of coalition government, he had given a painting to the Communist Party headquarters that Zhou Enlai had reportedly liked. From entries in his father's diary, Gordon thought that he was actually more inclined toward the Communists, having mentioned his desire to return to the mainland someday.

Despite growing up in one of the only nonwhite families in Piedmont, Gordon experienced what he considered a typical middle class childhood with lots of friends, though his mother later told him that some of the other residents were wary about their presence; after putting up Christmas lights the year they moved into the community, she was asked by a neighbor half seriously whether she was sending signals to the Chinese Communists. As he aged, however, the development of high school cliques and social divisions left him feeling unwelcome; at Piedmont High School he was never asked to join one of the fraternities, and he saw little of the friends he had enjoyed when younger. Nevertheless, throughout his school years Gordon was an outstanding student, interested in politics at an early age. As a primary school student barely 10 years old, he participated in a model United Nations program, assigned by his teacher to argue against the admission of the People's Republic of China, which was a major controversy at the time. Chagrined because he favored "Red China's" admission, Gordon later concluded that, knowing his sympathies, the "smart teacher" had required him to argue the opposite position as an "intellectual challenge."[4]

President of his high school class each of the last three years, as a senior Gordon became the student body president as well as valedictorian, giving formal speeches in both roles. In the former capacity he addressed a conference of student leaders from other suburban towns, pointing out that there was less than one percent racial minority enrollment in their schools and that the affluence of their communities insulated them from the problems of the "economically underprivileged" quarter of the nation. "To break away from middle-class provincialism," he called on them to organize student exchanges and assembly programs with the neighboring Oakland schools, attended largely by minorities. Following his own advice, Gordon developed a "Program of Awareness," allowing for exchange days between the Piedmont and Oakland high schools, but this innocuous idea produced a storm of protest and, he "was called a Commie." Then as the commencement speaker—in June 1966, amid rising unrest in the inner city and increasing protest against American involvement in Vietnam—Gordon warned the audience composed largely of parents that, if they didn't take these problems seriously, the "searching generation" of youth could become "the cursing and kicking generation." Gordon's own activities would soon become evidence for the accuracy of his prediction.

Gordon was encouraged to apply to Princeton by his high school biology teacher, Leonard Waxdeck, famous for his annual appearances on Johnny Carson's *Tonight Show*, where his students would demonstrate their contest-winning bird calls. Already interested in international relations or diplomacy and inspired by John F. Kennedy's call for public service, Gordon's career goal was "to do something connected to my father's legacy: U.S.–China relations." Arriving at the university in the fall of 1996, he found himself one of only six students of Asian background in a class of 800.[5]

At Princeton Gordon majored in history, focusing on East Asian studies and, for his senior thesis, produced a biography of the founding chairman of the Chinese Communist Party. Although in high school Gordon had thought of history as "the boring memorization" of names and dates, his opinion soon changed, influenced in particular by Arno Mayer, the professor named as an influence on their thinking by more than half the undergraduate interviewees, but none with more enthusiasm than Gordon. "Arno was a wonderful intellectual presence," he reminisced, "a man who opened my eyes about what history and human life could be. All of a sudden I realized that history was interconnected, complicated, that people made history, that there was causality in history."

Although before entering Princeton he already had "this liberal position" on the war—trying to balance American commitments against the lack of rationale for a presence in Vietnam—during his freshman year Gordon became steadily more horrified at the carnage. But what really spurred his radicalization was his experience in the October 1967 march on the Pentagon during the fall of his sophomore year, when he and some other Princeton students "almost got the shit beat out of us." Despite facing U.S. marshals and national guardsmen with bayonets, the demonstrators were not concerned for their safety as long as television cameras were there to record the events, but around 9 p.m. the crews started to pack up, ignoring pleas for them to stay. As soon as the electronic media departed, the soldiers and marshals waded into the crowd, swinging their truncheons indiscriminately. "I remember the sound," Gordon recalled, "these long things hitting people on the knees and shoulders, and the sound was really unsettling—crack, crack, crack." When he got up to run, a heart defect that had first been diagnosed in high school caused rapid beating, and he and his friends had to wait until an ambulance arrived to transport him to a clinic in Maryland, while during the trip the driver and the attendants cursed at them.

Around the time of the march, Gordon joined SDS. Convinced that racism and exploitation could only be eliminated by abolition of the capitalist system, he considered himself a revolutionary, though one motivated by the desire for "a more humane world"; "the butchering that was going on in Vietnam," in particular, "was so horrendous," he said, "that I just rebelled against the status quo," which seemed so "corrupt and evil and racist." The fact that the war was "identified with the best and the brightest"—the very people with whom Gordon thought he would associate as a member of the Princeton community—suggested to him that they were "not the solution but the problem."

Gordon traced his adherence to humanistic values to the influence of his mother, who had always emphasized the importance of "decency and respect." When some of his relatives made racist remarks, she always reminded him that such statements were wrong. Nevertheless she was upset by his political activity, both because she was worried about his safety and because, despite familial roots in California that dated back to the mid–19th century, she still felt insecure about the place of Asian Americans in the United States. "Well, you know, this is really not our country," Gordon remembered her saying; "this is their country," and radical political involvement might harm him "in the sense of racially." There was a sense on her part that "we are marginal, and we are seen as marginal, and people don't care"—comments foreshadowing Gordon's later scholarly work on Asian American identity and the extent of their acceptance in the society.

After playing an instrumental role in the formation of Princeton's Third World Liberation Front, Gordon announced his departure from SDS, explaining to his friends in the organization that race was a factor in his decision and that he didn't always feel comfortable as a member. Besides, as he recounted to me, he had "wanted to be serious about dedicating my life to revolutionary change" and thought that within SDS "there was an unseriousness among some" and an unfortunate influence of the Yippie style emphasis on counterculture and the substitution of pranks for politics.

In fact, Gordon was the only interviewee not a member of the WSA caucus who had kind words for PL's presence in SDS, precisely because he perceived them as more serious about political change. While he considered them "factionalists," there was also, he acknowledged, "an aspect that I admired: what I saw was their dedication, that they were willing to go join the army and organize, and to give up their Princeton education and their career." In retrospect, he expressed even greater understanding of PL's emphasis on a more conventional appearance. Although at the time he was turned off by "how straight arrow" they looked, he later decided that it was his own appearance that had been too influenced by the counterculture, sometimes blurring the distinction between political protest and personal statement.

In his senior year Gordon developed ties with Asian American radicals on other campuses, and by the spring semester he had become part of the New York City based group that formed I Wor Kuen, a Chinese American revolutionary nationalist organization similar to the Black Panthers or the Young Lords, its name derived from the Cantonese translation of the Boxers, Chinese nationalists who rebelled against the influence of foreign imperialists at the end of the 19th century. Engaged in completing his thesis at the time, Gordon was not attending classes and spent much of his senior year in New York's Chinatown. Soon after joining I Wor Kuen, he married another member of the collective, who had been an SDS leader at Sarah Lawrence.

Over the next decade the organization merged, first with another radical Asian American group on the West Coast, and then with a succession of Chicano and African American communist groups in California, the coalition emerging in 1978 as the League of Revolutionary Struggle, which lasted for another decade before dissolving itself. Asked whether there was some specific incident that had caused it to disband, Gordon replied with a laugh, "in 1989, yeah." The fall of the wall ended not only the League but his marriage as well; because it had been "held together by politics," he commented, "when politics became something else, the marriage fell apart." Peter Kaminsky and his first wife had remained a couple as long as they had drugs in common; Gordon and his first wife as long as they had politics.

Immediately after finishing his degree at Princeton, Gordon began graduate work at Stanford, specializing in Chinese history, but soon left the program with no intention of returning. For much of the next decade he taught courses as an adjunct at junior colleges in the Oakland area; at the time he had no plans for a career in academia, and teaching was just a way to survive financially while being politically active. For a brief period he also worked in restaurants in San Francisco, joining the service workers union, which included waiters and hotel workers; involved in support work for the union, he considered himself a professional organizer. By 1982, however, Gordon had changed his mind and decided to pursue a doctorate. Re-entering Stanford, he switched from Chinese to American history, returning to his earlier interest in international relations and diplomatic history; his doctoral dissertation studied American attempts, from the Truman administration through Richard Nixon's 1972 trip to Beijing, to exploit the differences between the Soviet Union and the People's Republic of China. Based on his dissertation, Gordon's first book, *Friends and Enemies*, received the Stuart L. Bernath Book Prize for "distinguished research and writing by scholars of American foreign relations."

Relying on previously classified documents, *Friends and Enemies* demonstrated that, in contrast to the official government position that "international communism" represented a monolithic threat to the United States, in fact American policymakers were well aware of the bitter conflicts between the two largest communist powers and plotted to exacerbate them. The Limited Test Ban Treaty between the United States, Great Britain, and the Soviet Union during the Kennedy administration, for example, was promoted to the public as a breakthrough in the quest for peace and stability, but the acknowledged purpose behind the scenes was to aggravate tensions between the Soviet Union and China, the latter of which saw the treaty, correctly, as an attempt to blunt its nuclear ambitions and was infuriated at the perfidy of its former ally. Indeed, the United States contemplated joint military action with the Kremlin against China, including the possibility of the two adversaries cooperating in a pre-emptive airstrike against China's nuclear weapons facilities.[6]

Though ancillary to its main theme, one issue discussed in the book had interesting implications for the antiwar movement. As Gordon's research indicated, the assumption informing policy at the highest levels of government was that failure to defeat the NLF in Vietnam would inevitably cede control of the country to China; there was even a hope that, to prevent Chinese expansionism, the Soviet Union might pressure the Vietnamese to the negotiating table.[7] Of course, anyone in SDS could have explained that the NLF and the North Vietnamese were nationalists as much as communists and that they were independent of both Moscow and especially Beijing, which had been the country's traditional enemy; the war between Vietnam and China occurring shortly after the withdrawal of American troops may have come as a shock to Washington, but few SDS activists were surprised. How was it that all these government experts and policy wonks discussed in Gordon's book— Dean Rusk, Walt Rostow, George Kennan—seemed so unaware of the basic facts of the region well known to those of us in the movement? Gordon explained that "they were ideologically captured." They didn't lack for information but made choices that were "bounded" by their ideologies—by their "assumptions about the nature of Chinese communism or communism generally"—as well as by their own initial claim that the Vietnamese uprising was an extension of Chinese communist influence.

After completing his doctorate Gordon spent two years at the Stanford Center for International Security and Arms Control—CISAC—while teaching Asian American history at the university. At CISAC, an academic think tank, he worked with people such as Condoleezza Rice and William Perry, who had served as Bill Clinton's secretary of defense. Given its mission, the center might have seemed a curious place for someone with a voluminous FBI file. However, Gordon had been brought in by a prominent political scientist, who authorized his position as Coordinator of the Project on Peace and Cooperation in the Asian-Pacific Region, supporting efforts to encourage academic dialogue among security specialists on East Asian nations—China, Japan, and the two Koreas. Although Gordon suspected that his co-workers at both the Arms Control Center and the Peace and Cooperation Project knew something about his radical past, "they really didn't pursue it," he said, "and I think over time I became genuinely respectful of academic values, of inquiry, of the integrity of most of my colleagues." Having returned to graduate school primarily to ensure "a more stable livelihood," he was surprised to find how much he had come to "respect and value and honor academia."

When Gordon was offered a tenure track position at the University of California–Irvine, a group of Stanford students who had been pressuring the

administration to establish an Asian-American studies program saw his imminent departure as a blow to their efforts and in protest barricaded themselves
in the president's office for eight hours. Although their insistence that he
receive a tenure track line at Stanford was but one demand in a larger list concerning the ethnic studies program, Gordon's continued presence at the university was an important part of the package. While the campaign to keep
him seemed unsuccessful, after only a year at his new university Gordon
returned to Stanford—at first while on leave from Irvine, but soon thereafter
in the capacity that the students had demanded—and has remained there ever
since. In 1997 he became the first director of the university's newly developed
Asian American Studies Program.

Gordon's scholarly work has focused on two areas, each with personal
significance. Early in his academic career he wrote on China, much of the
work an extension of his dissertation examining Sino-American relations in
the first two postwar decades. Exploring the nuclear brinkmanship that came
close to provoking armed conflict, for example, he analyzed the Eisenhower
era confrontation over Quemoy and Matsu—the offshore islands controlled
by the Nationalist Chinese but under attack by the mainland People's Republic—concluding that, in contrast to most previous interpretations, "war was
avoided due more to Chinese Communist caution than to the diplomatic
skills" of the Eisenhower administration. In one of his publications on this
issue, Gordon collaborated with a scholar from the People's Republic, allowing
the use of archival material from both China and the United States.[8]

Many former SDS activists had looked to China as the model of a nation
on the socialist path, and waving the so-called "Red Book"—its actual title
was *Quotations from Chairman Mao Tse-tung*—was common at SDS events,
a gesture not intended ironically. Thus, the boilerplate questions for interviewees included their opinion of China when they were active in SDS and
what they now thought of that opinion, but few of them had anything noteworthy to say beyond the obvious—that many of us had fallen for a naively
romanticized view of the country and its leader at the time, willfully ignorant
of the chaos we later learned was actually occurring.

However, since modern Chinese history was one of Gordon's areas of
scholarly expertise, his assessment of China and Mao was of particular interest, especially in view of the spate of books that had appeared in previous years
depicting the communist leader as a monster, both politically and personally.[9]
Gordon had conflicted feelings. On the one hand, he had felt "inspired by
Mao," calling him "such an important part of my maturation as a radical" that
there was "a part of me that is defensive about him." Having read Mao's work—

his more philosophical essays, such as "On Practice," "On Contradiction," and "Talks at the Yenan Forum on Literature and Art"—Gordon thought that Mao was "really brilliant" and acknowledged the Chinese leader's influence on his own approach to academic work: "the concern about performance, about art, about thinking dialectically, thinking about things as a historian thinks about time, place, circumstance, about how one can never be completely dispassionate from one's historical subject but has to be intimately involved in some way." On the other hand, he found it "really disheartening" to read of Mao's extremism and "the amount of suffering he caused." While Gordon warned that the recent critical publications should not be taken "entirely verbatim"—that they were plagued with "inaccuracies"—nevertheless, he realized, "the picture that comes out is ugly." Gordon had particularly harsh words for the Cultural Revolution, which, in his opinion, had begun as "quite idealistic, even romantic" but soon descended into such "terrible inhumanity and suffering" that he needed to resort to "philosophical terms" to summarize its effects: "it was a tragedy."

Since Mao's death, however, Gordon thought that China had made substantial progress. His opinion of Deng Xiaoping, who had been purged during the Cultural Revolution but regained power in the post–Mao period and led China through its subsequent economic reforms, was considerably less complicated. After visiting China during the student protests in 1985, Gordon had concluded that Deng's reforms were "revolutionizing Chinese society, not just economically but socially,"[10] and in our discussion he characterized Deng as "extraordinarily capable and probably deserving of all the credit he's been given."

At the time we spoke, shortly before the 2008 Beijing Olympics, the press was reporting on the suppression of rights in China and the crackdown on "undesirables"—a term applied to defenders of human rights and political dissidents.[11] Gordon thought that, while limitation on free expression was a genuine problem, it was being exaggerated by the media. More important, he emphasized that the fixation on such suppression had lost sight of the "bigger picture, which is a tremendous liberalization of the society from the lowest all the way up to the highest levels." Asked what constituted democracy in a socialist society like China's, Gordon responded that he was not convinced that a multi-party system was necessary and that "you can have forms of political democracy within a society which has a dominant, if not predominant party, as long as that party allows and practices a vigorous inner-party discussion, debate, election." But what Gordon found troublesome about contemporary China was the "negative consequences of industrialization that we don't hear about"—the "ubiquitous venality" and subsequent "void of value" that had accompanied economic growth and the increase in prosperity.

Soon after the fall of the wall, Gordon changed his scholarly focus. He certainly did not believe that dissolution of the communist bloc meant "the end of history"—a notion he dismissed as "silly." Rather he viewed it more as the return of history—the reemergence of all those messy "non-ideological aspects" that had been obscured by the Cold War: religion, ethnicity, regional differences. It was also the sort of history toward which Gordon turned his own interest, becoming one of the nation's most prominent scholars in Asian American studies. As director of the university's newly developed program, he suggested to the editor of Stanford University Press that a book series would help to institutionalize the new discipline; appointed the series editor, he has presided over the publication of work not just in history but in most of the disciplines within the humanities and social sciences—anthropology, sociology, law, literary criticism, politics, and the arts. At the time we spoke Gordon was preparing for publication an illustrated coffee table book on the recovery and interpretation of work by artists of Asian ancestry in the United States—his father among them—who had been celebrated during their period of productivity but had since been neglected because their artwork did not fit neatly into a racialized genre.[12] Between his own writing—articles and books that he has written and collections that he has edited—and the more than 30 volumes in the book series, since the early 1990s Gordon has been instrumental in producing a substantial body of work in the field.

The concept of ethnic studies resulted from campaigns carried on in the late 1960s at Berkeley and San Francisco State University by the Third World Liberation Front, which brought together groups representing African American, Asian American, Latino, and Native American students to demand courses on the experiences and struggles of ethnic minorities in the United States. At San Francisco State the TWLF led the longest student strike in the nation's history, culminating in establishment of the university's School of Ethnic Studies; the second longest strike, supported by the faculty union, took place at Berkeley and resulted in creation of the Department of Ethnic Studies.

The term "Asian American" was coined in 1968 by the historian Yuji Ichioka, a personal friend of Gordon's. At the time, this new rubric, replacing "Oriental" or "Asiatic," carried with it radical connotations in much the same way that the replacement of "colored" or "Negro" with "black" or "African American" had done, suggesting in either case the emergence of a new self-assertiveness. But for Asian Americans the designation also announced a new sense of pan-ethnic identity, one that unified groups from many different national backgrounds—Chinese, Japanese, Korean, Indian, Pakistani, Filipino, Vietnamese, and numerous smaller countries and peoples—emphasizing the commonality of their historical experience in the United States. As Gordon explained in a 2001 publication, "More than an ethnic label, the term 'Asian American' also was a statement about perceived social position and group interest," and, while no longer used exclusively by radical activists, it has continued "to suggest a consciousness about place in American society— a consciousness that appears to be growing, not diminishing."[13]

Gordon's decision to specialize in a field centered on race and ethnicity brought him full circle. Having come of age as the only Asian American and one of the only non-whites in Piedmont, what he called "the idea of racial divide" had always been an important concern in his life. Conscious of the extent to which his community had been "literally walled off" by the freeway system from nearby Oakland, even in high school his proposal for an exchange program with the neighboring, largely black school system had been an early attempt to bridge the divide. While he may not have experienced the kind of life-determining moment in which a 5-year-old Stephen Jay Gould famously saw his first Tyrannosaurus rex in the American Museum of Natural History and decided in that instant to become a paleontologist, from an early age Gordon has been particularly sensitive to the significance of race in American society.

However, it was his statement announcing formation of Princeton's TWLF that defined the specific direction Gordon's concern with ethnic differences would take, declaring that the "unity of non-white problems is foremost" in understanding the nature of racism in the United States and formulating a strategy for defeating it. Though phrased less tendentiously, three and a half decades later an author of one of the books in the Stanford series summarized the ideal of scholarship in ethnic studies in conceptually identical terms, describing it—in a characterization that Gordon affirmed— as the promotion of "anti-racist 'inter-ethnic identities and alliances' that cut against the most narrow and essentialist forms of identity politics."[14] At the heart of Gordon's work in Asian American studies have been the twin themes embodied in both these statements: the history of discrimination against Asian Americans in the United States and the nature of their ethnic identity.

All activist-scholars face a similar challenge: how to bring the values that informed their activism to bear on their academic research without sacrificing scholarly rigor. Gordon wanted his work to be "dispassionate" but still "very much imbued with my radical experience and outlook." Ichioka, Gordon's close friend and a dozen years his senior, had always been candid about the fact that his scholarship was inseparable from his political commitments. In published reflections after his friend's death, Gordon described Ichioka's approach in words that, he acknowledged, characterized his own perspective. The older historian's "efforts to uncover a 'buried past,'" Gordon wrote, "served the broader purpose of intellectually exposing and opposing racism and empowering those who had suffered such oppression." Ichioka "saw no contradiction between engaging in the most rigorous and truthful scholarship and political principle. For Yuji, true history advanced the politics of anti-racism and social justice; and in turn he believed that such political values guided his own historical work."[15]

Much of Gordon's own work has followed in the tradition pioneered by his friend, focusing on the history of discrimination against Asians and Asian Americans. Combining his interest in diplomatic history with that "broader purpose" that Yuji had encouraged, he has studied, for example, the so-called "Korean Expedition" of 1871, the little known episode in which an American naval force, initially dispatched in support of a diplomatic delegation, wound up in armed conflict, its superior firepower resulting in hundreds of Koreans killed but only three Americans. Gordon described how the violation of Korean territorial sovereignty—based on the presumption that "the principles of international law, such as respect for national boundaries, applied in full only to 'civilized,' Christian nations"—led to the misunderstanding that produced the conflict.[16]

However, most of Gordon's scholarship in this area has explored specific instances of discrimination against Asian Americans and their responses—though "exclusion" might be a more appropriate term for this history than "discrimination." While other minorities have suffered from policies designed to marginalize them, only Asian groups have been banned from American citizenship by federal legislation or forced to abandon their property and herded into work camps behind barbed wire despite having committed no legally actionable offense; indeed, as a study on Asian-white miscegenation in the Stanford series noted, at one point in the nation's history, an American woman of any race who married an Asian male "alien" was automatically denaturalized—deprived of her own citizenship.[17] In particular, Gordon has examined the wartime internment of Japanese Americans, demonstrating that—with the exception of the Quakers and the Socialist Party leader, Norman Thomas—it was liberals and leftists, including the Communist Party, who endorsed mass relocation on the basis solely of race and provided the propaganda to justify the policy. And in an analysis presaging the postwar role of social science, he has also explored the dynamics of what he called the "liberal, techno-managerial ethos," which rationalized the study and manipulation of this captive population by white liberal educators and social scientists, pleased to have the "immense coercive power of the state" at their disposal in "molding, reshaping, remaking a people in ways they determined best and consistent with their own ostensibly higher values and superior way of life."[18]

Unlike the usual racial narrative acknowledging a history of discrimination but recognizing the society's more egalitarian present, Gordon's work has not always arrived at such a hopeful conclusion. As contributors to one of his edited collections pointed out, Asian Americans have been stigmatized as the permanent other, "immutably foreign and unassimilable with whites," in order to rationalize their "civic ostracism." As a result of their linkage to this "idea of permanent foreignness," one author wrote, Asian Americans had been subjected to "citizenship nullification," rendering "genuine Asian American citizenship an impossibility," at least "for the foreseeable future."[19] Another volume in the Stanford series described the present condition of Asian Americans as "abjection": they were no longer subject to the kind of formal, institutional exclusion that had characterized the past but were still defined by mass media and public education as "aliens, thus both precluding their sense of national entitlement and inhibiting their American actualization." In a book review Gordon himself referred to "the 'dream' that America will one day see genuine multi-cultural democracy," implying that such a goal was still far off.[20] Though not entirely "pessimistic" about the future, at the moment he felt that Asians were still regarded as "perpetual foreigners—that somehow an Asian cannot be a real American."

Events around the time of my visit provided evidence for Gordon's bleak outlook. Some political ads portrayed the Chinese as beneficiaries of the Great Recession, exultantly anticipating the decline of the American economy, in some cases accompanied by footage of Chinese New Year celebrations in the United States. In some quarters Asian Americans were perceived as people to be victimized. A *Time* story discussed the outrage expressed by other delinquent adolescents at a treatment center after learning that an elderly woman had been mugged by some of their group. Asked whom it would be acceptable to mug, one of them answered, "A Chinese delivery guy."[21]

Yet the Asian American as abject has not prevented their depiction as the "model minority" in a conscious effort to counterpose their educational success and upward mobility to that of blacks; as far back as the 1960s, some opponents of the civil rights movement pointed to Asian Americans as the anti-blacks, improving their lot through hard work and self-reliance rather than demands for government assistance. Gordon's political activism had always emphasized the solidarity of all non-white groups, and he thought that blacks and Asian Americans still shared a common struggle, though it was "less clear," he acknowledged, now that the histories of the two groups had diverged. In the 1960s and 70s, he observed, blacks and Asian Americans had grown up side by side in the inner cities, but a combination of upward mobility and the influx of Asian professionals in the intervening three decades had transformed the Asian American community, situating it "mainly in these well-educated enclaves around urban areas."

These changes in the Asian American community suggest the other theme explored by Asian American studies: the nature of ethnic identity. While Gordon has not himself written extensively on identity, as series editor he has shepherded to publication a number of works on the topic. These books have examined the diverse identities formed by Asian Americans adapting to different circumstances in the United States—for example, analyses of the effects of globalization and technology in creating what one book called "the New Cosmopolitans" and another referred to as a "trans–Pacific commuter culture." Some of these works have also emphasized the intrapersonal dimension of identity formation. One author posited that, because of their designation as "aliens," Asian Americans have found it necessary "to perform into existence their identities *as Asian Americans* [emphasis in original]" through "acts of impersonation."[22]

Asked whether he had personally experienced this phenomenon, Gordon replied emphatically, "Oh, yeah; through much of my life." "I've become more comfortable in my own skin in recent years," he elaborated, "but I think finding an actual place—what is one's place, what is my place in America—is something I've thought about a lot, and still think about a lot, and still feel somewhat uncomfortable." In part this reaction had to do with the lack of diversity among the faculty; "I go to meetings all the time," he remarked, "and it just strikes me how often I am the only nonwhite member sitting there." This had nothing to do with the behavior of his colleagues, who were all "decent" people and often friends, but rather with "the fact that our society remains in de facto ways separated, not segregated. In some sense here I still am after in high school I was the only Asian American, I'm still sitting here by myself." But the paucity of other nonwhite colleagues was not the entire explanation. In discussions with his Asian American students at Stanford— not only an "extraordinarily talented and successful group" but also, in contrast to Gordon's isolation at Princeton, present at the university in substantial numbers—they too all "expressed something about being uncomfortable," a sense of "not belonging." Perhaps even now their reaction "goes back to what my mother said," he mused—the feeling that this was not their country.

Gordon's own thinking about Asian American identity has moved toward what he called a "transnational approach," which "strives to understand Asians in America as part of a growing number of 'internationalized' people in the Pacific Rim whose lives do not fall neatly into a specific national pattern."[23] Yet at the same time he worried that transnationalism might encourage the kind of "binary attitude" that could once again convey an impression of "Asians as foreign, as not really embedded in America." Thus the challenge and the dilemma that Gordon saw in Asian American studies and similar programs: how to "recognize that one's self has been shaped by group identity" without allowing the discussion to lapse into essentialism or ethnic generalizations.

Not everyone views ethnic studies programs as a positive intellectual development. David Horowitz has condemned them as representing "the political debasement of the university"—one of the ways in which 1960s activists "have colonized a significant part of the university system and transformed it to serve … political ends." While Horowitz could be dismissed as an opportunist, conducting an artless campaign based on incidents that often turned out to be distorted, some prominent academics have also been critical. Tony Judt, a respected scholar known for his commitment to the politics of social democracy, has been a harsh critic of ethnic studies—specifically naming "Asian-Pacific-American studies"—but not because of their presumed political content. Rather, according to Judt, "they encourage members of that minority to study *themselves*—thereby simultaneously negating the goals of a liberal education and reinforcing the sectarian and ghetto mentalities they purport to undermine [emphasis in original]."[24]

Of course, as Gordon pointed out, ethnic studies programs with a "high level of intellectual rigor" have been established in "all the first-tier universities" in the United States, including the Ivy League schools, Stanford, and the University of Chicago. But the notion that such programs conflict with the goals of a liberal education also seemed puzzling, since liberal arts institutions typically offer majors in the literature and culture of various European nations; the scholarly study of the historical experience and cultural productions of a minority group should be no less academically respectable than the corresponding study of, say, the French, Germanic, or Russian peoples. However, the criticisms appear to have been provoked by what is assumed to be a particular perspective of ethnic studies programs, one indicated by Judt's reference to "ghetto mentality," which suggested not only essentialist notions but the acceptance of their most objectionable aspects. In fact, Gordon's work has strived to do exactly the opposite, emphasizing the diversity of Asian American identities joined together by the common thread of "self-protection, … self-affirmation, and … aspiration."[25]

The values that motivated Gordon's radical activity remain central to him today: "decency, morality in the sense of being ethical, of being someone who attaches value to life and that one of the hallmarks of life should be ethical living, which means decency to other people, respect for others, tolerance." But while his values have not changed, his politics have moderated, perhaps because in the intervening decades the society has moved further toward the tolerance at the core of his own ethical code. "There has been so much progress almost undetected or uncelebrated," Gordon observed; "generally the country is antiracist, the country is anti-male chauvinist, the acceptance of people regardless of their race, religion, gender, even sexual preference." In addition, his assessment of capitalism, once regarded as the major source of the society's evils, has become more nuanced; he acknowledged that the system had done "wonderful, good things," creating extraordinary wealth and productivity, but also "terrible things," resulting in widespread suffering. But he also foresaw the convergence of systems thought to be antagonistic to each other, in which over time capitalist societies become more social democratic and socialist societies, including China, more market oriented.

Gordon has enjoyed an extraordinarily productive career, all the more remarkable since, in his own words, he "became an academic kind of by chance." And when we spoke, he had numerous projects of different kinds in varying stages of progress. Indeed, his most significant contribution may have been undertaken since the interview. In 2015 Gordon published *Fateful Ties*, tracing the history of American perceptions of China over three centuries— from a source of wealth and model of "an enlightened society ruled by reason" during the colonial era, through the racist alarm over the "yellow peril" that informed immigration policy in the late 19th and early 20th centuries, to China's status first as ally in World War II and then adversary during the Cold War before being recognized as a 21st century superpower. Having wanted to "do something" connected to U.S.–China relations since high school, he has now produced what may be the definitive book on the subject.

8. Being Useful

One of the most forceful SDS spokespersons during the anti–ROTC campaign was Robert ("Bobby") Cohen. In a letter to the *Daily Princetonian*, he explained how SDS saw the larger political context. The administration, he wrote, was responsible to "the trustees and their interests," and the trustees, "the men who control the corporations running this country," needed ROTC "because they must continue the war in Vietnam to protect their investments in Southeast Asia." Thus, "in the end," Bobby continued, "the trustees will always fall back on the apparatus of state power which they control," whether it was calling in the police to quash actions by opponents of the war or using the judiciary to indict them.[1] Though the letter never used the Marxist phrase, it was clearly a description of how the "ruling class" exercised its will under capitalism and a call for the rest of the population to resist.

After the split in the organization, Bobby became one of the leaders of SDS-RYM at Princeton. In the spring of his senior year, Walter Hickel, secretary of the Interior in the Nixon administration, was invited to Princeton to give the keynote address for an environmental conference. For some time members of the administration had been unwelcome on college campuses, and RYM viewed the topic of Hickel's speech as an attempt to divert attention from the war and make the presence of a White House representative again "legitimate." In an effort to refocus attention on the war, the group decided to interrupt his speech. Identified, along with two other students, as one of the leaders of the protest, Bobby was placed on probation and his degree was withheld until the February after commencement.[2]

The Internet revealed that Bobby was now a physician in Manhattan and one of the nation's most prominent advocates for improved health care for prisoners, having been named by federal courts as the monitor of prison medical care in half a dozen states and the District of Columbia; he had also written extensively on correctional medicine, drug use, and the treatment of AIDS. I arranged to meet Bobby at his office, and on a fall day in 2007 took the train to Penn Station, walking the last mile downtown to his office in a narrow building wedged between a pharmacy and a Chinese massage center, "specializing in relief from pain-stress-tension fatigue and insomnia." Because Bobby had not yet arrived, I sat down in the reception room, where, instead of the usual glossy magazines, the current issue of *The Nation*—the "flagship of the Left"—was available for waiting patients.

In 15 minutes Bobby—a little heavier but also more rugged looking than his youthful self—walked hurriedly through the door, and we headed past the examining rooms to his private office. There was a serious tone to our discussion, appropriate to Bobby's medical specialty, but there were also flashes of black humor. When I asked about the response to his letter in the *New York Times* calling for immediate closure of the prison at Guantanamo,[3] Bobby replied dryly, "It's still open."

Robert Cohen grew up in a middle class Jewish family in the Bayside section of Queens—a borough of New York City with a less metropolitan feel than Manhattan. His mother had been a junior high school typing teacher, though, in keeping with technological change, her subject had been renamed "keyboarding." In a unique combination of professions, Bobby's father was both an optometrist and a lawyer. He had gone to optometry school before the war and practiced for three decades, but then in the 1960s decided to go to law school. However he found the study of law much more appealing than the practice, especially after being offered a judgeship for a price even though he had almost no legal experience.

While Bobby's mother was apolitical, his father had leftist sympathies; he brought home books on Marxism and Leninism, and joined a study group, but, in Bobby's judgment, his level of involvement never even amounted to "fellow traveler status." As is true for many Jews, when the extended family got together, certain topics—the teachers union, Israel, among others—could not be mentioned for fear of conflict. But there was no doubt where the battle lines were drawn *within* the Cohen household: Republicans and the Yankees were the "devil's" side; the (Brooklyn) Dodgers, the Democrats and socialism the forces of goodness. By 1956 and not yet 10 years old, Bobby had already experienced "great political tragedies": the Yankees beat the Dodgers in the World Series, and the Eisenhower/Nixon administration won its second term. "It just showed we had a lot of work to do," he recalled; "we were losing."

Bobby grew up as "an avowed leftist." Even in elementary school he believed in the principle "From each according to their ability, to each according to their needs," but though elected school president, he acknowledged being unable to effect "any redistribution of wealth." Part of a politically active group in high school, he joined a human rights club and, as editorial page editor of the student newspaper, wrote in support of the Free Speech Movement, the protest at Berkeley considered the starting point for the student activism of the 1960s. Bobby entered Princeton originally intending to study mathematics and physics but became too involved in SDS to concentrate on such subjects and wound up majoring in English.

Despite having arrived at the university already inclined toward Marxist ideas, Bobby never considered himself a revolutionary and was distressed at the arrogance of students who viewed themselves in such a role. It was not that he opposed the idea of revolution, but rather that he realized the absurdity of thinking that students would lead it. Bobby felt that he was playing his part in a movement concerned with important issues—ending the war, providing some kind of remuneration for racism, viewing "apartheid and imperialism as problems within capitalism," and looking to socialism as a solution—but leafleting, sit-ins, and encouraging people to read *Containment and Change* could hardly be characterized as revolutionary acts. At one point he considered joining a Venceremos Brigade because he thought it "cool and romantic"—the brigade poster with its machetes was still displayed on the wall of his home—but decided against the trip out of concern that he didn't have the "physical skills" for the task.

Bobby's parents did not so much disapprove of his activities as they were scared for him—a feeling that he appreciated more now as a father himself than he did when he was "just a leech." His father in particular thought that Bobby "had too much to offer to be destroyed" or "made impotent politically" by taking risks—a fear that was exacerbated by the rumor that the National Guard, which had killed four students at Kent State University, would be called out to safeguard IDA. The worst that happened to him, however, was an arrest after the demonstration at IDA and then postponement of his degree as a result of the Hickel incident.

After graduating, Bobby traveled around the country—Detroit, where a relative was also an SDS activist, San Francisco, Seattle—seeking a political collective that he could join, and finally ended up in Philadelphia, where Jimmy Tarlau, one of the leaders of SDS-RYM at Princeton, had put together a group attempting to organize youth in the white working class Kensington neighborhood. Among other projects the collective brought Jane Fonda to the area for an antiwar event, put out a community newspaper—the "Kensington People's Press"—and established a food co-operative, which Bobby characterized as "pure opportunism"; he and the other activists purchased the food and then sold it for less. "There was nothing cooperative about it," he recalled, "but it was good; these were poor white working-class people" who needed assistance.

However, not everyone in the neighborhood was pleased at the collective's presence. Members of the group were arrested on trumped-up charges, all eventually dismissed with the help of noted civil rights attorneys, David Kairys and David Rudovsky. On two occasions the police came to the house while off duty and started a fight, in one instance knocking Bobby out. The windows in the collective's house were broken regularly—also by the police, he suspected. As Bobby put it, "we were busted, and we were busted up."

Deciding that this was not the milieu in which he could make a contribution, Bobby did not remain in the collective very long. Although he played a significant role in producing the newspaper, he didn't think of himself as a fighter, at least in the physical sense, and had difficulty relating to the neighborhood youth that he was supposed to be organizing. "I don't know if I was decaying or maturing," he reflected, "but at some point I realized that I had nothing in common with these kids; I didn't understand what they were talking about, and, particularly, I didn't even know what music they were listening to—the universal language of youth." Most of all, despite his respect for the efforts at working class organizing by other members of the group, Bobby did not feel comfortable during the house meetings when someone would emphasize the need "to get up with the workers, to sweat with the workers." He felt the same way about industrial organizing as he had about wielding machetes. It was not who he was; "I couldn't pretend I was a worker," he said.

Once it became evident to Bobby that he was not going to become a working class organizer, he had to decide on a new direction—to "become some kind of professional where I can do something useful"—a significant consideration in his career decisions. Having taken organic chemistry, physics and other science courses before changing his major to English, Bobby realized that he "was supposed to be a doctor," a career that had always been "in the cards and in some way I was just putting off." He even had the fantasy that he would return to Kensington, buy a pair of adjacent row houses—a gentrifier before his time—and open an office or work in a free clinic.

Now "back on the petit bourgeois track," Bobby pursued his medical degree at Rush Medical College in Chicago, part of Rush Presbyterian St. Luke's Hospital. While sharing their experiences, Bobby and some other students discovered that emergency caesarean sections on pregnant black women with preeclampsia, a life-threatening condition, were being interrupted for the collection of blood as part of a research project. Though the interruption was brief, it was nonetheless risky because it was important to get the baby out as quickly as possible; moreover, none of the patients had been informed that they were part of the study, nor, a fortiori, had they given consent. Upon bringing this situation to the medical school's attention, the students were told that it would be to their advantage not to talk about it. "So we thought about that," Bobby recalled, "and then we held a demonstration and sent all the information to the media."

Completing medical school, Bobby interned at Cook County Hospital when its chief of medicine was Quentin Young, an activist physician, known as founder and once chair of the Medical Committee for Human Rights, formed to provide medical care for civil rights workers during the Freedom Summer of 1964; he had also helped to establish neighborhood health clinics for the Black Panthers and Young Lords. With Young as a drawing card, according to Bobby, people were coming "from all over the country to work at Cook"—activists who had been members of SDS, PL, the CP, and a number of Trotskyist organizations. One of their first acts was to go on strike, not over wages, about which they were willing to accept whatever the hospital decided to give them—$11,600 a year for an intern in 1975—but over better conditions for patients; they refused to sign a contract until there were more clean sheets and towels, more laboratory services and improved patient transportation. Over the objection of even many other leftists in the hospital, Young also argued that they should add health care for prisoners in the Cook County Jail to their responsibilities. Agreeing with Young, Bobby interned in the jail and then became the attending physician for the prisoners—the beginning of his path towards becoming one of the nation's recognized experts in "correctional medicine."

One of the other physicians recruited by Young and named director of medical care at the jail was Lambert King, who became one of Bobby's close friends. The two doctors were part of a research group that looked at the link between epilepsy and violence among males incarcerated in the Illinois prison system—a study intended in part as a response to attempts to convert social problems into biological defects. In the *Journal of the American Medical Association*, three Harvard neurologists had suggested that it was not racism, unemployment, substandard housing, and inadequate education at the root of urban unrest, but "brain dysfunction in the rioters," and two of these scientists had advocated psychosurgery as a "cure" for individuals involved in violence. Yet another researcher later proposed a study to determine whether anticonvulsant medications might constitute an effective treatment for "episodic violence" putatively caused by seizure disorders. Finding no relationship between epilepsy and violence, the studies in which Bobby participated helped to disprove the notion that crime was biologically determined.[4]

Lambert King soon left Chicago to accept a position as director of health services at Rikers Island—New York City's main complex for pretrial confinement of people either denied or unable to make bail. A year later he wrote to Bobby, asking if he would like the job; the plan was for Bobby first to become King's deputy and then take over the directorship. Bobby decided, again, that it would be "a useful thing to do." Montefiore Medical Center, the health care provider for the facility, enjoyed a well-deserved reputation for its social democratic tradition; one of the first hospitals to have a Department of Social Medicine, Montefiore had sent medical students to Cuba and had found staff positions for exiled Chilean doctors after the 1973 coup. In keeping with King's plan, in 1981 Bobby returned to New York to become the associate medical director of Rikers Island Health Services; a year later he assumed the directorship.

As director, Bobby represented Montefiore at the quarterly meetings with the New York City Department of Juvenile Justice, which operated the Spofford youth detention center, where Montefiore also provided medical care. At these meetings he got to know Madeline ("Maddy") deLone, the department's contract monitor, and a few years later they were married. Maddy eventually became the executive eirector of the Innocence Project, founded by Barry Scheck and Peter Neufeld, which, by 2014, had exonerated more than 300 wrongfully convicted persons.

In 1981, the same year that Bobby arrived at Rikers, the Centers for Disease Control and Prevention recognized the existence of a new and often fatal infectious illness, and a month later he saw his first case of AIDS at the jail. It was not long before this new discovery turned into an epidemic, its epicenter located in New York and San Francisco; because the disease could be transmitted by needle sharing, it was particularly common among detainees at Rikers, many of whom had been arrested for intravenous drug use. After five years at Rikers, during which he had considerable experience with AIDS patients, Bobby applied to be director of the AIDS program at New York City Health and Hospitals Corporation, which administered all the public hospitals and public nursing homes in New York and at the time had more patients with HIV infection than any other medical facility in the world, but he never received a response. Then he applied to be the corporation's vice president—ironically, the person supervising the director of the AIDS program—and was appointed to that position, which he held for two years, before being named, first medical director at St. Vincent Hospital's AIDS Center for a year, and then the center's attending physician for a decade.

Bobby held these positions despite lacking the appropriate background. The problem, as he saw it, was that "nobody wanted to take care of these people," certainly not the infectious disease specialists, who "just ran in the other direction." "I mean, why should I be the director of the AIDS Center at St. Vincent's?" Bobby asked; "I was not trained in infectious diseases." For a moment I thought the question rhetorical, until he immediately added that, "the answer is because no one else would do it, and it was very important"— another useful activity on his part. And so the issue for Bobby was "How do you *not* do this? What are you supposed to do as a doctor?" Nor had the situation improved for many people in the intervening years, he emphasized, even with the advent of more effective antiretroviral drugs to manage the disease. To prove the point he pulled out an article published only the previous week, demonstrating that the mortality rate for whites with HIV infection was declining over time, while the mortality rate for African Americans continued to rise. Especially after 1996, as he summarized the study, "if you got drugs, you lived; if you didn't get drugs, you died. So access to treatment meant everything." It was one thing to design a curriculum to give medical students the necessary skills, Bobby pointed out, "but how do you pull people into this when they have other options"—and, in many senses, more rewarding ones. I thought of Tom Lehrer's line about doctors who specialized in diseases of the rich.

Almost three decades later, it is easy to forget how, at the onset of the AIDS epidemic, public hysteria threatened the civil liberties of the disease's victims, making draconian proposals for their identification and segregation alarmingly popular. In the mid–1980s, at the beginning of his tenure as vice president of the Health and Hospitals Corporation, Bobby was told by the NYU provost and chief of medicine at the university's Bellevue Hospital— someone accustomed to getting what he wanted—that AIDS was like being at war, and because the volume of death was just too intense for interns, medicals students, and residents, the Provost had an idea how to deal with the problem: to house everyone with an HIV infection, the city should construct a hospital on Randall's Island—a rectangle in the East River less than a square mile in size. A week later Bobby received a letter signed by the deans of all the medical schools in New York, endorsing the proposal. In addition, the Republican mayoral candidate in 1985 ran on a platform demanding HIV screening of all the city's health workers, teachers and beauticians. At the national level, too, some public figures contributed to a sense of the menace that "they"—gay males and drug users—posed to "us." Margaret Heckler, Ronald Reagan's secretary of health and human services, encouraged AIDS researchers to keep the disease confined within the "epidemiologic" risk groups. And William F. Buckley, still raising the prospect of casual communication of the disease in 1986, called for "universal testing" and famously proposed that "everyone detected with AIDS ... be tattooed"—on the upper forearm for needle-users, the buttocks for homosexuals.[5]

As one of the most prominent physicians on the front line of AIDS treatment, from the beginning of the epidemic Bobby was an outspoken opponent of these measures, arguing against what he called an attempt to divide the country "into two camps, antibody positive and antibody negative." Rather than allowing public health policy to be determined by "homophobic and erotophobic cultural biases," he wrote, it was important to recognize that AIDS was "a disease that affects human beings, not high risk groups" and he predicted, accurately, that, while AIDS might spread more slowly among heterosexuals, it would eventually "establish ... itself within a world-wide non-immune human host." Mass screening, he insisted, would "only bring harm to people, particularly gay men and poor populations with a high incidence of drug addiction and prostitution" by establishing the basis for their exclusion from insurance coverage and allowing the creation of "a list of those who could be placed in quarantine." Instead of policies that would stigmatize groups of people, Bobby called for educational programs, in schools as well as communities and workplaces, to "teach everyone how to live in a world with people with AIDS," including "techniques, such as safe sex and sterile needles"; in particular, he encouraged the "distribution of free needles and syringes" as a way to enable "drug addicts to avoid exposure to the AIDS agent."[6] Though now less controversial, at the time these recommendations represented an often unwelcome attempt to substitute scientific information for public prejudice.

Nor was Bobby's opposition to mass testing confined to exhortation in articles or public statements; after becoming vice president of the Health and Hospitals Corporation, the largest municipal healthcare organization in the country, he was in a position to exert influence on actual practice. "According to several local health experts," the New York Times reported in 1988, "Dr. Cohen has single-handedly blocked testing" in municipal hospitals, where poor women were most likely to receive care.[7] I asked Bobby about the quote. "To the extent that what they're saying is true," he replied modestly, "I'm proud of it."

While Bobby promoted sterile needle distribution as part of a program to prevent the spread of AIDS, the policy was also related to another issue on which he has been an outspoken advocate: decriminalization of drug use.

Although he had professional reasons for opposing criminalization, Bobby's belief that drug use should not be illegal predated his medical training; while in Philadelphia, a number of the working class youth in the Kensington neighborhood were heroin addicts, and the members of the collective organized a campaign to allow them to shoot up in the park without interference from the police. Bobby summarized his beliefs on drug use succinctly: "It doesn't make sense to arrest people. People who don't want to use drugs should not be forced to use drugs; people who use drugs recreationally should be allowed to use drugs recreationally; people who lose control of their ability to use drugs should be offered assistance in stopping it. And if they can't stop, which they often can't, they should be given the drug's substitution, so they don't have to steal to buy things that are illegal which they need to have." Drug use for Bobby was a right—perhaps not exactly "a human right, the way freedom to travel is," he conceded, but the ability for people "to drink or use whatever they want" was not something he thought should be legally proscribed. Libertarian drug policy had its appeal at both ends of the political spectrum: Chip Sills's support for decriminalization was combined with religious conservatism, Bobby's with democratic socialism.

However, Bobby was also outraged by the complicity in the war on drugs of his own professional field, which had bought into the "arbitrary moral/legal principle" that "drug use is illegal, therefore drug use is against the public health." While drug treatment programs may have helped a few people who wanted to stop, he acknowledged, many youthful drug users just preferred illegal drugs to abstinence, and it then became an unavoidable sequence: "abstinence programs don't work for 20-year-olds," and thus it made no sense to place them in "alternatives to incarceration on day one, the first time you bust them for using heroin, and the next time put them in jail for doing exactly the same thing, when you know that they're going to be doing it." After all, he continued, "that's what people who are addicted to drugs do; they use drugs." But there was also a simple and demonstrably successful solution— "as sciencey as you can get," Bobby called it, unlike the generally ineffective AA model: either provide addicts a substitute drug, such as methadone or buprenorphine, to reduce their craving for heroin, or if the craving still persists, provide them heroin. As he urged in a letter to the *Times*, "heroin and methadone should be dispensed in supportive settings on a monthly basis." The right policy on drugs, according to Bobby, was to tolerate them when they were safe and to minimize harm—through needle exchange programs, for example—when they posed a risk.[8]

Yet by "demonizing drug use as drug abuse," Bobby argued, the field of public health had facilitated the "joining of the moral and the medical," providing the basis for the social construction of drug use as criminal behavior, and thus allowing itself to be used "to legitimize the mass incarceration of drug users." And the result, he wrote in 2000, was a staggering increase in the number of persons arrested and incarcerated for drug use during the previous quarter century, the great majority of them African American. "Is one in three black men under the age of 30 under state criminal custody or alternative sentencing enough?" Bobby asked at the end of the article. "When is enough enough?"[9]

Both his interest in AIDS and in drug use have been outgrowths of the area in which Bobby is most well-known: health care for prisoners. From his initial experience in the Cook County jail, he has been a staunch supporter of what the Oath of Athens—the standards for clinical work in prisons, promulgated by an international group of physicians—called "the right of incarcerated individuals to receive the best possible health care." Indeed, his first published work raised ethical concerns about a program inviting inmates to sell their plasma twice a week to a commercial company for $6.25 per session and some fruit juice. In addition to the possible health risks of such frequent donation—the regular loss of large amounts of protein—he maintained that payment for jail inmates, confined precisely because of their inability to make bail, was inherently coercive and called into question the validity of their consent.[10]

However, it was at Rikers that Bobby became nationally visible. "Running Rikers is the top of the game," he declared; "it was the national model for jail health care." As its director, not only did he become a specialist in AIDS treatment, despite having no training in infectious diseases, but, again with no training in psychiatry, he wrote the standards for mental health care in the New York City jails and established a mental health program at the facility. As a recognized expert in prison care, his opinion was solicited in controversies. When a prisoner serving time for third degree murder needed an expensive bone marrow transplant, for example, Bobby supported his right to the procedure, arguing that everyone, no matter the circumstances, deserved access to care whatever the cost. "It is to our country's dishonor," he wrote in explaining his position, "that universal access to care that is free at the point of delivery has not been codified as law."[11] He was also now on the list of potential monitors of prison health care compiled by organizations such as the ACLU. When civil rights litigation was successfully filed against a state, alleging shortcomings in the health care for prisoners, the court would order a settlement instructing the state to take specific steps. Then, as was frequently the case, if the state failed to comply with the court's decree, the plaintiffs' attorney acting on behalf of the prisoners would bring a contempt motion, in response to which the court would appoint a monitor, generally chosen from a list submitted by the parties, to oversee the system. As a result of this procedure, in the early 1980s Bobby was appointed the monitor for prison health care, first in Florida, and eventually in a number of other states.

Given the institutional barriers to medical care for prisoners, Bobby viewed the practice of correctional medicine as often an adversarial process, requiring physicians to resist what he called "the deformation of medical care caused by incarceration." As he urged in his contribution to a textbook on prison health care, physicians had to act as advocates on two fronts, addressing inadequate care within prisons while at the same time working to change "policies that contributed to mass incarceration." In his capacity as monitor of prison health care, Bobby experienced no shortage of outrageous examples of the former problem—inmates with serious illnesses, whose complaints were nevertheless dismissed by physicians who either refused to believe their patient's complaints of pain and suffering or neglected their patients out of ignorance or willfulness. In one case an inmate lost a large portion of his forehead due to chronic osteomyelitis after his prison doctor and the facility's medical director dismissed his complaints of persistent headaches and accused him of faking symptoms. In another instance Bobby was asked to intervene on behalf of a prisoner suffering from lymphoma—resulting in paralysis so severe that he became incontinent, lying in his own feces unable to move— but diagnosed as a case of hysterical conversion by the prison doctor, who chained him to the bed in order to force him to change positions.[12]

As the medical monitor, one of whose tasks was to review the credentials of prison physicians, Bobby also discovered numerous instances of doctors hired to provide care for inmates despite being unacceptable "to practice in the free-world civilian sector"—physicians "with significant character problems, including convictions for criminal offenses" related to their treatment of patients, resulting in the loss of their license to practice medicine. In his review of the treatment of prisoners with HIV infections in one southern state, he found that all the physicians providing care had lost their state license and were limited to practicing medicine in prisons. In another series of reports on health care in a Beekman, New York, institution, Bobby concluded that the prison doctor, whose medical license had been suspended for gross incompetence, had been "unresponsive" to the complaints of his patients and "callous" in the treatment of their emergencies, leading to the death of two inmates.[13]

In addition, Bobby urged correctional physicians to oppose institutional policies that adversely affected inmates' health. He called on them, for example, to work to limit or eliminate the fees commonly imposed on prisoners requesting attention from a doctor or nurse; intended to deter prisoners from seeking medical care, the practice was dangerous, he warned, discouraging them from obtaining assistance even for contagious illnesses. When the fee-for-service system in a Pennsylvania prison was challenged before a federal appeals court as a constitutionally prohibited punishment, Bobby testified for the plaintiffs—represented by the same civil rights attorney who had assisted him decades earlier in Kensington—only to have the practice upheld by a three judge panel, including Samuel Alito eight years before his nomination to the Supreme Court. Bobby also encouraged physicians to advocate for "harm reduction" measures in prison, chiefly the availability of condoms and sterile syringes for prisoners to prevent the transmission of HIV and hepatitis C; despite institutional rules prohibiting intravenous drug use and even consenting sex between prisoners, these behaviors were realities of prison life, and he felt that physicians should encourage policies designed to prevent the possible spread of disease.[14]

Many of the policies that Bobby urged correctional physicians to support were intended to reduce the excessive prison population—more than two million people in 2002, which was, he noted, larger, both by absolute number and by proportion of the population, than any other country. Thus, he called for physicians to oppose not only the incarceration of drug users but what he called "irrational punishment"—"incarceration of the dying, severely disabled, mentally retarded," or others incapable of understanding what they have done or harming anyone. In particular, he argued for them to oppose the use of prisons and jails as warehouses for the mentally ill. One of the most appalling cases in which Bobby was involved occurred in Michigan, where a "floridly psychotic" inmate, who didn't belong in prison to begin with, was chained, delusional and screaming incoherently, to a concrete slab in four-point restraints for 18 hours at a time over five days, when the heat index sometimes exceeded 100 degrees, leading to his death from dehydration and arrhythmia; his collapse and last moments shortly after being unchained were captured by a surveillance camera and shown in a *60 Minutes* segment on the incident.[15] In a district court hearing, Bobby testified that not only was the psychiatric care inadequate but that the restraints used on the prisoner constituted torture, which physicians were required to oppose by the ethical standards of their profession; use of the term "torture" was a calculated, tactical decision, designed to invoke the framework of human rights, in contrast to "abuse," which might suggest a perhaps understandable, rare exception in the face of provocation by difficult prisoners taunting the custodial staff. Agreeing with Bobby's characterization, the judge ruled that the restraints violated the Eighth Amendment prohibition against cruel and unusual punishment, and as a remedy he ordered prison staff to attend training sessions on the humane treatment of patients, the content of which had to be approved by Bobby. (When the court also appointed Bobby at the same prison to ensure that inmates with untreated serious illnesses received prompt medical care, Michigan closed the institution, transferring all the prisoners to other facilities.)[16]

Finally, Bobby emphasized that both the American Medical Association and the Society of Correctional Physicians had taken an official position opposing any participation of physicians in executions. But in addition, he argued that their ethical commitment to healing meant that physicians had a responsibility not just to refuse personal involvement but to support efforts to abolish a practice that he considered immoral and that was, he noted, employed by some of the most repressive countries in the world.[17] And though Bobby did not mention it, the hundreds of people on death row exonerated by the Innocence Project directed by his wife must have provided yet further reason for him to insist that health care professionals should oppose the death penalty.

"The best way to practice correctional medicine," Bobby concluded, "is to practice the best medicine." That is, there was to be no difference between medical care for prisoners and for anyone else; "the complete welfare of the patient" was always to be the primary consideration. Unsurprisingly, this was hardly a popular position in many quarters. In response to his recommendation that a prisoner receive a bone marrow transplant, a philosophy professor bluntly insisted that the criminal had forfeited "access to extraordinary care for disease that, untreated, would be fatal"; indeed, the professor suggested, the knowledge that a potentially fatal disease would not be treated might have deterrent value.[18] At the time we spoke, Bobby had also just argued, as the court appointed monitor in Michigan, that prisoners suffering from renal failure should receive a kidney transplant if medically indicated, outraging state authorities who responded that scarce organs should be reserved for people lacking such special skills as robbing jewelry stores and other criminal activity.

As he noted in his own writing, Bobby understood the reasons that correction officers, struggling to provide health care and medications for themselves and their families, might resent the access to care afforded to prisoners; some prison health practitioners, cognizant of the delays experienced by poor persons dependent on clinic-based care, candidly acknowledged to him their feeling that if poor non-prisoners had to wait, then "prisoners should have to wait too, maybe even more." Bobby viewed their frustration as the unavoidable consequence of an American health system, in which too many people could not afford the cost of insurance, thus making even the substandard care provided to prisoners seem like an unearned privilege beyond the reach of many others who had not committed a crime. "Prisoners will not have regular access to decent medical care," he realized, "until everyone else in the United States has access. Without universal health care for all, prisoners will not receive decent medical care."[19]

Asked about the health care system he favored, Bobby was quick to provide the details: "Universal access, cradle to grave; of course, a single payer. Drug companies nationalized. Health education, continuing education of physicians, being a function of their academic and professional organizations and not being put off to the drug companies." Although Obama had not yet been elected when we spoke, Bobby's comments anticipated with disapproval the direction legislation would take. Single payer was essential in his opinion "because the other plans all envision a role for the insurance companies, and it is just counterintuitive to put the fox in charge of the henhouse." Although the concept of insurance—using a large population to pool risks—made sense to Bobby, he didn't see private health insurance as pooling risks but rather as a way to displace the "risks onto those people who are at risk and take the surplus to do other things with." Again, he preferred the language of rights in discussing health care, insisting that every person "is entitled to the best medical care their society has to offer"—a position, he observed, that was supported by international human rights documents.

Bobby lived these beliefs in his own practice—and not only in his efforts to obtain the best care for prisoners. While director and then attending physician at St. Vincent's AIDS Center, he also opened his own clinic but then left the Center after being told that he could not keep both positions at the same time. Consequently, he brought his patients from the center to his own practice, telling them that he would treat them even if they could not pay. Bobby was also Medical Director for a non-profit organization that provided education on AIDS treatment and HIV related issues to other professionals, bringing physicians and nurses from all over the world to New York.

Clearly Bobby could point to a number of changes in policy traceable largely to his advocacy. He has been able, in his words, "to present a model of one of the better ways to provide health care to prisoners" and, through his work in litigation, has helped "to substantially raise the standards that are acceptable or considered constitutional." But he viewed his efforts as a "one step forward, two steps backward kind of struggle," as Congress continued to enact legislation limiting prisoners' rights to health care. On balance, however, he thought that "the standards at the bottom are much higher right now than when I started, and I've been part of that effort"; he felt fortunate to have had the opportunity "to be useful in lots of the work that I do" and hoped that he could get to the point where he didn't have to be paid for it.

Bobby's beliefs have remained largely unchanged from those that motivated his activity in SDS, perhaps even from those he developed in elementary school. He still favored the redistribution of wealth and believed that the Marxist dictum relating ability to need, which had informed his thinking as a child, remained appropriate especially now "when greed replaces religion as a moral basis." His preferred solution to other social problems was similar to his support for universal health care. Seeing that Bobby had once been a member of the board of directors for the Bowery Residence Committee, which provided assistance for New York's skid row population, I asked what he favored as a response to homelessness. "Housing," he shot back, snickering at the foolishness of a question, the answer to which was so obvious. "It would be a social policy that sees the housing of everybody as critical—not building luxury housing, where two people live in a space that could satisfactorily house 20 for a tenth of the cost."

Given his views, naturally Bobby remained proud of his involvement in SDS, though, perhaps as a consequence of his experience treating prisoners, he now expressed outrage about one issue that no longer seemed that important to other interviewees. Mention of the CIA pressed an emotional button for Bobby because of the agency's recent implication in torture. "We torture people in secret prisons around the world," he said angrily, and then "we write memoranda defending torture by calling it 'not torture'"; television shows like *24* suggest that "it's a good thing to torture people if they're against you." The CIA was "really bad," he added, "a malign institution of the ruling class," and "they have their own private foreign policy, which they pull the United States into on a regular basis" in places like Vietnam, Cuba and Iraq.

Though he has devoted much of his life to helping others—often people detested by much of the society—Bobby hardly seemed the warm, fuzzy type; he is not Mother Teresa with an MD. Instead there was an intensity, an impatience, to his observations, suggesting a barely restrained outrage over the injustices that he has seen and that he has spent his life trying to remedy. But whatever the roots of his dedication, it was impossible not to be impressed by how useful his efforts have been.

9. The Organizer

Although Doug Seaton and Peter Kaminsky were the two most visible SDS members at public events, at least as important to SDS's functioning was Jimmy Tarlau—behind the scenes organizer, planner, strategist, and record-keeper. When *Time* did a story on "The Emergence of SDS" as a national political force, Jimmy was the person they quoted from the Princeton chapter.[1] Twice arrested for attempting to block entrance to IDA and twice disciplined by the university—once for interfering with a Marine Corps recruiter and once for his role in heckling Hickel—Jimmy was named "Biggest Revolutionary" in the class poll at the end of his senior year.

A short Jewish leftist from New York City, self-conscious about his tendency toward being overweight, Jimmy would probably not have been admitted to Princeton a few years earlier and, even during his time at the university, was no doubt considered "unclubbable" in more traditional quarters—though his bicker prospects could not have mattered less to him. He also had a touch of what linguists call "rhotacism"—from the Greek letter "rho"—an idiosyncratic pronunciation of the letter "r" that gave Jimmy the slightest hint of the Barbara Walters syndrome parodied by Gilda Radner on *Saturday Night Live*. Though radical activity dominated his life at Princeton probably more than for any other SDS member, Jimmy also had a wry sense of humor about his Marxism. A recognizable figure to local authorities, at one demonstration he was greeted by a policeman who asked, "Whadaya say, Jimmy?" "I say," Jimmy replied with a smile, "things are always progressing dialectically."[2]

I knew something about Jimmy's career before beginning this project. Sometime in the 1970s while at home channel surfing I heard a familiar voice talking about "wuhkuhs' issues" and immediately I knew that Jimmy had not given up the struggle—he was appearing on a panel as a representative of some labor organization in the Philadelphia area. A few years later, having become more active in the faculty union at Rutgers, I also learned that he was known in union circles in New Jersey for his work with the Communication Workers of America. I contacted Jimmy before conducting any interviews, and we arranged to meet in Atlantic City. Easily identifiable in his ubiquitous New York Yankees cap, Jimmy couldn't wait to pull out his Blackberry and, with obvious pride, show me photos, not of his family but of his most recent arrests: the police handcuffing him or taking him away after various protests. He had been arrested five times since turning 50.

A year later, in spring 2008, I took the train to Washington, D.C., to interview Jimmy, who lived just outside the district in Maryland. We sat down to talk in his kitchen but suspended the conversation a number of times so that he could rummage through file cabinets to retrieve letters from 35 or 40 years earlier explaining his radicalization or discussing issues from the time.

James Tarlau grew up in a religiously unobservant, German Jewish family on Manhattan's Upper West Side; a decade after he graduated from Princeton, another undergraduate from the same neighborhood named Elena Kagan wrote in the *Daily Princetonian* that it was an area where "nobody ever admitted to voting Republican."[3] His father was an attorney, whom Jimmy described as a "strong figure" with a "third degree stare" that he used to "break down witnesses," but that also made Jimmy's sisters dread to bring their boyfriends home. His mother was warmer, a teacher for 35 years in the New York City public school system. Though both his parents were Stevensonian Democrats, Jimmy had a "Red uncle"—Sidney Finkelstein—who was the music and cultural critic for the Communist Party as well as the author of *Jazz: A People's Music*, a classic book on the genre.

Jimmy attended Elizabeth Irwin High School in New York's Greenwich Village, the secondary school component of the "Little Red School House," famous for its left-wing politics; among other well known alumni, Angela Davis had graduated five years earlier.[4] Based on John Dewey's progressive principles, the school offered small classes for the academically talented, and Jimmy's graduating class numbered only 35 students. As early as the ninth grade, Jimmy was involved in politics, and by junior year, he stated, politics had become "100 percent of my life." His early involvement was motivated not by any specific issue but rather by a concern for "fairness"; it was about what he could do to make a difference, "to make things better"—a phrase Jimmy used half a dozen times in our three hours of conversation. Ironically, he was one of the most conservative persons at his high school, emphasizing the importance of "legitimate"—i.e., electoral—politics in contrast to the demonstrations and sit-ins favored by many of his peers; in the student newspaper he argued that such protests had "dubious" effects on decision makers and that the election of new people with different positions was the best way to change policy. Acting on his own advice, during his last two years of high school Jimmy did volunteer work for Upper West Side Democratic candidates for congress: William Fitz Ryan, one of the earliest house members to oppose the Vietnam War, and Ted Weiss, another avid supporter of liberal causes. Already a skilled organizer, by the time he graduated Jimmy had been elected president of the student body.

Princeton was a shock for Jimmy. He thought it "disgusting that so many resources were expended on so few people," and, accustomed to a coeducational environment, he found "the whole social thing horrendous." But most difficult, there was no Democratic organization of any strength; the only real political alternative to the left of the Young Republicans was SDS. For a time Jimmy considered dropping out of school and joining Vista—the national service program designed to fight poverty—but decided that the purpose of Vista was to make people "socially useful" to a system that he was beginning to reject.

By the end of his freshman year, Jimmy had moved closer to SDS, influenced in part by discussions with a student a year ahead of him whom he looked to as a political mentor: Doug Seaton, soon Jimmy's closest friend at Princeton and later to become the "lawyer for employers," helped to persuade him of the necessity for radical change rather than electoral reform. But even more of an impact on his thinking was the reality of Vietnam. Having idolized first JFK and the New Frontier, and then LBJ and the Great Society, Jimmy became disillusioned by what his heroes had wrought; as he observed in a letter to his old friends at Ted Weiss's office, "the most liberal administration in the history of the country is carrying out a war that can easily be described as genocidal." As it became clear to him that foreign and domestic policy, from Vietnam and Latin America to Harlem and Detroit, was "contrary to the interests of the rest of the world," he struggled with the question of what he personally should be doing. Anticipating a career in politics or public service, he had originally intended to study at the university's Woodrow Wilson School, which provided undergraduates the opportunity for an interdisciplinary major focused on public policy, but rejected that plan after concluding that the school was training students to become part of the "power structure." Preparing for one of the traditional helping professions—medicine, education, social work—might enable him to "do some little good" but not really "change anything important," especially when he felt "closer to rebelling black ghettoes and Guatemalan guerrillas than to American white liberals." As preposterous as Jimmy realized it might sound, "overthrowing the American power structure" seemed to him "the only rational conclusion." Indeed, not to be working for radical change, in his view, even if engaged in activities that helped people, made one an "accomplice" to the system's "crimes against humanity."

In this analysis Princeton was part of the problem—a ruling class institution that, as Jimmy and Doug noted in a letter to the school newspaper, acted as "a recruiting center for corporate executives, government bureaucrats, the CIA, and military officers" and was "deeply involved in weapons research."[5] If Jimmy was going to remain at the university, then his chief purpose would be to change it, and he made a conscious decision to dedicate his life as a student to organizing a movement that would "stop Princeton from supporting the war." His success at the task became one of Jimmy's greatest sources of pride, but in retrospect it came at a cost: his failure to "take advantage of the intellectual resources" at Princeton became a source of regret.

Although Jimmy was involved in all of SDS's activities, he played a particularly important role in the organization's most successful effort: the campaign against the university's affiliation with IDA. At an SDS national convention near the end of Jimmy's freshman year, a small group of people from around the country discussed the idea of a multi-university project opposing participation in IDA, an initiative that had special appeal at Princeton, the only university at which IDA had a physical presence. At the time Jimmy was still spending the summer in Washington as an intern for Congressman Ryan, and, knowing that Princeton SDS would be focusing on IDA in the fall, he used the position to gather as much information as possible, not just on IDA but on the many ways that universities had links to the Department of Defense. According to Jimmy, Ryan, who really liked his young intern, would "look the other way when I would ask DOD generals for a list of all the contracts that the Defense Department had with all these different universities."

Despite his importance as an organizer and planner, Jimmy had very little ego about his role, unconcerned that he rarely spoke at rallies; secure in the knowledge of his own significance, he did not need public attention for his contributions. Indeed, he commented, his influence behind the scenes at Princeton established a pattern of "playing second fiddle" that has persisted in his career in the labor movement, in which he has often performed work for which some higher union official received recognition.

As an SDS member, Jimmy considered himself a "radical" in the sense of the word's Latin origin; after years of liberal politics had failed to address the "root" of the society's problems, he concluded that the only real solution was a movement to bring about "participatory socialism." A revolution, he believed, was necessary to the extent that the state stood in the way of radical changes or defended its oppressive policies. Thus, when National Guardsmen were deployed in black neighborhoods after the assassination of Martin Luther King, Jr., Jimmy wrote to the *Daily Princetonian*, recommending that, to aid blacks, whites should raise money, for "medical aid, relief supplies, building materials and weapons. Guns must be sent to the black community for self-defense." Nor did he have reason to find this advice misguided when, on election day seven months later, he participated in a peaceful march in Newark and had to be treated for scalp lacerations and body blows after being clubbed to the ground by the police.[6]

Yet despite this goal, Jimmy nevertheless thought it essential to work for reform in order to engage liberals and suggest to them the necessity of a more radical vision. He has remained bitter about the internal conflicts in SDS because he believed that PL's inflexible rhetoric had alienated liberals, making it impossible to expand the movement beyond its narrow base. Jimmy "used to cry at night" because of what he perceived as attempts to "undermine" his efforts, and years later his feelings about PL still seemed raw; "I hated them; I did," he told me. It struck me as ironic that, although Jimmy eschewed PL's brand of Marxism, in contrast to so many other former radicals, he was one of the few who had gone on to lead a life that exemplified the party's insistence on organizing the working class as crucial to serious political change.

At the beginning of his senior year Jimmy became chair of Princeton SDS-RYM, though he relinquished the position at the end of the first semester when his mother was diagnosed with cancer. Nevertheless, he remained one of the most active members and participated in the "Heckle Hickel" incident, for which, along with Bobby Cohen and a third SDS member, he was forced to wait until the February after commencement to receive his degree in the mail. The delay caused no inconvenience, considering his plans for a career as a working class organizer. As Jimmy dryly observed, he had chosen "one of the few occupations where having a Princeton degree doesn't help."[7]

Immediately after leaving Princeton Jimmy moved to Philadelphia, where he became part of a collective composed of friends from high school or college; originally located in the Powelton Village neighborhood—then a drawing point for countercultural types—the group soon moved to Kensington, a white working class neighborhood, where Bobby Cohen would later join it. The idea was to combine a communal living arrangement, which would allow the inhabitants to change their personal lives, with an attempt to build a radical labor movement. However, as it turned out, some people were more interested in the former, and others—traditional leftists like Jimmy—more in the latter. While the collective launched a number of projects—a food co-op, a community newspaper—there were regular conflicts with the neighborhood youth. In Jimmy's opinion the collective was "too in-your-face in this community," and it soon disbanded, Jimmy and some of its members forming a new, more straightforwardly political organization: the Philadelphia Workers Organizing Committee. Led by Clay Newlin, a young labor organizer and member of the Communist Party, PWOC was composed of people focused on trade union work.[8]

Jimmy was arrested a number of times during this period, all of them on trumped up charges that were later dismissed. It was the Rizzo era in Philadelphia; Frank Rizzo, the city's police commissioner and soon to become its Mayor, was known for the strong-arm tactics that eventually led a United States District Court to charge him with a pattern of committing or condoning police brutality. In one case the police searched Jimmy's house and claimed to have found a package of heroin under the rug, a ludicrous charge to anyone who knew him. In another instance Jimmy was watching a rally for Rizzo when a fight broke out, and though he had nothing to do with the altercation, he was pointed out as one of the "anti–Rizzo" persons in the crowd, leading to charges of conspiracy to riot.

Although Jimmy first worked as a cab driver in a "ritzy" section of Philadelphia, taking "little old ladies to get their groceries," his goal was to get a job in a factory. He soon found a minimum wage position in an electrical factory making refrigerators, but in order to be taken seriously by other blue collar workers, he had to have skills of a sort unlikely to have been acquired at an Ivy League institution. As a consequence, the Princeton graduate enrolled in a technical school and learned how to run various kinds of machine equipment, including a turret lathe and a drill, which led to a position in a General Electric tool and dye apprenticeship program. It was Jimmy's first real factory experience, and he felt he did "effective political work," recruiting a number of fellow workers to become active in the movement and, along with Clay Newlin, putting out a rank and file newspaper. Eventually, however, the apprenticeship program was eliminated and Jimmy was laid off.

It was around this time—late 1971—that Jimmy himself joined the Communist Party, attracted by its membership in Philadelphia. Up to this point all the political groups with which he had been involved—Princeton SDS, the collective in Kensington, and most of the New Left—had consisted of young, white middle class types. In contrast, the local CP was a genuinely integrated organization, with a number of African-Americans active in its leadership. In addition, he saw that people in the party, many of them adults with children, "were serious about trying to make this a life"; this was not the student movement, consisting of temporary radicals devoting a couple of years to activism before becoming a doctor or lawyer. Moreover, although the CP had "missed the excitement of the outburst of youth in the 60s," he was impressed by the fact that the party had more working people than were ever involved in the New Left. Finally, and particularly important to Jimmy's decision, was his view of the CP's larger importance, despite the taint of its historical association with the Soviet Union. In order to build an effective movement, he reasoned, it wasn't realistic to expect that he would agree with every one of the party's positions or everything it had done in the past; if someone left the party every time there was disagreement, it would never be possible to achieve any substantial political change. He wasn't joining the CP because of something that had or hadn't happened in the Soviet Union—he had never been to Russia and could care less about such issues. What mattered to Jimmy was that "if you look at what the CP actually stood for in America, if you look at American labor history, if you look at American domestic politics, the party had always been the most principled people who have led a lot of the social movements."

Even though Jimmy's politics did not change when he joined the party, he quickly lost half his friends, who were horrified by the decision. And, as he learned years later, the FBI suddenly took a much greater interest in his activities. Of course, as an active SDS member, he already had an FBI file, and his father, whom he described as "a very careful and very ethical man," suddenly found his tax return audited—an action that Jimmy thought attributable to his anti-war activity. But as a CP member, his FBI file "jumped up tenfold" from its level when he was a radical activist with the exact same opinions.

Jimmy's account of his experience in the CP was a reminder of how much its influence had diminished since its pre-war heyday, when—as detailed in Vivian Gornick's wonderful book *The Romance of American Communism*[9]—whether or not they agreed, people were eager to hear the party's analysis, and members were so attached to the party that their departure, whether voluntary or enforced because of some doctrinal violation, could have an emotional impact similar to the end of a lengthy marriage. Jimmy's attitude toward the party, however, could not have been more casual. Sometimes "I was very active," he told me, but "there were other times when the party didn't mean anything." He went to meetings but "took it all with a grain of salt." The party was often inconsistent, one day telling members to raise some issue with co-workers, the next day asking them to switch to a different issue, but it didn't matter to Jimmy, who ignored the party in both cases. Besides, sometimes the party decided that members should take what he considered foolish positions, opposing, for example, the Equal Rights Amendment on the grounds that it might result in the elimination of worker protections for women and children. In such cases, he just disregarded the party line entirely—no one cared what the CP thought about the ERA—and, in any event, it was irrelevant to factory organizing. Although he believed in "talking over issues with others" in the party, when it came to his own work, Jimmy insisted, "I knew more about my job and how to organize and what to do politically than almost any of the others." Nevertheless, he remained in the party for almost two decades, because he felt that leaving would only "make it smaller and more insulated." In 1990, however, he was expelled, together with a number of other trade unionists, because of their support for a more moderate democratic socialist orientation in the wake of the changes in the Soviet Union; as he put it, he was only trying "to have people come to their senses." Jimmy was hardly displeased; "the party had become absurd," he declared.

As he became more active in various unions, a major concern for Jimmy was how much he should say to fellow workers about his politics and his membership in the CP. When the GE apprenticeship program was terminated, he found a position as a mechanic at Strick Trailer, a truck factory in Levittown, where he was involved in the UAW—the United Auto Workers. He quickly realized that "you couldn't really talk to anybody about politics before you actually knew how to do your job"; there was a lot of teamwork at the factory, and "if you couldn't do your job, no one is going to respect you." At first, by his own admission Jimmy was very clumsy, and it took him a year to get the job "down pat," but after doing so, he could talk to others about politics, and they would listen. The question was what to bring up. The easiest topic, of course, was wages and working conditions, but broadening the conversation to, say, war or racism was more difficult, demanding a sensitivity to how open a particular individual was likely to be to Jimmy's politics. It was a slow process, and he had "no illusions about how difficult it would be to build a radical movement among the white working class."

Moreover, Jimmy had to decide at what point he would acknowledge to other workers, "yes, I am a Communist, I am a radical"—a necessary admission, in his opinion, "or else people will never understand why that isn't such a bad thing." To hide the affiliation only to have it revealed by the FBI would make him completely isolated. "You have to have a bunch of people in this country," he emphasized, who say "'I am a socialist and that is a good thing, not a bad thing.'" At the truck factory, he actually reached that point; some of his friends from the party were also hired, and they formed a communist club in the factory that had regular meetings attended by some of the workers with whom he had been talking.

At the end of 1974 the truck factory closed, and Jimmy became involved in a campaign to organize the unemployed, participating in the formation of the Committee for Full Employment, which worked to increase unemployment coverage and to create jobs programs; he was appearing as a representative of this committee when I saw him on television. One of his most satisfying political experiences, the campaign produced a bill of rights for the unemployed and provided assistance to people who had been denied benefits. Years later Jimmy was gratified to learn that his efforts had favorable results he didn't realize at the time. Recently a state legislator, who had once chaired the Pennsylvania House Labor Relations Committee, contacted him on Facebook, explaining that his meeting with Jimmy three decades earlier had caused a change in his political views, making him more sympathetic to labor; it was after listening to Jimmy that this legislator had sponsored a bill mandating that companies planning to close their doors give workers six months notification.

Although in practice he had already performed as an organizer—for example, helping Philadelphia's Community Legal Services employees to join local 1199, the Healthcare Workers' Union—Jimmy finally assumed an official position as a union representative in 1977, when he moved to Roanoke, Virginia, to work for the International Ladies Garment Workers Union. However, he was not fond of the way the ILGWU relied so heavily on their attorneys, and soon went to the United Furniture Workers in Richmond, a small union attempting to organize a huge unorganized industry. As a result, he was sent willy-nilly to wherever it seemed there was "a hot campaign" at the moment—one month in Tennessee, the next in California. While he counted it as one of his most significant organizing experiences, he felt that it was hardly the way to build a union movement, an objective about which Jimmy was beginning to develop his own philosophy quite different from the usual approach.

After a couple of years with the furniture workers, during which time he was married and had his first child, Jimmy moved to Detroit, where his wife found a job with the United Auto Workers, while he remained at home tending to child care. At the same time he completed the Master's degree in Labor Relations that he had been pursuing and began work on a second Master's degree—this one in computer science; it was the early 1980s, but Jimmy had already recognized the potential for computer technology to facilitate union work and was soon traveling around the country teaching organizers how to use databases, leaflet writing software, and electronic methods of communication.

Returning to the Philadelphia area in 1983, Jimmy took a position with the Communication Workers of America, the union for which he has worked ever since. His first CWA assignment required him to organize the highway transportation engineers and computer programmers, a technologically oriented group not known to be sympathetic to the union movement. Nevertheless, he was able to increase membership from 30 to 70 percent, aided in part by his computer science degree, which helped him relate to the engineers, but also because he was learning how to connect union activity to the specific needs of that sector of the workforce that has since become his field of specialization: middle-class, college educated white collar workers with scientific or technical expertise, who, along with more typical union issues, were also likely to be interested in H1B visas, pension benefits and infrastructure improvements. Jimmy viewed such workers as the new "face of the working class"—a group of people who generally did not see themselves as part of a union but who had the same kind of relationships with their employers as more conventional union members. Organizing these non-traditional groups, he believed, was the "key challenge" for the union movement, and Jimmy had some non-traditional ideas about how to do it.

Jimmy's approach originated in his experience with the furniture workers, where he found interest in the union but not sufficient to reach the 50 percent mark legally necessary to achieve formal recognition and thus the right to collective bargaining. This requirement was not the case in many other countries, but in the United States it meant that the labor movement had to write off lots of factories and workplaces. His plan was to identify those people at a workplace interested in a union, whether or not their numbers were sufficient to warrant formal representation, and have them join a different kind of union—one that might not be recognized by the National Labor Relations Board as having the legal authority to negotiate a contract but that nevertheless could be an effective force, able to achieve improvements by exerting pressure on employers in various non-contractual ways. After all, Jimmy pointed out, the famous IWW—the Industrial Workers of the World, once the most powerful union in the country—never signed a contract with an employer. Instead of the present 12 percent of the labor force currently in a union, he expected that this approach would attract the 25 percent that were interested but lacked the opportunity to join under the present requirement for representation.

Eventually Jimmy was placed in charge of High Tech Organizing for CWA, a position that allowed him to put his philosophy into practice. Applied to the information technology sector, this model for re-energizing the union movement has been termed "Open-Source Unionism" (OSU), the name derived from open source computer programming, a philosophy promoting free and open access to a program's source code. In an article in a labor studies journal, Jimmy explained the concept, describing how his own OSU–type attempts at organizing had worked with some of CWA's affiliates, none of which enjoyed collective bargaining rights. At IBM, for example, a nationwide local with seven chapters was formed following protests against the company's attempt to slash pension benefits. Although the union did not bargain with IBM, it utilized non-traditional tactics, such as packing shareholder meetings, where union members enjoyed the right to speak because they owned stock. With some amusement Jimmy recounted to me how workers from IBM made speeches in front of other shareholders attacking the company's policies and calling the CEO a jerk, while he had no choice but to sit there and make faces. In another non-traditional approach reminiscent of the CIO's industry-wide organizing in the 1930s, WashTech—the Washington Alliance of Technical Workers—employed a geographical model, attempting to organize all IT personnel in the state of Washington, whether they worked for Amazon, Microsoft, an Internet service provider, or some other high tech company, or even if they were self-employed or unemployed; members were primarily interested in such less typical union issues as outsourcing, opportunities for training, and the practices of temp agencies. All of these non-traditional approaches to unionization allowed for two levels of membership: dues payers who voted on internal issues and non–dues-paying subscribers, who received information from the union but did not vote.[10]

As the hi-tech industry has become more of a global enterprise, these new and different types of unions that Jimmy helped to spawn have become international in scope. At the time of the interview, he had just been involved in the formation of TU, an international union representing T-Mobile workers in the United States, affiliated with both CWA and the two million strong German union, Ver.di—Vereinte Dienstleistungsgewerkschaft—the "United Services Union." Now known for his role in developing innovative approaches to unionization, Jimmy himself has spoken to German audiences on organizing in the IT sector.[11]

While Jimmy's accomplishments in the union movement were impressive, I wondered about their relation to his larger political goals for a radical transformation of the society. There was a time, he replied, when he believed that "labor was the key agent for social change and that it would be in the lead," but had now developed doubts about such a possibility. He still regarded unions as progressive—more so than in the 1960s—and reeled off the names of current leaders of major unions whom he described as "Ivy League progressives." But unions were not large enough to be effective by themselves, he acknowledged, and in the larger movement for social change, he viewed them as one component in a coalition with other, often overlapping organizations; black activists and church leaders, for example, might also be union members.

In 2000, Jimmy took a position in CWA's national office in Washington, D.C., and a few years later he and his wife bought a house in nearby Mt. Rainier, Maryland, a small town with a reputation as a progressive, multi-ethnic community. He quickly became involved with local issues and ran for a seat on city council, motivated in part by the council's attempt to abolish collective bargaining with its police union; elected to office, for the first time he now held an official position, allowing him to put some of his beliefs into practice. He set out right away to pressure for greater transparency. The problem, as Jimmy saw it, was that "a lot of people think they're big shots, and they think everything is hush-hush, and they're super important" even though, in his opinion, "most of the stuff that they talk about in closed meetings can be talked about in open meetings." Whatever substantive improvements he might or might not be able to make, Jimmy felt he could "at least tell people what's going on in council." In addition to seeking more open meetings, he went door-to-door in his ward, collecting hundreds of e-mail addresses, and began sending out regular reports containing descriptions of the council's discussions, information for residents, explanations of his own position on issues before the council, and requests for feedback, including the infrastructure projects people would like the city to undertake.[12] He also worked to have the city's newsletter published in a Spanish edition and arranged for one of the council meetings to be held at a senior citizens facility, allowing people to attend who would have difficulty traveling to city hall. Much to his dismay, however, Jimmy found himself "completely ostracized on council" and "hated" by the other members, who thought that he was "showing them up," though it was of some consolation that these actions made him well liked in town. He was also popular with constituents for donating his $4,000 annual salary as a member of city council back to community groups, such as an organization that provided music and dance programs for children; "I've become the Bill Gates of our town," he said proudly.

The most controversial issue to have arisen in the council when we spoke was a proposal to make Mt. Rainier a "sanctuary city." Citing the community's tradition of welcoming people of diverse ethnic backgrounds, the proposed ordinance prohibited anyone associated with the city—police officer, city official, employee, or contractor—from inquiring into the citizenship or immigration status of any person, providing such information to federal agencies, or discriminating against anyone on the basis of such status. I thought that the ordinance might have posed a problem for Jimmy because he supported the non-discriminatory principle on which it was based but had also pledged that he would not vote for a resolution opposed by a substantial portion of the people he represented—the classic conflict between egalitarian belief and a commitment to respect the people's will. When it turned out that public opinion was sharply divided, Jimmy decided that it left him free to vote his conscience, but the issue became moot when the resolution was tabled.[13]

While Jimmy has become more "practical" about what it was possible to accomplish, his "core political beliefs" have changed little since the 1960s, a moment during which "a crack in the system" provided him a "visionary glimpse" of the possibility of a different kind of society, an alternative to American capitalism. He still believed in socialism—in "people working cooperatively" rather than the "competitive system" of capitalism—and wanted to make a difference, whether it's "how to give back to the town we love" or how "to make this country a better place." He harbored no illusions about the difficulty of radical change, given that "we are not in a revolutionary period." "We live in the belly of the beast," Jimmy observed—a phrase attributed to Che Guevara referring to the United States as the major source of imperialism—and "people who live in the dominant country in the world are going to feel basically supportive of what the country is doing." Jimmy, however, "really hate[d] the kind of patriotism we have in the United States" and referred to himself as "emotionally anti–American"; "in many ways I dislike what this country stands for," he admitted. Even during the Olympics he refused to join in the jingoistic support for the United States because, in Jimmy's experience, winning tended to "bring out more pride and more conservative values," while after a loss people were "more interested in discussions about change,"

Though Jimmy's goals have remained the same, the means have become considerably more moderate, emphasizing more conventional methods for creating change. Indeed, one of his many arrests occurred when, as president of the New Jersey AFL-CIO, he was part of a union effort to register potential voters in front of the Trenton baseball stadium, where the minor league Thunder play their home games; the Republicans in charge of the county government wouldn't allow voter registration to take place there, but the stadium was a publicly funded venue, and the charge was quickly dismissed. Eventually, however, Jimmy decided that he was spending too much time supporting Democratic candidates. One of the lessons he had gleaned from the 60s was the importance of building a grass roots movement rather than supporting a specific politician. From this perspective the focus of union political efforts should be not to get candidates elected but to apply pressure on them once in office to enact progressive measures, such as a reformed tax structure. Besides, there have been few mainstream political figures that Jimmy has found appealing. What he really wanted was to build a political movement strong enough to make a third party a viable alternative.

Whether the context was global, local or personal, Jimmy was still driven by the concern for fairness that had informed his involvement in politics while in high school. "It's something basic with me, it's what I'm all about," he emphasized, "what's fair and helping people." What made him so "anti-patriotic" was his perception that the United States had *not* treated other people fairly. And when faced with a situation he considered unfair, he did not hesitate to go to great lengths to protest. In addition to his arrests for political activities, Jimmy was also once arrested for what he called "bank rage." In 1989, along with two other graduates he founded Princeton Progressive Alumni/ae to provide financial support for present Princeton students involved in progressive causes. As custodian of the organization's money, one morning Jimmy went to the bank holding its checking account and, noticing the signs for "free checking," asked the bank manager to retract the service charges that had already been deducted from the account. Upon having his request refused, he went home, printed out some fliers warning that the bank didn't live up to its promises, and returned to pass them out at the strip mall where the bank was located. The manager called the police, who told Jimmy that he couldn't distribute the fliers and that he would have to move; while he was prepared to comply with the former, he was adamant about not leaving, only to find himself in a police car being taken away for "disobeying an order"—an arrest for which he later received an apology from the town. Jimmy's response might have seemed disproportionate to the bank's offense, but he saw the refusal as a matter of fairness, and felt compelled "to do something about it."

Though not easy, Jimmy has maintained his relationship with Doug Seaton, his closest friend from the 1960s, the prominent Minneapolis Republican who now held seminars on how to defeat unions. Although Doug sent Jimmy a lengthy, heartfelt explanation of the reasons for his political metamorphosis, Jimmy has had difficulty coming to terms with "how he could change all his previous views"; it has been more difficult for Jimmy to accept Doug's transition than for Doug to accept Jimmy's resolve. They have remained good friends by avoiding all discussion of what Jimmy called "core issues."

More than any other interviewee, the course of Jimmy's life was changed by his involvement in the movement. "If I had gone to Princeton five years earlier or five years later," he reflected—in both a justification for what was and a poignant lament for what might have been—"I'd have had a completely different path in my life.... I'd still have been involved in politics but it would have been a different kind of politics." If not elected to office himself, Jimmy was certain he would have been a staffer for some congressperson or senator, or part of the Carter or Clinton administrations—not an unrealistic expectation, given his experience working for William Fitz Ryan as a high school student; "I would have been one of those guys in West Wing," he predicted, and "part of me misses the fact that I didn't get that kind of prestige; I sometimes wonder whether I could have been a big shot. On the other hand, when I look in the mirror and say, 'How do you actually change this country?' That's not how you change the country.... Basically, it's union organizations that elect progressive candidates and also push candidates to take better positions." Rather than being one of those "big shots," Jimmy preferred "building a movement" to ensure that such people "do the right thing." "It's a much harder task," he acknowledged, but "it has been quite fulfilling."[14]

Five years after our interview Jimmy decided to seek the Democratic nomination for the Maryland House of Delegates, emphasizing such issues as tax reform, increased state aid to education, a minimum wage of $15 per hour and a "blue-green alliance" between labor and environmentalists; with a lengthy list of endorsers, including his Congresswoman, the state's lieutenant governor, the Sierra Club, a number of local mayors, NARAL, the AFL-CIO, the Maryland Chapter of NOW, and the *Washington Post*, he finished first in a field of five and easily won the general election in his heavily Democratic district. Upon becoming the nominee, he immediately began to approach other state legislators in an attempt to create a progressive caucus. It may not be too late for Jimmy to combine political office with grassroots organizing.

10. Counteracting
the U.S. Role

In fall 1969, the first semester after the split in SDS, Neal Koblitz, a new graduate student in mathematics, joined the WSA caucus at Princeton. Neal had been an active member of SDS as an undergraduate at Harvard and a participant in the spring 1969 building occupation and subsequent strike; one of his last acts before leaving Cambridge was to co-edit a polished 27-page booklet, explaining the issues and the ideology behind the strike. At Harvard, too, SDS had launched a campaign seeking to eliminate ROTC from campus as a way to help end what the booklet called the "daily Guernicas" taking place in Vietnam. At Princeton Neal quickly became one of the most active members of SDS-WSA, leading its initiatives to establish connections with campus workers—especially the predominantly black, poorly paid janitorial staff—and to support striking General Electric workers in Trenton.[1]

Other SDS members viewed Neal as a prodigy. Being accepted for graduate work in mathematics at Princeton might have been reason enough for such high regard; one of the best math departments in the world, eight faculty members have won the Fields Medal—the math world's version of the Nobel Prize—and such luminaries as Albert Einstein and John von Neumann from the nearby Institute for Advanced Study, had also enjoyed offices in the department. But in addition, Neal's youth made him seem that much more of a wunderkind; only 20 when he began graduate work, he looked even younger, with a touch of chubby cheeks suggesting that he was barely post-pubescent. Yet despite his brilliance—or perhaps because of it—Neal could seem a little on the nerdy side, especially in comparison to hip activists like Peter Kaminsky. Although he had come of age in the generation of sex, drugs, and rock and roll, Neal candidly acknowledged that as an undergraduate he had little experience with the first two, and he acquired an interest in the third only late in his senior year.

It was simple to find Neal, now a professor of mathematics at the University of Washington. Not only was he famous within his field as a prolific scholar, but he had recently published a 375-page autobiography, a charmingly self-deprecating work that missed no opportunity to emphasize instances in which, compared to himself, his wife was more insightful or perceptive.[2] As a result, I knew more about Neal beforehand than I did about any of the other interviewees; the following profile is based on both the interview and the autobiography.

Having arranged to meet with Neal immediately after interviewing Gordon Chang, I flew directly from San Francisco to Seattle. As a native New Yorker, who had always viewed Gotham as America's ultimate international city, I suddenly felt embarrassingly provincial upon hearing the public address announcements at Sea-Tac Airport broadcast in English and Japanese, and finding the handbill on the public transportation system available in English and six foreign languages. Neal picked me up from my motel the next morning, driving a beat up and cluttered vehicle that could have passed for a four-door suitcase; he still looked younger than his age, but the chubby-faced graduate student had been replaced by someone with the lean, fit appearance of the serious runner that he later became. We drove to his house, a small immaculately kept structure in a modest neighborhood near the top of a steep hill overlooking the city, where we were joined by Neal's wife, Ann Hibner Koblitz, a professor in the Women's Studies Program at Arizona State University, specializing in the history of science; as an equal participant in many of his activities, during the interview she interjected occasional clarifications or additions.

———⊗⊗⊗———

Neal Koblitz was raised by well-educated parents. A World War II veteran who then earned a doctorate at Harvard, his father was a professor of political science at Bard College, a small, liberal arts school 90 miles north of New York City. Neal's maternal grandfather had been a union activist and member of the Communist Party, who took his 11-year-old daughter with him to the picket lines at a time when police were clubbing strikers, and later insisted that she attend college—a decision viewed in the early 1940s as "crazy" by his neighbors. Neal's mother became an elementary school teacher, active in the leadership of the National Education Association, the nation's largest teachers' union, and particularly involved with the organization's annual Human Rights Award; she also served on a committee that took a strong position against standardized testing in the 1970s, concerned that overreliance on the tests was unfair to minorities.

Neal characterized his parents' politics as "the left end of liberalism." Strong believers in civil liberties, they were unsympathetic to both communism and anti-communism, opposing McCarthyism and the Red scare of the 1950s. He was well aware of their opinions at an early age, if only because leftist entertainers were an important part of their cultural life. During his youth the family attended Pete Seeger concerts and listened to Paul Robeson records.

When Neal was six, his father was awarded a Fulbright fellowship to teach government at the University of Baroda in India, and his experience during the year abroad, even at such a young age, began pointing him toward a career in mathematics. Though the family was Jewish, Neal was enrolled in a Catholic school—the only opportunity to be taught in English—where he was exposed to a math curriculum far advanced in comparison to instruction in the United States. When, upon his return, the teacher at his public school saw the level at which he was doing arithmetic, he was immediately assigned a fifth-grade textbook, though not yet eight years old. According to Neal, the teacher erroneously believed that he had a "special gift," and her belief then became a self-fulfilling prophecy when he received encouragement and additional instruction not offered to others. Nor was this notion false modesty on Neal's part; 99 percent of mathematicians, he insisted, were "doing things that basically anybody could do, given an appropriate upbringing, environment, and opportunities." Neal also credited the year in India for the beginning of his progressive politics. At six years old he became "acutely conscious of the horrible injustice of poverty," as everywhere he went, he saw children begging in the streets—a memory that became even more disturbing to him when, shortly after returning to the United States, his family moved to the affluent community of Scarsdale.

Two grades ahead of others his age, Neal was nicknamed "Baby Univac" by classmates in his Scarsdale public school—a reference to the first American commercial computer. Studying calculus on his own, he soon knew more math than his high school teachers and was referred to Mark Kac, a brilliant mathematician, who had taught at Cornell and Rockefeller University. After seeing Neal solve a series of calculus problems that had proved too difficult for all but the very best Cornell students, Kac became his tutor and mentor. When Neal applied to colleges, Kac wrote letters of support to friends in the math departments at Harvard, Princeton, and Cornell; accepted at all three schools, Neal chose Harvard.

Before he headed off to Cambridge, Neal and his family spent the summer in Ithaca, New York, so that his father could attend a workshop on Southeast Asia taught by George Kahin and John Lewis, specialists in the topic at Cornell. Neal's father brought home an article by the two scholars, arguing that Vietnam was a single nation and that "South Vietnam" was an artificial creation dependent on American support for its existence. Although Neal now concluded that the communists in Vietnam *should* win, at the time he still considered radical activists ineffectual, believing that the way to change policy was to vote for "the lesser of the evils." Even as late as 1968—the election termed "a hoax" by many SDS members—he thought it "foolish and irrational" not to support Hubert Humphrey against Richard Nixon.

During the summer after his freshman year at Harvard, Neal traveled to Mississippi to work for Martin Luther King, Jr.'s Southern Christian Leadership Conference as a voter-registration volunteer. Originally intending to stay for several weeks, he left after only 12 days feeling utterly useless. The leaders of SCLC made a fuss over the fact that a volunteer had come from Harvard and treated Neal, he wrote to a friend at the time, "as if I had some mystical power which could help them." SCLC brought him to Birmingham to meet with a group of professionals involved in constructing a black-owned business, but he had nothing to contribute to their efforts. Even more awkward, when everyone else gathered for the nightly parade, clapping and dancing around the town square, the socially inhibited Neal couldn't bring himself to join in, feeling "like a fish out of water"; "I never danced," he said matter-of-factly.

Apart from math, Neal's other academic interest at Harvard was Russian language and literature. Realizing that some of the best mathematicians in the world were located in the Soviet Union, in his freshman year in high school he had begun to study Russian with the idea that he would then "have a unique role to play." There might be people who were better mathematicians than himself and people who were more familiar with the Russian language and culture, but "there would be very few Americans who were in both categories"; at age thirteen, he had already envisioned himself "as some sort of future mathematical ambassador who would help bridge the gap caused by the Cold War." Always a disciplined student, Neal immersed himself in Russian, not only taking courses in the language in high school, but buying recordings of excerpts from classic writers—Gogol, Tolstoy, Chekhov, Pasternak—read aloud by native speakers, which he would listen to dozens of times until he could repeat them from memory. Though at Harvard he never took a course in the language for credit, he sat in on Russian conversation sections conducted by émigrés. During the summer after his junior year, Neal learned that the American Mathematical Society had embarked on a project to translate Soviet journals into English and were paying $6 a page. Now fluent in

Russian, he earned $8,000 in three months ($53,000 adjusted for inflation), which he used to travel to Leningrad and Moscow, where he made contact with well-known mathematicians and spent time with math students. Amazed at the incredible concentration of talent, he experienced something of a shock at finding that, though being "one of the five or six best math majors in my year at Harvard," in the Soviet Union, "I was out of my league."

Not until the spring semester of his senior year did Neal become active in SDS. Before that time his most radical act had been to reject membership in Phi Beta Kappa on the grounds that the honor society promoted "an unjustified attitude of superiority and condescension"; after being congratulated by many other students for his refusal, Neal had hoped to organize a mass resignation but became disillusioned when not even the people who had praised his act wished to emulate it. Though opposed to the war and increasingly horrified by the atrocities in Vietnam, he was put off by SDS's anti-imperialist rhetoric; when the radicals tried to interest him in their literature, Neal responded that he was more likely to sympathize with their cause if he did *not* read any of their pamphlets. What finally persuaded him to join them was a sense that the movement might actually have an effect. In his view, to be an activist it was necessary not just to have a set of beliefs, but "also to have confidence that something can happen"—a conclusion he reached just in time to participate in the building occupation at Harvard. Gassed by the police he was dragged into a paddy wagon and taken off to jail along with almost 200 other occupiers.

Neal soon went from ridiculing the radicals' leaflets to writing them. Believing that the American action in Vietnam was "a Holocaust so disgusting that virtually anything would have been justified to put a stop to it," he was drawn to the PL/WSA faction of SDS, which had shown itself to be "hardnosed, practical, effective, determined, militant, and radical"—the group most likely to "shake things up." As a member of the WSA caucus, his experience on a picket line in support for striking workers was particularly influential in persuading him to accept PL's views. The company attempted to get scabs into the factory, escorted by 100 police, who pushed aside the striking workers and were accompanying the replacements toward the gates until 500 more workers converged on the scab convoy. The police took one look and immediately retreated; no one was arrested, and the scabs were prevented from entering. No amount of PL "rhetoric about the 'power of the working class' could have had the effect of that visit to the strike lines," Neal later wrote, especially in contrast to what he had witnessed two months earlier when students at Harvard had been beaten by the police and arrested.

When Neal began graduate work, he was not yet a member of PL, though attracted to the party by its commitment to represent the "downtrodden"— the type of people that he had seen "impoverished in India" and "who were fighting against the United States in Vietnam." His imminent induction into the army finally became the impetus for Neal to join. In agreement with PL that activists should allow themselves to be drafted in order to organize other servicemen against the war, he had not sought a deferment of any kind nor considered going to Canada, which had been his earlier plan. Now facing "the pressures of being a political activist in the Army," he felt that, to have any chance of success organizing other soldiers, he "needed the guidance and discipline" that the party could provide.

Fearing that college graduates would be given desk jobs isolating them from rank and file GIs, PL encouraged its members to extend their military commitment from two years to three, thus allowing them to choose the sort of military specialty for which they would be trained. Even though he had not yet learned to drive a car, and had no idea "what the various things under the hood were for," Neal, a skilled test-taker, nevertheless scored high enough on the auto mechanics portion of the army's test battery to qualify for his first choice of training: helicopter repair. However, he was quickly thrown out of the program by a lieutenant who would not trust a helicopter repaired "by an anti–American agitator," and shortly thereafter was arrested and court-martialed on several counts of "unauthorized distribution of publications"; Neal had been observed handing out PL literature to other soldiers—pamphlets with subtle titles like "Smash the Bosses' Armed Forces." Following PL's principles, he and a co-defendant—another party member—attempted to organize around the trial, circulating leaflets calling for supporters to attend. When hardly anyone aside from a couple of family members showed up, however, there was no receptive audience for the unapologetic political statements they offered the court in place of any legal defense, and the two men were sentenced to six months in the stockade.

Undaunted, Neal set out to organize other prisoners. As I knew from my own experience as stockade cadre while a military policeman, the overwhelming majority of soldiers confined to the stockade have committed offenses that led to incarceration only in the army; civilians who do not show up for work or disobey the boss's orders get fired, not imprisoned. Besides, upon completion of their sentences, such soldiers, typically guilty of no more than immaturity, were returned to their units to complete their military commitments. However, instead of organizing these prisoners, Neal found himself attacked by them because of his political activity, and he was placed into solitary confinement, followed by transfer to a different facility, where most prisoners were going to be discharged rather than returned to duty. Neal himself was soon released, the recipient of an oxymoronic "less than honorable" discharge "under honorable conditions"; at an appeal five years later the discharge was upgraded to fully honorable.

Immediately upon leaving the military, Neal resigned from PL, having been a member for less than a year. It was not that his political opinions had changed, nor did he have any major disagreements with the party. Rather the reason for departure was his sense that he had failed as a radical, a conclusion reinforced by the knowledge that other party members in the military had led protests and demonstrations. Neal's analysis of his decision seemed fittingly quasi-mathematical, essentially a syllogism whose premises produced an ineluctable conclusion: To be a member of a revolutionary communist party, one must be an effective organizer. I was a failure as an organizer. Therefore I should not be a member of a revolutionary communist party.

However, leaving the party did not mean leaving political activity. Upon his return to graduate study at Princeton, SDS had dwindled as a political force, but Neal, along with his girlfriend Ann—soon to become his wife—and a few holdovers from the WSA caucus, remounted some of the organization's campaigns, and for the first time in more than a year the university again experienced antiwar protests. When the trustees scheduled a closed meeting to discuss reinstituting the ROTC program, this new activist group blocked the entrance to Nassau Hall, and when a subsequent meeting was called for the same purpose, the group occupied the building beforehand. They also disrupted an invited talk by the chairman of the Joint Chiefs of Staff on the grounds that he was a war criminal, having authorized the bombing of North Vietnam; Neal was particularly proud of this action because a film crew had accompanied the visit, intending, he believed, to depict the appearance of the chairman at Princeton without protest as an indication that the antiwar movement was now dormant. Finally, in response to Nixon's escalation of the bombing and his mining of Haiphong Harbor, the group organized a blockade of IDA for four days, resulting in the arrest of almost 200 protesters; 10 faculty members joined the blockade and were also arrested. Convicted on a "disorderly persons" charge, more than 30 of the students, largely at Neal's urging and including Neal and Ann, declined to pay the $100 fine, opting for the alternative of 10 days in jail.

One other political activity had nothing to do with the war but eventually led to dramatic consequences in the academic world. In March 1972, Richard Herrnstein, a professor of psychology at Harvard, had been scheduled by Princeton's department to give a colloquium on his field of expertise: vision in pigeons. The previous fall Herrnstein had published a controversial article in *Atlantic Monthly*, arguing that the United States was on the way to becoming a hereditary meritocracy, in which the genetically most intelligent would enjoy financial success and social standing, while, at the other end of the IQ spectrum, unemployment would "run in the genes of a family about as certainly as bad teeth"; almost a quarter century later this thesis, elaborated at length, became the core of his book *The Bell Curve*.[3] Although they promised that Herrnstein would be able to give his talk unimpeded, Neal and his co-activists announced their intention to press him about the *Atlantic* article in the question and answer period following the colloquium, causing Herrnstein to cancel his appearance. In place of the scheduled event, the Princeton psychology department held an open forum on academic freedom, at which Neal challenged the department chair, Leon Kamin, to see what his disciplinary colleague had written in the name of their science. Acknowledging that Neal had a point, Kamin began the process of looking at the studies cited by Herrnstein, which led him to discover the flaws in British psychologist Cyril Burt's famous study of separated twins, widely regarded as the most important evidence for the heritability of intelligence; though first resistant to Kamin's criticisms, not only were other researchers in the field soon persuaded, but eventually evidence mounted that Burt had committed outright fraud, having invented his subjects' IQ scores—a conclusion stemming directly from Neal's challenge. Coincidentally, my own writing on the discovery of Burt's misbehavior described how Kamin had become involved at the prodding of a graduate student, though not until the interview did I know that Neal had been that student.[4]

After earning his doctorate, Neal and Ann spent a year in Moscow, mainly working with the prominent Soviet mathematician, Yuri Manin; Neal translated Manin's textbook *A Course in Mathematical Logic*, convincing the author to omit an offensive section on "Women's Logic." To Neal, it appeared that socialism had brought improvements to the lives of many people in the Soviet Union: a high degree of economic equality, a high literacy rate, progress in women's rights, subsidized culture—theater, ballet, literature—and a renaissance of government supported scientific research. At the same time, he had no illusion about the Soviet Union's Stalinist past or its repressive characteristics—the "idiotic bureaucratic policies and restrictions" that victimized many of his academic friends. He was also aware of the anti–Semitism limiting the number of Jews in Soviet universities, both as students and professors, and the repression of dissident mathematicians and other intellectuals;

in one case with which he was familiar, a famous logician was arrested and confined in a mental hospital, and colleagues who petitioned for his release—including Manin—were banned from foreign travel. Allowed to send and receive mail through the diplomatic pouch, Neal and Ann used the privilege to assist a number of dissidents to contact supporters in the West and apply for academic positions, though they were not pleased with some of the dissidents' racist attitudes toward African students and their desire to see the United States prevail in Vietnam.

Returning to the United States to accept a position at Harvard, Neal arrived just in time to participate in the first of a number of anti-racist activities during his four years at Cambridge. The major political issue in the Boston area at the time was court ordered busing to achieve school integration, which elicited protests from some whites who stoned the buses transporting black children into their neighborhoods. Neal joined a convoy organized by PL to support the bused children, only to have the whole group arrested for "disturbing the peace," based on the expectation that they would be attacked by the anti-busing demonstrators; although these bizarre charges were dismissed, he began his experience as a Harvard faculty member with his picture on the front page of the student newspaper for having been arrested. Neal also led a campaign to support a black food service worker at the university, a union shop steward who was suspended after having submitted a list of grievances involving safety and working conditions. He helped the union activist print and distribute newsletters describing the issues and spoke at a rally on his behalf. The food service worker was eventually reinstated.

Perhaps most important, during his last year at Harvard Neal became active in the anti-apartheid movement, resuscitated after a number of events again focused international attention on the South African regime: the Soweto uprising of black students, the killing of anti-apartheid leader Stephen Biko by the South African police, and announcement of the Sullivan principles exerting pressure on corporations for equal treatment of all South African employees regardless of race. In a replay of the SDS effort at Princeton a decade earlier, a group called the Southern Africa Solidarity Committee called for divestiture of the university's stock in companies doing business in South Africa. When the Harvard president produced a report similar to the Malkiel committee's document, declaring his opposition to apartheid but explaining why divestment was not the best way to produce change, Neal worked with other activists to publish an eight-page newspaper style reply with text, photos, sidebars, and even a cartoon. A subsequent anti-apartheid demonstration drew 3,000 participants in the largest campus protest since the 1969 uprising.

As a result a faculty meeting was called to discuss South African investments, and Neal spoke in favor of divestiture in the same room that he had once occupied as an SDS member.

In the summer before his last year at Harvard, Neal and Ann arranged a trip to Vietnam, flying from Moscow to Hanoi, their first of many visits over the next three decades. Unlike most other activists, whose interest in Vietnam was limited to opposing the war, Neal had long been following accounts of mathematical education in a country under attack by the world's largest military power. Then after his discharge from the service, he participated in projects to assist mathematicians in Vietnam by collecting books and journals, and raising money for a Vietnamese delegation to attend an international conference in Canada. During their year in the Soviet Union, Neal and Ann became friends with a Vietnamese mathematics student, who provided their first instruction in his language; they would eventually become, if not fluent, then at least able to communicate in Vietnamese. Neal was impressed by his first experience in Hanoi. Only three years after the war, he saw none of the beggars that had been so common in India and thought that Vietnam "compared well with other poor countries according to the most basic criteria—freedom from hunger, disease, illiteracy."

A year later, after joining the University of Washington where he has remained ever since, Neal agreed to head up the mathematics subcommittee of the U.S. Committee for Scientific Cooperation with Vietnam, a position in which he coordinated visits of Vietnamese mathematicians to the United States. This activity soon produced an FBI agent at his own door, motivated by the presence of Vietnamese scholars on a campus where classified research was being conducted. Neal responded by inviting the agent in for tea and giving him a two-hour lecture on why he opposed such research by universities: it gave the FBI an excuse to investigate a faculty member's foreign contacts. He was never bothered by the FBI again.

In 1985 Neal and Ann began a project, originally intended solely for Vietnam but later expanded to include six other developing countries. Based on her doctoral dissertation, Ann had published a biography of the prominent 19th century Russian mathematician and feminist, Sofia Kovalevskaia, the first European woman to be appointed to a university professorship. Both ardent feminists, Neal and Ann decided to use the royalties from the book sales, later supplemented by money from consulting fees and other sources, to create the Kovalevskaia Fund to encourage the work of women in science and technology. They began by working with the Vietnam Women's Union to co-sponsor a Southeast Asian women-in-science conference and the Vietnam Women's Museum, which grew out of the conference. The fund went on to make annual awards of the Kovalevskaia Prize to individuals and groups in Vietnam for more than a quarter of a century, the recipients chosen by a committee in which Neal and Ann have no involvement. While some of these projects have involved theoretical science, others have led to important applied results, producing new varieties of rice and vegetables, different types of vaccines for prevention of diseases, and utilization of local medicinal herbs in pharmaceutical products. As a result, the Kovalevskaia Prizes are well known throughout the country, and if there were a name-recognition poll in Vietnam, according to Neal and Ann, "the Kovalevskaia Fund would easily beat out the Ford and Rockefeller Foundations."

Moreover, as heads of the fund, Neal and Ann were treated as visiting dignitaries. At the women-in-science conference, they were invited by the Cambodian delegates to be guests of the Foreign Ministry at the tenth anniversary celebration of the country's liberation from Pol Pot; at the time the murderous Khmer Rouge was still recognized by the United States as Cambodia's legitimate government, and Pol Pot's representative still held the nation's seat at the UN. Along with other foreign delegations—none from Western nations—Neal and Ann were met at the airport by the Cambodian foreign minister and, as if the Kovalevskaia Fund were a small country, housed in the same diplomatic quarters as the official delegations from Angola, Nicaragua, and Mozambique. At the state dinner Ann exchanged toasts with the heads of state of the three countries comprising the former Indo-China, and the morning of the main festivities the couple joined official representatives from other nations on the reviewing stand.

Particularly well known in Vietnamese government circles, Neal and Ann have met with the major figures in the founding of the nation, including now deceased prime minister, Pham van Dong, second in importance only to Ho Chi Minh in the struggle for independence, and the legendary General Vo Nguyen Giap, commander of both the Viet Minh in the war against France and the Vietnam People's Army in the conflict with the United States. They have been particularly close friends with Madame Nguyen Thị Binh, who had been lead negotiator for the NLF during the war—signing the Paris Peace Accords on the organization's behalf—and then became the Minister of Education of the unified Vietnam, before being twice elected the nation's vice president by the National Assembly; Madame Binh also chaired the Kovalevskaia Prize Committee, working with other committee members to evaluate prospective candidates for the award. At a ceremony marking the 25th anniversary of the prizes in Vietnam, attended by high ranking government officials and covered by Vietnamese television, radio and newspapers, Madame Bình made a formal presentation of the President's Friendship Medal to Neal and Ann—the nation's highest honor for foreigners. During the same visit Neal received an honorary doctorate from the Vietnam Academy of Science and Technology.

Though held in esteem and enjoying cordial relations with many Vietnamese leaders, Neal and Ann were nevertheless unhesitant to criticize policies and practices that they considered detrimental, especially those concerning women; as Neal explained, they viewed their Vietnamese hosts "as colleagues, as equals," and did not wish to "patronize" them by remaining silent. Even before the fund had been established, after being invited to lecture at the Math Institute in Vietnam Neal crafted a lengthy "Confidential Report" to leaders of the scientific establishment in Hanoi, detailing a range of problems in Vietnamese education; the report eventually landed on the desk of General Giap, then head of the State Committee for Science and Technology. Along with other shortcomings, Neal noted that too few women were being prepared for careers in math, science, and technology.

After establishment of the fund, Neal and Ann became even more assertive. As financial supporters of the Vietnam Women's Museum, they were sharply critical of a number of exhibits planned for the museum's expansion. One exhibit under preparation glorified a Confucian image of women, focusing entirely on their traditional roles as wives and mothers, whose major accomplishments outside subservience to their families were limited to handicrafts, such as textiles and embroidery; another portrayed beauty contests and fashion shows, then beginning to be held in Vietnam, in a favorable light. In response to their objections the plans were modified: although there was a display of handicrafts and national costumes, it was relegated, along with the fashion show, to a less prominent position, ironically sharing space with an exhibit about the work of recipients of the Kovalevskaia Prize. Even in his speech accepting the Friendship Medal, Neal used the opportunity to point out to the audience of Vietnamese officials that, in the debate about higher education then taking place in the country, "unfortunately almost all of the participants have been men," who had "ignored the fundamental issue of gender equity." He went on to suggest that the government institute a policy favoring female applicants to universities as a counterbalance to the existing disproportionate admission of males.[5]

Neal's most serious—and most public—disagreement with official Vietnamese policy also occurred in the context of the debate over reform of higher education, in which the government was considering movement toward an

American style privatization of colleges and universities. He was vehemently opposed to such a change, especially after what he had seen in Russian universities, where, in his experience, a similar abandonment of socialist principles had led to a "tailspin" in the science, culture, and education that had once been "great strengths" of the Soviet Union"; as a result, in Neal's view, the system that had once brought together "a concentration of brilliant mathematicians unequaled anywhere else in the world" had now become "a scientific backwater," producing little work of any value or prestige. In his speech accepting the Friendship Medal, Neal referred sarcastically to the "foreign so-called 'experts,'" who had been advising the Vietnamese government—an allusion to a report written by two members of the Ash Institute for Democratic Governance and Innovation at the Harvard Kennedy school, recommending the creation of a university in Vietnam designed by Americans, for which, the report stated, "bluntly put, Vietnam must be willing to pay." Skewering the authors of the document, only one of whom had even earned a master's degree, as "completely unqualified" for consideration as an "expert consultant on improvement of higher education" in the United States, Neal called their employment in that capacity in Vietnam "an example of neocolonialism." In his own response to their report, he warned against following the American example with its "cancerous growth of bureaucracy," resulting in "as many administrative employees as faculty." The "American-style university" they hoped to create, he wrote, would have as its main purpose "low-level vocational training and also ideological indoctrination," in order to "undermine Vietnamese socialism and eventually make Vietnam subservient to U.S. economic interests."[6]

Having publically ridiculed a proposal that appeared to enjoy the support of the Ministry of Education and Training, Neal thought that perhaps he had gone too far but was soon invited to make the case against the proposal by Vietnam's deputy prime minister and head of the Ministry; he also was told by the chair of the National Assembly's Committee on Science and Education that other government officials agreed with his analysis. Whatever one thought of Neal's criticisms, it was remarkable that the opinion of a private citizen from another country with no official standing appeared to carry such influence in official circles.

Although the Kovalevskaia Fund's involvement in Vietnam represented its largest and longest commitment, two years after the fund's creation Neal and Ann expanded its sphere of activity, sponsoring projects first in Nicaragua but soon adding a presence in Cuba, El Salvador, Peru, and later Mexico and South Africa. These were not haphazard choices. As Neal put it, "when the first countries we went to were Vietnam and Nicaragua, we didn't pull those names out of a hat"; at the same time that the fund sponsored worthwhile projects, "we also are trying to oppose the U.S. role in the world." As private citizens opposed to their government's policies, they had chosen "to go precisely to those countries where the government is doing the most damage and try to do something in the other direction"—a decision informed by both "a certain feeling of guilt that we didn't do enough to try to stop the Vietnam War sooner" and a sense of "responsibility to do something to counteract the role that our government has played and is playing." There was a "vague analogy," Neal suggested, between these projects and the movement of German youth after World War II, who planted trees in Israel or provided other assistance to the Jewish state in order to atone for the actions of their parents' generation.

After visiting Nicaragua for the first time, Neal realized that, in order to function effectively, it would be necessary to learn Spanish, and he and Ann began study of yet another language. Although he was almost 40 at this point, within a couple of years he was able to deliver a professional talk in the language. However, just as he had dismissed his exceptional mathematical ability, he insisted that he was really not very good at languages but, unlike many Americans, was not resistant to learning them. Besides, he was happy "to give credit to the U.S. government when they do something right": the tapes developed by the State Department to train their own employees in a foreign language had been particularly helpful.

In Vietnam, of course, it was well known that Neal and Ann had opposed the war and were often at odds with their own government's foreign policy. Indeed, in Madame Binh's speech presenting them with the Friendship Medal, she had noted that both recipients had spent time in jail because of their opposition. In addition, the Russian sounding name of their fund provided another indication that it was not intended to enhance America's reputation. Neal thought that there was a similar effect in Cuba, which, in his description, had "stood up to a half-century of bullying by the colossus 90 miles to the north," as well as in Nicaragua, especially during the Sandinista period when the United States–backed Contras were committing acts of terrorism against civilians. (The murder victims included a young civil engineer who had graduated from the University of Washington before traveling to Nicaragua to help construct a hydroelectric plant in a rural community[7]; Neal attempted to get the university's faculty senate to observe a moment of silence after the killing, but when "the bureaucrat in charge" rejected the request, he resigned from what he called "a powerless, pointless, and pompous assemblage.") However, in countries with no history of conflict with the United States, much to Neal's and Ann's chagrin, their motivations were sometimes misunderstood. In an elementary school in Peru, where they had established a math enrichment program, upon their arrival they were dismayed to find the toddlers waving little homemade American flags to welcome them. The last thing Neal and Ann wanted was to be perceived as good will ambassadors for the United States.

Using what they had done in Vietnam as a model, Neal and Ann began the Kovalevskaia Fund's activities in the Americas by organizing a Central American Conference on Women in Science, Technology, and Medicine in Nicaragua, at which the first pair of prizes were awarded. Also as in Vietnam, where prime minister Pham Van Dong had been helpful in publicizing a similar event, they persuaded the Sandinista minister of the interior, Comandante Tomas Borge, to address the conference—an hour-long talk on the history of misogyny and the importance of feminism. However, without an institution comparable to the Vietnam Women's Union to sustain the momentum, the Kovalevskaia Prizes were awarded for only a few years in Nicaragua. Shortly thereafter Neal and Ann made their first visit to Havana, their expenses paid by the Cuban Academy of Sciences to avoid violation of the U.S. embargo prohibiting not travel to the island but expenditure of money there. Extending the prizes to Cuba proved to be more difficult because of the embargo's restrictions, but the Treasury Department informed Neal that he could proceed as long as the fund did not support a training program. The first prizes were awarded in 2003 with the leaders of the Cuban Academy of Science in attendance.

When the fund began to award prizes in El Salvador, unlike Nicaragua and Cuba, the country was ruled by a right-wing government, whose American trained military had engaged in indiscriminate murder of the regime's opponents, including the infamous El Mozote massacre, in which all the residents of a rural village were systematically tortured and executed. In this case Neal and Ann situated one of the projects sponsored by the Kovalevskaia Fund at a Catholic university, whose Jesuit faculty members had been among the government's severest critics, with the result, according to Neal, that the university's campus had been declared "hostile territory" by the U.S. embassy; despite claiming to approve of what the program was doing, the American ambassador refused an invitation to send an embassy representative to the prize ceremony—normally a routine appearance when a U.S. foundation sponsors an event at a foreign national university. Shortly after the first prizes had been awarded, Neal was "shocked and numbed" to learn that six priests at the university—two of them personal friends—along with their housekeeper and her teenage daughter had been murdered by an army unit, which occupied the campus and would not allow it to reopen for seven months.[8] During their next visit to El Salvador, Neal and Ann found the campus completely trashed from a combination of vandalism and military bombardment. Nevertheless, the fund resumed its activities, making awards and sponsoring conferences for another decade.

In Peru, along with awarding prizes to women scientists Neal and Ann also broadened the fund's activity, providing travel money for Peruvian youth—many from indigenous (Quechua) families—to participate in the International Mathematical Olympiads and scholarships for girls to attend the Gauss School, a specialized institution for the study of mathematics. They also began a program of math enrichment lessons, in which they visited elementary and middle school classes, presenting children with challenging puzzles and unsolved problems to demonstrate that mathematics could be taught as an exciting branch of science. They have now taught these classes in a dozen countries in Asia, Africa, and Latin America, ranging from Quechua speaking children in an isolated village in the Peruvian Andes to Xhosa speaking youth in Cape Town, South Africa. Neal and Ann didn't think of themselves as primarily helping others, he emphasized, because they benefited so much themselves, not only in the personal relationships they have formed but in the classroom experiences that have influenced Neal's thought and writing about mathematics education.

In the United States Neal saw the main reasons for the low mathematical level of so many students as the substitution of self-esteem for accomplishment and boring classes that relied on rote memory in place of thinking. He has also maintained that "computers should not be a major component" in math education, reinforcing, as they do, "the fascination with gadgetry, as opposed to intellect, that is endemic in American popular culture."[9] In the early 1990s he began making regular visits to sixth grade classes at a local Seattle school in an inner-city neighborhood and a few months later designed a special course for math majors at the university intending to teach the subject in the public schools. The course required undergraduates to help present "math enrichment material" to sixth or seventh graders in one of the city's poorest schools—topics from fields such as cryptography, graph theory, and geometry, all presented without the hype of high-powered electronic technology.

Although Neal was one of the world's experts on the branch of number theory called p-adic analysis and a household name in cryptography for his co-creation of elliptic curve cryptography—a mathematical technique for securing electronic communications—his autobiography made only a scant and self-effacing mention of his contributions to the former field and relegated his accomplishments in the latter to a brief anti-penultimate chapter. Actually Neal had come up with the idea for ECC even before email was in common use, and he thought of it as an interesting theoretical construction with no commercial significance. A few years later, however, three professors at a Canadian university formed the Certicom Corporation to market ECC, which became the method of electronic encryption used, ironically, by the National Security Agency among others; Neal's regular consultant fee from Certicom is sent from the company directly to the Kovalevskaia Fund. Within the field of cryptography he has also played an important role in opposing the NSA's heavy-handed attempt to restrict open research.[10] However, Neal regarded these professional contributions as much less significant than the activities of the fund and his political involvement. More important than his personal accomplishments, he insisted, were the "things I did collectively with other people to oppose the U.S. in Vietnam and subsequently to oppose apartheid in South Africa, to oppose U.S. policies in Central America. I was proud to be part of that."

Indeed, the more academically oriented issues that Neal did focus on in his autobiography invariably had a political dimension. With obvious relish he described the sequence of events by which an article assigned to Ann during her graduate study eventually led to the rejection of its author, Samuel Huntington, for membership in the prestigious National Academy of Sciences; Huntington had been the Harvard Professor and advisor to the State Department during the Vietnam War, who had provided the rationale for forcing the civilian population out of rural villages and into cities. The article presented an algebraic equation in which the variables represented such amorphous concepts as social mobilization, social frustration, and political institutionalization. Neal, who regarded the term "social science" as an oxymoron and had been skeptical of its practitioners misuse of quantitative methods, wrote a critique of Huntington's work titled "Mathematics as Propaganda" and sent a copy to the prominent mathematician and NAS member Serge Lang, who was known to hold such work in similar contempt. When Huntington was nominated for membership in the academy almost a decade later, Lang led the opposition. Calling Huntington's work "pseudoscience" and "nonsense," he distributed copies of Neal's critique to Academy members, and two years in a row Huntington was rejected before his supporters gave up the attempt to have him admitted.[11]

Neal's politics have remained consistent since senior year at Harvard."
His "overall ideology changed more in the first 6 months of 1969," he
observed, "than it has in the four decades since." He has remained sympathetic
to socialist countries, though not unaware of their flaws. There was much
about Castro and Cuba that he didn't like but felt that, "if you look at the
most basic criteria such as freedom from hunger, freedom from illiteracy,
reproductive rights of women, having a safety net, and in the case of the
Caribbean being prepared for hurricanes, Cuba looks pretty good," especially
in comparison with other countries with roughly similar conditions. And
since the demise of the Soviet Union—which Neal still considered "to some
extent" a socialist country—he claimed that there had been a return of
inequality and poverty, along with "rampant public health problems that are
far worse than anything they had" during the time he spent there years earlier.
As an advocate for women's rights in particular, he insisted that "generally
where the state sector is strong, it's much better for women, and when things
get privatized, then the women get shafted. And that's certainly been true in
Russia."

Because of her position at Arizona State University, Neal and Ann spent
a good deal of time in Phoenix, and, captivated by the beauty of the surrounding area, in 2000 they decided to buy a 20-acre piece of land in the Picacho
Mountains. A couple of years later, however, they became disenchanted with
the purchase when a landfill company began construction nearby of one of
the largest dumps in the Southwest. Prepared to take a loss on the property,
they sold it at what turned out to be the peak of the real estate bubble for
almost six times what they had paid for it. Though a dedicated socialist, Neal
had no misgivings about making such a huge profit. "I suppose I should feel
sorry for the guy who bought that worthless piece of property," he remarked,
but "he was a real estate speculator who got caught standing up when the
music stopped, and I don't feel any moral qualms" about the sale.

Even before the sale, Neal and Ann had bought a different and surprisingly inexpensive 20-acre parcel on the flank of Copper Mountain that no
one seemed to want, because it was thought to be just steep rock with "no
insurable access." Using his knowledge of calculus, however, Neal realized
from the topographical map that there had to be a saddle point in the middle
of the property, and when he hiked through the brush up the steep incline,
he not only found a giant saddle but unobstructed views more spectacular
than he had anticipated. In addition, he discovered early 14th century Native
American ruins, making the property of historic interest as well. When I
spoke with them, Neal and Ann had arranged to have a dirt road access the

land and were planning to use their windfall profit for construction of a "dream house," intending for it to be sold in the future to the kind of wealthy person who would use it as a getaway. Although this seemed like a strange project for a couple of socialists, the idea was that, being childless, they would leave the proceeds from sale of the house to the Kovalezskaia Fund in perpetuity, which would coordinate a grant program for women in Third World countries. In his autobiography Neal noted wryly that a gourmet kitchen and whirlpool tub would thus be "the cross we have to bear, the altruistic sacrifice we have to make for the good of our charity!" But, as he concluded in a more serious vein, this investment in the fund's future was the more adult response to the challenge of a privileged life amid the existence of impoverishment than that of the child who had once "picked the jacket pockets of his parents' guests" in order to hand the money out to beggars on the streets of Delhi.

11. The Anti-Anti-Communist

The founding meeting of the Princeton chapter of SDS was considered significant enough to draw a journalist from the *National Observer*, a conservative weekly published in the 1960s and 70s by Dow Jones & Company as a more general news supplement to its better known financial daily, the *Wall Street Journal*. Although the resulting front page story focused primarily on the "draft ruckus"—the relationship between patriotism and protest—it noted the anomaly that one of the "bearded SDSers ... wore earrings,"[1] an adornment not generally associated with a Y chromosome at the time. The subject of this observation was Grover Furr, a graduate student in comparative literature, who was in fact sporting a single earring, acquired after a few glasses of wine had helped convince him to let some girl at a party take a needle to his earlobe.

At Princeton all the students were smart in the traditional sense of having strong verbal and analytic skills, but some were more knowledgeable—i.e., better informed—than others. Whatever the topic—history, politics, literature, and especially Marxism—few people knew more than Grover, who was familiar not only with most of the standard works on a subject in English but had a reading knowledge of half a dozen foreign languages. In his spare time he was learning Chinese, and at the lengthy SDS meetings he would often pass the time drawing Chinese characters in the air, much like some people play air guitar. As one of the chapter's leading intellects, he was called upon when it was necessary to craft a more detailed statement than the usual flier. In response to Goheen's statement on university investments in South Africa, for example, Grover produced SDS's response, an eight-page single spaced document dismantling the president's argument point by point, while driving toward the obligatory conclusion that, whether in South Africa or the United States, "we can fight racism only by attacking its material basis—the capitalist system."[2]

Even before attempting to locate old SDS members, I knew that Grover was a Professor of English at Montclair State University, having been named by David Horowitz as one of the "101 Most Dangerous Academics in America." Among other reasons for his inclusion, Grover had been "allowed ... to teach a course on the Vietnam War" despite having "no training or credentials ... as a historian," and he had been an apologist for Stalin. The course in question, actually titled the "Vietnam War and American Culture," examined the legacy of the war "reflected ... primarily in American literature"—an indisputably appropriate offering in an English department. However, an inspection of Grover's extensive web page indicated that he had indeed been a staunch defender of Stalin's, having authored numerous publications maintaining that the Soviet leader never perpetrated any of the crimes or mass murders with which he has been charged. In addition, Grover's "Politics and Social Issues" page left no doubt about his ideological sympathies, providing a list of sites he had found valuable in his attempt to understand "class struggle, exploitation and all the attendant horrors of capitalism," each link prefaced by a little photo of Lenin acting as a bullet point; many of the links connected to articles from *Challenge*, the biweekly newspaper of the "Revolutionary Communist Progressive Labor Party," which Grover described as the "best source of class analysis of the world's events."[3] Obviously his politics were no less radical than they had been four decades earlier.

More than a year after the first interview—with Doug Seaton, the most conservative of the former activists—I drove to Grover's house in a North Jersey suburb for the last interview, this time with the most radical. Grover lived with his significant other in her house in an unpretentious, middle class neighborhood on a winding, narrow one-way street, separated from its counterpart heading in the opposite direction by an island wide enough to serve as a small park, landscaped with a curving walkway through its vegetation and benches at regular intervals—a miniature version of a Frederick Law Olmstead creation. At the end of the block the two one-way streets skirted the outside of a traffic rotary encircling a small man-made lake stocked with fish. The houses were built close to the curb and to each other—separated by driveways barely the width of a car—but their meticulously well-kept appearance together with the charm of the island conveyed an impression not of crowdedness but of community. Allowing for the effects of age, Grover looked very much like I remembered him, though his earring was gone along with much of his hair.

Grover Furr was born in Washington, D.C., to parents who were both from North Carolina, but at the time his father was serving in the army air corps during the "Good War," and his mother had temporarily moved in with her parents in a Virginia suburb of the district. Grover's father, like his father before him, was a Republican—an iconoclastic political identification in the old "Solid South," where persisting resentment over the "War of Northern Aggression" and its bitter aftermath had made the party of Lincoln into a dirty word. However, when the textile industry moved to North Carolina in search of a nonunion work force, the grandfather had seen its presence as his opportunity to get off the farm and, while rising to a managerial position, came to identify with the Northern Republican factory owners. Grover's father followed a similar path, both occupationally and politically, though his mother and her family were Democrats like most of their North Carolina neighbors.

When the war ended, the textile company that had employed Grover's father offered him the opportunity to help open a new branch in Montreal, and Grover grew up as an American living in Canada, attending grade school, high school, and even college—McGill University—in the City of Saints. The experience was a culture shock for his parents, accustomed as they were to small "supersegregated" Southern towns, but, according to Grover, "they wanted to fit in, and they changed." The family lived in a middle class suburb, where most of the other fathers, too, had white collar positions and few of the mothers worked outside the home.

Grover's parents "were very supportive, the best parents you could want," he called them. His father was involved in activities like cub scouts and boy scouts with the neighborhood's children, and when Grover became interested in skiing, his father took up the sport at the age of 40 in order to share the experience with his son. While they were not themselves academics or intellectuals, his parents were "very respectful of people who were good academically," a group that they were pleased to find included their son, and when Grover began to excel in school, they "didn't try to micromanage what I did, didn't worry if I had somewhat unconventional ideas."

Grover didn't find high school particularly stimulating, though as an intellectually curious teenager he had already begun to pursue his own academic path. Latin was a favorite subject, and he soon became even more attracted to languages after his mother bought him a dictionary containing, inside the front cover, alphabets from different linguistic systems—Hebrew, Arabic, Russian, Greek. Fascinated to learn that, like Latin, Russian had cases and declensions, he decided that he would study the language on his own and bought a teach-yourself Russian book, the first of a number of foreign languages in which he would become fluent. One other event exerted an influence, not on Grover's intellectual interests, but on his political direction. During his junior year, the Sharpeville Massacre occurred, in which the South African police opened fire on a crowd of peaceful demonstrators. Because Canada, along with what was then the Union of South Africa, were both members of the British Commonwealth at the time, the slaughter received more attention in the Canadian media than in the United States. Officials from South Africa even spoke at an assembly at his high school, during which they were challenged by one of his classmates, an incident that made quite an impression on Grover.

At McGill, one of Canada's most prestigious universities, Grover majored in English but was uninvolved in political activity until his senior year. Then after "Bloody Sunday"—the brutal beating of civil rights marchers in Selma— Grover drew up a sign expressing his shock as an American citizen, which he held while marching in front of the embassy. Also, during McGill's model parliament exercise, for the first time he met people who called themselves "communists"—students running under the banner of "Young Communists"—though he later realized that they "didn't strike me as anything I would recognize as a communist since then." But what impressed Grover at the time was the fact that, in contrast to the other student parties—liberals, progressives, conservatives, all of which seemed focused on parochial concerns— only the communists were raising significant political issues. He decided to vote for them, not necessarily because he agreed with their positions but as a "vote for seriousness."

Grover entered Princeton just in time to attend the first meeting of the university's SDS chapter; friends at McGill had told him enthusiastically about the organization after attending the SDS sponsored march in Washington the previous spring, where Paul Potter had made his famous statement denouncing the "system" while declining to name it. Three weeks after joining SDS, Grover was marching in the next major Washington protest, this time under the "Even Princeton" banner. However, participating in SDS was not his only political activity at the time; during his first year Grover was also involved with the Friends of SNCC, raising money for the Student Nonviolent Coordinating Committee's efforts at voter registration in the South. In retrospect he considered himself quite politically naïve, having written a letter to Lyndon Johnson in the fall of 1965, explaining that there had been "a big misunderstanding": the Vietnamese were no threat to the United States. Even then he felt a little silly, wondering whether anyone would actually read his four-page analysis, but "that was the level of political understanding I was at," he remarked.

It was not until after Grover had participated in a number of SDS campaigns—protesting ROTC, getting arrested at IDA—that he began the transition to a more radical position on both the war and the larger society. When he first heard intervention in Vietnam attributed to American imperialism, "a little light bulb went off in my head," he recalled, "because I had been raised in Canada." In the Canadian educational system there had never been an attempt to deny the fact of British imperialism but rather to demonstrate that it had been "benign and altruistic," in contrast to the American system, which "taught that the United States is not imperialist." But after three years of opposing the war and not finding any plausible explanation, viewing the conflict "in the context of imperialism made a lot of sense" to Grover. Now predisposed to be receptive to a radical analysis, he joined a Marxist study group organized by Macklin Smith, his fellow graduate student in comparative literature and a member of PL. By this time Grover had finished all the courses necessary for his doctorate and was starting work on his dissertation, but with no classes to take, he used the free time to immerse himself in a study of Marxism, which impressed him as "intellectually profound"; whether or not one agreed with it, he concluded, Marxism was not "a simpleminded way of looking at the world." Perhaps a year or two earlier the combination of his own reading and the study group would not have had the same effect, he mused, but "at that particular time and place it all came together for me, and I started to think, this is what makes sense."

This political transition was further strengthened by Grover's experience in SDS's summer work-in program, which encouraged student radicals to find blue collar jobs. He wound up at a local chemical plant, working on the loading dock, where powdered substances were delivered before being combined into their final form as pesticides and insecticides. The working conditions were horrible. The air in the plant was filled with tiny particles from the powder, making it impossible to avoid inhaling them, and Grover, who suffered from asthma, found himself sitting up much of the night unable to breathe; even today he continued to struggle with symptoms resulting from the summer job more than four decades ago.

Grover's parents had gone through a difficult divorce just around the time he had begun graduate school and were each soon remarried. Focused primarily on getting reestablished in their new lives, they nevertheless remained supportive of his political activity. Indeed, his father was undergoing a similar if not quite as extreme political transformation of his own, having abandoned his republican roots and changed from a Goldwater conservative in 1964 to a Gene McCarthy liberal four years later.

By the time he left Princeton at the end of 1969, Grover had become committed to Marxism as an intellectual framework for understanding social problems and to communism as their solution. He also had become the leading member of Princeton SDS's WSA caucus and shared the views of its PL leadership. A participant at SDS's tumultuous national convention in Chicago, he interpreted the attempt to expel WSA as a result of "anti-communism"—a term of opprobrium to Grover, who prides himself on being a staunch anti-anti-communist. In his opinion it was resentment at PL's presence, a sense on the part of its opponents that "there was something illegitimate about a communist party within an organization like SDS" that caused the rift. Of course, by 1969 the majority of the people attending an SDS national convention considered themselves communists, and, like many internal conflicts among leftists, both sides claimed to be the true custodians of the red banner. However, while most other former SDS members have given up this particular ghost, Grover has remained supportive of communism as the ultimate goal and opposed to anti-communism as the major obstacle to social progress.

Although he would not complete his doctoral dissertation until almost a decade later, beginning with the spring 1970 semester Grover was offered a tenure track position at what was then Montclair State College; the institution was designated a university in 1994. Having been a state teachers college for its first half-century up to 1958, Montclair was still organized according to the public school system's career clock, which meant that in his third year Grover was evaluated for and received tenure, though without the usual promotion to associate professor, which came later.

Throughout his time at Montclair State—that is, throughout his life since leaving Princeton—Grover has remained committed to working for a radical transformation of society. For the first few years he was still involved in SDS and its spin-offs. While none of the factions would ever again exercise the organization's pre-split level of influence, the PL-led WSA branch could call itself the "real" SDS at least in the sense that it alone maintained the original policy of welcoming anyone who wished to participate; besides, RYM disbanded not long after the Chicago convention, and Weatherman went underground, leaving SDS-WSA as the only group still claiming the SDS mantle. However, when American withdrawal from Vietnam deprived SDS of its chief issue, again at PL's initiative, what remained of the organization changed its focus from anti-imperialist to anti-racist, morphing into the Committee Against Racism, a campus based anti-racist group with SDS–style local chapters, soon expanded to become the International Committee Against Racism. As Grover explained the reasoning for this political reorientation, "racism is sort of the fundamental issue in the United States; forget about revolution, it holds back social reform in so many ways and always has."

During the 1970s CAR and then InCAR were involved in a number of campaigns both on and off campuses. Within the academy its members opposed the biologically rooted theories promulgated by a number of scientists: Arthur Jensen's claims that blacks were genetically less intelligent than whites; Richard Herrnstein's predictions that the heritability of intelligence was producing a stratified society in which the upper class was merely the socioeconomic reflection of genetic ability; and E.O. Wilson's sociobiological theory arguing that all sorts of social behaviors were biologically based. They also demonstrated against rallies called by the Klan and other segregationist groups. With Grover as its faculty advisor, the local chapter at Montclair State organized protests on behalf of some minority faculty who were being terminated and against a publication by a faculty member that, according to Grover, contained "some horribly racist anti–African and anti–Arab" material. He considered all these activities "reform" struggles; they attempted to make existing social structures more egalitarian but did not change the society in any fundamental way. While Grover believed it essential to work for reforms, he emphasized that it was a "mistake" to see them as "the end point, the only thing worth fighting for." The objective of antiracist activity in his view was not only to gain real improvements in people's lives but also to encourage an analysis of racism as an aspect of capitalism; to truly eradicate the former one had to do away with the latter.

To anyone familiar with leftist rhetoric, this perspective sounded like routine dogma, but what kept Grover from seeming like a caricature of a Marxist ideologue has been the depth of his personal commitment to antiracism. After marrying in 1976, Grover and his wife—a white woman who shared his political beliefs and from whom he is now divorced—adopted two interracial boys, one before and one after the birth of their biological daughter. Intent on living in a racially diverse community, they left their upper middle class all-white suburb of Upper Montclair and bought a house in the Vailsburg section of Newark's West ward, an integrated neighborhood at the time. Within the next few years all the whites moved out, replaced by mainly black and a few Hispanic families—not only African Americans but immigrants from Haiti, Guyana, Jamaica, Nigeria, and other Caribbean and African countries—so that, as Grover put it, "it was not long before it wasn't integrated anymore, except for us."

For 23 years Grover lived in the Vailsburg house, the first 12 with his wife, raising the children, making lots of friends and spearheading efforts to improve neighborhood safety, municipal services, and public education; when he and his wife separated, he remained there as a single father for more than another decade. "Sure, we were a little bit odd" in the neighborhood at first, he said, but he soon found that "the vast majority of black people are not nearly as anti-white as there are white people who are anti-black; they were not afraid or ashamed to live with a couple of white people there, they didn't say, 'there goes the neighborhood.'" Faced with inner city problems of crime, drugs, and security, Grover and his wife organized a block association that created a neighborhood watch, published pamphlets on topics such as how to secure your home, and held block parties in the summertime.

As his own children progressed through the public school system, Grover became active in the Parent Teacher Student Organization—Newark's version of the PTA—demanding improvements in both the physical facilities and the curriculum. His children attended University High School, one of the small, supposedly college-oriented high schools in the city for gifted and talented students, and Grover and his wife were appalled to see the horrible condition of the building: leaking classrooms, large holes in the ceiling, broken windows that were never fixed, chained doors violating fire regulations, and a gym in such bad shape that there were no physical education classes. They spent five years trying to get the school board to fix the leaks and put stalls in the bathrooms, which had toilets without partitions or doors around them; at one point their children organized a walk-out of students as a protest. In comparison to the "gorgeous" high school two miles up the street in a nearby suburb, the conditions at his children's school reflected what Grover called "the face of racism."

The pedagogical experience was no better than the physical plant. When Grover's oldest child entered the high school for gifted and talented students fresh from a similar program in the lower grades, not only were there no math textbooks but the math curriculum was composed of subject matter that the students had already taken two years earlier. When activist parents demanded that calculus be offered in the high school curriculum, according to Grover, the director of mathematics education—later to become the superintendent of schools—visited the school and told the parents that black kids couldn't learn calculus. The fact that the director herself as well as the majority of the board of education were black suggested to Grover that the institutional nature of racism had nothing to do with the color of the people in control; the schools had been neglected when the board was dominated by whites, he observed, but "the black school board was just as bad." Despite Grover's Marxist analysis of the ruling class's interest in perpetuating racial inequity, he was pleased at the state takeover of the Newark school system—a comment on how horrible he considered the conditions his children had to endure.

After all three children had become adults, Grover left Newark, and his daughter and her fiancé, soon to become her husband, moved into the Vailsburg house. Certified as a school nurse after earning her masters degree, she became head of the block association that Grover and his wife had organized decades earlier, carrying on the family tradition of community activism.

In addition to his efforts in the community, Grover has also been politically active as an academic, in part by attempting to influence professional organizations to take a more progressive stand on issues. The Modern Language Association's Radical Caucus, for example, was organized, according to its manifesto, in order to offer to the MLA—the most prominent organization for teachers and scholars in English and foreign languages—"a class analysis of both economic and ideological issues in our profession, in higher education generally, and in society at large." In practice, this objective largely meant the presentation of resolutions at the association's annual meetings. Thus, the caucus regularly called for improved treatment of adjuncts—part-time faculty, who are poorly paid, receive no benefits, and have no job security. In the years after 9/11 the caucus also submitted a number of resolutions opposing the administration's foreign policy. However, because the MLA's constitution allowed it to consider only resolutions addressing matters that fell within its professional mission—the teaching of language and literature— the caucus had to focus its efforts not on the policy itself but on the language in which the policy was expressed. Thus, a typical resolution—submitted by Grover but drafted collectively by the caucus—urged repeal of the Patriot Act because the government's insistence on defining terrorism "however it wishes," and the resulting investigation of the reading habits and electronic correspondence of academics, could lead to "intellectuals who engage in critical inquiry and political activism ... be[ing] dubbed terrorists." Declaring that the phrase "War on Terrorism" had been used to justify "military action anywhere in the world," another resolution encouraged members of the MLA, as "professionals committed to scrupulous inquiry into language and culture," to conduct "critical analysis of war talk" in classrooms when appropriate.[4]

While both of these resolutions were approved by the MLA's Delegate Assembly and then ratified by the membership, more controversial was a proposed resolution—again drafted by Grover on behalf of the caucus—that sought to defend the academic freedom of critics of Zionism and Israel as a response to incidents in which some scholars found their speaking invitations withdrawn, were accused of anti–Semitism, or were denied tenure despite support from their departmental colleagues after individuals or groups outside their university exerted pressure on their administration. Grover was infuriated when the prominent literary scholar, Cary Nelson—who was also president of the American Association of University Professors at the time and known as a leftist himself—employed parliamentary maneuvers to prevent the resolution from being brought up for a vote. Some months after the interview, another resolution drafted by the Radical Caucus, expressing support for "teaching and scholarship about Palestinian culture," passed despite Nelson's attempt again to offer a substitute.[5]

Although Horowitz's profile of Grover included a brief allusion to his involvement in the radical caucus, it was more the thought of a Marxist professor using the classroom for ideological indoctrination that warranted his inclusion on the "most dangerous" list. A specialist in medieval literature who had completed a dissertation requiring him to read articles in Latin, French, and German as well as Middle English, Grover found that at Montclair State there was little demand for such an esoteric subject; especially after the requirements for the English major were liberalized to allow more choice, not many of the largely first-generation, occupationally oriented students chose medieval literature, and Grover found himself in the awkward situation of having been hired to teach a subject that few undergraduates wanted to study. Faced with the necessity to fill out his teaching schedule, along with developing new courses of his own Grover took over some that had been designed by others—standard offerings in an English department such as survey courses in English literature and world literature. His syllabi for these courses listed conventional readings—uncontroversial anthologies or established textbooks. The world literature course did assign some novels by Third World authors that could be considered anti-colonialist, but these were critically acclaimed books, such as Chinua Achebe's *Things Fall Apart*—arguably the most important work of African literature, which has been translated into 50 languages—and Ousmane Sembene's *God's Bits of Wood*, another seminal African novel.

In any event, Grover had not evoked controversy for his traditional courses but rather because of the courses he had designed focusing on his own interests, such as the Literature of Social Protest, or the Vietnam War and American Culture—it was the latter in particular, taught by someone with professed Marxist beliefs, that had so outraged Horowitz. A few years after Grover joined the faculty, Montclair State revamped its general education curriculum, adding a course called "Contemporary Issues" as a new requirement intended to encourage an interdisciplinary approach to subjects.

According to Grover, his proposal for a course on Vietnam to be listed as one of the options under this rubric was initially rejected until a lengthy article in the *New York Times Magazine* noted that more than two dozen universities were offering similar courses[6]; once it proved good enough for schools like Harvard and Michigan, then Montclair State dropped its objections.

Horowitz claimed that Grover "uses the course to vent his political passions on his helpless students," quoting a number of his observations harshly critical of both the war and the United States government, although Horowitz neglected to mention that the statements came from Grover's writing, not anything he was reported to have said in class. Grover insisted that, while he acknowledged his Marxism to students, he did not impose his views on them but emphasized the importance of their own effort to discover the truth and took special care to express appreciation to students who disagreed and to encourage them to continue speaking out. His web page indicated that he also assigned readings on the war from many different perspectives, including work by a prominent defender of the war published in *Parameters: Journal of the U.S. Army War College*. Although it was not possible to know what actually transpired in his classes, a letter, posted online from a former student who took "Professor Furr's much-maligned Literature of the Vietnam War course in spring 1994," provided support for Grover's claims. Conservative members of the class disagreed with Grover without any adverse consequences, the student wrote, and assignments included sources "from both sides of the conflict." Most remarkable, the student described Grover's response to an exchange in the student newspaper that occurred during the course: after Grover's letter to the editor making some observations about the Vietnam War elicited a retort from a faculty member who was a Vietnam veteran, Grover invited his colleague to address the class to present "the pro-war view." Although the invitation was declined, the incident was nevertheless instructive.[7]

However, Grover's most significant political activity—both in terms of the effort invested on his part and the controversy it has elicited—has been his work on the history of the Soviet Union under Stalin, arguing that the deceased communist head of state has been unfairly maligned. Absent Grover's defense of Stalin, it is unlikely that a leftist faculty member at a regional institution would have become such a target of conservatives' anger. Indeed, the outrage has become even more widespread after Grover participated in a 2012 debate on campus, during which he called the claim that Stalin was responsible for mass murder "a lie"; despite years of research, Grover told the audience, he had yet to find "one crime that Stalin committed." A YouTube video of the statement drew tens of thousands of hits, producing calls for

Grover's immediate termination on the grounds that he was using his position to impose Stalinism on students. In fact, his writing on Stalin had never been part of reading assignments or class materials, and Grover's students affirmed that he had never introduced these views in class. As an agent of the state, the university responded, properly, that it could not interfere with his first amendment rights.[8]

Grover first became interested in the Stalin era shortly after leaving Princeton, when he read the historian Robert Conquest's 1968 book, *The Great Terror*, the first comprehensive study of the purges that took place in the Soviet Union in the late 1930s, based largely on information that became available only after Khrushchev's famous "Secret Speech" denouncing the brutality under Stalin's rule; the title of the book became a commonly used term for the entire constellation of repressive policies implemented in the Soviet Union at the time.[9] As someone already committed to communism, Grover was initially disturbed by these revelations, but before coming to a conclusion he decided to conduct his own investigation of Conquest's claims. Spending all his spare time at the New York Public Library and fluent in Russian, Grover systematically checked on every footnote in Conquest's mammoth book, finding, he maintained, that many of them were "phony in various ways—out of context, or didn't say what he said they said, or didn't prove what he said it proved." It amounted, he insisted, to "a fraudulent use of the apparatus of scholarship to deceive people."

However, it was not until the late 1990s that Grover changed his own academic focus from medieval literature to Soviet history, deciding that his greatest contribution—one that he in particular could make—would be to determine whether Stalin was a "monstrous criminal or a significant leader," who made mistakes in the course of "honestly trying to build a better society." Immersing himself in Soviet archives released since the fall of the Berlin wall, he came to the conclusion, in contrast to every other scholar's reading of the evidence, that the canonical version of the history of the Soviet Union in general and the role played by Stalin in particular had been "falsified." Moreover, in Grover's analysis, this "demonization" of Stalin and Soviet history had been employed, first by Khrushchev and then by Gorbachev, "to justify the return to capitalism" in Russia. "With all its weaknesses," he declared, "the communist movement was, during the 20th century, by far the major force for human liberation and the empowerment of working people ... the only bright spot in a century of capitalist horrors." As a consequence, according to Grover, it was "axiomatic that all defenders of capitalist exploitation, and of the various ideologies that sustain it, will be strongly anti-communist, and will not hesitate to lie about the history of the communist movement."[10] His own goal thus became to "stick a dagger in anti-communism's heart," at least in one part of it, by changing the way people thought of communism in the Soviet Union. For the last 15 years Grover has applied his formidable polemical abilities in pursuit of this curious objective.

Much of Grover's work on Soviet history has appeared in Russian before being published in English, perhaps unsurprising given the *New York Times'* account of "the wave of ... nostalgia for the Soviet Union in Russia—and even for Stalin himself," which had led to a movement for the former ruler to be "fully rehabilitated." In 2007 he produced an ambitious book, published in Moscow: *Antistalinskaia Podlost* ("Anti-Stalin Villainy"), according to Grover, climbed as high as seventh on Ozon's bestseller list, the Russian version of Amazon. Three years later, it appeared in English (and has since been translated into Vietnamese and Turkish) as *Khrushchev Lied*, with the expansive subtitle *The Evidence That Every "Revelation" of Stalin's (and Beria's) "Crimes" in Nikita Khrushchev's Infamous "Secret Speech" to the 20th Party Congress of the Soviet Union on February 25, 1956, Is Provably False.* Calling Khrushchev's address—the actual title of which was "On the Cult of Personality and its Consequences"—"the 20th Century's Most Influential Speech," Grover characterized it as "foundational" to "the whole historical paradigm of Soviet history of the Stalin period." Thus by claiming to have disproved each of its 61 assertions, he felt he had effectively dismantled the case for Stalin as murderous dictator.[11]

Grover realized how far outside the mainstream his conclusions have placed him; he acknowledged "basically saying that anybody who teaches Soviet history in the United States and anyplace else are all full of shit." In our exchange of emails prior to the interview I had promised to be provocative but not argumentative; I was there to ask Grover about his thinking, not to debate him, but naturally I wanted to know how he justified being such a heretic. For some hours we ranged over the litany of charges against Stalin: the purges and liquidation of party members for minor deviations, the forced collectivization and the consequent decimation of the Kulaks, the Ukrainian famine that cost millions of lives, the Katyn Massacre of Polish officers, the Lysenkoist control of science and imprisonment of geneticists, the repression of writers and intellectuals, the gulags where political dissidents were sentenced to forced labor, the "Doctors' Plot" alleging an effort by physicians to kill Soviet officials, widely regarded as part of an anti–Semitic campaign since most of the accused were Jewish, even the Soviet betrayal of the Republicans in the Spanish Civil War. In each case Grover had some sort of explanation for why the established version was incorrect. He did not deny that millions of people died as a result of official actions in the Soviet Union, though he dismissed even the lowest estimate of 10 million—many historians believe the actual number to be three to five times larger—as grossly inflated. But he maintained that Stalin was never personally responsible—at least not "in the sense in which most people think," but only in the larger, impersonal "sense that if it happens on your watch, you're culpable."

For at least one issue Grover could point to the existence of a genuine academic controversy. The Ukrainian famine of 1932–1933, probably the worst single calamity measured by number of deaths, has traditionally been described as the result of premeditation, an official plan to commit genocide against the peasantry in order to suppress nationalism and overcome resistance to collectivization. On the basis of more recent archival data, however, some scholars have argued that the 1932 harvest was much smaller than had previously been thought, which made the subsequent year's famine, perhaps not inevitable, but more likely.[12] Soviet authorities might have been incompetent and certainly insensitive from this perspective, but there was no official policy designed to produce starvation.

But Grover's rejection of most of the other charges against Stalin typically relied on claims of recently discovered documents outlining plots and conspiracies against the government. He granted, for example, that huge numbers of people were wrongly executed during the purges, but claimed that these atrocities were carried out by a combination of party leaders seeking to overthrow Stalin and members of the NKVD—the Soviet police—who were themselves "involved in a conspiracy to kill as many people as possible, because they were collaborating with the Germans and the Japanese." Thus, in Grover's analysis, the executions were committed not by the true Soviet communists but by the people plotting against them. And as soon as Stalin realized what was taking place, according to Grover, he replaced the head of the NKVD with Lavrenti Beria, and the number of executions immediately plummeted. Every other historian of the period has concluded that, in fact, Beria presided over the execution of Stalin's political rivals, real or imagined, along with tens of thousands of Red Army officers, and hundreds of thousands of ordinary citizens convicted of false charges. Similarly, almost all other scholars have determined that the so-called "Moscow Show Trials"—resulting in the execution of almost every one of the "Old Bolsheviks" who had participated in the revolution, along with many high ranking military officers—were a sham, relying on forged evidence and false confessions extracted under duress. Again on the basis of archives not yet released by the Russian government, Grover insisted that all these people were guilty as charged—that they really *had* conspired with foreign governments to overthrow Stalin. Even the claim of Trotsky's collaboration with the Germans and Japanese, almost universally ridiculed as absurd, Grover maintained, was substantiated by new information.

Grover's latest project has been an effort to disprove "the 'official' version of the Katyn Massacre." Sometime in early 1940 some 22,000 Polish nationals—officers, policemen, and intelligentsia taken prisoner during the Red Army invasion of Eastern Poland the previous fall—were murdered in the Katyn Forest in Russia. When their bodies were unearthed three years later, Stalin blamed the massacre on the Nazis, a position maintained by successive Soviet governments for almost the next half-century until the release of previously closed state records divulged thousands of documents pertaining to the Polish prisoners. The most important of these documents have been translated into English and published by Yale University Press, leading the volume's editors to call "the Katyn massacre ... now the most amply documented Stalinist crime," a conclusion shared by almost every other scholar.[13] Nevertheless, Grover's article on the subject stated that accusations of forgery in 1995 (made by a Russian conspiracy theorist who also called the moon landing a hoax perpetrated by NASA with the assistance of Soviet scientists) had triggered a "fierce partisan debate." The statements of former NKVD operatives involved in the massacre he rejected as "not entirely voluntary," informed by fear of not confirming what their interrogators expected to hear. But what clinched the case for him was the discovery that a few Polish victims thought to have perished at Katyn were in fact killed elsewhere two years later. For Grover the fact that some people had not met their fate where expected made it indisputable: "the best proven 'crime of Stalinism'" had been debunked.[14]

To most other scholars Grover's claims are regarded much as the communist equivalent of Holocaust denial. But in Grover's view, "'mainstream'— i.e., anticommunist—academia" had no "desire to discover the truth," and the "vast majority of books" written by recognized historians he called contaminated by "anti-communist bias," typically including sections that were just "dishonest." For example, he dismissed Timothy Snyder—author of the critically praised *Bloodlands*, a study of the mass killings caused by both Stalin's Soviet Union and Hitler's Germany in the area between the two regimes— as "notorious ... because he blatantly lies about Soviet history"; indeed, Grover protested Snyder's appearance as an invited speaker at a nearby university. Tony Judt, another scholar who has written critically about the Soviet Union, Grover disparaged as only "a journalist, not a researcher." In fact, Judt, now deceased, was an acclaimed scholar, who occupied a named chair in European history at New York University, directed the university's Remarque Institute supporting multi-disciplinary studies, and had authored or edited 15 books, many of them published by university presses; *Postwar: A History of Europe Since 1945*, his magisterial overview based on research in six languages received the Council on Foreign Relations' Arthur Ross Award for the year's best book on international affairs and was shortlisted for the UK's Samuel Johnson Prize presented to the year's best non-fiction work in English.[15]

Quite apart from this uncharitable characterization of other academics, much of Grover's argument was based on belief in a complex and extensive web of forged documents, conspiracies, and secret archives. The appeal to such an implausible explanation might serve to account for a specific incident, but when invoked in one instance after another to discredit the canonical version of history, it becomes more difficult to take seriously. Although Grover insisted that he began his investigations with an open mind, ready to follow wherever the facts might take him, it was difficult to escape the impression that the evidence would always lead him where he was predisposed to go. In any event, the newly available archives that he has been expecting to result in a sea change have so far led to the opposite. An outpouring of recent scholarly works on the Soviet Union have only provided additional evidence in support of the established view.[16]

One wonders how someone as extraordinarily intelligent as Grover and as genuinely dedicated to improving the lives of others could become such an ardent defender of a figure almost universally regarded as responsible for a system of soul-crushing tyranny. Grover viewed his campaign to revise this historical verdict as inextricable from his commitment to the larger goal: the radical transformation of society, which he saw presently hindered by the received judgment about Stalin. Since he viewed anti–Stalinism as ipso facto anti-communism, the importance of defeating the latter made it essential to defeat the former; the charges against Stalin *had* to be false for communism eventually to prevail.

While Grover acknowledged that all communist states to date had "failed," he still believed in a society based on production for human needs rather than profit, and organized around a slightly amended version of the classic Marxist dictum: instead of "ability," from each according to "commitment," to each according to need. That is, presuming that people contributed as best they could, some would receive more than others because they needed more—perhaps because of illness or disability. Communists, in Grover's vision of this system, would not be dictators but rather role models, setting an example for others "by fighting the good battle selflessly for communism."

Grover voted but only because, as someone involved in local, reform organizations, "it's expected of me to do it"; though electorally based reforms could be helpful to people, "getting rid of capitalism" had to remain the goal. Indeed, he viewed elections under capitalism, involving such huge expenditures of money, as "just another way of circumventing democracy." For Grover, nothing less than communism could create the truly egalitarian society.

Four months after the interview, I had reason to visit Montclair State and made arrangements to have lunch with Grover. The evening before our appointment Grover called to share horrible information: he had found his younger son—28-year-old, Joe—lying dead from a diabetic attack and coma. Joe had lacked the health insurance necessary to have his condition treated. A week later my wife and I attended the funeral. In an unfortunate coincidence we had gone to a different funeral earlier in the day—the mother of my wife's best childhood friend—after which we immediately drove the more than 100 miles from one ceremony to the other.

The memorial service for Grover's son was held at a Universalist Church in Orange, New Jersey. We arrived to find hundreds of people jammed into a chapel built for an audience half that size; they filled all the benches and stood packed together in the aisles, no doubt in violation of the fire laws. The crowd included some left activists and academics—presumably colleagues of Grover's—but mostly Newark neighbors, people from diverse races and cultures. The "celebration" of Joe's life was overtly political, beginning with the explanation of his middle name in the program: Joseph Gracchus Furr was an allusion to Gracchus Babeuf, a French political agitator and journalist guillotined during the revolution, whose ideas were characterized by subsequent scholars as "socialist" or "communist," though such words did not exist during his lifetime. Grover's ex-wife spoke about the right of all children to have health care and the importance of the "mainstream taking control of the upstream" to guarantee that no one would die needlessly. People had various names for such a transformation, she told the group, but "to me it's communism"; obviously whatever issues caused their divorce, political differences were not among them. Grover's speech linked his son's triumph over a learning disability to the right to receive "the special care, instruction, and support that every child in this country, in this world, deserves but which so very, very many are denied" and honored the pride and dignity of Joe's work as a diesel mechanic. Other people came to the microphone to contribute their memories, including an elderly black woman, once a neighbor of the Furrs in Newark, who had traveled from North Carolina to attend and needed assistance to get up the steps to the rostrum.

The contrast between the two funerals could not have been more striking. At the earlier event, a traditional Catholic service, a well-intentioned priest had made boilerplate remarks about how belief in Jesus brought an eternity in paradise, inserting the deceased's name at the appropriate points; it was form letter as funeral service. At the commemoration of Joe's life, God was never mentioned, but people laughed, cried, hugged, sang versions of the old union song "Bread and Roses" and the civil rights song "I'm Gonna Sit at the Welcome Table" before gathering around a community meal as diverse as the crowd, as people from different cultures brought their traditional dishes to share. It was truly the "beloved community" that Todd Gitlin had found so compelling about early SDS, though not rooted in the easy idealism of youth but involving people of different ages who knew something about life's struggles. On the way home my wife, an observant Catholic who had been offended by the impersonality of the funeral for her friend's mother, remarked that the service for Joe was one of the most Christian events she had ever attended. Whatever one thinks about Grover's Marxist theory, his practice has obviously touched a lot of lives for the better.

Conclusion: Past and Present

Shortly after the collapse of the Eastern European communist regimes, the prominent Russian historian Louis Menashe reported seeing a poster with a caricature of a puzzled looking Marx and the caption (in German), "It seemed like a good idea at the time"[1]; it certainly did too for these nine former Princeton SDS members. Four decades later two of the nine—Doug Seaton, the lawyer for employers, and Chip Sills, the Anglican priest—have undergone dramatic transitions, taking them to the opposite end of the ideological spectrum. Three people may no longer be true believers but still have politics left of center. Professor of English Macklin Smith has liberal opinions, though politics is no longer a central concern in his life. The other two—journalist and producer Peter Kaminsky and professor of history Gordon Chang—have continued to be politically active on issues related to their professional positions; their involvement can be viewed to some extent as a continuation, though considerably tempered, of their earlier, radical activity. The remaining four former activists—physician Bobby Cohen, union organizer Jimmy Tarlau, professor of mathematics Neal Koblitz, and professor of English Grover Furr—are either still working for or at least would welcome a more socialistic society, though, with the exception of Grover, they now voiced their opinions in less inflammatory language. Despite Clemenceau's belief that such views were a consequence of youthful idealism, a number of this group have not followed the progression to more conservative beliefs that he expected from sensible people.

Yet whatever direction their politics have taken, except for Doug Seaton no one expressed any misgivings about having participated in the SDS campaigns intended to hinder the war effort. Indeed, many of these former activists cited their involvement in the antiwar movement as among the most significant accomplishments in their life, regretting only that they had not done more to end the conflict. The fact that this pride in their activism was mentioned even by those who would never support the same demands on campus today, provides testament to the degree to which the war was regarded as an atrocity justifying otherwise unacceptable measures. Peter put it succinctly. He no longer opposed the presence of ROTC on campus because "a nation needs an army," but "opposing it was the right thing" at a time when it was impossible "to excuse or condone the millions of deaths that the war produced"; the Vietnam War was "so evil," he continued, "that as a matter of practical policy anything you could do to throw a monkey wrench into it was okay." Similarly, the attempt to prevent CIA recruiting was justifiable at the time but made no sense to Peter today when the availability of nuclear weapons technology made good intelligence crucial. And, of course, the same reasoning applied to the sit-ins at IDA. "Again, it's contextual," he remarked; "Werner von Braun doing rocket research for the Nazis was different from Werner von Braun doing rocket research for us."

Most of the interviewees, however, still supported severing the relationship between the university and the military. Of the four people who have spent their professional lives as academics, only Macklin Smith now expressed ambivalence about opposition to ROTC's presence on campus, not because he favored it but because he considered the issue less important than the current approach to military recruitment, which he described as specifically targeting "people who are victimized because of their class situation," people "with few alternatives" available to them; even the draft, he believed, was preferable as a fairer system. But all the academics favored the termination of university involvement with defense department funded research, the closest contemporary equivalent of association with IDA.

While South African investment is no longer a controversial issue since the fall of the apartheid regime, all these former activists still supported the notion of using the university's portfolio in some circumstances to pursue political goals, though a couple of them thought that such attempts were nothing more than symbolic; "it makes you feel better," Peter observed, "but I don't know that it does anything." Perhaps because it is a market-based approach, not even the two conservatives opposed such a tactic if applied against regimes whose behavior they found objectionable. South Africa may have changed, but Doug Seaton would support similar economic pressure exerted against Iran and North Korea. As a libertarian, Chip Sills thought that "investment in general is something that's got to be allowed to happen," but if the university could be "persuaded" rather than "strong-armed" into participating, he would enthusiastically support the BDS movement—boycott, disinvest, sanction—against Israel.

This extent of agreement is perhaps unsurprising, given that the use of an institution's portfolio as a tool for social change is hardly a radical act anymore; ethical investing has become a common concern on campuses, the definition of such a consideration being more controversial than the issue of whether it should play a role in financial decisions. At Princeton, for example, in 2012 undergraduates voted overwhelmingly in favor of an oversight committee "to ensure socially responsible investment of the university's endowment." The most recent national campaign, involving students at more than 300 campuses, has focused on divestment from companies in the fossil fuel business; at Harvard alone there are two different student groups—Responsible Investment at Harvard and Divest, Harvard—calling for the university's portfolio to be scrubbed of stocks that profit from the release of carbon. (To which Harvard president Drew Gilpin Faust gave the same response as had President Goheen four decades earlier concerning South African investments: though "deeply concerned about climate change," divestment would have substantial economic costs and it would be more effective for the university to address the issue by efforts as shareholders to encourage companies to be "a positive force.") Even President Obama, in his Georgetown University speech on climate change, urged the audience to pressure those in power "to adopt smarter practices. Invest. Divest"—an unmistakable signal of encouragement for the divestment movement.[2]

For a number of interviewees, the most striking change had nothing to do with their opinion on any specific issue but rather with the extent of their commitment to a political system they had once rejected as incapable of effecting any meaningful change. Naturally the people whose views have moderated—not only the two conservatives but those people, though still left of center, for whom the bloom has long disappeared from the socialist rose—look to electoral politics for solutions to social problems; once the end has become less radical, the means inevitably follows suit. But, again with the lone exception of Grover Furr, who believes that only a revolution will bring about the desired result, even those still pursuing the socialist dream, or sympathetic to others' attempt to do so, now tended to pin their hopes on the conventional political process. This is not to say that there was enthusiasm for any specific political figure, and a number of the people on the left side of the spectrum were hard put to name anyone in electoral politics since the 1960s whom they supported, but even their disappointment at being unable to do so—indeed, especially their disappointment—was an indication of their desire for such a figure to emerge. Those who did mention someone often referred to their initial hopes for Jimmy Carter or Bill Clinton, which were dashed when the former proved feckless and the latter reckless.

As a corollary of their greater investment in the electoral system, the liberals also seemed more interested in the personal characteristics of political leaders than they had been during their student activist period. While their dismal opinion of George W. Bush's policy in Iraq was not unexpected, the visceral level of their dislike for the president differed sharply from the movement's reaction to an earlier commander-in-chief pursuing an unpopular war. Despite opposing the "imperialist" intervention in Vietnam, SDS members had viewed Lyndon Johnson as someone whose policies merely pursued the interests of the capitalist class that he represented. In contrast, a number of people characterized Bush (and Dick Cheney, too) as personally "evil." Macklin Smith called the administration "a bunch of thieves and liars," and Peter Kaminsky characterized the 43rd president as "a mean dry drunk," with "an abusive personality." The antiwar movement obsessed over Johnson's refusal to stop prosecution of the war in Vietnam, but no one ever cared a whit about his traits as a person.

While the politics of a number of the interviewees have changed over the intervening decades, their values have remained stable—an indication that the same values can inform dramatically different political positions. His belief in the importance of freedom and liberty led Doug Seaton to SDS in the 1960s but later to Reagan and George W. Bush. A similar emphasis has taken Chip Sills from collectivist notions to opposing even benign forms of government assistance; also important to Chip was solidarity with others, though the Marxist oriented connection to his comrades in the movement has been replaced by the religious imperative to give himself "to God and then to everybody else." In contrast, the liberal or radical interviewees mentioned social justice, fairness, respect for others, concern for the "downtrodden," and anti-racism—all values tending to focus more on equality than individual freedom.

The four people who have spent their professional life in academic positions all viewed the uproar over political correctness as overdone, silly, or malign. Although no one expressed any sympathy for speech codes, there was a sense that opposition to the desire for sensitive language represented, as Gordon Chang phrased it, a "cynical attack on people trying to do the right thing." It was hardly "a terrible imposition," in Neal Koblitz's opinion, to expect people "to use language that's respectful of minority groups, women, and the disabled." Besides, as the professor of English at the University of Virginia Mark Edmundson pointed out in *Why Teach*, his jeremiad on the state of the liberal arts, the real threat to serious inquiry in the 21st century college classroom emanates not from the politically correct left but from a free market ideology that has recast higher education as a business, whose primary mission is to satisfy its customers: the students. Thus, Edmundson observes, the "admirable impulse" underlying political correctness, the desire not to offend, has expanded to the point where professors have become "careful retailers who have it as a cardinal point of doctrine never to piss the customer off," creating less demanding intellectual environments, ensuring that no one fails, and making students exempt from criticism.[3] From this perspective politically correct language, the decline in standards, and the programs in identity studies and pop culture that so exercise conservative critics like Horowitz as well as liberals like Judt all merely reflect the market at work.

Of course, the most interesting question concerns what these brief biographies reveal about the factors that have influenced the political trajectories of these nine people, all from middle class or professional families. After being attracted to such a radical analysis of the society during their student days, what accounts for the varied directions that their politics have taken—for the fact that some former activists were still dedicated to the cause while others felt embarrassed to admit that they were once attracted to such an ideology.

Given the small sample, any attempt to identify the determining factors must necessarily be suggestive rather than conclusive. Individual experience since the end of the student movement has certainly played a role. Doug Seaton's six years as staff for the Minnesota state legislature's Labor Committee led to his transformation from a supporter of socialism to the lawyer for employers; while it is true that his opinions had begun to moderate as a result of his doctoral research on the Association of Catholic Trade Unionists, his exposure to the workings of the committee seemed to have exercised a transformative influence, taking him further down the conservative path.

However, different experiences by themselves are insufficient to account for the variability in political outcomes. Doug and his best friend, Jimmy Tarlau, were ideologically identical as undergraduates, but if, somehow, Jimmy had wound up working for the Minnesota Labor Committee, it is inconceivable that he would have gone through a similar political transition; in the years he spent on the factory floor, Jimmy must have seen his share of the sort of irresponsible behavior—the "scams and shams" that so shocked his old comrade—but it did not shake his political commitment. For these persons, whether or not experiences that might challenge liberal or radical beliefs actually exerted an effect seemed to depend largely on their background before joining the movement—before attending college. Despite being Marxist firebrands at Princeton, the two most conservative interviewees came from the two most conservative home environments. Doug's father had been involved in struggles against the left wing of his electronics union, and Doug himself had been a Goldwater supporter in high school, while Chip Sills had been raised in a military family.

Indeed, over time almost everyone in the group exhibited a tendency to gravitate toward the sociopolitical environment in which they had been raised. While Macklin Smith's liberal sympathies diverged somewhat from his parent's political disinterest, like them he has remained generally inactive. With one exception this same trend held true for the active liberals or radicals; not only were they raised in generally leftist environments, but the further left the environment, the more radical they tended to be. While none of them could be described as red diaper babies, in most cases either a relative—a grandfather or an uncle—or a friend of the family had been a member of the Communist Party, making the notion of Marxist ideology less threatening than the popular image. Peter Kaminsky, whose parents had liberal politics, described himself as a "classic Isaiah Berlin liberal." The importance for Gordon Chang of decency, respect for others, and tolerance mirrored the humanistic values emphasized by his mother. Bobby Cohen, whose father participated in leftist study groups and read the socialist classics, has considered himself a Marxist ever since elementary school; Bobby's sister, too, had been an SDS activist and attended medical school before first establishing a project for women and children with AIDS, which she directed for 25 years, and then joining a project in Rwanda to provide assistance for women who had been raped. Union activist Jimmy Tarlau was not only raised in a Stevensonian household but attended the most politically progressive school in New York. And Neal Koblitz, who with his wife has provided so much support for socialist countries, came from a family in which his mother was an activist in the National Education Association, the nation's largest teachers' union, and both his parents had politics at the left end of liberalism.

The lone exception to this association is Grover Furr, an unabashed communist despite having been raised in a fairly conservative home. However, his parents' situation is rather unusual. They both came of age in the South during the pre–civil rights era, acquiescing to its segregated society more as a cultural accommodation than a firmly held personal belief, and, once relocated to Montreal, their views became more progressive, culminating in Grover's father's support for liberal, anti-war senator Eugene McCarthy's campaign for the Democratic presidential nomination in 1968; father and son moved to the left simultaneously, though the former ended near where the latter had begun.

In her provocative book *The Nurture Assumption*, Judith Rich Harris argues that whatever similarity in personal traits exists between parents and children results not from the shared family environment but rather is caused by genetic factors. And the emerging new field of "genopolitics" employs the techniques of behavior genetics in the belief that genetic variation can explain some portion of the variation in political behavior—a controversial approach considered scientifically significant by some researchers but dismissed by others as "the modern day equivalent of phrenology."[4] Even more controversial, Harris goes on to insist that the non-genetic variation in personality characteristics reflects the influence of peers rather than parents; that is, children and adolescents look to each other rather than to parents for role models and sources of identification. Whatever one thinks of the genetic component of this theory of development, its emphasis on peer influence helps explain the earlier radicalism of these nine people at a time when so many of their contemporaries were rebelling.

Moreover, one additional factor, also related to peer influence, helps to differentiate between those interviewees who became more mainstream liberals and those further to the left: the existence of some sort of social or organizational support. A substantial body of research in social psychology has documented the tendency called "group polarization"—for the position arrived at by a group after discussion to be systematically more extreme than the initial inclination of its individual members. Thus, the presence of others with similar politics not only provides ideological reinforcement for one's views facilitated by the bonds of camaraderie, but, in the case of leftists, tends to make the group as a whole more radical than its members. Among the nine people profiled here, those who have remained further to the left have all been part of a collective of some kind—either a formal organization or a looser association of people of like mind. Gordon Chang spent the better part of two decades as a member of various radical minority groups; for some years Bobby Cohen practiced medicine surrounded by other activist physicians who viewed health care as a universal right; and for two decades Jimmy Tarlau was a member of the Communist Party. Neal Koblitz, not affiliated with any leftist group since resigning from the Progressive Labor Party, might seem to be an exception, but his focus on supporting women scientists in Third World countries has made him and his wife part of a number of groups in foreign countries in which socialism is a national ideal. Finally, Grover Furr, the most radical former SDS member, has been involved with one PL-led effort after another and, whether or not he is a member in some official sense, obviously has close ties to people in the party.

Thus, the picture that emerges of the person who, contrary to Clemenceau's expectation remains committed not just to leftist ideas but to activism long after the period of youthful idealism: someone from a liberal or radical family background, raised around peers with similar views and, even later in life, part of a group, formal or informal, that encouraged radical thought and supported corresponding policies.

～∞∞～

On the spectrum of 1960s movement activity, these nine Princeton radicals were all much closer to the organized political pole than to the individualistic one, more dedicated to structural change in the society and the polity rather than interested in "doing their own thing"; for the most part, these people were Marxists, not hippies or bohemians. However, this orientation did not prevent them, some more than others, from indulging in drug use, primarily marijuana and various hallucinogens; among the interviewees, only the intellectually precocious but socially less developed Neal Koblitz could be counted an abstainer. Nor did any of them claim to have "experimented" with drugs—that ridiculous verb used by politicians in an attempt to refashion their normal, youthful experience toking up as if it were some kind of research project. Most people in the movement, even those sympathetic to PL's more disciplined style, enjoyed getting high and tripping, and for the most part Princeton SDS members were no exception.

As an aside, this acknowledged use of drugs provides a graphic reminder of both the insanity of the War on Drugs and its selectively oppressive effect. Whatever one thinks of their politics, each of these former SDS members has gone on to a productive career; indeed, the person who apparently indulged the most—Peter Kaminsky—can point to probably the longest list of accomplishments in multiple fields. The fact that they used drugs has had no deleterious effect on their lives and offers persuasive evidence for Bobby Cohen's contention that drug policy is entirely arbitrary—that, like the parental "because," drugs are illegal only because they are illegal; no rational purpose nor any conceptualization of justice would have been served by their treatment as criminals. But, of course, none of these people was likely to suffer any legal consequences. As Michelle Alexander has convincingly demonstrated, despite studies suggesting that white professionals are the most likely of any group to have used illegal substances,[5] drug laws are enforced in a way that ensures the arrest and mass incarceration mainly of blacks and Latinos not fortunate enough to confine their use of drugs to Ivy League campuses. Not even at the height of the activist era among students, when drug use was an integral aspect of political rebelliousness, would it have been tolerable for police to swarm onto campus rounding up everyone with a joint in his or her possession, though similar tactics are standard procedure in minority neighborhoods.

The writer Kurt Andersen argues that the changes in society in the last half-century, economic as well as cultural, represent a triumph of the individualist wing of the 1960s movement. "Doing your own thing" in this analysis became the basis for "every man for himself"; the privileging of individual desires over collective interest led not only to the sensory gratifications of drugs and sex but to an unrestrained capitalism comfortable with executives paid 400 times the salary of an average employee, factories relocated overseas, and the kind of financial speculation that made accruing huge fortunes an end in itself. There is no doubt that at elite universities the idealism of the 1960s has been replaced by more acquisitive motivations. Instead of becoming scientists, physicians, inventors, or entrepreneurs, according to the *Harvard Crimson*, 58 percent of the men and 43 percent of the women in the class of 2007 took positions in finance or consulting. Although Andersen meant to link the individualist ethos of the 60s to the greed of subsequent generations, in fact this trend was epitomized *within* the life of Jerry Rubin. An anti-war activist, co-founder (with Abbie Hoffman) of the Youth International Party, and one of the "Chicago Eight," tried for incitement to riot at the 1968 Democratic National Convention, Rubin evolved from Yippie to Yuppie, encouraging business networking as the route to wealth creation and managing an operation accused of being a pyramid scheme.[6]

Despite their indulgence in drugs, none of the nine Princeton activists have made career choices influenced by the selfishness that Andersen saw resulting from the individualist end of the movement spectrum. Whatever direction their politics have taken, their decisions have been informed largely by remunerations other than financial, most of them pursuing not careers but callings. And in most cases that calling has offered the same attraction first provided by the movement decades earlier: the opportunity to lead a life of meaning, one that incorporates the person's deepest values. Chip Sills performing "corporal acts of mercy," Gordon Chang attempting to bridge the racial divide, Neal (and Ann Hibner) Koblitz working to improve the opportunities for women scientists in the Third World, Jimmy Tarlau and Doug Seaton fighting for the respective interests of workers and small business people, the groups with which they identify—these former SDS members and others in this sample have found ways to achieve the harmony of living their beliefs, creating a unity between their personal and professional selves.

Indeed, at least one of the persons in this group meets the formal criteria for a "moral exemplar" outlined by Anne Colby and William Damon, developmental psychologists at Stanford specializing in the study of moral development. Based on their discussions with theologians, philosophers, and scholars of ethics and morality, Colby and Damon propose that a moral exemplar is someone who demonstrates "a sustained commitment to moral ideals or principles that include a generalized respect for humanity"; "a disposition to act in accord" with these ideals or principles; "a willingness to risk one's self-interest for the sake of one's moral values"; "a tendency to be inspiring to others"; and "a sense of realistic humility about one's own importance," reflecting a "lack of concern for one's own ego."[7] This is a fairly accurate description of Bobby Cohen, the physician who has devoted his life largely to the treatment of prisoners and people with AIDS.

For two centuries the role of the Left in the United States, concludes the political historian Michael Kazin, has been to effect major changes in the nation's culture without itself ever coming to power.[8] That is certainly true of the 1960s movement, which never elected anyone to high office or made socialism a realistic possibility, but was nevertheless instrumental in creating a more humane and egalitarian society. As the nine former SDS members profiled here indicate, the student Left of the 1960s produced not only changes in the society but in the kind of lives chosen by the people who participated in it.

Chapter Notes

Introduction

1. Sarkozy is quoted in S. Schmemann, "Paris on the Anniversary of the 1968 Protests," *New York Times*, May 10, 2008, A18. On the confrontation at the Democratic convention, see the so-called "Walker Report": D. Walker, *Rights in Conflict* (National Commission on the Causes and Prevention of Violence, 1968). N. Mailer, *Miami and the Siege of Chicago* (Cleveland: World Publishing, 1968), 223.

2. E. Langer, "Notes for Next Time: A Memoir of the 1960s," in *Toward a History of the New Left: Essays from Within the Movement*, ed. R.D. Myers (Brooklyn, N.Y.: Carlson Publishing, 1989), 65. C. A. Reich, *The Greening of America: How the Youth Revolution Is Trying to Make America Livable* (New York: Random House, 1970), 340–341.

3. T. Gitlin, *The Sixties: Years of Hope, Days of Rage* (New York: Bantam Books, 1987), 433.

4. Z, Heller, *The Believers* (New York: HarperCollins, 2008), 26.

5. R. Kimball, *Tenured Radicals: How Politics Has Corrupted Our Higher Education* (New York: Harper & Row, 1990), xv.

6. *Ibid.*, 165.

7. *Ibid.*, 166–167. K. Andersen, "The Age of Apoplexy," *New York Magazine* (October 15, 2007): 22–23.

8. D. Horowitz, *The Professors: The 101 Most Dangerous Academics in America* (Washington, D.C.: Regnery), ix–x. For an example of distortion, Horowitz quoted Michael Berube as describing the university as "the final resting place of the New Left" and the "progressives' only bulwark against the New Right" (*ibid..*, 73). Berube actually wrote that, if one read 20 new books on the academy, one would find "the contemporary university is so amorphous that it can be described as the research wing of the corporate economy, the final resting place of the New Left, the last best hope for critical thinking, the engine room of global technological advance, the agent of secularization and the advance of reason, the training ground for the labor force, the conservatives' strongest bastion of antifeminist education, the progressives' only bulwark against the New Right, the natural home of intellectual isolates, the natural home of goosestepping groupthinkers, and the locus of postmodern skepticism and fragmentation." M. Berube, "The Abuses of the University," *American Literary History* 10 (1998): 147.

9. Horowitz, *The Professors*, 340. On Dorothy Day, see, S. Otterman, "In Hero of the Catholic Left, a Conservative Cardinal Sees a Saint," *New York Times*, November 27, 2012, 1.

10. T. Hayden, *Rebel: A Personal History of the 1960s* (Granada Hills, California: Red Hen Press, 2003); Gitlin, *The Sixties*. B. Ayers, *Fugitive Days: Memoir of an Antiwar Activist* (Boston: Beacon, 2001); M. Rudd, *Underground: My Life with SDS and the Weathermen* (New York: HarperCollins, 2009); C. Wilkerson, *Flying Close to the Sun: My Life and Times as a Weatherman* (New York: Seven Stories Press, 2007). The second memoir is B. Ayers, *Public Enemy: Confessions of an American Dissident* (Boston: Beacon, 2013). The quotes are from Rudd, *Underground*, 316, 121–122.

11. Reich, *The Greening of America*, 276.

12. K. Sale, *SDS* (New York: Random House, 1973), 16. The statement, originally distributed in mimeographed form by SDS, has been published as T. Hayden, *The Port Huron Statement: The Visionary Call of the 1960s Revolution* (New York: Thunder's Mouth Press, 2005); the quote is from p. 53. On SDS's early history, see Sale, *SDS*.

13. For year-by-year membership statistics

see the appendix, in *Ibid.*, p. 663–664. The "recruiter" quotation comes from p. 173.

Chapter 1

1. See D. Yankelovich, Inc., *The Changing Values on Campus: Political and Personal Attitudes of Today's College Students* (New York: Washington Square Press, 1972), 62. Yankelovich gives the statistics in response to these items for 1969, 1970, and 1971; the cited numbers are from 1970, the smallest percentage of disagreement in most cases, though the percentages in the other years are not much larger.

2. G.W. Domhoff, *Fat Cats and Democrats: The Role of the Big Rich in the Party of the Common Man* (Englewood Cliffs, NJ: Prentice-Hall, 1972), 157. See Sale, *SDS*, 484.

3. The history of prison labor system is documented in D.A. Blackmon, *Slavery by Another Name: The Re-Enslavement of Black Americans from the Civil War to World War II* (New York: Doubleday, 2008). D. Oshinsky, *"Worse Than Slavery": Parchman Farm and the Ordeal of Jim Crow Justice* (New York: Free Press, 1996).

4. For a detailed account of the black experience under segregation, see N.R. McMillen, *Dark Journey: Black Mississippians in the Age of Jim Crow* (Urbana: University of Illinois Press, 1989). M.E. Dyson, *April 4, 1968: Martin Luther King's Death and How It Changed America* (New York: Basic Civitas, 2008), 62. For an example of the gruesomeness of the event, see D.M. Oshinsky, *"Worse Than Slavery,"* 102–105.

5. *Boynton v. Virginia*, 364 U.S. 454 (1960). For photos of the Freedom Riders at the time of their arrest, see E. Etheridge, *Breach of Peace: Portraits of the 1961 Mississippi Freedom Riders* (New York: Atlas, 2008).

6. On the appointment of segregationist judges, see V. Navasky, *Kennedy Justice* (New York: Athenum, 1971), ch. 5.

7. H. Sitkoff, *The Struggle for Black Equality 1954–1980* (New York: Hill and Wang, 1981), 106. J. Farmer, *Lay Bare the Heart: An Autobiography of the Civil Rights Movement* (New York: Arbor House, 1985), 219. Farmer is quoted in Wofford, *Of Kennedys and Kings: Making Sense of the Sixties* (Pittsburgh: University of Pittsburgh Press, 1992), 153.

8. J.L. Jackson, Jr., *Racial Paranoia: The Unintended Consequences of Political Correctness* (New York: Basic Civitas, 2008), 63–64.

9. See J. Nelson and J. Bass, *The Orangeburg Massacre* (New York: World, 1970).

10. See "New Furor over an Old Informant," *Time* (July 24, 1978): 17. Both the defense attorney and Hoover are quoted in G. Collins, *When Everything Changed: The Amazing Journey of American Women from 1960 to the Present* (Boston: Little, Brown, 2009), 144, 145. On the SNCC coordinator, see "Curfew Imposed by Governor in Orangeburg, S.C.," *New York Times*, February 10, 1968, 23 and J. Bass, "Documenting the Orangeburg Massacre," *Nieman Reports* (Fall 2003): 8–11. The call to investigate the alleged black power movement is cited in D. Robinson, "Orangeburg Calm as Guard Patrols," *New York Times*, February 15, 1969, 29.

11. Quoted from the *St. Louis Globe-Democrat* in T. Branch, "The Last Wish of Martin Luther King," *New York Times*, April 6, 2008. See Dyson, *April 4, 1968*, 58–60 and "The FBI: The Crusade to Topple King," *Time* (December 1, 1975): 15. Thurman and Reagan are quoted in R. Perlstein, *Nixonland: The Rise of a President and the Fracturing of America* (New York: Scribner, 2008), 257.

12. G.E. Gilmore, *Defying Dixie: The Radical Roots of Civil Rights, 1919–1950* (New York: W.W. Norton, 2008), 6. Quoted in D. Caute, *The Great Fear: The Anti-Communist Purge Under Truman and Eisenhower* (New York: Simon and Schuster, 1978), 168.

13. On Levison, see D.J. Garrow, "The FBI and Martin Luther King," *Atlantic Monthly* 290 (July/August 2002): 80–88. T.F. Jackson, *From Civil Rights to Human Rights: Martin Luther King, Jr., and the Struggle for Economic Justice* (Philadelphia: University of Pennsylvania Press, 2007).

14. See T. Branch, *At Canaan's Edge: America in the King Years, 1965–68* (New York: Simon & Schuster, 2006), 684–685.

15. R. Suskind, "Without a Doubt," *New York Times Magazine*, October 17, 2004, 51.

16. Transcript is published in R. Reagan, "The President's News Conference, February 18, 1982," *Public Papers of the Presidents of the United States: Ronald Reagan, 1982 Volume I* (Washington, D.C.: U.S. Government Printing Office); the quote occurs on 184–185.

17. J.S. Olson and R. Roberts, *Where the Domino Fell: American and Vietnam, 1945 to 1990* (New York: St. Martin's Press, 1991), 9–10.

18. *Ibid.*, 8–12.

19. *Ibid.*, 226.

20. *Ibid.*, 23.

21. A.L.A. Patti, *Why Vietnam? Prelude to America's Albatross* (Berkeley: University of California Press, 1980), 56, 125, 374.

22. *Ibid.*, 248–249.

23. The entire Declaration appears in, *Vietnam Documents: American and Vietnamese Views of the War*, ed. G. Katsiaficas (Armonk, N.Y.: M.E. Sharpe, 1992), 7–9.

24. Patti, *Why Vietnam?*, 251.

25. Olson and Roberts, *Where the Domino Fell*, 20; Patti, *Why Vietnam?*, 367.

26. Quoted in E. Snow, *Journey to the Beginning* (New York: Random House, 1958), 389.

27. Quoted in J. Buttinger, *Vietnam: The Unforgettable Tragedy* (London: Andre Deutsch, 1977), 20.

28. R.E. Herzstein, *Henry R. Luce, Time, and the American Crusade in Asia* (New York: Cambridge University Press, 2005), 142.

29. See Olson and Roberts, *Where the Domino Fell*, 36. D. Schoenbrun, *Vietnam: How We Got In; How to Get Out* (New York: Atheneum, 1970), 33.

30. See Olson and Roberts, *Where the Domino Fell*, 48, 46. They give the figure of 300,000 Viet Minh deaths and a million Vietnamese civilians, compared to 95,000 French deaths.

31. See R. Drummond and G. Coblentz, *Duel at the Brink: John Foster Dulles' Command of American Power* (Garden City, N.Y.: Doubleday, 1960), 121–122.

32. Both parts of the Geneva Accords—the "Agreement on the Cessation of Hostilities in Vietnam" and the "Final Declaration of Geneva Conference"—are contained as appendices in the report by the Lawyers Committee on American Policy Towards Vietnam, *Vietnam and International Law* (Flanders, N.J.: O'Hare Books, 1967); the quotes appear on 148 and 149.

33. *Ibid.*

34. The "Statement by United States Representative on Final Declaration at Closing Session of Geneva Conference" appears in *ibid.*, 150.

35. On the surreptitious activity in the North, see the "Lansdale Team's Report on Covert Saigon Mission in 1954 and 1955," in *The Pentagon Papers: The Defense Department History of United States Decisionmaking on Vietnam, Volume 1* (Senator Gravel Edition) (Boston: Beacon, 1971), 573–583; also Olson and Roberts, *Where the Domino Fell*, 58. The

ICC finding is cited in B. Spock and M. Zimmerman, "How We Got Involved—The Vietnamese and the French," in *Vietnam Documents*, 42–43.

36. On Diem's background and selection as prime minister, see Olson and Roberts, *Where the Domino Fell*, 55–58 and Schoenbrun, *Vietnam*, 41–42.

37. D.D. Eisenhower, *Mandate for Change 1953–1956* (Doubleday: Garden City, N.Y., 1963), 372. Patti, *Why Vietnam?* 240. J. Alsop, "A Reporter at Large," *New Yorker* 31 (June 25, 1955): 35, 39, 48, 63, 58.

38. J. Osborne, "The Tough Miracle Man of Vietnam," *Life* (May 13, 1957): 164.

39. "South Vietnam: Revolt at Dawn," *Time* (November 21, 1960): 27. E.K. Lindley, "An Ally Worth Having," *Newsweek* (June 29, 1959): 31. Kennedy is quoted in Buttinger, *Vietnam*, 36; Baker, "Eisenhower Greets Vietnam President," 16. G. MacGregor, "Vietnam Economy Termed Stagnant," *New York Times*, November 4, 1957, 57. Diem is quoted in Spock and Zimmerman, "How We Got Involved," 43.

40. In a 1955 referendum, Diem received 5,722,000 votes out of a total of 5,785,000, according to "South Vietnam: The Firing Line," *Time* (August 4, 1961): 29. T. Buckley, "What Life's Like in Vietcong Territory," *New York Times Magazine*, November 23, 1969, 136. On the election for National Assembly and the abolition of village councils, see Olson and Roberts, *Where the Domino Fell*, 68, 63; also, D. Luce and J. Sommer, *Vietnam: The Unheard Voices* (Ithaca, N.Y.: Cornell University Press, 1969), 48. On the one successful opposition candidate, see Buttinger, *Vietnam*, 35–36. Osborne, "The Tough Miracle Man of Vietnam," 164.

41. For profiles of the Diem family, see Olson and Roberts, *Where the Domino Fell*, 64–65, 99–100. On Nhu, see also S. Castan, "Vietnam's Two Wars," *Look* (January 28, 1964): 35. D. Halberstam, "Charges Threat by Embassy," *New York Times*, August 8, 1963, 3. H.J. Morgenthau, "We Are Deluding Ourselves in Vietnam," *New York Times Magazine*, April 18, 1965, 86.

42. Olson and Roberts, *Where the Domino Fell*, 66. Buttinger, *Vietnam*, 36. See also R.S. McNamara, J.G. Blight, and R.K. Brigham with T.J. Biersteker and H.Y. Schandler, *Argument Without End: In Search of Answers to the Vietnam Tragedy* (New York: Public Affairs, 1999), 179; G.M. Goldstein, *Lessons in Disaster: McGeorge Bundy and the Path to War in*

Vietnam (New York: Times/Henry Holt, 2008), 51.

43. Olson and Roberts, *Where the Domino Fell*, 63. R. Scheer, "Behind the Miracle of South Vietnam," in *Vietnam and America*, ed. M.E. Gettleman, J. Franklin, M.B. Young, and H.B. Franklin (New York: Grove, 1995), 144.

44. See Luce and Sommer, *Vietnam: The Unheard Voices*, 114–117; also, Goldstein, *Lessons in Disaster*, 75–76.

45. The United Nations special commission is mentioned in Castan, "Vietnam's Two Wars," 35.

46. On the coup, see Goldstein, *Lessons in Disaster*, 77–91, and Olson and Roberts, *Where the Domino Fell*, 104–105. Some of the coups are described in Olson and Roberts, 122–127, and the total number is given in *Vietnam Documents*, 62.

47. The White Paper is quoted in Scheer, "Behind the Miracle of South Vietnam," 141. On the assassinations, see Olson and Roberts, *Where the Domino Fell*, 67.

48. G. Porter, "Distorting History," *Society* 21 (November-December, 1983): 19. Buckley, "What Life's Like in Vietcong Territory," 136. On NLF organization and practice, see K. Knoebl, *Victor Charlie: The Face of War in Vietnam* (New York: Frederick A. Praeger, 1967), chapter 5 and J. Schell, *The Village of Ben Suc* (New York Alfred A. Knopf, 1967), 3–11. The estimate of NLF control is cited in *Vietnam Documents*, 63. G.R. Hess, "The Unending Debate: Historians and the Vietnam War," *Diplomatic History* 18 (1994): 259.

49. The most thorough examination of the incident is J.C. Goulden, *Truth is the First Casualty: The Gulf of Tonkin Affair—Illusion and Reality* (Chicago: Rand McNally, 1969); the commander is quoted on 152. Goulden quotes Johnson (160) as saying "For all I know, our Navy was shooting at whales out there."

50. The White Paper is reprinted in *Vietnam and America*, 255–268. Morgenthau, "We Are Deluding Ourselves in Vietnam," 86–87. Johnson's address, delivered at Johns Hopkins University, was recorded and reprinted as "Text of the President's Address on U.S. Policies in Vietnam, *New York Times*, April 8, 1965, 16.

51. Johnson, "Text of the President's Address," 16. The quoted portion of Johnson's address was also cited as the American purpose 2 years later by General Maxwell Taylor, who had been the Ambassador to South Vietnam at the beginning of the escalation; see M.D.

Taylor, "General Taylor Says: The Cause in Vietnam Is Being Won," *New York Times Magazine*, October 15, 1967, 37. Bundy was quoted in "The Use of Power With a Passion for Peace," *Time* (June 25, 1965): 28. Acheson was quoted in B.B. Fall, "'This isn't Munich, it's Spain,'" *Ramparts* (December 1965): 29. J. Reston, "Washington: The Guiding Principle in Vietnam," *New York Times*, February 26, 1965, 28.

52. Ky and Thieu are profiled in Olson and Roberts, *Where the Domino Fell*, 131–132; the Assistant Secretary of State for East Asian and Pacific Affairs, William Bundy—National Security Advisor McGeorge Bundy's brother—is quoted on 132. N. Sheehan, "Not a Dove, But No Longer a Hawk," *New York Times Magazine*, October 9, 1966, 132; Sheehan also makes the "Captain Marvel" observation, 137. See also J. Randal, "Vietnam's Army: Sometimes It Only Seems to Fight," *New York Times*, June 11, 1967, 198.

53. The election and the subsequent arrests are described in F. Fitzgerald, *Fire in the Lake: The Vietnamese and the Americans in Vietnam* (Boston: Little, Brown, 2002), 332–338 and in L. Berman, *Lyndon Johnson's War: The Road to Stalemate in Vietnam* (New York: W.W. Norton, 1989): 79–80. See also Olson and Roberts, *Where the Domino Fell*, 164–165.

54. The quotation comes from D. DeVoss, "The Other prisoners," *Time* (March 19, 1973): 41. The prisons are also described in Luce and Sommer, *Vietnam: The Unheard Voices*, 157–158 and in J. Leslie, "Saigon's Political Prisoners Tell of Torture," *Los Angeles Times*, Match 4, 1973. Estimates of the number of political prisoners held by the Thieu/Ky government, range as high as 200,000.

55. The role of government officials in drug smuggling in South Vietnam, including the heroin epidemic among American troops, is detailed in A.W. McCoy, *The Politics of Heroin in Southeast Asia* (New York: Harper & Row, 1972), chapter 5. The report by the customs advisor is quoted in "Saigon Airport a Smugglers' Paradise," *New York Times*, April 22, 1971, 1. J. Anderson, "Is South Vietnam's Gen. Ky now a refugee 'godfather?'" *Courier-Post*, December 22, 1983, 11a.

56. Pham Van Dong is quoted in Schoenbrun, *Vietnam*, 79. The details of the South Vietnamese military are provided in Olson and Roberts, *Where the Domino Fell*, 250.

57. Reagan's speech, including the "noble cause" comment is reported in H. Raines,

"Reagan Calls Arms Race Essential To Avoid a 'Surrender' or 'Defeat,'" *New York Times*, August 19, 1980, 1; the full text of the speech is available onlineat http://www.presidency.ucsb.edu/ws/index.php?pid=85202. The text of Bush's speech appears in "Transcript of the Comments by Bush on the Air Strikes Against the Iraqis," *New York Times*, January 17, 1991, A14.

58. P. Feeny with J. Allaway, "The Ecological Impact of the Air War," in *Vietnam and America*, 462–463. E.S. Herman, *Atrocities in Vietnam: Myths and Realities* (Philadelphia: Pilgrim Press, 1970), 55.

59. Feeny with Alloway, "The Ecological Impact of the Air War," 463. Quoted in F. Harvey, *Air War-Vietnam* (New York: Bantam, 1967), 58. G.H. Orians and E.W. Pfeiffer, "Ecological Effects of the War in Vietnam," *Science* 168 (1970): 552.

60. Herman, *Atrocities in Vietnam*, 45. Olson and Roberts, *Where the Domino Fell*, 160–161.

61. Ellsberg makes this observation in Peter Davis's Oscar-winning 1974 documentary *Hearts and Minds*.

62. South Vietnamese desertion rates are discussed in Olson and Roberts, *Where the Domino Fell*, 130–131; the same source (97) reports use of the expression "Vietcong PXs." For reports of robbery, see, for example, N. Sheehan, "Luxury a Fading Echo in Banmethuot," *New York Times*, October 18, 1965, 4; R.W. Apple Jr., "Saigon's Troops Plunder Hamlet," *New York Times*, November 28, 1966, 4; and Luce and Sommer, *Vietnam: The Unheard Voices*, 272, 270.

63. The general's account appears in Sheehan, "Not a Dove, But No Longer a Hawk," 133. The major is quoted in C. Mohr, "Siege at Pleime: Americans Marvel at Tough Foe, *New York Times*, October 28, 1965, 1. Sheehan, "Not a Dove, But No Longer a Hawk," 27, 132–133.

64. D. Pike, *Viet Cong: The Organization and Techniques of the National Liberation Front of South Vietnam* (Cambridge, Mass.: MIT Press, 1966), 110, 111. A. de Borchgrave, "Then and Now—the Difference," *Newsweek* (March 14, 1966): 42. On the Rand Corporation and the M&M studies, see R. Robin, *The Making of the Cold War Enemy: Culture and Politics in the Military-Industrial Complex* (Princeton, N.J.: Princeton University Press, 2001), 46–50, 190–192. "Loyalties of the Hamlets," *New York Times*, August 7, 1967, 14.

65. The shooting of villagers who refused to leave is reported in Castan, "Vietnam's Two Wars," 35. The demolition is described in Schell, *The Village of Ben Suc*, 131–132. The refugee conditions are described in T. Buckley, "Rural Vietnamese Swept Up by War Into Refugee Camps," *New York Times*, October 28, 1967, 1 and in Schell, *The Military Half* (New York: Alfred A. Knopf, 1968), 70. Quoted in D. Halberstam, "Crucial Point in Vietnam," *New York Times*, December 23, 1963, 1.

66. H. Bigart, "U.S. Helps Vietnam In Test of Strategy Against Guerillas," *New York Times*, March 29, 1962, 1. Schell, *The Village of Ben Suc*, 94. H. Bigart, "Vietnam Sets Up Fortified Towns," *New York Times*, April 1, 1962, 3. M.D. Taylor, "The Cause in Vietnam Is Being Won," 137, 138.

67. On the warning leaflets, see Schell, *The Military Half*, 5–25. The quotation is from Schell, *The Village of Ben Suc*, 104.

68. The anti-personnel bombs are described in Harvey, *Air War-Vietnam*, 55–57 and in Herman, *Atrocities in Vietnam* 70–75. M.W. Browne, *The New Face of War* (Indianapolis: Bobbs-Merrill, 1965), 118. The effort to transport napalmed children to medical care is described in W.F. Pepper, "The Children of Vietnam," *Ramparts* 5 (January 1967): 44–67.

69. O. Schell, "'Pop Me Some Dinks,'" *New Republic* (January 3, 1970): 29. See also Herman, *Atrocities in Vietnam*, 50 and D. Robinson, "Ex-Pilot Alleges Civilian Slayings, *New York Times*, April 7, 1970, 5. Schell, *The Military Half*, 53; the same quote as widespread among American soldiers appears in S. Hersh, *My Lai 4: A Report on the Massacre and Its Aftermath* (New York: Random House, 1970), 13.

70. Quoted in T. Smith, "Anti-Vietcong Cordon Disrupts Life of a Village," *New York Times*, September 24, 1969, 6.

71. Conditions in Saigon and other urban areas are discussed in a number of essays in B. Weisberg, *Ecocide in Indochina* (San Francisco: Canfield Press, 1970): O. Schell and B. Weisberg. "Ecocide in Indochina," 17–32; F. Fitz-Gerald, "The Tragedy of Saigon," 142–156; and T. Bodenheimer and G. Roth, "Health and Death in Vietnam," 163–168. Sheehan, "Not a Dove, But No Longer a Hawk," 137.

72. S.P. Huntington, "The Bases of Accommodation," *Foreign Affairs* 46 (1968): 653, 650, 649.

73. The herbicide program as well as the

attempt to burn down forests are described in W.A. Buckingham, Jr., *Operation Ranch Hand: The Air Force and Herbicides in Southeast Asia 1961–1971* (Washington, D.C.: Office of Air Force History, 1982). On the change in Vietnamese agricultural production, see the pamphlet by B. Bartholomew, M. Bradley, P. Caldarola, P. Cohen, H. Edenberg, L. Glibert, P. Grobstein, D. Kennedy, E. Merrell, P. Morrow, and C. Pittendrigh, "A Legacy of our Presence: The Destruction of Indochina" (Stanford: Stanford Biology Study Group, 1970), 4. The twin purposes of the program are described in J. Raymond, "Weed Killers Aid War on Vietcong," *New York Times*, March 28, 1965, 2. Statistics on the program appear in Buckingham, *Operation Ranch Hand*, 199–201 and in T. Whiteside, *Defoliation* (New York: Ballantine Books, 1970) 84–85. Whiteside (8) also mentions the program's original name.

74. On concentration of the chemical, see Whiteside, *Defoliation*, 30–32, 108 and T. Fuller, "4 Decades on, U.S. Starts Cleanup of Agent Orange in Vietnam," *New York Times*, August 10, 2012, A4. The necessity for a pilot to dump the whole chemical load at once is mentioned in R. Blumenthal, "U.S. Shows Signs of Concern Over Effect of 9-Year Defoliation Program in Vietnam, *New York Times*, March 15, 1970, 14 and in Orians and Pfeiffer, "Ecological Effects of the War in Vietnam,"553. On the NIH study and the attempt to suppress its results, see Whiteside, *Defoliation*, 16–22. The study by the Japanese agronomist is discussed in S.M. Hersh, "Our Chemical War," *New York Review of Books* (April 25, 1968): 33, 34.

75. The petition, together with a list of the Nobel Laureates who signed it, appeared as "Text of Scientists' Petition to Johnson," *Washington Post*, February 15, 1967, A13. The statement by the Federation appeared in "Chemical Agents in War Are Criticized," *F.A.S. Newsletter* 19 (Febrary 1966): 1–2 and in "Scientists Protest Crop Destruction," *Science* 151 (1966): 309. The AAAS resolution, "Use of Herbicides in Vietnam," can be found in the association's online archives at http://archives.aaas.org/docs/resolutions.php?doc_id=283. Orians and Pfeiffer, "Ecological Effects of the War in Vietnam," 544–554. The report of the AAAS investigators is summarized in "Manmade Wasteland in Vietnam," *New York Times*, January 2, 1971, 16. The call for an agreement is reported in "...and a Plea to Ban 'Ecocide,'" *New York Times*, February

26, 1970. See also B. Weisberg, "On ecocide," in Weisberg, *Ecocide in Indochina*, 1–14.

76. On the VA campaign of denial, see R. Severo and L. Milford, *The Wages of War: When American Soldiers Came Home—From Valley Forge to Vietnam* (New York: Simon & Shuster, 1989), chapters 24–27; the official is quoted on 390. The first review was Committee to Review the Health Effects in Vietnam Veterans of Exposure to Herbicides, *Veterans and Agent Orange: Health Effects of Herbicides Used in Vietnam* (Washington, D.C.: National Academy Press, 1994); updated versions of the report appeared in 1996 and 1998. The list of diseases associated with Agent Orange exposure can be found on the Department of Veterans Affairs website, http://www.publichealth.va.gov/exposures/agentorange/diseases.asp.

77. P.J. Griffiths, *Agent Orange: "Collateral Damage" in Vietnam* (London: Trolley, 2004), 38, 108.

78. For descriptions of the killings, all based on eyewitness recollections, see S. Hersh, *My Lai 4*, 54–58, 74–75; R. Hammer, *One Morning in the War: The Tragedy at Son My* (New York: Coward-McCann, Inc., 1970), 130–138, 144; and H. Wingo, photographed by R.L. Harberle, "The Massacre at Mylai," *Life* 67 (December 5, 1969): 36–45.

79. The press officer is quoted in Hersh, *My Lai 4*, 78. "G.I.'s, in Pincer Move, Kill 128 in a Daylong Battle," *New York Times*, March 17, 1968, 1. The praise for the officers is quoted in M. Bilton and K. Sim, "My Lai: A Half-Told Story," (London) *Sunday Times Magazine* (April 23, 1989): 34. The official investigation, the (General William R.) Peers Report, which quotes from the combat-action report, is available online at http://www.law.umkc.edu/faculty/projects/ftrials/mylai/suppression.html.

80. Ridenhour's letter is reprinted in J.S. Olson and R. Roberts, *My Lai: A brief History with Documents* (Boston: Bedford, 1998), 147–151.

81. "Colonel Says Every Large Combat Unit in Vietnam Has a Mylai," *New York Times*, May 25, 1971, 13. Hersh, *My Lai 4*, 31–35, 178, 184. Hammer, *One Morning in the War*, 145. The investigation is the subject of D. Nelson, *The War Behind Me: Vietnam Veterans Confront the Truth About U.S. War Crimes* (New York: Basic Books, 2008). N. Turse, *Kill Anything That Moves: The Real American War in Vietnam* (New York: Metropolitan Books, 2013).

82. Gavin is quoted in B. Buzzanco, "The American Military's Rationale Against the Vietnam War," *Political Science Quarterly* 101 (1986): 572. See T. O'Brien, "The Vietnam In Me," *New York Times Magazine*, October 2, 1994, 52 and H. Kamm, "G.I.'s Near Songmy Doubt Any Massacre," *New York Times*, December 1, 1969, 12. The analyst, Douglas Pike, is quoted in G.D. Solis, *Son Thang: An American War Crime* (Annapolis, Md.: National Institute Press, 1997), 144–145.

83. C.L. Sulzberger, "Foreign Affairs: Corpse on Horseback," *New York Times*, May 12, 1967, 46. B. Levin, "Bertrand Russell: Prosecutor, Judge, and Jury," *New York Times*, February 19, 1967, 234. The result of the hearings was published as B. Russell, *War Crimes in Vietnam* (New York: Monthly Review Press, 1967). S, Melman (Research Director) M. Baron and D. Ely (Research Associates), *In the Name of America: The conduct of the war in Vietnam by the armed forces of the United States as shown by published reports, compared with the Laws of War binding on the United States Government and on its citizens* (Annandale, Va.: Turnpike, 1968).

84. N. Sheehan, "Should We Have War Crime Trials?" *New York Times Book Review*, March 28, 1971, 1–3, 30–34. T. Taylor, *Nuremberg and Vietnam: An American Tragedy* (Chicago: Quadrangle Books, 1970). See also Taylor's comments, quoted in N. Sheehan, "Taylor Says by Yamashita Ruling Westmoreland May Be Guilty," *New York Times*, January 9, 1971, 3.

85. J. Raymond, "Veteran of Special Forces Denounces U.S. Policy in Vietnam as a 'Lie,'" *New York Times*, February 10, 1966, 2. J. Duncan, "'The whole thing was a lie!,'" *Ramparts* 4 (February 1966): 23, 15; on Duncan's service record, see D. Duncan, *The New Legions* (New York: Random House, 1967), 275.

86. W.D. Ehrhart, *Ordinary Lives: Platoon 1005 and the Vietnam War* (Philadelphia: Temple University Press, 1999), 19, 20. The reflections on his experience in Vietnam were made in episode number 4 of the 11-part PBS series, "Vietnam: A Television History"; a copy of the transcript appears online at http://www.pbs.org/wgbh/amex/vietnam/series/pt_04.html.

87. On the generals' opposition to the war, see Buzzanco, "The American Military's Rationale Against the Vietnam War," 559–576; the quotes from Gavin and Shoup come from 567 and 571–572. H.B. Hester, letter to the editor, *New York Times*, April 3, 1971, 28.

88. D, Cortright, *Soldiers in Revolt: The American Military Today* (Garden City, N.Y.: Anchor Press, 1975), 10–16, 35–36, 123–124, 43–47. On fragging, see also Solis, *Marines and Military Law in Vietnam: Trial by Fire* (Washington, D.C.: History and Museums Division Headquarters, U.S. Marine Corps, 1989), 110–111. R,D. Heinl, Jr., "The Collapse of the Armed Forces," *Armed Forces Journal* 108 (June 7, 1971): 30.

89. Cortright, *Soldiers in Revolt*, 286–302 gives a list of 259 underground newspapers with, in some cases, dates of publication. Heinl, "The Collapse of the Armed Forces," 31. See also J. Lembcke, *The Spitting Image: Myth, Memory, and the Legacy of Vietnam* (New York: New York University Press, 1998), 42 for a characterization of the underground newspapers. The Concerned Officers Movement is discussed in Cortright, 109 and Heinl, 33.

90. A.E. Hunt, *The Turning: A History of Vietnam Veterans Against the War* (New York: New York University Press, 1999), 50–51, 112–116.

91. See Cortright, *Soldiers in Revolt*, 53 and Hunt, *The Turning*, 34. On the show, see R. Greenspun, "Jane Fonda's 'F.T.A.' Show Now a Film," *New York Times*, July 22, 1972, 14.

92. See Lembcke, *The Spitting Image*, especially 32 and 71–83. C. Andersen, *Citizen Jane: The Turbulent Life of Jane Fonda* (New York: Henry Holt, 1990), 209. A. Hoffman, *Revolution for the Hell Of It* (New York: Dial, 1968), 25. An article on the October 1969 moratorium described how hecklers responded to some opponents of the war attempting to read the names of men who had been killed in Vietnam by yelling, "Spit at those people," though it does not record that anyone acted on the demand; "America gathers under a sign of peace," *Life* 67 (October 24, 1969): 39.

93. "The Vietnam Agreement and Protocols" was published in *New York Times*, January 25, 1973, 15.

94. The tapes are discussed in R. Perlstein, "'They'll Open Up for This,'" *Newsweek* (December 15, 2008): 38; the quote from Kissinger on the tape appears in G. Rose, "What Would Nixon Do?" *New York Times*, June 26, 2011, SR3. The analyst, Howard Glaser, was quoted in D, Streitfeld, "A Bold U.S. Plan to Help Struggling Homeowners," *New York Times*, March 27, 2010, B1. "Briefing," *Time* (December 19, 2011): 15.

95. H.B. Franklin, "Antiwar and Proud of

It," *Nation* (December 11, 2000): 6. Nixon's taped discussion with Henry Kissinger is quoted in D. Ellsberg, *Secrets: A Memoir of Vietnam and the Pentagon Papers* (New York: Penguin, 2002), 418–419. Acknowledgement of the movement's influence in Nixon's memoir is quoted in H. Zinn, *The Zinn Reader: Writings on Disobedience and Democracy* (New York: Seven Stories Press, 1997), 401.

96. For a detailed study of FBI activities just at Berkeley, see S. Rosenfeld, *Subversives: The FBI's War on Student Radicals and Reagan's Rise to Power* (New York: Farrar, Strays & Giroux, 2012). J.M. Crewdson, "F.B.I. Burglarized Leftist Offices Here 92 Times in 1960–66, Official Files Show," *New York Times*, March 29, 1976, 1. N. Chomsky, Introduction to N. Blackstock, *COINTELPRO: The FBI's Secret War on Political Freedom* (New York: Vintage, 1976), 4.

97. For typical letters sent by the FBI to parents, see J.K. Davis, *Assault on the Left: The FBI and the Sixties Antiwar Movement* (Westport, Conn.: Praeger, 1997), 54, 91–93, 117, 119, 126, 145–146; also D. Cunningham, *There's Something Happening Here: The New Left, the Klan, and FBI Counterintelligence* (Berkeley: University of California Press, 2004), 142–143. For examples of dismissals resulting from FBI efforts, see N. Chomsky, "Engineering of Consent," the foreword to *Counter-Intelligence: A Documentary Look at America's Secret Police, Volume I* (Chicago: Citizens in Defense of Civil Liberties, 1982), v. The false information on housing is described in Cunningham, *There's Something Happening Here*, 53–54.

98. Copies of the original FBI materials— internal memos, and anonymous letters—are available at http://www.icdc.com/~paulwolf/cointelpro/b/aclnationalist.htm. A number of them are also reproduced in *Counter-Intelligence*. For coverage at the time of the killings, already indicating a deliberate government plot, see C. Chandler, "Black Panther Killings in Chicago," *New Republic* (January 10, 1970): 21–24. The larger story of the years long legal battle to get at the truth is told in J. Haas, *The Assassination of Fred Hampton: How the FBI and the Chicago Police Murdered a Black Panther* (Chicago: Lawrence Hill, 2009).

99. On Tommy the Traveler, see "Hobart College Upset by Police Agent," *New York Times*, June 7, 1970, 62 and "Police: Tales of Three Cities," *Time* (June 22, 1970): 18. On Grantwohl, see S.M. Hersh, "F.B.I. Informer Is Linked to Bombings and Protests by Weath-

ermen Groups," *New York Times*, May 20, 1973, 56. For the offer of explosives, see the article photocopied in *Counter-Intelligence*, 46. The killing of the veteran is described in R.J. Goldstein, *Political Repression in Modern America from 1870 to present* (Cambridge, Mass.: Schenkman, 1978), 473–474 and in P. Chevigny, *Cope and Rebels: A Study of Provocation* (New York: Pantheon, 1972), 264–265.

100. See S.V. Roberts, "F.B.I. Informer Is Linked to Right-Wing Violence," *New York Times*, June 24, 1973, 30 and E.R. Holles, "A.C.L.U. Says F.B.I. Funded 'Army' to Terrorize Young War Dissidents," *New York Times*, June 27, 1975, 4.

Chapter 2

1. Princeton was founded in 1746, after Harvard (1636), William & Mary (1693), and Yale (1701). Princeton's history during the colonial period is described on the university's website at http://www.princeton.edu/main/about/history/american-revolution/.

2. J. Karabel, *The Chosen: The Hidden History of Admissions and Exclusion at Harvard, Yale, and Princeton* (New York: Houghton Mifflin, 2005). Wilson's opinion of blacks and slavery is quoted in D. Blackmon, *Slavery by Another Name* (New York: Doubleday, 2008), 358; H.W. Bragdon, *Woodrow Wilson: The Academic Years* (Cambridge, Mass.: Belknap Press of Harvard University Press, 1967), 237–238; and K. A. Clements, *Woodrow Wilson: World Statesman* (Boston: Twayne, 1987), 7. E.E. Slosson, *Great American Universities* (New York: Macmillan, 1910), 104.

3. Karabel, *The Chosen*, 232–236, 379.

4. R. Evans, "Nassau St. Pickets Attacked by Mob," *Daily Princetonian* (hereinafter *DP*), March 14, 1960, 1. The Dean's description of blacks' characterization was reported in F. Stuart Jr., "Report Cites Evolution of Negro at Princeton," *DP*, January 19, 1963, 1. I personally observed the confederate flags during my time as a student at Princeton from 1967 through 1970. On the committee, see the articles in the *DP*: J. Armstrong, "Group Promotes Segregation," March 13, 1964, 1; J. Armstrong, "Race Reconciliation Group Elects Negro Vice-President," April 10, 1964, 1; J. MacGregor, "Goheen Scores Treatment of Race Reconciliationists," April 14, 1964, 1; R. J. Biunno, "Putnam says Anthropological Facts Prove Genetic Inferiority of Negroes," May 15,

1964, 1. On Putnam and the scientific campaign against civil rights, see W. H. Tucker, *The Funding of Scientific Racism: Wickliffe Draper and the Pioneer Fund* (Champaign, Ill.: University of Illinois Press, 2002), ch. 4.

5. Slosson, *Great American Universities*, 105. The university secretary is quoted in Karabel, *The Chosen*, 124.

6. See Karabel, *The Chosen*, 298–310. C.W. Mills, *The Power Elite* (New York: Oxford University Press, 2000), 67.

7. J. Parsons, "Notes from Nowhere," *DP*, February 8, 1960, 2. H. Meserve, "Item: Discrimination," *DP*, February 10, 1960, 2. P. J. Ponomarenko (recipient of the Freshmen First Honor Prize), letter to the editor, *DP*, February 20, 1964.

8. Slosson, *Great American Universities*, 107. F. S. Fitzgerald, *This Side of Paradise* (New York: Charles Scribner's Sons, 1920), 40. There were regular stories about head shaving in the *DP* every fall up till 1965, though sometimes a stencil and paint replaced the shears; see, for example, J. H. Glick, "Frosh Rally Invaded by Sophs," *DP*, September 24, 1962, 1. On the interclass gang fight, see S. F. Medina Jr., "600 Riot in Resumed Class Rivalry," *DP*, September 22, 1960, 1.

9. . C. Creesy, "'Spring Riot': 1,500 Participate, 12 Arrested," *DP*, May 7, 1963, 1, 4. The governor was quoted in "14 Are Arrested in Princeton Riot," *New York Times*, May 8, 1963. The university president was quoted on the cause of an earlier and similar if not quite as destructive riot in "700 Riot at Goheen House, Railroad Station; President Forced to Help Quell Disturbance," *DP*, May 17, 1960, 1. The rioters in 1960 shouted that they wanted extended hours for women in the dorms and permission to have cars on campus; see "1,500 at Princeton Go on Noisy Spree," *New York Times*, May 17, 1960.

10. "Proctors Investigate Midnight Raid On Room of Socialist Club Leader," *DP*, December 19, 1961, 1. The characterization of Princeton in the early 60s appeared in J. Johns, "Activists Challenge Princeton to Modernize with the Times," *DP*, January 21, 1971, 1. Assistant Dean George D. O'Brien, quoted in P. Sandman, "Princeton Charlie: An Educational Success?" *DP*, October 20, 1964, 1.

11. On the advertisement signed by faculty, see M.W. Miles, "Sixty Faculty Members Sign Protest Against American Policy in Vietnam," *DP*, February 24, 1965, 1. When the ad actually appeared it was signed by 93 members of

the Princeton faculty; see "An Open Letter to President Johnson on Vietnam," *New York Times*, March 1, 1965, 17. An ad from the student group supporting U.S. policy in Vietnam, signed by more than 200 undergraduates appeared as "An Open Letter from the Other Ad HOC Committee," *DP*, March 12, 1965, 5. On the telegram, see J. Dippel, "Vietnam Telegram Prepared," *DP*, October 27, 1965, 1. "SDS Attends Washington Rally," *DP*, November 30, 1965, 1. "Princeton Students for a Democratic Society: Radical Activism in an Unlikely Place," *DP*, May 12, 1966, 4–5.

12. P.T. Chew, "What the Draft Ruckus Is All About," *National Observer*, October 25, 1965, 1. See also P. Sandman, "200 Would-Be Debaters Invade Organizational Meeting of SDS," *DP*, October 20, 1965, 1. "Service from SDS" (editorial), *DP*, October 28, 1965, 2. L. MacNamara, R. Land, W. P Curtis, and J. M. Gillespie, letter to the editor, *DP*, October 6, 1965, 2. The exclusion clause, which was voted down 16–10, was discussed in P. Sandman, "Local SDS Select Governing Offices," *DP*, October 19, 1965, 1, 4; Sandman, "200 Would-Be Debaters Invade Organizational Meeting of SDS," 3; "SDS Rules Cannon Green," *DP*, October 25, 1965, 1, 3. "Princeton Students for a Democratic Society: Radical Activism in an Unlikely Place," 5.

13. R.K. Rein, "Princeton SDS jolts university, IDA with sit-in and vociferous demands," *DP*, February 23, 1968, 1. The demonstration is described in M. Finston, "Princeton Tigers Growl but Campus Stays Calm," *Star Ledger* (Newark), May 3, 1968, 1, 11. The editorial was "SDS or UGA?" *DP*, May 6, 1968, 2. The SDS member who later joined Weathermen tells his story in B. Burlingham, "Paranoia in Power," *Harper's* 249 (October 1974): 26–37; the quote is from 30. Burlingham's opposition to allowing communists to be members of Princeton SDS was described to me by Grover Furr, who was present at the meeting where the issue was discussed.

14. C. Oglesby, "An Open Letter: Dear McCarthy Supporters," mimeographed paper reprinted from *New Left Notes*, August 19, 1968 and "distributed during the Chicago convention." "Elections Are a Hoax—Don't Vote, Organize!" mimeographed paper, Students for a Democratic Society Princeton Chapter. Copies of both documents in my personal possession.

15. The nation-wide teach-in was described in M. Frankel, "Bundy to Defend Vietnam

Policies," *New York Times*, May 12, 1965, 2; "A Daylong Debate On Vietnam Policy To Be Held Today," *New York Times*, May 15, 1965, 4; F. Whitehouse, "Vietnam Policy Scored at N.Y.U.," *New York Times*, May 16, 1965, 62; and M. Frankel, "Vietnam Debate Heard on 100 Campuses," *New York Times*, May 16, 1965, 1, 62. A number of statements by speakers at the Berkeley event are available on "Berkeley Teach-In: Vietnam" (CD), Smithsonian Folkways Recording, Washington, D.C.

16. Kennedy is quoted in "Robert Kennedy Assures Vietnam," *New York Times*, February 18, 1962, 1, 10; also H. Bigart, "A Very Real War in Vietnam—and the Deep U.S. Commitment," *New York Times*, February 25, 1962, E3. On his position on the war, see also T.H. Anderson, *The Movement and the Sixties* (New York: Oxford University Press, 1995), 204–206, and D. Greenberg, "After the Assassination: How Gene McCarthy's response to Bobby Kennedy's Murder crippled the Democrats," *Slate* (June 4, 2008): http://www.slate.com/id/2192865/.

17. The full text of Cronkite's commentary from February 27, 1968 is available at http://faculty.smu.edu/dsimon/Change%20—Cronkite.html. A. Lewis, "Look on My Works...," *New York Times*, May 1, 1975, 41.

18. Kennan is quoted in P.H. Smith, *Talons of the Eagle: Dynamics of U.S.-Latin American Relations* (New York: Oxford University Press, 1996), 126.

19. On Iran, see S. Kinzer, *All the Shah's Men: An American Coup and the Roots of Middle East Terror* (Hoboken, N.J.: John Wiley & Sons, 2003). On the Dominican Republic, see P. Gleijeses, *The Dominican Crisis: The 1965 Constitutionalist Revolt and American Intervention* (Baltimore: Johns Hopkins University Press, 1978). On Indonesia, see B.R. Simpson, *Economists with Guns: Authoritarian Development and U.S.-Indonesian Relations, 1960–1968* (Stanford, Cal.: Stanford University Press, 2008).

20. On the coup in Guatemala, see P. Gleijeses, *Shattered Hope: The Guatemalan Revolutions and the United States, 1944–1954* (Princeton, N.J.: Princeton University Press, 1991); the State Department official is quoted on 365. Also, S. Kinzer, *Overthrow: America's Century of Regime Change from Hawaii to Iraq* (New York: Henry Holt, 2006), ch. 6. On the CIA's specific activities, see Smith, *Talons of the Eagle*, 137 and T. Weiner, *Legacy of Ashes: The*

History of the CIA (New York: Doubleday, 2007), 97. On the junta's repressive measures, see Smith, *Talons of the Eagle*, 138. The call for the plebiscite was described in "Guatemala: A Test of Power," *Time* (October 4, 1954): 38. The 99.99 percent figure is given in Gleijeses, *Shattered Hope*, 383; Smith (138) gives the actual numbers as 485,531 "yes," 393 "no." The characterization of the result appeared in "Who Won," *Time* (October 25, 1954): 33.

21. On the interconnections between government/military and United Fruit, see Kinzer, *Overthrow*, 129–130 and Gleijeses, *Shattered Hope*, 361. C. Oglesby and R. Shaull, *Containment and Change* (New York: Macillan, 1967), 132; the book was actually two essays—Oglesby's lengthy "Vietnamese Crucible" and Shaull's much shorter "Revolution: Heritage and Contemporary Option"—but the latter was largely ignored and Oglesby's contribution became synonymous with the book.

22. C. Oglesby, "Notes on a Decade Ready for the Dustbin," *Liberation* 14 (1969): 6. Oglesby's essay is reprinted in R.D. Meyers, *Toward a History of the New Left: Essays From Within the Movement* (Brooklyn, N.Y.: Carlson Publishing, 1989), 21–48.

23. Portions of Potter's speech are reprinted in K. Sale, *SDS* (New York: Random House, 1973), 187–189; his subsequent observation about failing to use the word "capitalism" is quoted on 188. The entire speech is available online at http://www.sdsrebels.com/potter.htm.

24. On the demonstrations at the Pentagon and the University of Wisconsin, see D. Dellinger, *More Power Than We Know: The People's Movement Toward Democracy* (Garden City, N.Y.: Anchor/Doubleday, 1975), 53.

25. R. Durkee, "Goheen Cautions Against Activism; Emphasizes Study," *DP*, September 18, 1967, 1, 4. D.P. Seaton and J.J. Tarlau, "SDS Replies" (letter to the editor), *DP*, September 20, 1967, 2.

26. The change in Selective Service regulations is discussed in D. Carmody, "Educators Oppose Draft Rule for Graduate Students," *New York Times*, February 17, 1968, 10. "Occupational Deferments: how you can get one," spirit duplicated (i.e., "dittoed") Princeton Graduate Draft Union brochure, n.d. The literature list appears on "Information for Princeton Graduate Draft Union members," spirit duplicated sheet, May 12, 1968. Both documents in my personal possession. "Prince-

ton Graduate Draft Union: Statement of Purpose," spirit duplicated sheet, n.d. in my personal possession. "We Won't Go," *DP*, May 6, 1968.

27. "The Drafting of Students" (editorial), *DP*, January 12, 1966, 2; R. Wells, "Uncle Sam Wants You," *DP*, January 10, 1966. "J. Tweedy" (pseudonym), "The Nation's Service?" *DP*, February 9, 1967; "J. Tweedy," "The Princeton Pfc.," *DP*, February 13, 1967, 2.

28. "We Won't Go," *DP*, April 14, 1967. The Draft Resistance Union of SDS and its joint activity with the Graduate Draft Union are discussed in D. Huber, "SDS to March in Protest at Newark Draft Center," *DP*, March 4, 1968, 1.

29. Potter's observation—actually, a challenge—is reported in B. Ayers, *Fugitive Days: Memoirs of an Antiwar Activist* (Boston: Beacon, 2001), 62. According to Todd Gitlin, the phrase came originally from SNCC's James Forman but was popularized by Lynd; see T. Gitlin, *The Sixties: Years of Hope, Days of Rage* (New York: Bantam, 1987), 107.

30. Among the many leaflets produced by Princeton SDS, some typical examples were "The United States in Latin America," "The Tragic Nature of United States Economic Imperialism," and "Princeton in the Service" (on the role of ROTC); in my personal possession. None of them is dated, though all were written between 1966 and 1969.

31. P. Berman, *A Tale of Two Utopias: The Political Journey of the Generation of 1968* (New York: W.W. Norton, 1996), 62.

32. "The History of the Progressive Labor Party, Part One," *PL Magazine* 10 (August-September 1975): 55, 56, 61–62. On PL's early history, see also Sale, *SDS*, 121–123, 160–161, 235–236, 263. For the record of testimony before HUAC, see *Hearings on H.R. 12047, H.R. 14925, H.R. 16175, H.R. 17140, and H.R. 17194—Bills to Make Punishable Assistance to Enemies of U.S. in Time of Undeclared War: Investigative Hearings Before the Committee on Un-American Activities*, HR 89–2, August 16–19. 1966. The specific quote comes from the testimony of Steven Charles Hamilton on 1178.

33. On the RYM proposal, see Sale, *SDS*, 506–510.

34. Berman, *A Tale of Two Utopias*, 84. S. Kelman, *Push Comes to Shove: The Escalation of Student Protest* (Boston: Houghton Mifflin, 1970), 142. Sale, *SDS*, 456. C. Wilkerson, *Flying Close to the Sun: My Life and Times as a*

Weatherman (New York: Seven Stories, 2007), 166. Gitlin, *The Sixties*, 209, 191, 382.

35. "New York, New York," *The Last Poets* (self-titled album, Douglas 3 label).

36. On Lee Otis Johnson, see "S.N.C.C. Officer Gets 30 Years in Texas," *New York Times*, August 28, 1968, 22 and "The Agitator," *Time* (March 13, 1972): 58. On John Sinclair, see A. Salpukas, "Freed Poet Hails Michigan Ruling," *New York Times*, March 12, 1972, 35. Hoover's memo is quoted in N. Blackstock, *Cointelpro: The FBI's Secret War on Political Freedom* (New York: Vintage Books, 1976), 124.

37. "On the Campus: Fear and Anger," *Newsweek* (July 10, 1967): 87. The demand for university resources in support of the draft union comes from "'Don't Mourn, Organize!'" mimeographed sheet, n.d., in my personal possession. "Channeling," Selective Service public relations paper, Government Printing Office document 899–125, July 1, 1965; after it became public, this document was withdrawn from circulation but mimeographed copies, one in my personal possession, were available from the Princeton Draft Information Center.

38. "Among Vietnam's Victims: The Draft," *Newsweek* (July 10, 1967): 42. Both Princeton undergraduates were quoted in Chew, "What the Draft Ruckus Is All About," 10. J. Fallows, "What Did You Do In the Class War, Daddy?" *Washington Monthly* 7 (October 1975): 6, 7.

39. M. Rudd, *Underground: My Life with SDS and the Weathermen* (New York: William Morrow, 2009), 127–128.

40. C. Fink, P. Gassert, and D. Junker (eds.), *1968: The World Transformed* (New York: Cambridge University Press, 1998). M. Kurlansky, *1968: The Year that Rocked the World* (New York: Ballantine, 2004). P. Gassert and M. Klimke (eds.), *1968: Memories and Legacies of a Global Revolt* (Washington, D.C.: German Historical Institute, 2009).

41. For detailed descriptions of the Columbia rebellion, see Rudd, *Underground*, 57–103 and Sale, *SDS*, 430–447. "France: Battle of the Sorbonne," *Time* 91 (May 17, 1968): 43–44. W. Bastedo, "SDS Meeting Calls for Protest at Nassau Hall This Afternoon," *DP*, May 2, 1968, 1.

42. On the history of IDA, see the organization's internal document, "The Purpose and Nature of IDA," n.d., in Special Committee on the Structure of the University Records, box 7 folder 5, "Institute for Defense Analysis [sic]: Purpose and Nature," Princeton Univer-

sity Mudd Manuscript Library (hereinafter "MML"). See also D.S. Greenberg, "IDA: University-Sponsored Center Hit Hard by Assaults on Campus," *Science* 160 (1968): 744–748. For the ads, see *Notices of the American Mathematical Society* 13 (1966): 177 and *Physics Today*, 17 (1964): 12.

43. Quoted in Greenberg, "IDA: University-Sponsored Center Hit Hard by Assaults on Campus," 746. On the projects, see C. McAffee, "IDA: The Academic Conscripts," *Viet-Report: An Emergency News Bulletin on Southeast Asian Affairs* (1968): 8, 10. The report title and summary appears on a DD Form 1473, "Document Control Data," June 1966, in Special Committee, MML, box 7 folder 1, "Faculty Opinions on the Institute for Defense Analysis [sic]." Although the report is listed on the form as "secret," the form itself is labeled "unclassified."

44. See "Wider Guard Use in Riots Is Urged," *New York Times*, December 21, 1967, 25 and "A Study Reports on Riot Weapons," *New York Times*, November 12, 1967, 53.

45. The original recommendation not to join IDA is described by Raymond J. Woodrow, the university's Assistant Treasurer, in the transcript of the Special Committee to Examine Princeton's Relations with the Institute for Defense Analyses, November 28, 1967, in Special Committee, MML, box 7, folder 1, "Faculty Opinions on the Institute for Defense Analysis [sic]." The building's opening was described in "Von Neumann Name of IDA Building; Dedication Set," *DP*, October 20, 1960, 5. A copy of the contract between IDA and the university appears in Special Committee, MML, box 7 folder 4, "Institute for Defense Analysis [sic]: Contract and Amendment."

46. Among the mimeographed SDS leaflets—none of them dated—were "Princeton in the Nation's Service or Princeton in the Service if the Warfare State: An Analysis of Princeton's involvement in the Institute for Defense Analyses," "Thoughts on the Responsibility of Scientists in the Nation's Service," and "Institute for Defense Analyses: An SDS Research Paper"; all in my personal possession. Among the student paper's coverage was C. Kerr, "IDA: Princeton's Military Secret," *DP*, October 12, 1967, 1, 3; "Princeton and IDA," editorial, *DP*, October 12, 1967, 2; and R.K. Rein, "Faculty, SDS Attack University Tie to IDA," October 13, 1967, 1, 5.

The request to meet with the board appears

in J.R. Hoffman (for Princeton SDS), letter to the Board of Trustees, October 18, 1967, and the subsequent request for an open hearing appears in Princeton SDS to Chairman, Board of Trustees, October 20, 1967; both documents in Special Committee, MML, box 8, folder 6. On the demonstration, see S.V. Roberts, "31 at Princeton Held in Protest," *New York Times*, October 24, 1967, 1, 11 and R.K. Rein, "Local Police Seize, Arrest 31 Protesters," *DP*, October 24, 1967, 1, 3. R. Rein, "Tams Issues $50 Fine to Each IDA Protester," *DP*, November 27, 1967, 1, 4. R.K. Rein, "Faculty Shows Support for SDS' IDA Activities," *DP*, October 30, 1967, 1.

47. On Goheen's background, see J.B. Oakes, "New Man and New Vistas at Princeton," *New York Times Magazine*, September 22, 1957, 26–31; "On Academic Heights: Robert Francis Goheen," *New York Times*, December 8, 1956, 22; M. Noden, "A Life at Princeton," *Princeton Alumni Weekly* (November 8, 2006); and the entry for "Goheen, Robert Francis," A. Leitch, *A Princeton Companion* (Princeton, N.J.: Princeton University Press, 1978), 218–221.

48. On his emphasis of the moral dimension of education, see, for example, "Morals Stressed to Princeton '58," *New York Times*, June 16, 1958, 19 and "Goheen Stresses Moral Maturity," *New York Times*, September 21, 1964, 33. On avoiding activism, see "Dr. Goheen Warns 'Student Activists' Can Fail in College," *New York Times*, September 1966, 51 and "Princeton University," *New York Times*, June 12, 1967, 50. On Goheen and the admission of women, see Noden, "A Life at Princeton"; "Daily Princetonian Asks Coeducation as 'Healthy Move,'" *New York Times*, January 9, 1965, 27; "Dr. Goheen Rejects Coeds at Princeton In Spite of Pleas," *New York Times*, February 8, 1965, 27; and the entry for "Women," *A Princeton Companion*, 527–530. Goheen's changed opinion of the war is quoted in S.M. Tilghman, "Commencement 2008: The Spirit of Bob Goheen," *Princeton Alumni Weekly* (July 16, 2008): 3.

49. The meeting was announced in "President Goheen Calls Meeting to Consider IDA-Princeton Ties" and "President Goheen's Open Letter," both in *DP*, October 27, 1967, 1. The meeting was covered in two articles sharing the same headline: B. Durkee, "Goheen Debates Critics on IDA, Announces Faculty Review of Ties: Discussion" and C. Kerr, "Goheen Debates Critics on IDA, Announces

Faculty Review of Ties: President Policy," *DP*, November 1, 1967, 1.

50. G.F. Thomas, J.P. Reeder. Jr., V. Preller and F.W. Young (Religion Department), Memorandum, December 18, 1967; M. Bazin to S. Kelley, Jr., Memorandum, December 8, 1967; both documents in Special Committee, MML, box 7, folder 1, "Faculty Opinions on the Institute for Defense Analysis [sic]." "Faculty Committee Recommends Possible Withdrawal from IDA," *DP*, February 29, 1968, 1, 3. The committee's majority report appears in full in Special Committee, MML, box 8, folder 2, "Reports of the Majority and the Minority of the Special Committee to Examine Princeton's Relationship to the Institute for Defense Analysis [sic]." The recommendation for the University of Chicago to withdraw appears in "Chicago Group Seeks to Sever IDA Tie," *Science* 150 (1968): 860.

51. B. Davis, "Faculty Approves Report on IDA," *DP*, March 5, 1968, 1,4.

52. R.F. Goheen, "Salient Points: Meeting of Special Committee of IDA Trustees on Institutional Relationships," February 23, 1968, in Special Committee, MML, box 7, folder 10, "Reaction to the Report of the Special Committee on IDA." The "Proposed Reorganization of IDA," March 1968, and the cover memorandum sent to members of the faculty, R.F. Goheen, "University-IDA Relations," April 26, 1968 are in Special Committee, MML, box 7, folder 2, "Faculty Opinions on the Institute for Defense Analysis [sic]." See also B. Davis, "Report Proposes End for Official Links," *DP*, April 29, 1968. With the exception of Chicago, where the university president called the faculty recommendation to pull out of IDA "reasonable and sound," the other member schools followed Princeton's lead and converted the status of their presidents' membership on IDA's board from institutional representative to individual. See "Chicago U. Quits Defense Studies," *New York Times*, May 9, 1968, 41 and D.R. James, "Research Unit Cuts Link to Universities," *New York Times*, June 5, 1968, 1.

53. A copy of the resolution, dated April 27, 1968, appears in Special Committee, MML, box 8, folder 2, "Reports of the Majority and the Minority of the Special Committee to Examine Princeton's Relationship to the Institute for Defense Analysis [sic]." See also "Princeton Faculty Rejects Defense Research Terms," *New York Times*, May 8, 1968, 26. The possibility of a strike by faculty was men-

tioned in B. Davis, "Faculty Resolution, SDS Letter Recommend More Action on IDA, Other Crucial Issues," *DP*, May 1, 1968, 1. See also "Princeton Agitation Over IDA Continues," *Newark Evening News*, April 30, 1968, 19.

54. C. Creesy, "Trustees Liberalize Car Ruling," *DP*, June 3, 1963, 1. J.M. Jones, "Poll Shows Students Oppose Chapel Rule," *DP*, December 4, 1962. D. Winterbottom, "Trustees Eliminate Chapel Rule," *DP*, September 15, 1964. On the gradual increase in hours, see, for example, T.J. Bray, "UGC Members Seek to Extend Women-in-Dorms Time Limit," *DP*, November 30, 1960, 1; W.A. McWhirter, "Trustees Pass 11 O'Clock Rule; New Hours Effective Saturday," *DP*, April 27, 1961, 1; J.H. White, "Trustees Liberalize Dormitory Curfew: Women in Rooms Until 12 O'Clock," *DP*, March 19, 1962, 1; J. McCollum, "UGC Will Present Faculty With New Parietal Request," *DP*, December 3, 1964, 1; and C. Jones, "Faculty Committee Rejects Proposal for Extension of Friday Dorm Rule," *DP*, December 14, 1964, 1. B. Paul, "Parietal Hours Set Back to 2 a.m., 10 p.m.," *DP*, April 22, 1968, 1. "The Trustees' Travesty," *DP*, April 22, 1968, 2.

55. Letter, Princeton Students for a Democratic Society to Robert F. Goheen, n.d. but distributed at the May 2, 1968 demonstration, copy in my personal possession. This strategy was also stressed in "Rally for Princeton Reform," *DP*, May 2, 1968, 2, and "Demonstration, March, Rally," leaflet, n.d. but distributed to announce the May 2nd demonstration, copy in my personal possession. M.F. Diamond, J. Schrecker, L.F. Hoffman, and V. Preller, letter to the chairman, *DP*, May 2, 1968, 2. Farber's essay was originally circulated in mimeographed form before being published in the underground newspaper, the *Los Angeles Free Press*, in 1967 and then in a book of essays, J. Farber, *The Student as Nigger* (North Hollywood, Calif.: Contact Books, 1969); the quotes are from 116, 115. C. Davidson, "University Reform Revisited," *Educational Record* 48 (1967): 5, 8.

56. B. Davis, "Princeton Could Face Columbia Disaster" (continuation of "Faculty Resolution" article on p. 1), *DP*, May 1, 1968, 4. The statement appeared as "President Goheen's Remarks at the Demonstration Organized by SDS," *Princeton Alumni Weekly* (May 21, 1968): 6–7. On the committee see C. Rankin, "UGA Suggests Committee to Study Decision-making," *DP*, May 10, 1968, 1 and R. Schnell, "Faculty Elects 8 to Analyze Struc-

ture," *DP*, May 29, 1968, 1. W.H. Paul, "Board to Study Power Structure," *DP*, May 20, 1968, 1, 5.

57. W. Bastedo, "Kaminsky, Sittenfeld, Watts Head UGA Slates," *DP*, April 9, 1968, 1. W. Bastedo, "Kaminsky Elected by 366 Votes; Miller, Arbogast, Moorman Win," *DP*, April 24, 1968, 1. Kaminsky is quoted in G. Conderacci, "Campus SDS Springs Offensive," *DP*, April 18, 1969, 1.

58. Though his last name is misspelled, Robby's background is described in A. Adelson, *SDS* (New York: Charles Scribner's Sons, 1972), 142–145.

59. D.B. Kipp, Charter Trustee, quoted in the transcript of the Princeton University Committee on the Structure of the University, June 27, 1968, copy in my personal possession.

60. "A Parietal Plan" (editorial), *DP*, April 23, 1968, 2. On divestment as one of SDS's issues, see Finston, "Princeton Tigers Growl but Campus Stays Calm," 1 and E.R. Weidlein III, "On the Campus," *Princeton Alumni Weekly* (May 21, 1968): 7.

61. G. Griffin, "SDS Leaves Kelley Group in Dramatic Protest," *DP*, October 9, 1968. All three statements were printed in "Kelley Committee: Liberal Illusion Exposed by Walk-out," *Dissenter: Newsletter of Princeton SDS* (October 17, 1968): 1–4.

62. The committee proposed the council in its preliminary report, "A Proposal to Establish the Council of the Princeton University Community: A Report of the Special Committee on the Structure of the University," May 1969, and fleshed out the proposal in "The Governing of Princeton University: Final Report of the Special Committee on the Structure of the University," April 1970, copies of both in my personal possession. The reports were summarized, respectively, in R. Balfour, "Kelley Group Report Proposes Community Council," *DP*, May 21, 1969, 1, 4 and B. Highberger, "Sharing Power: Kelley Releases Study," *DP*, April 7, 1970, 1.

63. On SDS's growth, see R. Balfour, "SDS Walk-out Threatens Structure Committee," *DP*, October 2, 1968, 4. SDS sat in at IDA again in April, 1969; see B. Beckner, "SDS at IDA," *DP*, April 24, 1969, 1. "No CIA Recruiting!" mimeographed paper, n.d., copy in my personal possession. C. Connell, "SDS Protest Scheme Stalls CIA Recruiter," *DP*, February 11, 1969, 1; T. Crocker, "CIA Cancels Visit Here; SDS Unveils New Plans," *DP*, February 12, 1969, 1.

64. From the 1968 ROTC recruitment brochure, "Where the Leaders Are," quoted in "Princeton in the Service," Princeton SDS mimeographed paper, n.d., but from early November 1968; copy in my personal possession.

65. The demonstration is described in R. Balfour, "SDS, Protestors Hit ROTC, Trustees," *DP*, December 16, 1968, 1. R. Ollwerther, "Dean Urges Academic Exclusion of ROTC Units from University," *DP*, November 11, 1968, 1. B. Highberger, "Report Urges End to ROTC Academic Credit: Proposal Includes Title Change," *DP*, February 26, 1969, 1. The ROTC contract was quoted in R. Ollwerther, "The ROTC contracts," *DP*, December 5, 1968, 1. T. Henderson, "ROTC Bounced; Goheen Calls Open Meeting," *DP*, March 4, 1969, 1. J. Collier, "Trustees Reconfirm ROTC Policies, Extend Junior Faculty Voting Rights" *DP*, April 20, 1970, 1. B. Highberger, "Council Votes End to ROTC, Supports Strike," *DP*, May 4, 1970, 1.

66. See M. Meredith, *In the Name of Apartheid: South Africa in the Postwar Period* (New York: Harper & Row, 1988).

67. For a list of UN resolutions condemning apartheid, see K. Samuels, *Political Violence and the International Community* (Leiden, The Netherlands: Koninklijke Brill, 2007), 359–366. Oglesby, *Containment and Change*, 97–100.

68. L.F. Jay, "Students to Picket Bank in Protest of Apartheid," *DP*, March 19, 1965, 3.

69. ABC's formation was announced in J.A. Field, "Negro Undergraduates Unite," *DP*, April 18, 1967, 1. The interaction between Goheen and the students is described in C. Connell, "Princeton Spring," *Princeton Alumni Weekly* (July 16, 2008).

70. "Report of the Ad Hoc Committee on Princeton's Investments in Companies Operating in Southern Africa" in Special Committee on the Structure of the University Records, MML, Box 1, Folder 1.

71. W.R. Scott and C. Spight, "Princeton University, South African Investments and the Black Experience," (report of the two black students on the committee) and R. Butler, "University Investments and the Situation in Southern Africa" (report of the SDS member of the committee) are available in *Ibid*. C. Rankin, "Student Charges 'Conflict of Interest,'" *DP*, Nov 20, 1968, 1, 5, and C. Rankin, "Investigation Shows Trustee Holdings," *DP*, November 21, 1968, 1, 4.

72. Kaminsky was quoted in C. Rankin,

"Students, Faculty Butt Heads over Report on Investments," *DP*, January 10, 1969, 1. On the building occupation, see T. Crocker, "New South Goes Black: Exact Timing Facilitates Seizure," *DP*, March 12, 1969, 3–4 and G. Conderacci, "ABC Abandons New South after 11 Hours of Orderly South African Demonstration," *DP*, March 12, 1969, 1, 3. The event was also covered in "Students Occupy a Princeton Hall," *New York Times*, March 12, 1969, 30. ABC's comments appeared in the organization's letter to the editor, *DP*, March 18, 1969, 2. Formation of the Princeton chapter of the Third World Liberation Front was announced in G. Chang and eight others, letter to the editor, *DP*, March 6, 1969, 2.

73. The demands were listed in L. Munford, "SDS Schedules Hometown Offensive," *DP*, April 15, 1969, 1.

74. P. Parnell and B. Nickerson, "Nassau 'Patriots' Stymie SDS," *DP*, April 21, 1969, 3. The quote, from ABC leader, Jerome Davis, is from my own recollection.

75. B. Beckner, "SDS at IDA," *DP*, April 24, 1969, 1.

76. Quoted in Sale, *SDS*, 510.

77. See "Local SDS Journeys to Texas to Attend National Conference," *DP*, April 8, 1969, 1.

78. K. Ashley, B. Ayers, B. Dohrn, J. Jacobs, J. Jones, G. Long, H. Machtinger, J. Mellen, T. Robbins, M. Rudd, and S. Tappis, "You don't need a weatherman to know which way the wind blows," *New Left Notes* (June 18, 1969): 3–8. Ayers, *Fugitive Days*, 164.

79. See the editorial "Revolutionaries Must Fight Nationalism," *PL Magazine* (August 1969): 3–13.

80. This and the subsequent description of the convention is based on both Sale, *SDS*, 563–579 and my personal recollection.

81. Quoted in Sale, *SDS*, 567.

82. *Ibid.*, 627.

83. See Sale, *SDS*, 579–613. Also, Ayers, *Fugitive Days*, 159, 207, 214–215.

84. The bomb is described in Ayers, *Fugitive Days*, 281. Wilkerson, *Flying Close to the Sun*, 343.

85. J. Raymond, "SDS Members Visit Strikers in Trenton," *DP*, February 10, 1970, 1; J. Raymond, "SDS-WSA Rally Attracts 60 to Clio," *DP*, April 14, 1970, 4. B. Highberger, "'Repression Teach-in' Crowd Jams Dillon Gym," *DP*, 1,6; SDS-RYM, "'Panthers' Freedom Must be Purchased," February 27, 1970, *DP*, March 3, 1970, 2. B. Highberger, "SDS

Heckles Hickel's Ecology Keynote Talk," *DP*, March 6, 19701,6.

86. J. Collier, "Mass Chapel Meeting Votes University Strike," *DP*, May 1, 1970, 1, 4. B. Highberger, "5,000 Attend Jadwin Assembly," *DP*, May 5, 1970, 1,6. R. Fondiller, "UNDO Plans National Mobilization to Teach Legal Ways of Opposing Draft," *DP*, May 6, 1970, 5. B. Nickerson, "Unlikely Revolution, *DP*, May 18, 1970, 1. F. LaMay, "Faculty Condemns Indochina War Expansion," *DP*, May 6, 1970, 1.

87. C. Hitchens, *Hitch-22: A Memoir* (New York: Twelve, 2010), 331. Berman, *A Tale of Two Utopias*, 33.

88. Gold is quoted in Gitlin, *The Sixties*, 400. Weatherman's meeting with the Vietnamese is described in Ayers, *Fugitive Days*, 168.

Chapter 3

1. These quotes appear, respectively, in R. Balfour, "SDS to Protest Election," *DP*, October 22, 1968, 1; R. Balfour, "SDS Scores 'Election Hoax' in Dramatic Teach-in Oratory," *DP*, November 4, 1968, 6; R. Balfour, "SDS Slates Election Protests," *DP*, November 1, 1968, 5; T. Crocker, "CIA Cancels Visit Here; SDS Unveils New Plans," *DP*, February 12, 1969, 1; L. Munford, "Forum Debates War, Princeton," *DP*, April 30, 1969, 1; D.P Seaton, letter to the editor, *DP*, February 20, 1969, 2.

2. See the profile for Douglas P. Seaton, part of the web site for Seaton, Beck & Peters, http://www.seatonlaw.com/team/seaton.shtml.

3. The photo accompanied the article on the takeover, G. Conderacci, "ABC Abandons New South after 11 Hours of Orderly South African Demonstration," *DP*, March 12, 1969, 1.

4. B. Herbst, "Farrell Accepts Office after Seaton Declines," *DP*, September 22, 1967, 1. On the election as SDS chair, see R. Balfour, "SDS Cries 'Foul,'" *DP*, October 7, 1968, 1.

5. Quoted in M. Noden, "A War Still with Them," *Princeton Alumni Weekly* (March 23, 2005).

6. Quoted in *ibid.*

7. The dissertation was published as D.P. Seaton, *Catholics and Radicals: The Association of Catholic Trade Unionists and the American Labor Movement, from Depression to Cold War* (Lewisburg, Penn.: Bucknell University Press, 1981).

8. The quotes in this and the next two paragraphs come from letters from Doug to Jimmy in January 1982 and December 1984.

9. D.P. Seaton, "The Worst Documentation Mistakes Made by Employers and How to Avoid Them," *Lawfax* No. 41 (April 2003), available at http://www.seatonlaw.com/pubs/may10.pdf.

10. *Ibid.*

Chapter 4

1. "Proposed Budget for Princeton SDS—September 1968–June 1969" with "Dear Friend" cover letter from C. Sills, December 9, 1968; copy in my personal possession.

2. Quoted in "Local SDS Journeys to Texas to Attend National Conference," *DP,* April 8, 1969, 1.

3. On the Greenbrier, see C.W. Mills, *The Power Elite* (New York: Oxford University Press, 2000), 159; D. McGinn, "The Last Resort" *Newsweek* (January 25, 2010): 42–43; and D. Garner, "Nothing Boutique About It," *New York Times,* August 12, 2010, TR1.

4. See the comment on "Clarity," posted on listserv discussion of "Jungian psychological type & teaching of composition," October 7, 1996 at http://listserv.tcu.edu/cgi-bin/wa.exe?A2=ind9610&L=typwrt-l&P=215.

5. H. Marcuse, *Eros and Civilization: A Philosophical Inquiry into Freud* (Boston: Beacon, 1966). N.O. Brown, *Life Against Death: The Psychoanalytic Meaning of History* (Middletown, Conn.: Wesleyan University Press, 1959).

6. C. Sills, review of *White Racism: A Psychohistory* by Joel Kovel, *Telos* 12 (1972): 143.

7. K. Marx and F. Engels, *The German Ideology: Parts I and II* (New York: International Publishers, 1968), 22.

8. Sills, review of *White Racism,* 141, 142.

9. C. Sills and G.H. Jensen (eds.), *The Philosophy of Discourse: The Rhetorical Turn in Twentieth Century Thought, Volume 1 and Volume 2* (Portsmouth, NH: Boynton/Cook, 1992).

10. C. Sills, "Introduction" (to the Frankfurt School), in *ibid.., Vol. 1,* 97.

11. K.B. MacDonald, *A People that Shall Dwell Alone: Judaism as a Group Evolutionary Strategy* (Westport, Conn.: Praeger, 1994); K.B. MacDonald, *Separation and Its Discontents: Toward an Evolutionary Theory of Anti–Semitism* (Westport, Conn.: Praeger, 1998); K.B. MacDonald, *The Culture of Critique: An Evolutionary Analysis of Jewish Involvement in Twentieth-Century Intellectual and Political Movements* (Westport, Conn.: Praeger, 1998).

Chapter 5

1. M. Smith, "To my fellow inductees," mimeographed letter, n.d.; copy in my personal possession.

2. J. Nordheimer, "A Rare Tern Sets the Blood Racing for Birders," *New York Times,* July 25, 1993, 1, 36. S. Weidensaul, *Of a Feather: A Brief History of American Birding* (New York: Harcourt, 2007), 287.

3. For a poem related to birding, see, for example, M. Smith, "Birding the Battle of Attu," *Ploughshares* 10 (1984): 146. M. Smith, *Transplant* (Ann Arbor, Mich.: Shaman Drum Press, 2003). P.N. Malani, "Poetry" (review of *Transplant*), *JAMA* 290 (2003): 1385.

4. His experiences at the copper mill are described in M. Smith, "Princeton SDS-er Working in Copper Mill," *Summer Dissenter: The Newsletter of Princeton SDS* (August 1968).

5. M. Smith, *Prudentius' Psychomachia: A Reexamination* (Princeton: Princeton University Press, 1976).

6. Quoted in A. Chen, "Students Gather on Diag in Memory of Cancer Victims," *Michigan Daily,* March 17, 2004. Smith, *Transplant,* 68.

Chapter 6

1. P.J. Kaminsky, "West College Wind," *DP,* October 5, 1967, 2. Peter's statement is included in "The Three Statements of Dissent Leading to the SDS-Student Walk-Out of the Kelley Committee," mimeographed paper, n.d. but distributed at open meeting of the Kelley Committee, October 8, 1968, copy in my personal possession.

2. P. Kaminsky, *Culinary Intelligence: The Art of Eating Healthy (and Really Well)* (New York: Knopf, 2012).

3. C. Hagel with P. Kaminsky, *America: Our Next Chapter* (New York: HarperCollins, 2008), 5.

4. P. Kaminsky, *American Waters: Fly-Fishing Journeys of a Native Son* (New York: Stewart, Tabori & Chang, 2005), 16.

5. N. Lemann, "Campaign '96: America's New Class System," *Time* 147 (February 26, 1996): 42.

6. Kaminsky, *American Waters*, 18. P. Kaminsky, *The Fly-Fisherman's Guide to the Meaning of Life: What a Lifetime on the Water Has Taught Me about Love, Work, Food, Sex, and Getting Up Early* (New York: Rodale/St. Martin's, 2002), 2, 119, 8.

7. P. Kaminsky, "A Late Comeback for East End Stripers," *New York Times*, November 4, 2001, SP16. Kaminsky, *The Fly-Fisherman's Guide to the Meaning of Life*, 23–24.

8. P. Kaminsky, "The Fish of His Dreams," *New York Times*, November 18, 1990, S7. P. Kaminsky, "Look What's for Dinner," *New York Times*, October 23, 2002, F1. Kaminsky, *The Fly-Fisherman's Guide to the Meaning of Life*, 33, 35, 39–40.

9. Peter wrote about the opening of Boulud's new restaurant in P. Kaminsky, "Four-Star Farm Boy," *New York Magazine* (December 14, 1998). For Peter's collaboration with Boulud, see D. Boulud and P. Kaminsky, *Chef Daniel Boulud: Cooking in New York City* (New York: Assouline, 2002) and D. Boulud and P. Kaminsky, *Letters to a Young Chef* (New York: Basic, 2003).

10. J. Madden and P. Kaminsky, *John Madden's Ultimate Tailgating* (New York: Viking, 1998). F. Mallmann and P. Kaminsky, *Seven Fires: Grilling the Argentine Way* (New York: Artisan, 2009). On the grill in Peter's back yard, see O. Schwaner-Albright, "Grilling Over Wood as a Sweaty, Smoky Sport," *New York Times*, May 20, 2009, D1, D9.

11. G. Kunz and P. Kaminsky, *The Elements of Taste* (New York: Little, Brown, 2001).

12. Kaminsky, *The Fly-Fisherman's Guide to the Meaning of Life*, 118. P. Kaminsky, *Pig Perfect: Encounters with Remarkable Swine and Some Great Ways to Cook Them* (New York: Hyperion, 2005), 11. 187. See also P. Kaminsky, "On the Trail of Fine Ham: First, Plant an Acorn," *New York Times*, October 6, 2004, F11.

13. Kaminsky, *Pig Perfect*, 22, 233–247.

14. *Ibid.*, 255.

15. I. Berlin, *The Crooked Timber of Humanity: Chapters in the History of Ideas* (London: John Murray, 1990), 11.

Chapter 7

1. G. Chang, A.S. Farah, A.A. Issa, D. Kapur, G.P. Miwa, J.D. Semida, A. Lopez-Videla, Z. Ibrahim Husami, and M.H. Ibrahim, "Towards the Third World" (letter to the editor), *DP*, March 6, 1969, 2.

2. The photo accompanied G. Conderacci, "ABC Abandons New South after 11 Hours of Orderly South African Demonstration," *DP*, March 12, 1969, 1.

3. G.H. Chang, "Deployments, Engagements, Obliterations: Asian American Artists and World War II," in *Asian American Art" A History, 1850–1970*, ed. G.H. Chang, M.D. Johnson, and P.J. Karlstrom (Stanford: Stanford University Press, 2008), 121–122; see, also the biographical entry on 299–300.

4. See G.H. Chang, "Are There Other Ways to Think about the 'Great Interregnum'?" *Journal of American—East Asian Relations*, 7 (1998): 117.

5. See "A Moment with ... Gordon Chang '70," *Princeton Alumni Weekly* (November 21, 2007).

6. G.H. Chang, *Friends and Enemies: The United States, China, and the Soviet Union, 1948–1972* (Stanford: Stanford University Press, 1990), 249, 245, 252.

7. *Ibid.*, 166, 266–269.

8. Chang, "To the Nuclear Brink," 122. G.H. Chang, and H. Di, "The Absence of War in the U.S. China Confrontation over Quemoy and Matsu in 1954–1955: Contingency, Luck, Deterrence?" *American Historical Review* 98 (1993): 1500–1524.

9. For example, J. Becker, *Hungry Ghosts: Mao's Secret Famine* (New York: Free Press, 1996). L. Zhisui, *The Private Life of Chairman Mao: The Memoirs of Mao's Personal Physician* (New York: Random House, 1996).

10. G.H. Chang, "A Report on Student Protests at Beijing University," *Bulletin of Concerned Asian Scholars* 18 (1986): 31.

11. See, for example, "Empty Olympic Promises" (editorial), *New York Times*, February 4, 2008, A22.

12. *Asian American Art*, ed. Chang, Johnson, and Karlstrom.

13. G.H. Chang, "Asian Americans and Politics: Some Perspectives from History," in *Asian Americans and Politics: Perspectives, Experiences, Prospects*, ed. G.H. Chang (Washington, D.C.: Woodrow Wilson Center Press and Stanford: Stanford University Press, 2001), 29.

14. Chang, et al., "Towards the Third World," 2. D.Y. Kim, *Writing Manhood in Black and Yellow: Ralph Ellison, Frank Chin, and the Literary Politics of Identity* (Stanford: Stanford University Press, 2005), xix.

15. G.H. Chang, "Epilogue: Remembering Yuji," in *Before Internment: Essays in Prewar*

Japanese American History, ed. G.H. Chang and E. Azuma (Stanford: Stanford University Press, 2006), 301, 302.

16. G.H. Chang, "Whose 'Barbarism'? Whose 'Treachery'? Race and Civilization in the Unknown United States—Korea War of 1871," *Journal of American History* 89 (2003): 1350.

17. S. Koshy, *Sexual Naturalization: Asian Americans and Miscegenation* (Stanford: Stanford University Press, 2004), 1, 7.

18. G.H. Chang, "'Superman is about to visit the relocation centers' and the Limits of Wartime Liberalism," *Amerasia Journal* 19 (1993): 37–59. G.H. Chang, "Social Darwinism vs. Social Engineering: The 'Education' of Japanese Americans During World War II," in *Landscaping the Human Garden: Twentieth-Century Population Management in a Comparative Framework*, ed. A. Weiner (Stanford: Stanford University Press, 2003), 195.

19. C.J. Kim, "The Racial Triangulation of Asian Americans," in *Asian Americans and Politics*, 41. N.T. Gotanda, "Citizenship Nullification: The Impossibility of Asian American Politics," in *ibid.*, 80, 99.

20. D.L. Li, *Imagining the Nation: Asian American Literature and Cultural Consent* (Stanford: Stanford University Press, 1998), 6. G.H. Chang, Review of *Asian American Dreams: The Emergence of an American People* by H. Zia, *Journal of American Ethnic History* 22 (2003): 106.

21. Quoted in J. Kluger, "What Makes Us Moral," *Time* (December 3, 2007): 60.

22. *New Cosmopolitans: South Asians in the U.S.*, ed. G. Rajan and S. Sharma (Stanford: Stanford University Press, 2006). S. Chang, *The Global Silicon Valley Home: Lives and Landscapes Within Taiwanese American Trans-Pacific Culture* (Stanford: Stanford University Press, 2006). T. Chen, *Double Agency (Acts of Impersonation in Asian American Literature and Culture* (Stanford: Stanford University Press, 2005), xvi.

23. G.H. Chang, "Asian Immigrants and American Foreign Relations," in *Pacific Passage: The Study of American-East Asian Relations on the Eve of the Twenty-First Century*, ed. W.I. Cohen (New York: Columbia University Press, 1996), 113.

24. D. Horowitz, *The Professors: The 101 Most Dangerous Academics in America* (Washington, D.C.: Regnery, 2006), xxv. T. Judt, *The Memory Chalet* (New York: Penguin, 2010), 202.

25. Chang, Review of *Asian American Dreams*, 106.

Chapter 8

1. R.L. Cohen, "Any Day Now," *DP*, April 17, 1969.

2. B. Highberger, "SDS Heckels Hickel's Ecology Keynote Talk, Goheen Promises Discipline," *DP*, March 6, 1970, 1. On the probation and withholding of the degree, see S. Orso, "Bowen Modifies Disrupters' Suspensions; Affirms Judicial Unit's 'Substantive Issues,'" *DP*, April 27, 1970, 1.

3. R.L. Cohen, letter to the editor, *New York Times*, June 13, 2006, A22.

4. S. Whitman, L.N. King and R.L. Cohen, "Epilepsy and Violence: A Scientific and Social Analysis," in *Psychopathology in Epilepsy: Social Dimensions*, ed. S. Whitman and B.P. Hermann (New York: Oxford University Press, 1986), 284–302. Also, S. Whitman, T.E. Coleman, C. Patmon, B.T. Desai, R. Cohen, and L.N. King, "Epilepsy in Prison: Elevated Prevalence and No Relationship to Violence," *Neurology* 34 (1984): 775–782.

5. Heckler's position is described in R.L. Cohen, "AIDS: The Impending Quarantine," *Health/PAC Bulletin* 16 (1985): 9. W.F. Buckley Jr., "Crucial Steps in Combating the AIDS Epidemic: Identify All the Carriers," *New York Times*, March 18, 1986, A27.

6. *Ibid.*, 9–14. On Bobby's support for access to sterile needles, see, also, P.A. Selwyn, C. Feiner, C.P. Cox, C. Lipschutz, and R.L. Cohen, "Knowledge about AIDS and High-Risk Behavior Among Intravenous Drug Users in New York City," *AIDS* 1 (1987): 247–254.

7. J. Gross, "New York's Poorest Women Offered More AIDS Services," *New York Times*, March 6, 1988, 1, 38.

8. R.L. Cohen, "Mass Incarceration: A Public Health Failure," in *Building Violence: How America's Rush to Incarcerate Creates More Violence*, ed. J.P. May and K.R. Pitts (Thousand Oaks, Cal.: Sage, 2000), 96, 98. R.L. Cohen, letter to the editor, *New York Times*, January 5, 1999, A16.

9. Cohen, "Mass Incarceration," 97, 96, 99. M. Alexander, *The New Jim Crow: Mass Incarceration in the Age of Colorblindness* (New York: New Press, 2010).

10. The Oath of Athens is reproduced in R.L. Cohen, "Health and Public Health Advocacy for Prisoners," in *Clinical Practice in*

Correctional Medicine, ed. M. Puisis (Philadelphia: Elsevier, 2006), 28. R.L. Cohen, "Imprisoned Plasma Donors: A Medical-Ethical Case and Comment," *Journal of Prison and Jail Health* 2 (1982): 41–46.

11. R.L. Cohen, "A Prisoner in Need of a Bone Marrow Transplant: Commentary," *Hastings Center Report* 17 (1987): 26.

12. Cohen, "Health and Public Health Advocacy for Prisoners," 38, 29–30.

13. *Ibid.*, 32. On the Green Haven Correctional Facility at Beekman, see M.B. Pfeiffer, "Fight for Better Prison Care Takes Years, Costs Lives," *Poughkeepsie Journal*, January 6, 2003, posted online at http://www.poughkeepsiejournal.com/projects/prison3/lo010603s3.shtml, and M.B. Pfeiffer, "Prison Doctor's Record Arouses Concerns, *Poughkeepsie Journal*, January 6, 2003, posted online at http://www.poughkeepsiejournal.com/projects/prison3/lo010603s4.shtml.

14. Cohen, "Health and Public Health Advocacy for Prisoners," 31–32. See also M. Petersen, "Charging Inmates for Care Raises Issue of Health Risk," *New York Times*, December 2, 1996, B1, B6. The court case was *Reynolds v. Wagner*, 128 F. 3rd 166 (1997).

15. Cohen, "Health and Public Health Advocacy for Prisoners," 33–34. On the inmate, Timothy Joe Souder, see L. Sander, "Inmate's Death in Solitary Cell Prompts Judge to Ban Restraints," *New York Times*, November 15, 2006, A20. Souder's collapse can be viewed at http://www.cbsnews.com/video/watch/?id=2458916n.

16. See *Hadix v. Caruso* (Hadix II) 461 F. Supp. 2d 574 (2006); *Hadix v. Caruso*, No. 4:92-CV-110 (W.D. Mich. March 6, 2007); and *Hadix v. Caruso*, No. 4:92-CV-110 (W.D. Mich. May 4, 2007).

17. Cohen, "Health and Public Health Advocacy for Prisoners," 37–38.

18. *Ibid.*, 38. J. Paul, "A Prisoner in Need of a Bone Marrow Transplant: Commentary," *Hastings Center Report* 17 (1987): 27.

19. Cohen, "Health and Public Health Advocacy for Prisoners," 36–37.

3. E. Kagan, "Fear and Loathing in Brooklyn," *DP*, November 10, 1980, 10.

4. See D. Hampton, *Little Red: Three Passionate Lives Through the Sixties and Beyond* (New York: Public Affairs, 2013).

5. D.P. Seaton and J.J. Tarlau, "SDS Replies" (letter to the editor), *DP*, September 20, 1967, 2.

6. J. Tarlau, "Weapons Bring Changes" (letter to the editor), *DP*, April 9, 1968, 2. R. Balfour, "Newark Policemen Beat Orderly SDS Demonstrators," *DP*, November 6, 1968, 7.

7. Quoted in M. Noden, "A War Still With Them," *Princeton Alumni Weekly* (March 23, 2005).

8. See M. Elbaum, *Revolution in the Air: Sixties Radicals Turn to Lenin, Mao and Che* (London; New York: Verso, 2006), 106.

9. V. Gornick, *The Romance of American Communism* (New York: Basic Books, 1977).

10. The term "OSU" was coined in R.B. Freeman and J. Rogers, "Open Source Unionism: Beyond Exclusive Collective Bargaining," *WorkingUSA: The Journal of Labor and Society* 5 (2002): 8–40. The non-traditional approaches are described in D. Nack and J. Tarlau, "The Communications Workers of America Experience with 'Open-Source Unionism,'" *WorkingUSA: The Journal of Labor and Society* 8 (2005): 721–732.

11. Jimmy's comments at the IG metal-Konferenz in Frankfurt am Main are reported in "Den Nerv Getroffen," *IT-Magazin* (March 2003): 18–19.

12. All of "Jimmy's Ward Reports" are available at http://www.jimmytarlau.org/.

13. For his discussion of the "sanctuary city" issue, see the reports in *ibid.*, December 24, 2007, and February 10, 2008. On the controversy, see J. Spinner, Mt. Rainier Council to Vote on becoming 'Sanctuary' City," *Washington Post*, January 20, 2008, C4, and P. Constable, "Anti-Immigrant Effort Takes Hold in Maryland," *Washington Post*, February 23, 2008, B1.

14. In addition to the interview some of these remarks were quoted in Noden, "A War Still With Them."

Chapter 9

1. "The Emergence of S.D.S." *Time* (May 24, 1968): 59.

2. Quoted in G. Conderacci, "SDS: From IDA's Steps to Goheen's Door," *DP*, November 13, 1969, 1.

Chapter 10

1. T. Hopkins, N. Koblitz, and R. Minot, *SDS* (Boston: SDS, n.d. but obviously written in 1969). On Neal's leadership of SDS-WSA's activities, see J. Raymond, "SDS-WSA Rally

Attracts 60 to Clio Steps," *DP*, April 14, 1970, 4 and J. Raymond, "SDS Members Visit Strikers in Trenton, *DP*, February 10, 1970, 1.

2. N. Koblitz, *Random Curves: Journeys of a Mathematician* (Berlin: Springer-Verlag, 2008).

3. R.J. Herrnstein, "I.Q.," *Atlantic Monthly* 228 (September, 1971): 43–64. R.J. Herrnstein and C. Murray, *The Bell Curve: Intelligence and Class Structure in American Life* (New York: Free Press, 1994).

4. L.J. Kamin, *The Science and Politics of I.Q.* (Potomac, Md.: Lawrence Erlbaum, 1974). W.H. Tucker, "Fact and Fiction in the Discovery of Sir Cyril Burt's Flaws," *Journal of the History of the Behavioral Sciences* 30 (1994): 335–347.

5. See "Visit to the Vietnam Women's Museum," *Kovalevskaia Fund Newsletter* 23 (April, 2008): 6–8 and A.H. Koblitz, *Kovalevskaia Fund Newsletter* 25 (May 2010): 4–6.

6. T.J. Vallely and B. Wilkinson, "Vietnamese Higher Education: Crisis and Response," Harvard Kennedy School, Ash Institute for Democratic Governance and Innovation, 6. Neal's response appears in N. Koblitz, "A Second Opinion by an American on Higher Education Reform in Vietnam," October 3, 2009, available online at http://www.math.washington.edu/~koblitz/vnhigheredE.pdf and Part II, October 20, 2009, available online at http://www.math.washington.edu/~koblitz/vnhighered2E.pdf. See also N. Koblitz, "Panel of 'Leading American Experts' Advises Vietnamese Government on Higher Education," *Kovalevskaia Fund Newsletter* 23 (April, 2008): 8–9.

7. See E. Sciolino, "U.S. Groups Lay Blame for Killing of Volunteer on Administration," *New York Times*, April 30, 1987, A12.

8. See M. Danner, *The Massacre at El Mozote: A Parable of the Cold War* (New York: Vintage, 1994). L. Gruson, "6 Priests Killed in a Campus Raid in San Salvador," *New York Times*, November 17, 1989, A1, A12 and "The Six Salvadoran Priests Slain by Uniformed Gunmen," *New York Times*, November 17, 1989, A13.

9. N. Koblitz, "The Case Against Computers in K–13 Math Education (Kindergarten through Calculus)," *The Mathematical Intelligencer* 18 (1996): 10, 13.

10. In addition to his autobiography, see, also, N. Koblitz, "The Uneasy Relationship Between Mathematics and Cryptography," *Notices of the American Mathematical Society* 54 (2007): 972–979.

11. See P.M. Boffey, "Prominent Harvard Scholar Barred by Science Academy," *New York Times*, April 29, 1987, A1, D4. The essay is reprinted as N. Koblitz, "Mathematics as Propaganda," in *Mathematics Tomorrow*, ed. L.A. Steen (New York: Springer-Verlag, 1981), 111–120.

Chapter 11

1. P.T. Chew, "What the Draft Ruckus Is All About," *National Observer*, October 25, 1965, 1.

2. Untitled mimeographed document responding to President Goheen's statement on university investment in South Africa, Princeton SDS (March 10, 1969), 7; copy in my personal possession.

3. For the entry on Grover, see D. Horowitz, *The Professors: The 101 Most Dangerous Academics in America* (Washington, DC: Regnery, 2006), 186–189. See also R. DiPippo, "A Scholar for Stalin," *Front Page Magazine* (March 16, 2005), available at http://archive.frontpagemag.com/readArticle.aspx?ARTID=9247; DiPippo is credited by Horowitz for research. For Grover's web page, see http://msuweb.montclair.edu/~furrg/.

4. The caucus's Manifesto is posted online at http://groups.yahoo.com/group/radcaucus/. The resolution on adjuncts appears in the "Convention News & Program Update," Modern Language Association of American, December 27, 2007, 1. The resolutions on the Patriot Act and on "War Talk" can be found at https://lists.lsit.ucsb.edu/archives/rfp/2003-November/001758.html.

5. The resolution on criticism of Zionism appears in "Convention News & Program Update," 1. The resolution on teaching Palestinian literature and culture is described in S. Jaschik, "MLA's Middle East Moves," *Inside Higher Ed*, December 30, 2008, http://www.insidehighered.com/news/2008/12/30/mla.

6. See F. Butterfield, "The New Vietnam Scholarship," *New York Times Magazine*, February 13, 1983, 60–61.

7. The assigned article was G. Lewy, "Some Political-Military Lessons of the Vietnam War," *Parameters: Journal of the U.S. Army War College* 14 (1984): 2–14. The student's letter was posted by DiPippo at http://archives.econ.utah.edu/archives/aut-op-sy/2008m04/msg00034.html.

8. Video of the statement can be seen at

http://www.youtube.com/watch?v=hRPTZF
5zSLQ. The controversy engendered by the
debate is described in the Montclair State student newspaper in J. Smith IV, "The Defama-
tion of Grover Furr," *Montclarion*, December
13, 2012, 1, 3.

9. R. Conquest, *The Great Terror; Stalin's
Purge of the Thirties* (New York: Macmillan,
1968).

10. See "Interview with Grover Furr," on
the blog "Reason in Revolt Now Thunders!"
http://msuweb.montclair.edu/~furrg/miller
interview0506.pdf.

11. A. Roth, "Russia Revives the Namesake
of 'Uncle Joe,'" *New York Times*, February 1,
2013, A4. See also D. Bilefsky, "Even After a
War With Russia, Many Georgians Revere
Stalin," *New York Times*, October 1, 2008, A6.
G. Furr, *Khrushchev Lied: The Evidence That
Every "Revelation" of Stalin's (and Beria's)
"Crimes" in Nikita Khrushchev's Infamous "Se-
cret Speech" to the 20th Party Congress of the
Soviet Union on February 25, 1956, is Provably
False* (Kettering, Ohio, Erythros Press, 2011).

12. See, for example, M.B. Tauger, "The
1932 Harvest and the Famine of 1933," *Slavic
Review* 50 (1991) 70–89 and the ensuing exchanges in the journal between Tauger and
Conquest: 51 (1992): 192–194 and 53 (1994):
318–320.

13. A.M. Cienciala, N.S. Lebedeva, and W.
Materski (eds.), *Katyn: A Crime Without Punishment* (New Haven: Yale University Press,
2007). See (literally) also Andrzej Wajda's film
based on the incident, *Katyn*.

14. G. Furr, "The 'Official' Version of the
Katyn Massacre Disproven?" *Socialism and
Democracy* 27 (2013): 96–129.

15. T. Snyder, *Bloodlands: Europe between
Hitler and Stalin* (New York: Basic Books,
2010). T. Judt, *Postwar: A History of Europe
since 1945* (New York: Penguin, 2005).

16. See, for example, D. Smith, *Former Peo-
ple: The Final Days of the Russian Aristocracy*
(New York: Farrar, Straus and Giroux, 2012);
L. Viola, *The Unknown Gulag: The Lost World
of Stalin's Special Settlements* (Oxford; New
York: Oxford University Press, 2007); J. Brent,
*Inside the Stalin Archives: Discovering the New
Russia* (New York: Atlas, 2008); A. Apple-
baum, *Gulag: A History* (New York: Double-
day, 2003).

Conclusion

1. L. Menashe, Review of "Faith of the
Century: A History of Communism" (Web
Exclusive), *Cineaste* 34 (2009), http://www.
cineaste.com/articles/emfaith-of-the-century-
a-history-of-communismem.

2. A. Greene, "Students Endorse Referendum for Oversight of Endowment," *Princeton
Alumni Weekly* (June 6, 2012): 17. R. Smith,
"A New Divestment Focus on Campus: Fossil
Fuels," *New York Times*, September 6, 2013, B1.
See D. Faust, "Fossil Fuel Divestment Statement," October 2, 2013, http://www.harvard.
edu/president/fossil-fuels. President Obama
is quoted in J. Gillis, "Old Tactic in New Climate Campaign," *New York Times*, July 8, 2013,
D3.

3. M. Edmundson, *Why Teach? In Defense
of a Real Education* (New York: Bloomsbury,
2013), 21.

4. J.R. Harris, *The Nurture Assumption:
Why Children Turn Out the Way They Do*
(New York: Free Press, 1998). See also J.R.
Harris, "Where Is the Child's Environment?
A Group Socialization Theory of Development," *Psychological Review* 102 (1995): 458–
489. The critical comment, made by Evan
Charney, a researcher at Duke University's Institute for Brain Sciences, is quoted in T.B. Ed-
sall, "Are Our Political Beliefs Encoded in Our
DNA?" online *New York Times* column, http:
//opinionator.blogs.nytimes.com/2013/10/
01/are-our-political-beliefs-encoded-in-our-
dna/?_r=0.

5. M. Alexander, *The New Jim Crow: Mass
Incarceration in the Age of Colorblindness* (New
York: New Press, 2012), 197.

6. K. Andersen, "The Downside of Liberty," *New York Times*, Jul 4, 2012, A23. D.J.
Hemel, "'07 Men Make More," *Harvard Crimson*, June 6, 2007, available online at http://
www.thecrimson.com/article/2007/6/6/07-
men-make-more-male-harvard/. On the pyramid scheme, see Webster v. Omnitrition International (1996) 79 F.3d 776.

7. A. Colby and W. Damon, *Some Do Care:
Contemporary Lives of Moral Commitment*
(New York: Free Press, 1992), 29.

8. M. Kazin, *American Dreamers: How the
Left Changed a Nation* (New York: Knopf,
2011).

Bibliography

Adelson, A. *SDS*. New York: Charles Scribner's Sons, 1972.
Alexander, M. *The New Jim Crow: Mass Incarceration in the Age of Colorblindness*. New York: New Press, 2010.
Andersen, C. *Citizen Jane: The Turbulent Life of Jane Fonda*. New York: Henry Holt, 1990.
Anderson, T.H. *The Movement and the Sixties*. New York: Oxford University Press, 1995.
Applebaum, A. *Gulag: A History*. New York: Doubleday, 2003.
Ayers, B. *Fugitive Days: Memoir of an Antiwar Activist*. Boston: Beacon, 2001.
Ayers, B. *Public Enemy: Confessions of an American Dissident*. Boston: Beacon, 2013.
Bartholomew, B., Bradley, M., Caldarola, P., Cohen, P., Edenberg, H., Glibert, L., Grobstein, P., Kennedy, D., Merrell, E., Morrow, P., and Pittendrig, C. "A Legacy of our Presence: The Destruction of Indochina" (pamphlet). Stanford: Stanford Biology Study Group, 1970.
Bass, J. "Documenting the Orangeburg Massacre." *Nieman Reports* (Fall 2003): 8–11.
Berlin, I. *The Crooked Timber of Humanity: Chapters in the History of Ideas*. London: John Murray, 1990.
Berman, L. *Lyndon Johnson's War: The Road to Stalemate in Vietnam*. New York: W.W. Norton, 1989.
Berman, P. *A Tale of Two Utopias: The Political Journey of the Generation of 1968*. New York: W.W. Norton, 1996.
Blackmon, D.A. *Slavery by Another Name: The Re-Enslavement of Black Americans from the Civil War to World War II*. New York: Doubleday, 2008.
Blackstock, N. *COINTELPRO: The FBI's Secret War on Political Freedom*. New York: Vintage, 1976.
Boulud, D., and Kaminsky, P. *Chef Daniel Boulud: Cooking in New York City*. New York: Assouline, 2002.
Boulud, D., and Kaminsky, P. *Letters to a Young Chef*. New York: Basic, 2003.
Bragdon, H.W. *Woodrow Wilson: The Academic Years*. Cambridge: Belknap Press of Harvard University Press, 1967.
Branch, T. *At Canaan's Edge: America in the King Years, 1965–68*. New York: Simon & Schuster, 2006.
Brent, J. *Inside the Stalin Archives: Discovering the New Russia*. New York: Atlas, 2008.
Brown, N.O. *Life Against Death: The Psychoanalytic Meaning of History*. Middletown, Conn.: Wesleyan University Press, 1959.
Browne, M.W. *The New Face of War*. Indianapolis: Bobbs-Merrill, 1965.
Buckingham, W.A. *Operation Ranch Hand: The Air Force and Herbicides in Southeast Asia 1961–1971*. Washington, D.C.: Office of Air Force History, 1982.
Burlingham, B. "Paranoia in Power." *Harper's* 249 (October 1974): 26–37.
Buttinger, J. *Vietnam: The Unforgettable Tragedy*. London: Andre Deutsch, 1977.
Buzzanco, B. "The American Military's Rationale Against the Vietnam War." *Political Science Quarterly* 101 (1986): 559–576.
Caute, D. *The Great Fear: The Anti-Communist Purge Under Truman and Eisenhower*. New York: Simon and Schuster, 1978.
Chang, G.H. "Are There Other Ways to Think about the 'Great Interregnum'?" *Journal of American-East Asian Relations* 7 (1998): 117–122.

Chang, G.H. "Asian Immigrants and American Foreign Relations." In W.I. Cohen, ed., *Pacific Passage: The Study of American-East Asian Relations on the Eve of the Twenty-First Century*. New York: Columbia University Press, 1996, 103–118.

Chang, G.H. *Friends and Enemies: The United States, China, and the Soviet Union, 1948–1972*. Stanford: Stanford University Press, 1990.

Chang, G.H. "A Report on Student Protests at Beijing University." *Bulletin of Concerned Asian Scholars* 18 (1986): 29–31.

Chang, G.H. Review of *Asian American Dreams: The Emergence of an American People* by H. Zia. *Journal of American Ethnic History* 22 (2003): 105–106.

Chang, G.H. "Social Darwinism vs. Social Engineering: The 'Education' of Japanese Americans During World War II." In A. Weiner, ed., *Landscaping the Human Garden: Twentieth-Century Population Management in a Comparative Framework*. Stanford: Stanford University Press, 2003, 189–204.

Chang, G.H. "'Superman is about to visit the relocation centers' and the Limits of Wartime Liberalism." *Amerasia Journal* 19 (1993): 37–59.

Chang, G.H. "To the Nuclear Brink: Eisenhower, Dulles, and the Quemoy Matsu Crisis," *International Security* 12 (1988): 96–123.

Chang, G.H. "Whose 'Barbarism'? Whose 'Treachery'? Race and Civilization in the Unknown United States—Korea War of 1871." *Journal of American History* 89 (2003): 1331–1365.

Chang, G.H., and Di, H. "The Absence of War in the U.S. China Confrontation over Quemoy and Matsu in 1954–1955: Contingency, Luck, Deterrence?" *American Historical Review* 98 (1993): 1500–1524.

Chang, G.H., ed. *Asian Americans and Politics: Perspectives, Experiences, Prospects*. Washington, D.C.: Woodrow Wilson Center Press and Stanford: Stanford University Press, 2001.

Chang, G.H., and Azuma, E., eds. *Before Internment: Essays in Prewar Japanese American History*. Stanford: Stanford University Press, 2006.

Chang, G.H., Johnson, M.D., and Karlstrom, P.J., eds. *Asian American Art" A History, 1850–1970*. Stanford: Stanford University Press, 2008.

Chang, S. *The Global Silicon Valley Home: Lives and Landscapes Within Taiwanese American Trans-Pacific Culture*. Stanford: Stanford University Press, 2006.

Chen, T. *Double Agency: Acts of Impersonation in Asian American Literature and Culture*. Stanford: Stanford University Press, 2005.

Chevigny, P. *Cope and Rebels: A Study of Provocation*. New York: Pantheon, 1972.

"Chicago Group Seeks to Sever IDA Tie." *Science* 150 (1968): 860.

Chomsky, N. "Engineering of Consent." In *Counter-Intelligence: A Documentary Look at America's Secret Police, Volume I*. Chicago: Citizens in Defense of Civil Liberties, 1982, foreword.

Cienciala, A.M., Lebedeva, N.S., and Materski W., eds. *Katyn: A Crime Without Punishment*. New Haven: Yale University Press, 2007.

Clements, K.A. *Woodrow Wilson: World Statesman*. Boston: Twayne, 1987.

Cohen, R.L. "AIDS: The Impending Quarantine." *Health/PAC Bulletin* 16 (1985): 9–14.

Cohen, R.L. "Health and Public Health Advocacy for Prisoners." In M. Puisis, ed., *Clinical Practice in Correctional Medicine*. Philadelphia: Elsevier, 2006, 28–38.

Cohen, R.L. "Imprisoned Plasma Donors: A Medical-Ethical Case and Comment." *Journal of Prison and Jail Health* 2 (1982): 41–46.

Cohen, R.L. "Mass Incarceration: A Public Health Failure." In J.P. May and K.R. Pitts, eds., *Building Violence: How America's Rush to Incarcerate Creates More Violence*. Thousand Oaks, Cal.: Sage, 2000. 95–99.

Cohen, R.L. "A Prisoner in Need of a Bone Marrow Transplant: Commentary." *Hastings Center Report* 17 (1987): 26–27.

Colby, A., and Damon, W. *Some Do Care: Contemporary Lives of Moral Commitment*. New York: Free Press, 1992.

Collins, G. *When Everything Changed: The Amazing Journey of American Women from 1960 to the Present*. Boston: Little, Brown, 2009.

Committee to Review the Health Effects in Vietnam Veterans of Exposure to Herbicides. *Veterans and Agent Orange: Health Effects of Herbicides Used in Vietnam*. Washington, D.C.: National Academy Press, 1994.

Conquest, R. *The Great Terror; Stalin's Purge of the Thirties*. New York: Macmillan, 1968.
Cortright, D. *Soldiers in Revolt: The American Military Today*. Garden City, N.Y.: Anchor Press, 1975.
Cunningham, D. *There's Something Happening Here: The New Left, the Klan, and FBI Counter-intelligence*. Berkeley: University of California Press, 2004.
Danner, M. *The Massacre at El Mozote: A Parable of the Cold War*. New York: Vintage, 1994.
Davidson, C. "University Reform Revisited." *Educational Record* 48 (1967): 4–8.
Davis, J.K. *Assault on the Left: The FBI and the Sixties Antiwar Movement*. Westport, Conn.: Praeger, 1997.
Dellinger, D. *More Power Than We Know: The People's Movement Toward Democracy*. Garden City, N.Y.: Anchor/Doubleday, 1975.
Domhoff, G.W. *Fat Cats and Democrats: The Role of the Big Rich in the Party of the Common Man*. Englewood Cliffs, NJ: Prentice-Hall, 1972.
Drummond, R., and Coblentz, G. *Duel at the Brink: John Foster Dulles' Command of American Power*. Garden City, N.Y.: Doubleday, 1960.
Duncan, D. *The New Legions*. New York: Random House, 1967.
Duncan, D. "'The whole thing was a lie!'" *Ramparts* 4 (February 1966): 12–24.
Edmundson, M. *Why Teach? In Defense of a Real Education*. New York: Bloomsbury, 2013.
Ehrhart, W.D. *Ordinary Lives: Platoon 1005 and the Vietnam War*. Philadelphia: Temple University Press, 1999.
Eisenhower, D.D. *Mandate for Change 1953–1956*. Garden City, N.Y.: Doubleday, 1963.
Elbaum, M. *Revolution in the Air: Sixties Radicals Turn to Lenin, Mao and Che*. London: Verso, 2006.
Ellsberg, D. *Secrets: A Memoir of Vietnam and the Pentagon Papers*. New York: Penguin, 2002.
Etheridge, E. *Breach of Peace: Portraits of the 1961 Mississippi Freedom Riders*. New York: Atlas, 2008.
Fall, B.B. "'This isn't Munich, it's Spain.'" *Ramparts* (December 1965): 28–39.
Fallows, J. "What Did You Do In the Class War, Daddy?" *Washington Monthly* 7 (October 1975): 5–19.
Farber, J. *The Student as Nigger*. North Hollywood, Calif.: Contact Books, 1969.
Farmer, J. *Lay Bare the Heart: An Autobiography of the Civil Rights Movement*. New York: Arbor House, 1985.
Fink, C., Gassert, P., and Junker, D., eds. *1968: the World Transformed*. New York: Cambridge University Press, 1998.
Fitzgerald, F. *Fire in the Lake: The Vietnamese and the Americans in Vietnam*. Boston: Little, Brown, 2002.
Fitzgerald, F.S. *This Side of Paradise*. New York: Charles Scribner's Sons, 1920.
Freeman, R.B., and Rogers, J. "Open Source Unionism: Beyond Exclusive Collective Bargaining." *WorkingUSA: The Journal of Labor and Society* 5 (2002): 8–40.
Furr, G. *Khrushchev Lied: The Evidence That Every "Revelation" of Stalin's (and Beria's) "Crimes" in Nikita Khrushchev's Infamous "Secret Speech" to the 20th Party Congress of the Soviet Union on February 25, 1956, is Provably False*. Kettering, Ohio: Erythros Press, 2011.
Furr, G. "The 'Official' Version of the Katyn Massacre Disproven?" *Socialism and Democracy* 27 (2013): 96–129.
Garrow, D.J. "The FBI and Martin Luther King." *Atlantic Monthly* 290 (July/August 2002): 80–88.
Gassert, P., and Klimke, M., eds. *1968: Memories and Legacies of a Global Revolt*. Washington, D.C.: German Historical Institute, 2009.
Gettleman, M.E., Franklin, J., Young, M.B., and Franklin, H.B., eds. *Vietnam and America*. New York: Grove, 1995.
Gilmore, G.E. *Defying Dixie: The Radical Roots of Civil Rights, 1919–1950*. New York: W.W. Norton, 2008.
Gitlin, T. *The Sixties: Years of Hope, Days of Rage*. New York: Bantam Books, 1987.
Gleijeses, P. *The Dominican Crisis: The 1965 Constitutionalist Revolt and American Intervention*. Baltimore: Johns Hopkins University Press, 1978.
Gleijeses, P. *Shattered Hope: The Guatemalan Revolutions and the United States, 1944–1954*. Princeton: Princeton University Press, 1991.

Goldstein, G.M. *Lessons in Disaster: McGeorge Bundy and the Path to War in Vietnam.* New York: Times/Henry Holt, 2008.

Goldstein, R.J. *Political Repression in Modern America From 1870 to present.* Cambridge, Mass.: Schenkman, 1978.

Gornick, V. *The Romance of American Communism.* New York: Basic Books, 1977.

Goulden, J.C. *Truth is the First Casualty: The Gulf of Tonkin Affair—Illusion and Reality.* Chicago: Rand McNally, 1969.

Greenberg, D.S. "IDA: University-Sponsored Center Hit Hard by Assaults on Campus." *Science* 160 (1968): 744–748.

Griffiths, P.J. *Agent Orange: "Collateral Damage" in Vietnam.* London: Trolley, 2004.

Haas, J. *The Assassination of Fred Hampton: How the FBI and the Chicago Police Murdered a Black Panther.* Chicago: Lawrence Hill, 2009.

Hagel, C. with Kaminsky, P. *America: Our Next Chapter.* New York: HarperCollins, 2008.

Hammer, R. *One Morning in the War: The Tragedy at Son My.* New York: Coward-McCann, Inc., 1970.

Hampton, D. *Little Red: Three Passionate Lives Through the Sixties and Beyond.* New York: Public Affairs, 2013.

Harris, J.R. *The Nurture Assumption: Why Children Turn Out the Way They Do.* New York: Free Press, 1998.

Harris, J.R. "Where Is the Child's Environment? A Group Socialization Theory of Development." *Psychological Review* 102 (1995): 458–489.

Harvey, F. *Air War-Vietnam.* New York: Bantam, 1967.

Hayden, T. *The Port Huron Statement: The Visionary Call of the 1960s Revolution.* New York: Thunder's Mouth Press, 2005.

Hayden, T. *Rebel: A Personal History of the 1960s.* Granada Hills, California: Red Hen Press, 2003.

Heinl, R.D. "The Collapse of the Armed Forces." *Armed Forces Journal* 108 (June 7, 1971): 30–38.

Heller, Z. *The Believers.* New York: HarperCollins, 2008.

Herman, E.S. *Atrocities in Vietnam: Myths and Realities.* Philadelphia: Pilgrim Press, 1970.

Herrnstein, R.J. "I.Q." *Atlantic Monthly* 228 (September, 1971): 43–64.

Herrnstein, R.J., and Murray, C. *The Bell Curve: Intelligence and Class Structure in American Life.* New York: Free Press, 1994.

Hersh, S. *My Lai 4: A Report on the Massacre and Its Aftermath.* New York: Random House, 1970.

Herzstein, R.E. *Henry R. Luce, Time, and the American Crusade in Asia.* New York: Cambridge University Press, 2005.

Hess, G.R. "The Unending Debate: Historians and the Vietnam War." *Diplomatic History* 18 (1994): 239–264.

"The History of the Progressive Labor Party, Part One." *PL Magazine* 10 (August-September 1975): 55–70.

Hoffman, A. *Revolution for the Hell Of It.* New York: Dial, 1968.

Horowitz, D. *The Professors: The 101 Most Dangerous Academics in America.* Washington, D.C.: Regnery, 2006.

Hunt, A.E. *The Turning: A History of Vietnam Veterans Against the War.* New York: New York University Press, 1999.

Huntington, S.P. "The Bases of Accommodation." *Foreign Affairs* 46 (1968): 642–656.

Jackson, J.L. *Racial Paranoia: The Unintended Consequences of Political Correctness.* New York: Basic Civitas, 2008.

Jackson, T.F. *From Civil Rights to Human Rights: Martin Luther King, Jr., and the Struggle for Economic Justice.* Philadelphia: University of Pennsylvania Press, 2007.

Judt, T. *The Memory Chalet.* New York: Penguin, 2010.

Judt, T. *Postwar: A History of Europe since 1945.* New York: Penguin, 2005.

Kamin, L.J. *The Science and Politics of I.Q.* Potomac, Md.: Lawrence Erlbaum, 1974.

Kaminsky, P. *American Waters: Fly-Fishing Journeys of a Native Son.* New York: Stewart, Tabori & Chang, 2005.

Kaminsky, P. *Culinary Intelligence: The Art of Eating Healthy (and Really Well).* New York: Knopf, 2012.

Kaminsky, P. *The Fly-Fisherman's Guide to the Meaning of Life: What a Lifetime on the Water Has Taught Me about Love, Work, Food, Sex, and Getting Up Early*. New York: Rodale/St. Martin's, 2002.

Kaminsky, P. *Pig Perfect: Encounters with Remarkable Swine and Some Great Ways to Cook Them*. New York: Hyperion, 2005.

Karabel, J. *The Chosen: The Hidden History of Admissions and Exclusion at Harvard, Yale, and Princeton*. New York: Houghton Mifflin, 2005.

Katsiaficas, G., ed. *Vietnam Documents: American and Vietnamese Views of the War*. Armonk, N.Y.: M.E. Sharpe, 1992.

Kazin, M. *American Dreamers: How the Left Changed a Nation*. New York: Knopf, 2011.

Kelman, S. *Push Comes to Shove: The Escalation of Student Protest*. Boston: Houghton Mifflin, 1970.

Kim, D.Y. *Writing Manhood in Black and Yellow: Ralph Ellison, Frank Chin, and the Literary Politics of Identity*. Stanford: Stanford University Press, 2005.

Kimball, R. *Tenured Radicals: How Politics Has Corrupted Our Higher Education*. New York: Harper & Row, 1990.

Kinzer, S. *All the Shah's Men: An American Coup and the Roots of Middle East Terror*. Hoboken, N.J.: John Wiley & Sons, 2003.

Kinzer, S. *Overthrow: America's Century of Regime Change from Hawaii to Iraq*. New York: Henry Holt, 2006.

Knoebl, K. *Victor Charlie: The Face of War in Vietnam*. New York: Frederick A. Praeger, 1967.

Koblitz, N. "The Case Against Computers in K–13 Math Education (Kindergarten through Calculus)." *The Mathematical Intelligencer* 18 (1996): 9–16.

Koblitz, N. "Mathematics as Propaganda." In L.A. Steen, ed., *Mathematics Tomorrow*. New York: Springer-Verlag, 1981, 111–120.

Koblitz, N. *Random Curves: Journeys of a Mathematician*. Berlin: Springer-Verlag, 2008.

Koblitz, N. "The Uneasy Relationship Between Mathematics and Cryptography." *Notices of the American Mathematical Society* 54 (2007): 972–979.

Koshy, S. *Sexual Naturalization: Asian Americans and Miscegenation*. Stanford: Stanford University Press, 2004.

Kunz, G., and Kaminsky, P. *The Elements of Taste*. New York: Little, Brown, 2001.

Kurlansky, M. *1968: the Year that Rocked the World*. New York: Ballantine, 2004.

Langer, E. "Notes for Next Time: A Memoir of the 1960s." In R.D. Myers, ed., *Toward a History of the New Left: Essays from Within the Movement*. Brooklyn, N.Y.: Carlson Publishing, 1989, 63–123.

"Lansdale Team's Report on Covert Saigon Mission in 1954 and 1955." In *The Pentagon Papers: The Defense Department History of United States Decisionmaking on Vietnam, Volume 1* (Senator Gravel Edition). Boston: Beacon, 1971.

Lawyers Committee on American Policy Towards Vietnam, *Vietnam and International Law*. Flanders, N.J.: O'Hare Books, 1967.

Leitch, A. *A Princeton Companion*. Princeton, N.J.: Princeton University Press, 1978.

Lembcke, J. *The Spitting Image: Myth, Memory, and the Legacy of Vietnam*. New York: New York University Press, 1998.

Lewy, G. "Some Political-Military Lessons of the Vietnam War." *Parameters: Journal of the US Army War College* 14 (1984): 2–14.

Li, D.L. *Imagining the Nation: Asian American Literature and Cultural Consent*. Stanford: Stanford University Press, 1998.

Luce, D., and Sommer, J. *Vietnam: The Unheard Voices*. Ithaca: Cornell University Press, 1969.

MacDonald, K.B. *The Culture of Critique: An Evolutionary Analysis of Jewish Involvement in Twentieth-Century Intellectual and Political Movements*. Westport, Conn.: Praeger, 1998.

MacDonald, K.B. *A People that Shall Dwell Alone: Judaism as a Group Evolutionary Strategy*. Westport, Conn.: Praeger, 1994.

MacDonald, K.B. *Separation and Its Discontents: Toward an Evolutionary Theory of Anti-Semitism*. Westport, Conn.: Praeger, 1998.

Madden, J., and Kaminsky, P. *John Madden's Ultimate Tailgating*. New York: Viking, 1998.

Mailer, N. *Miami and the Siege of Chicago*. Cleveland: World Publishing, 1968.

Malani, P.N. "Poetry" (review of *Transplant*). *JAMA* 290 (2003): 1385.

Mallmann, F., and Kaminsky, P. *Seven Fires: Grilling the Argentine Way*. New York: Artisan, 2009.

Marcuse, H. *Eros and Civilization: A Philosophical Inquiry into Freud*. Boston: Beacon, 1966.

Marx, K., and Engels, F. *The German Ideology: Parts I and II*. New York: International Publishers, 1968.

McAffee, C. "IDA: The Academic Conscripts." *Viet-Report: An Emergency News Bulletin on Southeast Asian Affairs* (1968): 6–12.

McCoy, A.W. *The Politics of Heroin in Southeast Asia*. New York: Harper & Row.

McNamara, R.S., Blight, J.S., and Brigham, R.K., with Biersteker, T.J., and Schandler, H.Y. *Argument Without End: In Search of Answers to the Vietnam Tragedy*. New York: Public Affairs, 1999.

Melman, S. (Research Director), Baron, M., and Ely, D. (Research Associates). *In the Name of America: The conduct of the war in Vietnam by the armed forces of the United States as shown by published reports, compared with the Laws of War binding on the United States Government and on its citizens*. Annandale, Va.: Turnpike, 1968.

Meredith, M. *In the Name of Apartheid: South Africa in the Postwar Period*. New York: Harper & Row, 1988.

Mills, C.W. *The Power Elite*. New York: Oxford University Press, 2000.

Nack, D., and Tarlau, J. "The Communications Workers of America Experience with 'Open-Source Unionism.'" *WorkingUSA: The Journal of Labor and Society* 8 (2005): 721–732.

Navasky, V. *Kennedy Justice*. New York: Athenum, 1971.

Nelson, D. *The War Behind Me: Vietnam Veterans Confront the Truth About U.S. War Crimes*. New York: Basic Books, 2008.

Nelson, J., and Bass, J. *The Orangeburg Massacre*. New York: World, 1970.

Oglesby, C. "Notes on a Decade Ready for the Dustbin." *Liberation* 14 (1969): 5–19.

Oglesby, C., and Shaull, R. *Containment and Change*. New York: Macmillan, 1967.

Olson, J.S., and Roberts, R. *My Lai: A brief History with Documents*. Boston: Bedford, 1998.

Olson, J.S., and Roberts, R. *Where the Domino Fell: American and Vietnam, 1945 to 1990*. New York: St. Martin's Press, 1991.

Orians, G.H., and Pfeiffer, E.W. "Ecological Effects of the War in Vietnam." *Science* 168 (1970): 544–554.

Oshinsky, D. *"Worse Than Slavery": Parchman Farm and the Ordeal of Jim Crow Justice*. New York: Free Press, 1996.

Patti, A.L.A. *Why Vietnam? Prelude to America's Albatross*. Berkeley: University of California Press, 1980.

Paul, J. "A Prisoner in Need of a Bone Marrow Transplant: Commentary." *Hastings Center Report* 17 (1987): 27.

Pepper, W.F. "The Children of Vietnam." *Ramparts* 5 (January 1967): 44–67.

Perlstein, R. *Nixonland: The Rise of a President and the Fracturing of America*. New York: Scribner, 2008.

Pike, D. *Viet Cong: The Organization and Techniques of the National Liberation Front of South Vietnam*. Cambridge, Mass.: MIT Press, 1966.

Porter, G. "Distorting History." *Society* 21 (November-December, 1983): 18–22.

Public Papers of the Presidents of the United States: Ronald Reagan, 1982 Volume I. Washington, D.C.: US Government Printing Office, 1983.

Rajan, G., and Sharma, S., eds. *New Cosmopolitans: South Asians in the US*. Stanford: Stanford University Press, 2006.

Reich, C.A. *The Greening of America: How the Youth Revolution Is Trying to Make America Livable*. New York: Random House, 1970.

"Revolutionaries Must Fight Nationalism." *PL Magazine* (August 1969): 3–13.

Robin, R. *The Making of the Cold War Enemy: Culture and Politics in the Military-Industrial Complex*. Princeton: Princeton University Press, 2001.

Rosenfeld, S. *Subversives: The FBI's War on Student Radicals and Reagan's Rise to Power*. New York: Farrar, Straus & Giroux, 2012.

Rudd, M. *Underground: My Life with SDS and the Weathermen*. New York: HarperCollins, 2009.

Russell, B. *War Crimes in Vietnam*. New York: Monthly Review Press, 1967.

Sale, K. *SDS*. New York: Random House, 1973.

Samuels, K. *Political Violence and the International Community*. Leiden, The Netherlands: Koninklijke Brill, 2007.

Schell, J. *The Military Half*. New York: Alfred A. Knopf, 1968.

Schell, J. *The Village of Ben Suc*. New York Alfred A. Knopf, 1967.

Schoenbrun, D. *Vietnam: How We Got In; How to Get Out*. New York: Atheneum, 1970.

"Scientists Protest Crop Destruction." *Science* 151 (1966): 309.

Seaton, D.P. *Catholics and Radicals: The Association of Catholic Trade Unionists and the American Labor Movement, from Depression to Cold War*. Lewisburg, Penn.: Bucknell University Press, 1981.

Selwyn, P.A., Feiner, C., Cox, C.P., Lipschutz, C., and Cohen, R.L. "Knowledge about AIDS and High-Risk Behavior Among Intravenous Drug Users in New York City." *AIDS* 1 (1987): 247–254.

Severo, R., and Milford, L. *The Wages of War: When American Soldiers Came Home—From Valley Forge to Vietnam*. New York: Simon & Shuster, 1989.

Sills, C. Review of *White Racism: A Psychohistory* by Joel Kovel. *Telos* 12 (1972): 141–143.

Sills, C., and Jensen, G.H., eds. *The Philosophy of Discourse: The Rhetorical Turn in Twentieth Century Thought, Volume 1 and Volume 2*. Portsmouth, NH: Boynton/Cook, 1992.

Simpson, B.R. *Economists with Guns: Authoritarian Development and U.S.-Indonesian Relations, 1960–1968*. Stanford: Stanford University Press, 2008.

Sitkoff, H. *The Struggle for Black Equality 1954–1980*. New York: Hill and Wang, 1981.

Slosson, E.E. *Great American Universities*. New York: Macmillan, 1910.

Smith, D. *Former People: The Final Days of the Russian Aristocracy*. New York: Farrar, Straus and Giroux, 2012.

Smith, M. "Birding the Battle of Attu." *Ploughshares* 10 (1984): 146.

Smith, M. *Prudentius' Psychomachia: A Reexamination*. Princeton: Princeton University Press, 1976.

Smith, M. *Transplant*. Ann Arbor, Mich.: Shaman Drum Press, 2003.

Smith, P.H. *Talons of the Eagle: Dynamics of U.S.-Latin American Relations*. New York: Oxford University Press, 1996.

Snow, E. *Journey to the Beginning*. New York: Random House, 1958.

Snyder, T. *Bloodlands: Europe between Hitler and Stalin*. New York: Basic Books, 2010.

Solis, G.D. *Marines and Military Law in Vietnam: Trial by Fire*. Washington, D.C.: History and Museums Division Headquarters, U.S. Marine Corps, 1989.

Solis, G.D. *Son Thang: An American War Crime*. Annapolis, Md.: National Institute Press, 1997.

Tauger, M.B. "The 1932 Harvest and the Famine of 1933." *Slavic Review* 50 (1991) 70–89.

Taylor, T. *Nuremberg and Vietnam: An American Tragedy*. Chicago: Quadrangle Books, 1970.

Tucker, W.H. "Fact and Fiction in the Discovery of Sir Cyril Burt's Flaws." *Journal of the History of the Behavioral Sciences* 30 (1994): 335–347.

Tucker, W.H. *The Funding of Scientific Racism: Wickliffe Draper and the Pioneer Fund*. Champaign: University of Illinois Press, 2002.

Turse, N. *Kill Anything That Moves: The Real American War in Vietnam*. New York: Metropolitan Books, 2013.

Viola, L. *The Unknown Gulag: The Lost World of Stalin's Special Settlements*. Oxford: Oxford University Press, 2007.

Walker, D. *Rights in Conflict*. National Commission on the Causes and Prevention of Violence, 1968.

Weidensaul, S. *Of a Feather: A Brief History of American Birding*. New York: Harcourt, 2007.

Weiner, T. *Legacy of Ashes: The History of the CIA*. New York: Doubleday, 2007.

Weisberg, B., ed. *Ecocide in Indochina*. San Francisco: Canfield Press, 1970.

Whiteside, T. *Defoliation*. New York: Ballantine Books, 1970.

Whitman, S., Coleman, T.E., Patmon, C., Desai, B.T., Cohen, R., and King, L.N. "Epilepsy in Prison: Elevated Prevalence and No Relationship to Violence." *Neurology* 34 (1984): 775–782.

Whitman, S., King, L.N., and Cohen, R.L. "Epilepsy and Violence: A Scientific and Social Analysis." In S. Whitman and B.P. Hermann, eds., *Psychopathology in Epilepsy: Social Dimensions*. New York: Oxford University Press, 1986, 284–302.

Wilkerson, C. *Flying Close to the Sun: My Life and Times as a Weatherman*. New York: Seven Stories Press, 2007.
Wofford, H. *Of Kennedy and Kings: Making Sense of the Sixties*. Pittsburgh: University of Pittsburgh Press, 1992.
Yankelovich, D. *The Changing Values on Campus: Political and Personal Attitudes of Today's College Students*. New York: Washington Square Press, 1972.
Zinn, H. *The Zinn Reader: Writings on Disobedience and Democracy*. New York: Seven Stories Press, 1997.

Index

www.ingramcontent.com/pod-product-compliance
Lightning Source LLC
Chambersburg PA
CBHW031411270326
41929CB00010BA/1414